Industrial Finance 1830–1914

P. L. COTTRELL

Industrial Finance
1830–1914

The finance and organization
of English manufacturing industry

METHUEN
LONDON AND NEW YORK

First published in 1980 by
Methuen & Co. Ltd
11 New Fetter Lane, London EC4P 4EE
First published as a University Paperback in 1983

Published in the USA by
Methuen & Co.
in association with Methuen, Inc.
733 Third Avenue, New York, NY 10017

Printed in Great Britain by
Thomson Litho, East Kilbride

British Library Cataloguing in Publication Data
Cottrell, P. L.
    Industrial finance, 1830–1914
        1. Corporations–Great Britain–Finance–History
        1. Title
    338.4'3   HG 4140
    ISBN 0-416-85680-2
    ISBN 0-416-36260-5 (University paperback 820)

Library of Congress Catalog Card Number: 81–178834

To the memory of
H. J. D., R. D. and F. E. H.

Errata

From *Table* 4.7, p. 96

	1860		1885	
Service Industries				
Shipowners	0.01		3.69	
Construction and inland transport	0.96		0.33	
Other service industries	0.58	⎯⎯	3.45	⎯⎯
Subtotal		1.55		7.47
Non-industrial skilled and semi-skilled				
artisans and workers		2.37		1.37
Employees				
Directors	—		0.21	
Managers	0.09	⎯⎯	0.43	⎯⎯
Subtotal		0.09		0.64

Table 7.6, p. 225

Table 7.6 Analysis of composition of overdrafts at Carlisle branch of the Cumberland Union Bank, 31 December 1885

To *Clients*	
Unoccupied: Male	5.3%
Female	0.4
Institutions and Public Authorities	2.2
Land	6.8
Professions	3.1
Trade and Services: Merchants	16.5
Agents	0.7
Retailers	1.2
Other	0.4
Manufacturing	59.5
West Cumberland Iron & Steel Co.	30.6/
Building	0.6
Unknown	3.2

Contents

Preface

This book has a number of origins. My interest in the topics and themes that it explores began in undergraduate seminars conducted by Janet Blackman and John Saville at the University of Hull. During my first year as a postgraduate I began to look at the finances of English industry in the third quarter of the nineteenth century, but the chance discovery of the papers of an investment bank diverted my attention to other fields and other areas. The notes collected then gathered dust until Arthur Thomas and myself were asked by John Naylor of Methuen to write jointly a book on the subject. The trustees of the Houblon-Norman fund kindly made available money to finance further research and their help and that of the Research Board of the University of Leicester made the writing of this book possible. Once research had got underway and some initial drafts had been sketched out, it soon became evident that the original intention to survey developments from about the 1830s to the present within the confines of one volume was not feasible. Our publisher, always helpful, agreed that the work could be split into separate volumes which would appear under single authorship. This formalized a working agreement where I was responsible for the nineteenth century and Arthur Thomas the twentieth. However, here I would like to take the opportunity of acknowledging the considerable help and assistance of my erstwhile collaborator in the project who read a number of drafts and commented both critically and constructively.

The approach that has been adopted in this book is both chronological and thematic. In briefly surveying the existing literature on the initial stages of industrialization, Chapters 1 and 2 provide an introduction to the rest of the book which consists of thematic sections or chapters. Chapter 2 has been deliberately restricted in scope to those industries which students, rightly or wrongly, are normally referred to; this decision was taken for reasons of space and in order not to repeat what may be forthcoming in a companion volume which will look solely at the industrial revolution. Chapters 3 to 6 stand together as a block dealing with the joint stock limited company and its adoption as a mode of organization by industry. Certain parts of Chapters 3 and 5 are rather detailed but the opportunity has been taken to look at the nearly forgotten long debate over company law during the second half of the nineteenth century and to place Chadwick's parliamentary evidence on mid-Victorian company promotion, so often quoted or paraphrased, in its proper perspective. It is perhaps important to point out at this early stage that a rather elastic and amorphous definition of what constitutes 'manufacturing' industry has been adopted. Extractive industry has been included even though some purists may point out that its proper place is in the primary sector. Although there was never any intention from the outset to be encyclopedic, it has proved possible to say at least something about the finances of nearly every branch of manufacturing proper, although usually in terms of illustrative material to a general point. As a result, in the case of brewing for instance, only a passing acknowledgment of the existence of this important processing industry is made in Chapter 2, but a detailed discussion of its finances in the late 1880s and 1890s occurs in the consideration of public company formation in Chapter 6, and further reference is made to the industry in Chapter 7. Such an approach may cause some frustration, but it proved to be the only one practicable and it is hoped that some of the problems and irritations that it may cause will be at least partially solved by resort to the index. Lastly, in terms of coverage, the word 'English' in the title is deliberate as Welsh, Irish, and Scottish developments have been generally excluded, not for any nationalistic or other reasons, but simply to reduce the scope of the work to manageable confines.

Chapters 7 and 8 are wholly thematic in their consideration of the roles of bank finance and internal funds. Given the unfavourable comparisons drawn between German and British banks both at the end of the nineteenth century and now, Chapter 7 contains a rather lengthy section on the operations of the German banking sector during the quarter of a century before the First World War. Chapter 8 is considered by the author at least to be the least satisfactory and the only consolation is that it may either encourage or provoke others to look at the topics again, especially profitability. In the main body of the book, that is from Chapter 3 on, an attempt has been made to combine the fruits of my own research, such as they are, with the body of literature established over the past years by many others. It has not been possible to fill all the remaining gaps and sometimes this has been due to serious source deficiencies. Here a note of apology is called for: the author, in 1972, publicly made a number of disparaging remarks about the extent of information in 'official' bank histories on lending to industrial firms. At that time he did not realize how well served he had been by the past secretaries of the one financial institution whose history he had investigated. As part of the preparation for this book, various bank archives were surveyed but despite the richness of their holdings, few readily useable sources dealing with the nature and mechanics of loans and advances came to light.

A very great number of people have assisted me in both the underlying research and the preparation of the manuscript for this book. Robert Frost, then at the Staffordshire County Record Office, Rosemary Ashbee, Archivist at the National and Commercial Banking Group, and Edwin Green, Archivist at the Midland Bank, gave considerable help in my initial researches. Miss Ashbee and Mr Green also played some part in shaping the final draft of Chapter 6 by both smoothing the difficulties involved in revealing a customer–bank relationship in print and bringing fresh acquisitions in their archives to my attention. Douglas Farnie, of the University of Manchester, in both conversation and in correspondence gave freely from his unrivalled knowledge of the development of the cotton industry during the second half of the nineteenth century. I owe a debt to those who organized, gave papers and took part in discussions at meetings of the Ealing Business History Seminar, the Midlands Economic Historians, and the Monetary History Group. Chapter 4 benefited from early 'airings' before a staff seminar at the University of Leeds and at a meeting of the Midlands Economic Historians at the University of Loughborough. My colleagues at both the University of Liverpool and the Univeristy of Leicester, especially Professor Seymour Broadbridge, Dr Joyce Ellis, Dr Peter Musgrave, Sheena Wilkinson and David Williams, without complaining suffered coffee sessions ruined by further discussions of my research, and then went on to read substantial sections of the raw manuscript. Similarly, Bill Kennedy of the University of Essex passed a critical eye over early drafts of Chapters 4, 5 and 6 while Roger Benedictus of the Department of Law, University of Leicester, kindly looked at Chapter 3. I am extremely grateful for all their comments on both content and style and I alone am responsible for the errors, confusions and lacunae that remain.

A considerable vote of thanks should also go to my long-suffering publisher, whose only words were those of encouragement, and to Miss Judith Watts and my wife, who undertook the laborious task of typing various drafts and the final manuscript.

Finally, thanks are due to Mr C. A. E. Goodhart and the Cambridge University Press for permission to reproduce tables 7.2 and 7.3 respectively.

1 Financing the industrial revolution I – institutional change

In the examination of the process of economic growth, the role of capital has received what can only be called a 'mixed press'. During the 1950s, largely as a result of the impact and development of Keynesian theory, primacy was given to investment as the key variable. This interpretation led to changes in the ratio of investment to income accepted as the indicator of industrialization. Analyses with this premise stimulated a search for empirical evidence with which to test the hypotheses on which they were based. Initially it seemed that too much emphasis had indeed been given to the relationship between the growth of investment, its consequent increased absorption of income, and structural change. It appeared that instead of the investment ratio rising from about 5% to 12–15% within the space of 30 to 50 years, the accumulation of capital assets during industrialization was far slower and less dramatic. Deane and Cole's work on British economic growth indicated that the needs of investment took up about 5% of national income in the decades before the 1780s, increased to only 7% by the 1800s, and only reached the level of 9–10% with the railway construction booms of the 1830s and 1840s. Although research by Hoffmann and others on the German economy found an appreciable rise in the ratio of net capital formation to national income from about 8.5% in the 1850s to 13.5% in the early 1870s, this was partly due to the abnormal amplitude of the upswing of the trade cycle in the latter decade. In the 1880s the ratio was still below 14%. Testing of what may be termed the Rostow–Lewis thesis of the explanation of industrialization appeared to find it wanting. The role of capital was also apparently diminished by findings from sources of growth analyses in which the growth of output was accounted for by the growth of factor inputs. Results, which initially met with some surprise, showed that generally at least a third of the growth of real output was attributable to a residual, not being explained by increases in the volume of land, labour, and capital employed.

The pendulum of interpretation may now be swinging back somewhat in favour of capital. Further estimates of capital formation have been laboriously assembled and those recently published by Feinstein for Britain are not in accordance with the Deane and Cole interpretation which had received growing acceptance during the 1960s. Feinstein's data, which will be discussed later, point to the investment ratio rising sharply during the eighteenth century from about 8% in the 1760s to 14% in the 1790s, almost doubling in a Rostow–Lewis manner. However, thereafter, with the exception of a dip during the Napoleonic Wars, investment's absorption of income in proportionate terms did not change and was not lifted to a new higher level by the coming of the railway. Recent estimates constructed by Lévy-Leboyer show a somewhat similar picture with the share of French national product invested increasing from about 7% in the 1810s to 12% by the 1850s and then remaining at this level for the next four or five decades. However although the Rostow–Lewis view may now be finding new foundations, the stress placed on the investment ratio has to be viewed in terms of a wider perspective. One reason for the appreciable rise in the ratio during the onset of industrialization is that at this stage in an economy's modernization, capital goods are relatively expensive compared with consumption goods. Initially there is no machine-producing industry and once producer goods have evolved beyond the point of being cheap, crude and self built, there may occur a period, albeit brief, when they are relatively costly. Subsequently the growing demand for capital goods will lead to the emergence of specialist builders. In addition to the play of specific factors, it may be important to turn to the movement of the consumption ratio. A rapid doubling or tripling of the investment ratio, partly caused by supply inelasticies, appears dramatic, an event consistent with a revolutionary interpretation of industrialization. Even though it may occur, it is accommodated by a small decline in the share of consumption, of the order of not much more than 10% during a period when income is continuously rising in the medium term relatively to population growth. Perhaps what is more important is not the comparison of the investment ratio at the beginning and end of the stage of the onset of industrialization but rather changes in its very long term behaviour.

The investment ratio in a pre-modern society is generally thought to be very low, of the order of 3% of income, although in England's case at least it could rise to about 6% for limited periods, as after the plague and the Great Fire of London. These short term movements may have of course been due to dishoarding, hoards having been accumulated precisely for such 'rainy day' periods, or to a reduction in conspicuous consumption. However during industrialization the investment ratio rises secularly, probably as a result of a changed view of what the future holds, and then remains stubbornly at a new higher level. The magnitude of the shift in the ratio is substantial but it has to be considered with the movement of other variables. Europe's industrialization took place against a background of rapid population growth and in Britain's case at least capital per head was only barely maintained, according to Feinstein's data, between 1760 and 1830, but over this period output per head almost doubled. Investment was required simply to maintain the existing capital: population ratio but changes in the nature and quality of the factors of production lead to increases in productivity which increased income and accommodated the need for investment. This raises questions not simply about the growth of the volume of the input of capital and its consequent absorption of income but rather about the nature, quality, and character of the new capital employed during industrialization.

Unfortunately sources-of-growth calculations provide little assistance in this area. Capital is assumed to be homogeneous, a premise which may be of some validity in the short term, but crumbles over longer periods, especially when they span marked discontinuities in an economy's development. Feinstein's data indicate that capital inputs were responsible for about 25% of the 2% per annum increase in British real output during the century after 1760, whereas the 'residual' accounted for about 35%. Such quantitative pointers to the sources of growth during industrialization should not cause alarm, despondency, or even surprise. At the outset before considering the implications, it should be realized that there are major problems in measuring the growth of the real capital stock. In particular the necessary price indices required for deflation are rare and unreliable and consequently any resultant series, and this is not to deny their worth, will not adequately reflect improvements in the quality of capital. These 'measurement' problems alone will produce a downward bias with regard to the role of capital. However a positive residual does not simply arise because of the pardonable failure of the input series to take into account changes in the quality of the factor employed. It is also a product of productivity growth, mainly arising from increasing returns to scale, the redistribution of factors of production, and technological change. All these factors can be assumed to have played a major role in growth during a period of structural transformation of an economy brought about by industrialization. Scale effects will arise as both production units develop and an economy becomes more fully integrated. The greater spread of market forces will lead to the migration of labour and capital to areas within the economy where they can obtain the highest return. This shift from low to high productivity employments will produce a rise in output not accounted for by increased inputs. Lastly there is technological change, moulded by the relative costs of factors of production, but usually embodied in capital and so the residual partly measures another side of the contribution of capital to growth.

As the capital stock grows during industrialization, its composition changes. Generally in the early stages of growth the biggest demands for capital arise from urbanization and the development of transport systems. The demand of manufacturing industry is normally small and a high proportion of its share of investment consists of inventories. The need for stocks declines with the integration of the economy brought about by improved transport but at the same time the volume of producer's equipment substantially increases. Consequently with the tailing off of construction expenditure, industry's share rises. It would seem that in Britain's case fixed industrial and commercial capital rose from 5% to 25% of domestic reproducible capital between 1760 and 1860. Business investment in Germany increased from a seventh to nearly half of total net investment between the early 1850s and the opening years of the twentieth century. These changes in the type of investment undertaken will produce mirror reflections in the mobilization of savings – in the demands placed upon the markets for credit and capital – which in turn will shape the pattern of institutional development that takes place to accommodate them.

A consideration of the methods used by manufacturers to raise capital and credit during the industrial revolution is important, not only in itself but also because the techniques adopted tended to mould financial behaviour throughout the nineteenth century. The greater development of financial practices was a consequence of the amount of resources absorbed by the growing industrial sector and especially of the type of assets involved. Attempts have been made to construct series displaying the growth of investment for both specific industries and the economy. All are exploratory exercises,[1] difficult forays to mount, into an era bereft of any reliable and continuous quantitative source material, and consequently their foundations, especially at the level of the economy, are very fragile. It is therefore not surprising that there is little agreement between them, though it is unfortunate for present purposes that the largest differences arise in the areas of industry and trade. The most recent estimates by Feinstein[2] are in conflict with earlier constructed series, their author considers them to be the product of conjecture, but they are the most comprehensive. They indicate that gross domestic fixed capital formation in the case of industrial and commercial fixed assets rose from £0.77m. per annum at current prices in the 1760s to £5m. per annum by the 1810s and reached the level of £13.29m. by the 1840s. Consequently the share of fixed investment absorbed by the industrial and commercial sector increased from about 20% in the decades around the 1770s to over a third by the middle decades of the nineteenth century. Fixed industrial investment appears to have grown at about 3% per annum in real terms for the first century of industrialization, and this secular increase from the 1790s was due primarily to investment in machinery rather than in buildings to house it. The key characteristic of this investment, which distinguished it from previous outlays, was its growingly specific nature. Chapman has found that fixed capital assets held by textile manufacturers in the middle decades of the eighteenth century had general rather than specific uses, this being an insurance against the vagaries of trade and the erratic course of economic change.[3] Such hedging also took place through involvement in other activities such as farming, malting and the ownership of inns.

Although there is considerable disagreement over the amount of demand for financial resources generated by the transformation of English manufacturing industry, it is generally accepted that savings within the economy were not inadequate to support industrialization.[4] This is not to imply that individual entrepreneurs in the eighteenth and nineteenth centuries did not face considerable difficulties in raising funds for either commencing or expanding production. However, generally the problem was the personal one of obtaining finance, rather than resources being either totally unobtainable or insufficient for envisaged needs. There were geographical and institutional barriers which impaired the mobilization of savings but during the eighteenth century financial markets began to emerge which brought savers and borrowers into contact. This chapter will review these general developments. The next will look at the growth of a number of major industries as it is evident that each industry and each industrial district had specific financing methods.[5]

★

The first step towards the creation of a formal capital market was the development of long-term borrowing by the state in order to finance war expenditure, a process begun by the Tontine of 1693. This market became fully developed during the first half of the eighteenth century and by the 1750s the London bourgeoisie, institutions and trustees were placing substantial sums in government securities.[6] The acquisition of government securities throughout the eighteenth century seems to have been predominantly a metropolitan habit. In the provinces the mortgage market was more important. Here the key figure was the attorney and although most of the transactions he arranged were for financing consumption or real-estate development, there are some recorded cases of savings being directed into the coal and glass industries.[7] Yorkshire land law was actually modified in the 1710s specifically in order that tradesmen in the cloth trade could provide acceptable security for loans to provide working capital for their businesses.[8] While nearly all of these changes, especially those in the metropolis, were remote from the needs of the industrialist, they do mark the beginnings of regional capital markets which in turn allowed the establishment of other financial institutions.

Similarly another important step forward was the absorption of the 'law merchant' into the formal legal system at the beginning of the eighteenth century. The Payment of Bills Act, 1698 and the Promissory Notes Act, 1704 put foreign and inland bills on the same statutory footing. During the next decade the foundations of modern commercial law regarding bills of exchange were laid. The doctrine of negotiability was recognized and the rights and liabilities of the parties to a bill were established legally in considerable detail. The finishing touches were added by Chief Justice Mansfield during the middle decades of the eighteenth century through establishing practice where it was still uncertain with the aid of special juries of merchants. This was a major advance over the situation in the 1690s when Sir Josiah Child commented: 'it is well if, after great expenses of time and money, we can make our own Counsel understand one-half of our case, we being amongst them as in a foreign country.'[9] These legal developments placed England in a unique position. The bill of exchange became the engine of commercial and industrial credit as a result of the flexibility of the legal code which acknowledged mercantile custom and practice to be the guiding rule. As a result in England it was not necessary to express on a bill that value had been given, a bill could be drawn and made payable in the same place, and from 1765 could be drawn payable to bearer. However in France the position of the bill remained fixed, the mere transfer of a trade debt, as a consequence of legal conservatism.[10]

The development of state funded and floating debt, the integration of the mortgage market through intermediaries such as attorneys, and the increased flexibility of commercial bills were important stages in the establishment of the conditions allowing the emergence of fully-fledged financial institutions. During the first half of the eighteenth century this occurred mainly in London through growth of state borrowing. There existed in the metropolis by 1720 an embryonic market for credit and capital in which the principal intermediaries were the Bank of England, a number of private bankers, and the stock exchange which provided a secondary market in government debt.[11] There were no similar developments in the provinces but the absence of people calling themselves bankers should not be taken literally. Although the great growth of country banking did not occur until half a century later, there were even in the 1720s many people in provincial towns and cities who would discount bills, remit funds and arrange loans.

One possible consequence of these financial developments of the first half of the eighteenth century was a fall in the rate of interest. The secular trend of the yield on government stocks was gently downwards from the 1690s until the 1750s and the rate on short-term securities followed a similar course, as did private rates. At the same time the differentials between long- and short-term rates, and between government and private rates narrowed. Interest rates rose from the 1750s but were at low levels from the mid-1770s and even fell between the mid-1780s and the mid-1790s.[12] It is difficult to establish the mechanism causing the fall in the rate of interest. Most probably it was due to special market conditions arising out of a conjunction of an increase in the volume of savings seeking a relatively secure placement with a decline in the amount of government bonds available for purchase. The markets in state and private debt were linked through the London banks and insurance companies which both invested in the funds and provided agricultural mortgages.[13]

The fall in the rate of interest appears to have had an important positive effect upon the volume of land sales, enclosures and transport and urban improvements. Pressnell has drawn a convincing picture of sympathy between low interest rates and high investment in these areas, at least at the major turning points. However, it is doubtful whether the secular decline of the first half of the eighteenth century had any major stimulative effect upon industrial investment as was once suggested. Industrialists in general appear to have raised very little capital externally other than through personal and filial connections. Such a pattern of behaviour diminished considerably their sensitivity to movements in the rate of interest. It is also probable that the rate of interest was not a crucial variable in their calculations, because normally industrial investment yielded a much higher rate of return and had a shorter 'life' than capital outlays in agriculture and public utilities. Probably what counted most in the pace and timing of manufacturing investment on the supply side was the sheer availability of funds rather than their price, given the restricted personal pools of savings on which entrepreneurs could draw.[14]

Commercial transactions, unlike government borrowing, were subject to the Usury laws. These restricted the extent of interest rate sensitivity of private business because when the yield on government securities rose above the legal maximum, funds did switch from private to government paper in sufficient volume to cause liquidity problems for landowners, merchants and manufacturers. The legal maximum of 5% could be stretched in the case of bills to 5.25% through the inclusion of commission to cover special expenses, such as the cost of postage. With regard to advances, bankers had found means by the late 1820s to stretch the legal maximum to 6.5% or 7%. However, the penalties for infringing the laws were severe. In the case of a bill, the right to protest was lost together with the right to use the bill as a proof of the existence of the debt involved, while the fines imposed amounted to three times the capital sum involved. The laws were modified in 1833 and 1837, but with regard to paper with a maturity longer than three months, they continued on the statute book until 1854.[15]

The Usury laws created one set of difficulties for a manufacturer seeking finance, another was posed by the Bubble Act of 1720. This criminal statute appears to have had the aim of preventing the free creation of a large stock of freely transferable shares. Consequently after 1720, company promoters had to apply to either the Crown or Parliament in order to establish a joint stock company, although ways were soon devised to sidestep this expensive process. Initially the Crown officers interpreted very harshly the clauses of what was a very ambiguous statute to the extent that shares in patents could not be assigned to more than five persons. The situation had eased by the middle decades of the eighteenth century and substantial numbers of unincorporated companies were being established privately, their trust deeds usually containing the clause 'Proviso that nothing therein shall be construed an Undertaking against 6th George I'. The numbers of unincorporated companies grew during the last three decades of the eighteenth century, especially in the fields of insurance and non-ferrous metal working. These concerns were, strictly, large co-partnerships whose assets were vested in trustees via deeds of settlement. While the trust device did allow English lawyers to circumvent the probable intentions of the framers of the Bubble Act, there were still considerable problems in establishing an unincorporated company. It was difficult to make the shares of these companies freely transferable, while their trustees bore great responsibilities yet generally received small rewards. The Scottish legal code was less rigid and companies could be formed north of the border by a 'Seal of Cause' from a municipality.

Until the 1760s the main aim of promoters of unincorporated

companies was to raise capital in larger amounts than could be obtained by a simple partnership. However, during the last quarter of the eighteenth century there were an increasing number of attempts to obtain the privilege of limited liability which could only be successful through incorporation by the Crown or Parliament. Most of the industrial unincorporated companies formed in the eighteenth century were involved in the non-ferrous metal trades of Birmingham and Bristol. The Birmingham Metal Company, established in 1781, came to be a model for further promotions, such as the Birmingham Mining and Copper Company of 1790 and the Rose Copper Company of 1793.[16] The experience of William Champion is illustrative of the problems that some industrial entrepreneurs faced in forming such companies. He had set up a copper-smelting concern in Bristol and by 1761 was working it in conjunction with three other partners. The partnership was then enlarged to twelve but this did not provide the finance that was required and by 1765 it was short of funds. This was due to the partners not contributing the capital that they had agreed to subscribe and the resulting shortfall had to be met by borrowing at high rates of interest. Actually at least an additional £200,000 was required to finance expansion. It was thought that this sum could be raised by making the company's partnership shares freely transferable but only if it had limited liability. Two warrants were obtained from Parliament in 1767 which gave authority for the preparation of a charter of incorporation but the grant of a charter was subsequently denied.[17] This attempt to obtain incorporation by the proprietors of the Warmley Company appears to have been the first where limited liability was one of the major objectives of the promoters.[18]

Two forms of business organization were entirely unaffected by the stipulation of the Bubble Act – the ship partnership[19] and non-ferrous metal mining partnerships – as the former came under Admiralty law and the latter under Stannary law. Stannary law developed mainly in Cornwall and Devon where it established the custom for other mining besides that of tin. Its original basis was a simple partnership of working 'adventurers' who were part owners of the products and assets of the streamwork that they exploited. However, by the beginning of the eighteenth century most 'adventurers' were usually blind investors, often merchants, employing a labour force. Alluvial mining had generally been replaced by drifts and shafts which became deeper as the century progressed and consequently generated a demand for substantial amounts of capital. This led to the development of the cost book company. These were constituted by shareholders who jointly agreed to the proportion of the costs that they were willing to bear and whose names were entered in a cost book for a share, usually an eighth. Such mining company shares were freely transferable because originally they were nothing more than a share of ownership. The companies were managed by pursers who called monthly or quarterly meetings at which either the profits were divided or further capital was raised. By 1777 there were 86 copper mines in Cornwall, of which 20 accounted for most of the output, with between 500 and 1,000 investors in the industry, most of whom were resident outside the county. Although the cost book company system allowed investors to spread risk, the frequent division of profits prevented companies from either building up reserves or pursuing long-term marketing strategies.[20]

A similar form of organization to the cost book company, known as the pay-share partnership, formed the basis of lead mining in the Pennines. Such concerns ranged from associations of a few wealthy partners to companies established by large groups of small shareholders. By the end of the eighteenth century the main investors were landowners, lead merchants, and local business and professional men. Many of the smaller investors had retired with the expansion of the industry, as in Cornwall, and were replaced by middle-class rentiers, including manufacturers from Leeds and Bradford who were preponderant in mines in Nidderdale and Wharfdale.[21]

Generally the Bubble Act had very little impact upon the finance and organization of manufacturing and extractive industry. The individual proprietorship or the small co-partnership had become the framework within which nearly all concerns could raise the finance that they required, and consequently the Act did not prove to be a restrictive straitjacket. Actually the partnership could be used as the basis for very flexible forms of organization, with new partners being recruited either to increase a firm's financial resources or provide management and technical skills. Extremely complex and capital intensive concerns involving multi-site operations and combining manufacturing, merchanting and even banking could and did operate as partnerships, as shown by the activities of the Foleys in the iron industry at the turn of the eighteenth century.[22] The Act of 1720 may have been inconvenient for some but it was not a major check to industrial development. Even after the Bubble Act was repealed in 1825, the partnership continued to be the unit of organization for most of English manufacturing industry for at least a further half-century.

★

The English legal framework in the form of the Usury laws and the Bubble Act constituted no institutional barrier to industrialization. Similarly the economy had a favourable general factor endowment. While certain categories of labour, particularly the skilled, may have been in short supply, labour generally, through rapid population growth, was abundant until at least the 1870s. This situation, coupled with the growth in agricultural productivity which kept pace with population growth, resulted in real wage rates not rising rapidly. Consequently the cost of labour recruitment did not act as a brake upon the growth of profits. As capital investment by firms was generally financed internally through the ploughback of profits, the economy's factor endowment did not retard capital accumulation in manufacturing and extractive industry. However, the relative abundance of labour compared with capital may have led firms to have pursued policies of capital widening rather than capital deepening. In the very much longer run this may have had the negative result of retarding technological development which in turn restrained the growth of investment.[23]

However, one further factor of production – land – has to be considered. In the extractive and processing industries, the niggardliness of nature did provide a spur to a second shift in capital intensity, particularly from the 1830s. By then surface seams had generally been exhausted in commercially worked coalfields and consequently deeper pits had to be sunk which required greater inputs of capital and technology. Similarly the exploitation of lower-grade ores in the iron industry necessitated larger blast furnaces for economical smelting. For example, the cost of two blast furnaces with their associated equipment, built at Congreaves in 1861, amounted to £6,000, a substantial increase compared with the 1840s. Their output was, of course, much larger but the number required to work them was approximately the same as in 1843, namely 44 men and 16 boys.[24] The most dramatic change in the capital intensity and the capital:labour ratio of the primary iron industry came in the 1850s with the opening up of the Cleveland ore field and the establishment of the industry at Middlesborough. The problem posed by the relative scarcity of land compared with capital arose at least 60 years after the onset of industrialization. The two main financial problems that most first-generation industrialists faced were first, raising the initial funds with which to buy buildings and plant, and second, obtaining credit to carry stocks.

★

The growth of industrial investment from the 1760s led to inter-sectorial shifts of savings within the economy. As the largest industry, agriculture would appear to have been the main source of resources to facilitate the growth of industry. However, the land both absorbed and released capital during the eighteenth century and it is difficult to estimate with any precision the actual direction of the net flow. Agricultural change took place alongside industrial change, and the improvement of farming consumed a large amount of savings. For example there was a burst of enclosure from 1780 to 1810, which ran in parallel with the establishment of the cotton industry, and although the cost per acre varied considerably, the national average was about £1 8s. (£1.40) per acre.[25] Some of the necessary funds were obtained through mortgages, hence the tie between fluctuations in the rate of interest and the timing of enclosures, but estate revenues provided a large amount of the finance required. This reduced agriculture's ability to release funds which could be used for industrial investment in stocks and plant. There was also a flow of resources·from industry into land as many industrialists bought estates for various reasons, but mainly to enhance their social status. Consequently it is difficult to establish the magnitude of the role played by 'agricultural' capital in industry during the critical decades of the last quarter of the eighteenth century. Similarly with regard to the regional flow of credit through the banking system that developed after 1750, it is probable that the significance of the surplus credit balances built up in agricultural areas before 1815 has been overestimated. Arable farmers themselves required credit to finance the period between sowing and threshing, and so during the summer months were net drawers of credit. It is possible that grain farmers became important 'lenders' only after they had accumulated capital through the windfall profits of the French war period.[26]

Landowners did play an important role in industrial development. Such activity was accepted as a normal part of estate exploitation and, unlike on the continent, carried no social stigma. However, they limited themselves mainly to the development of their own estates. In this they benefited from English law, which gave them the ownership of all minerals on their estates, except gold and silver, a unique legal position in Western Europe.[27] After agriculture and forestry, the exploitation of mineral deposits was the most common estate activity. The importance of noble landlords and gentry in mining and in the iron industry in some areas and regions was considerable. The Earls of Shrewsbury and Devonshire, the Duke of Rutland and Lord Paget played a major role in the industrial development of the North Midlands as did the Bute family on the Durham coalfield.[28] However, increasingly after 1750 landlords withdrew from direct participation in industrial concerns and by the 1820s the aristocratic entrepreneur was a rare figure. The increasing expense of exploitation together with the cost of employing professionals such as viewers, managers and mineral agents, was by 1800 sufficient to deter the gentry and lesser landowners. Instead mines and ironworks were leased off in order to avoid the risks of fraud, inefficiency and losses which not infrequently arose from any concern entrusted to a manager or agent.[29] The problems posed by the increasing amounts of capital required, coupled with the commensurate rise in risk, continued to grow through the nineteenth century causing more and more of the greater landlords to sell off their industrial interests, or at least to lease. The Marquess of Stafford changed from being an entrepreneur to a rentier at the height of the boom of the 1820s. In this particular case local social and political pressures were responsible for the decision but there was also a desire to insulate the family income against the increasing vagaries of the local trade cycle.[30]

By 1800 industrial incomes were an important part of the revenues of great estates. Landowners did place capital derived from agricultural pursuits in the development of industrial enterprises, overwhelmingly mines and ironworks. However, during the second half of the eighteenth century and particularly after 1775, agriculture in net terms was probably not releasing funds in the form of either capital or credit flows to be absorbed in the general expansion of industry. Agricultural improvement itself was a capital- and credit-consuming process, while the growth of population from the mid-century coupled with the problems of the war economy from the 1790s acted as further spurs to investment in the soil.

★

The major financial innovation of the industrial revolution was the growth of country banking after 1750. Two of the main functions performed by these institutions were the provision of means of payment through note issues and the generation of a supply of credit by discounting bills. These two activities were linked as notes were generally placed in circulation as a result of discounting. The largest part of the profits of the Smith Bank in Nottingham in the 1780s came from interest, discounts and commission. It charged a fixed rate for loans, overdrafts and discounts – either 4% or 5% – the precise rate being determined by the particular circumstances of each transaction. Generally all country banks preferred to ration credit rather than widely vary their loan charges. The Smith bank circumvented the Usury laws during the last quarter of the eighteenth century by granting overdrafts instead of straight loans during periods of high interest rates, being thus able to charge a commission on turnover in addition to interest. Three main types of security were taken by the bank for advances – mortgages which could be transferred by assignment or sale, personal bonds, and promissory notes in the case of smaller sums. The provision of short-term finance through discounts, loans and overdrafts by concerns like the Smith Bank was extremely important for early industrial firms, given their high ratios of inventories to fixed capital. The third main role performed by the country banks was the supply of remittance facilities, especially to London. Actually the Smith Bank had developed because of Thomas Smith I's ability to send funds to London through his connections with metropolitan goldsmith bankers.[31] By the 1780s the most important business of the London 'City' banks was their agency work for the rapidly growing number of country banks. It was the development of this correspondent system which transformed the unit country banks into a national banking system.

The number of country banks rose from about 12 in 1750 to more than 300 by 1800. Generally they were small, the typical concern in the 1800s having an equity capital of only £10,000, as a result of being restricted to having no more than six partners by the charter of the Bank of England. Few had branches, hence the importance of the correspondent system, and so their fortunes were tied closely to those of the local areas that they served. They were not evenly distributed across the country and even in the industrial North West there was by 1800 a marked absence of formal financial institutions. The place of banks in this area was taken generally by the merchant, and the need for currency was met by a circulation of bills.[32] The structure of English country banking with ease of access and paltry capitals was inherently unstable.

Industrialists comprised one of the main groups who established banks after 1750, another being attorneys. They became bankers in order to meet their need for currency and capital, with many manufacturers beginning their banking careers through issuing tokens and promissory notes, usually to meet wage payments. This was necessary because the English currency in the eighteenth century was generally in a chaotic situation and coin was usually in short supply. The most acute shortage occurred after the crisis of 1793 during which a quarter of the existing country bankers stopped payment, a situation which led many entrepreneurs to become at least quasi-bankers. Note-issuing became easier after the suspension of cash payments in 1797 but the shortage of small change continued.[33] This problem was at least partially solved through a greater use of trade tokens and a further development of the truck system. Industrialist bankers were found mainly in the metals and textile industries and in brewing. The manufacturer, through establishing a bank, attempted to satisfy his own financial requirements but by providing banking services to the public, especially through deposits, could augment the resources of his manufacturing enterprise. 'Industrial' banks rarely provided long-term loans to other concerns, while the granting of such facilities was in any case fraught with danger. One of the main reasons why 'industrial' banks failed was because the banker/entrepreneur borrowed, on the long term, resources from his bank with which to support his industrial interests.[34]

There is considerable controversy over the extent to which country banks were generally prepared to provide long-term capital to industry. A growing body of evidence now indicates that banks did provide medium- and long-term finance in addition to credit, especially in the textile, non-ferrous metal mining and primary iron industries.[35] As well as variations in the practice of individual banks and in the experience and needs of different industries, there were also regional differences in the willingness to lend long. It would almost appear to have been the standard practice in South Wales.[36] The existence of only a few wealthy mercantile firms in Hull led the banks there to grant extensive advances, sometimes with little or no security, over long periods.[37] It may be possible to begin to generalize from these regional variations which suggest that where local informal supplies of finance were inadequate for development, banks stepped in and provided capital in addition to credit. On the one side there would have been the demand for such finance while on the other its provision, given a degree of circumspection, could have been highly profitable. There is supporting evidence of a negative nature for this hypothesis in the case of the Lancashire cotton industry. Formal banking institutions were not established in the North West until the 1790s because there were many quasi-bankers, primarily merchants, who provided credit and capital and who continued to do so even when banks began to be formed. Consequently banks in east Lancashire from the 1790s until the 1820s were left with only the field of credit provision and, once accustomed to this business, were little prepared to step outside it.[38] Therefore it would appear that only when capital requirements had a degree of lumpiness, as with deep mining and primary metalworking, or in the case of areas where the informal supply of capital was extremely limited, did banks become important providers of fixed capital. What is more certain is that banks only very rarely provided long-term finance to newly formed enterprises seeking initial capital.[39]

The recurrent financial crises experienced by the economy, generated in part by the weak structure of country banking, resulted eventually in legislative intervention in the 1820s. Since 1815 the government had favoured the introduction of joint stock banking and had experience of its development in Ireland. However, until the panic of 1825 the opposition of the private bankers and the Bank of England had blocked Lord Liverpool's plans for reform. By the Act of 1826 large banking co-partnerships were allowed to be established outside a 65-mile radius London and in 1833 non-note-issuing joint stock banks were permitted to operate within that radius. The initial growth of joint stock banking was slow with only 33 banks being formed by 1833, but thereafter the number of banks increased rapidly during the 1830s boom, particularly in Lancashire and Yorkshire.[40] But the new joint stock banks were in size and nature very much like their private counterparts, having small capitals, few branches, and parochial outlooks.[41]

One distinguishing characteristic of the joint stock banks was their preference for deposits, mobilized by the cheque as well as by discounting, rather than note-issuing. Estimates indicate that the deposits of all London banks increased at 2.4% per annum between 1824 and 1844 while country deposits rose more rapidly at an average of 4.3%.[42] These funds were invested in bills of exchange instead of government securities, a commercial preference reinforced by the banks' parochial nature. This investment pattern, coupled with the growing tendency to place money at call with the emerging discount houses, widened the London money market.[43] Consequently by the end of the 1830s a national distributive mechanism for credit had been fully established which worked in the following way:

> The means by which the bills in the London market are discounted are derived from the surplus deposits of the agricultural banks?–To a very great extent; the money of the agricultural banks is thus brought down to the manufacturing districts and made useful there....
>
> Is it not the case that the agricultural banks furnish to the discount brokers in London a certain portion of their banking capitals, whereby those demands of the borrowers in Manchester are supplied?–That is the case.[44]

However, apart from this national credit network, the structure of banking in the 1840s in its essentials was very little different from that existing in the mid-1820s. The new joint stock banks were generally hardly distinguishable from the private country banks in terms of resources, management and branch networks. They were essentially weak local institutions and their frail fabric was a major contributive factor to the financial instability which continued to plague the economy until the 1870s.

Notes

(Place of publication is London unless otherwise stated)

1 P. Deane, 'Capital Formation in Britain before the Railway Age', *Economic Development and Cultural Change*, IX, 1961; S. Pollard, 'The Growth and Distribution of Capital in Great Britain, c. 1770–1870', *Third International Conference of Economic History* (Munich, 1965), Paris, 1968.

2 C. H. Feinstein, 'Capital Formation in Great Britain' in P. Mathias and M. M. Postan (eds) *Cambridge Economic History of Europe*, VII, *The Industrial Economies: Capital, Labour*, Part I, *Britain, France, Germany and Scandinavia*, 1978.

3 S. D. Chapman, 'Industrial Capital before the Industrial Revolution: an Analysis of the Assets of a Thousand Textile Entrepreneurs, c. 1730–1750' in N. B. Harte and K. G. Ponting (eds) *Textile History and Economic History*, Manchester, 1973.

4 M. M. Postan, 'Recent Trends in the Accumulation of Capital', *Economic History Review*, VI, 1935; H. Heaton, 'Financing the Industrial Revolution', *Bulletin of the Business Historical Society*, XI, 1937.

5 F. Crouzet, 'Capital Formation in Great Britain during the Industrial Revolution' in Crouzet (ed.) *Capital Formation in the Industrial Revolution*, 1972, p. 183.

6 P. G. M. Dickson, *The Financial Revolution in England*, 1967, pp. 300–2.

7 B. L. Anderson, 'The Attorney and the Early Capital Market in Lancashire' in J. R. Harris (ed.) *Liverpool and Merseyside: Essays in the Economy and Social History of the Port and its Hinterland*, 1969; B. L. Anderson, 'Provincial Aspects of the Financial Revolution in the Eighteenth Century', *Business History*, XI, 1969.

8 F. Sheppard and V. Belcher, 'The Middlesex and Yorkshire Deeds Registries', *Journal of the Society of Archivists*, 1978.

9 C. H. S. Ffoot, 'The Development of the Law of Negotiable Instruments and the Law of Trusts', *Journal of the Institute of Bankers*, LIX, 1938; J. Milnes Holden, *The History of Negotiable Instruments in English Law*, 1955, pp. 30–55, 99–114.

10 B. L. Anderson, 'Money and the Structure of Credit in the Eighteenth Century', *Business History*, XII, 1970, p. 90.

11 On the Bank of England see J. H. Clapham, *The Bank of England. A History*, I, *1694–1797*, Cambridge, 1944, and J. K. Horsefield, *British Monetary Experiments 1650–1710*, 1960; on private banking see R. D. Richards, *The Early History of Banking in England*, 1929, and D. M. Joslin, 'London Private Bankers 1720–1785', *Economic History Review*, 2nd series, VIII, 1956. On the stock exchange see E. V. Morgan and W. A. Thomas, *The Stock Exchange*, 1962, and Dickson, op. cit., pp. 486–520.

12 L. S. Pressnell, 'The Rate of Interest in the Eighteenth Century' in Pressnell (ed.) *Studies in the Industrial Revolution*, 1960, pp. 179–80.

13 Dickson, op. cit., pp. 483–4.

14 Pressnell, op. cit., pp. 190–5; D. S. Landes, *The Unbound Prometheus*, Cambridge, 1969, pp. 64–5.

15 S. Shapiro, *Capital and the Cotton Industry in the Industrial Revolution*, Ithaca, New York, 1967, pp. 64–73.

16 A. B. Du Bois, *The English Business Company after the Bubble Act 1720–1800*, 1938.

17 J. Day, *Bristol Brass. A History of the Industry*, Newton Abbot, 1973, pp. 83–93; see also S. Pollard, *The Genesis of Modern Management*, Harmondsworth, 1968, pp. 103–4.

18 Du Bois, op. cit., p. 95.

19 On the ship-owning partnership see R. Davies, *The Rise of the English Shipping Industry*, 1962, pp. 82–104; R. C. Jarvis, 'Fractional Shareholdings in British Merchant Ships with Special Reference to the 64ths', *Marriners' Mirror*, XLV, 1959; R. Craig and R. C. Jarvis, *Liverpool Registry of Merchant Ships*, Cheetham Society, XV, 3rd series, Manchester, 1967.

20 R. R. Pennington, *Stannary Law. A History of the Mining Law of Cornwall and Devon*, Newton Abbot, 1973, pp. 7–11, 147–53; J. Rowe, *Cornwall in the Age of the Industrial Revolution*, Liverpool, 1953, pp. 22–4, 47, 62–6, 86, 133–4; see also Pollard, op. cit., pp. 87–93.

21 A. Rastrick and B. Jennings, *A History of Lead Mining in the Pennines*, 1965, pp. 183–4, 253–8.

22 R. G. Schaffer, 'Genesis and Structure of the Foley "Ironworks in Partnership" of 1692', *Business History*, XIII, 1971; S. D. Chapman, 'The Peels in the Early English Cotton Industry', *Business History*, XI, 1969.

23 H. J. Habakkuk, *American and British Technology in the Nineteenth Century*, 1967, pp. 150–1.

24 D. B. Evans, 'The Iron and Steel Industry of South Staffordshire from 1760 to 1950', unpublished M.A. thesis, University of Birmingham, 1951, pp. 91–3.

25 See J. D. Chambers and G. E. Mingay, *The Agricultural Revolution 1750–1880*, 1966, pp. 82–5.

26 E. L. Jones, Introduction in Jones (ed.) *Agriculture and Economic Growth in England 1650–1815*, 1967, pp. 28–32.

27 D. Spring, 'English Landowners and Nineteenth Century Industrialism' in J. T. Ward and R. G. Wilson (eds) *Land and Industry. The Landed Estate and the Industrial Revolution*, Newton Abbot, 1971, pp. 16–17.

28 J. T. Ward, 'Landowners and Mining' in Ward and Wilson, op. cit., pp. 68, 70; Pollard, op. cit., p. 82.

29 See G. E. Mingay, *English Landed Society in the Eighteenth Century*, 1963, pp. 189–95.

30 E. Richards, 'The Industrial Face of a Great Estate: Trentham and Lilleshall, 1780–1860', *Economic History Review*, 2nd series, XXVII, 1974, pp. 414–30. See also D. Spring, 'The English Landed Estate in the Age of Coal and Iron, 1830–80', *Journal of Economic History*, XI, 1951; F. M. L. Thomson, *English Landed Society in the Nineteenth Century*, 1963.

31 J. A. S. L. Leighton-Boyce, *Smith the Bankers, 1658–1958*, 1958, pp. 14, 45–7, 58.

32 T. S. Ashton, 'The Bill of Exchange and Private Banks in Lancashire, 1790–1830', *Economic History Review*, XV, 1945; B. L. Anderson, 'Money and the Structure of Credit in the Eighteenth Century', *Business History*, XII, 1970, pp. 94–5.

33 L. S. Pressnell, *Country Banking in the Industrial Revolution*, Oxford, 1956, pp. 14–17, 23–6; R. E. Cameron, 'England, 1750–1844' in Cameron (ed.) *Banking in the Early Stages of Industrialisation*, 1967, pp. 18–19.

34 Pressnell, op. cit., p. 291.

35 In addition to Pressnell, op. cit., and Cameron, op. cit., see P. Mathias, 'Capital, Credit and Enterprise in the Industrial Revolution', *Journal of European Economic History*, II, 1973.

36 See A. H. John, *The Industrial Development of South Wales, 1750–1850*, Cardiff, 1949, pp. 43–9; R. O. Roberts, 'The Operations of the Brecon Old Bank of Wilkins & Co., 1778–1890', *Business History*, I, 1958.

37 J. M. Bellamy, 'Some Aspects of the Economy of Hull in the Nineteenth Century with Special Reference to Business History', unpublished Ph.D. thesis, University of Hull, 1966, chapter VII.

38 M. M. Edwards, *The Growth of the British Cotton Trade*, Manchester, 1967, pp. 198, 216–18.

39 Crouzet, op. cit., pp. 180–1.

40 *Circular to Bankers*, May 1836, pp. 330–1.

41 Cameron, op. cit., pp. 23–9.

42 D. K. Addie, 'English Bank Deposits before 1844', *Economic History Review*, 2nd series, XXIII, 1970, pp. 290, 292.

43 W. T. C. King, *History of the London Discount Market*, 1936, pp. 89–103.

44 *B.P.P.*, 1841, V, *Second Report of the Select Committee on Banks of Issue*, evidence of P. Moon James, Managing Director of the Manchester and Salford Joint Stock Bank, qq. 1533, 1535.

2 Financing the industrial revolution II – textiles, coal and iron

The industrial revolution did not take place uniformly either geographically or across the manufacturing sector of the economy. It was essentially a process of regional economic growth and of the transformation of a limited number of industries. At the forefront was cotton, whatever general interpretation is made concerning this industry's exact strategic role within the overall modernization of the economy. The production of cotton yarn and cloth developed in three areas: East Lancashire and North Cheshire, the North Midlands, and Central Scotland. The adoption of new machinery and growing centralization of production led to the amount of fixed capital invested in the industry rising from about £0.5m. in 1787 to approximately £6.3m. in 1817.[1] There were two investment booms in Lancashire[2] – 1788 to 1793 and 1799 to 1802 – while mill building was at very high levels in the Midlands during the following years: 1783 and 1784, 1788, and 1791 and 1792.[3] English cotton firms tended to be small partnerships with the average number of persons per bankrupt enterprise being 1.4 between 1786 and 1846.[4] Generally, Scottish concerns had more partners and, as company law was less restrictive north of the border, there was a greater use of the unincorporated company[5] to mobilize capital. In the Midlands, where the industry had to compete for funds with the established hosiery and lace trades, there appears to have been greater reliance on banks to finance fixed capital investment. Fifteen spinning firms in this region had either filial or partnership connections with banking and a further five developed such links. At the 1792 peak in mill building in the Midlands, overdrafts granted by Smiths' bank, Nottingham, to cotton firms amounted to £29,921 – 30% of the bank's total advances.[6]

Until the late 1790s the industry consisted primarily of small workshops, which housed carding and spinning machinery, and printing works, with weaving being carried on in domestic premises. Most early mills, of which there were at least 142 driven by water in 1788,[7] were modified existing buildings – either corn mills, where the water wheel was retained for power, or houses and cottages. Consequently entry into the industry in terms of the amount of finance required to begin manufacturing remained relatively easy until the turn of the century. Even Arkwright's water frame, which is generally regarded as a factory rather than a domestic machine, could be housed in comparatively small mills. Profit margins in all branches of the industry were at high levels between 1785 and 1792 and from 1799 to 1803, which allowed the accumulation of reserves to finance the building of larger mills specifically designed for carding and spinning. Water power predominated in spinning until the 1820s, and the use of steam power was a very gradual development with only the largest firms being able to afford a Boulton and Watt engine.[8] Continuing their father's fustian business, John Ashworth with his brother Edmund built the New Eagley Mill in 1802 for spinning by water power at a probable cost of £2,000. Fifteen years later the factory was valued at £2,254 and its machinery at £860.[9]

The Arkwright mill at Cromford marks the beginning of the factory system in the industry and it provided a model for other early water-powered spinning factories erected in the 1790s. At this stage, steam, when applied, was used generally to provide a constant flow of water over the wheel. A three- to four-storey mill, employing 1,000 spindles, cost about £3,000 while one of twice that capacity was £5,000.[10] The most important concern during the 1790s was the group of spinning mills, printing works, and warehouses owned by the Peel family and their partners. The fire insurance valuation of their total manufacturing assets in 1795 amounted to £191,690. The family had been interested in textile-merchanting and farming since the mid-seventeenth century and their background was typical of other Blackburn calico printers and cotton spinners. By the mid-1790s the Peels owned a number of mills and printing works at widely dispersed sites in Lancashire and the Midlands. These were operated and financed through a series of interlocking partnerships which brought together the necessary capital and management expertise. Most of the partners were either blood relations, in-laws, or trusted workmen. 'Outside' partners were recruited to obtain further capital and mercantile connections as was the case with the development

of the Tamworth site, where Robert Peel II went into partnership with
Joseph Wilkes, a Midlands merchant and financier, and Edward
Bickenson, a Burton brewer and capitalist.[11]

Most cotton entrepreneurs until at least the 1800s were both merchants
and manufacturers, with profits from trading activities being used to
finance the construction of a factory. Such merchant industrialists
predominated in both Lancashire and the Midlands, especially once
specialized mill building began. However, new entrants, whatever their
background, could raise capital in various ways. A partnership with either
an active or a 'sleeping' partner was common and existing manufacturers
frequently offered assistance, usually via mortgage, whereby they thus
acquired a foothold in the affairs of a competitor and, of equal
importance, a possible financial connection for their own future use.
Other sources were mill builders who were prepared to grant mortgages,
while factories were often sublet – a lucrative way of temporarily reducing
the capacity of an existing enterprise. M'Connel and Kennedy began in
the 1790s by renting, and 'room and power' could be had in Manchester
in 1814 at the cost of 4s. 6d. (22½p) to 5s. (25p) per spindle.[12]

The cost of mill building increased sharply with the building of the first
steam-powered urban factories at the turn of the century, although they
were not to be a principal feature of the industry until some decades later.
It has been estimated that a steam-powered mill cost three to four times
more than an early water mill.[13] The investment in the first M'Connel
and Kennedy mill between 1798 and 1800 amounted to £6,074 with its
steam engine. However, the unit cost of steam power did decline fairly
rapidly: a 16 h.p. Boulton and Watt engine cost £1,000 in 1797 while a 45
h.p. engine cost £2,178 five years later.[14]

Until the 1790s the amount spent on machinery was relatively small
and most spinning firms made their own, especially those in remote
situations.[15] With the rapid development of spinning and finishing
machinery in the 1790s, specialist machine makers appeared and the costs
of machinery rose. The 1795 fire insurance valuation of the Peel complex
at Burton reveals that its machinery was insured for approximately the
same sum as the buildings that housed it.[16] Machine makers did give
credit, usually six months with a 5% discount for a three-month bill.
However, many of the larger firms continued to build their own
equipment. M'Connel and Kennedy developed as both fine spinners and
machine builders, and this kept the firm in the van of technical progress.
They sold outdated machinery to other firms.[17] Second-hand machinery,
particularly for printing, could be bought on credit and, as the industry
grew, machinery could be rented along with 'room and power'.

The financing of fixed investment – buildings and machinery – was most burdensome during the early stages of the growth of an enterprise. Oldknow, Cowpe & Co. of Mansfield made no profit during its first four years and fixed capital comprised over 50% of its assets. Thereafter this ratio declined and within the next six years it had fallen to 33%. The proportion of fixed capital within the total assets of established firms did rise secularly as spinning and finishing became more technically advanced processes from the mid-1790s but it would appear on the basis of surviving business records that it seldom exceeded 50%.[18]

The need for working capital was met in a variety of ways which became more institutionalized as country banking developed and spread. The main credit instrument was the highly flexible bill of exchange while the other sources of short-term finance were tokens and truck, trade credit, and bank loans. Cotton before the 1820s had a seasonal demand for credit which reached a peak in the summer, particularly in the case of the finishing trades as a result of the physical difficulties of bleaching and washing cloth.[19]

The bill on London was the key credit instrument in Lancashire. Merchants, manufacturers and banks all dealt in and discounted bills, for they were generally regarded as being synonymous with currency. One main problem was obtaining bills of the right maturity as well as quality and there were often swap arrangements between merchants and manufacturers, especially to exchange long-dated bills for those of a shorter date or cash. However, the mutual credit club which permeated the industry and the region worked effectively only during the upswing of a boom. During periods of bad trade, credit contracted and it became difficult to raise large sums even by offering for discount, bills drawn on first class London houses.[20] Bank finance, in the form of either a discount account or an overdraft, became increasingly important during the 1790s. Actually many cotton entrepreneurs set up banks to meet their needs: the Peels had interests in four.

Merchants and wholesalers were important sources of working capital, particularly at times of expansion. Merchants allowed time for accounts to be settled and gave advances in cash or short-dated bills. Credit terms varied between different sections of the industry and between localities. One method by which fixed investment could be financed was through obtaining credit at a longer maturity than the firm in turn was granting. Initially M'Connel and Kennedy bought raw cotton on six months credit[21] but the normal terms in Liverpool until the 1850s were ten days credit followed by payment with a three months bill.[22] Generally, elsewhere a four months bill was the norm but in Manchester credit lines of up to eight months were current. In nearly every case discounts could be obtained by prompt payment.[23] Credit to weavers for yarn purchases varied considerably at the beginning of the nineteenth century and depended usually upon the relative size and standing of the spinner and weaver. The Ashworths in the 1840s sold yarn on six months credit but gave a 2.5% discount for cash.[24] Cloth was sold either to a wholesaler for cash or short-dated bills or through a commission house for an advance in either cash or bills.[25] Most of the large, dominant firms in the industry did not take credit. Once established M'Connel and Kennedy always paid promptly for raw cotton in order to secure the discount and preferred its own debtors to behave in a similar fashion. In order to stop disreputable firms obtaining large credit lines from it, M'Connel and Kennedy pursued a policy of credit screening.[26] Similarly Ashworths rarely took credit but from the 1830s became important suppliers of short-term finance. Between 1832 and 1851, debts to the New Eagley mill were equal to a third of annual yarn sales while between 1834 and 1846 this ratio rose to 50%.[27]

Cotton firms expanded mainly by the retention of profits, with occasionally partners not even taking interest, usually 5%, on their capital. Such practice was assisted by the wide profit margins current during the second half of the 1780s and the first five years of the nineteenth century. M'Connel and Kennedy grew in this manner but, after the completion of a third mill in 1820, an increasing proportion of the firm's profits were invested outside the industry in land and in the shares of insurance and water companies.[28] In the case of the Ashworth enterprise, profits were not always sufficient and at certain stages in the firm's development new partners had to be brought in and loans raised from outside the family. However, these were quickly repaid and the 'outside' partners bought out in order to keep the enterprise solely under family control. Profits, after the payment of interest on partners' capital, averaged 4.9% between 1818 and 1831 at the Ashworths' New Eagley Mill.[29]

From the 1830s weaving began to be a mechanized process. This led to the demise of the hand loom and the water-powered rural spinning mill. However, the latter could be viable economically even in the early 1850s if it had good communications with Liverpool and Manchester, while outside Lancashire the rural water mill remained a feature of the industry for at least another decade.[30] As a result of these developments, fixed capital invested in the manufacturing branches of the Lancashire cotton increased from approximately £14.8m. in 1834 to £31m. in 1856.[31] An investment in a 'typical' mill of the 1830s amounted to between £20,000 and £50,000, and at the beginning of the decade Manchester mills were employing on average 400 hands as opposed to half that number two decades before.[32]

Early power looms were expensive to operate and only really suitable for coarse fabrics. The number of hand looms declined from the mid-1830s, and after the intense depression of the late 1830s all coarser cloths were woven by power. The necessary capital for the introduction of power looms came mainly from existing cotton spinners. The mechanized weaving shed set up alongside the spinning mill slowly and gradually replaced the putting-out and sale of yarn. These 'combined' firms were most common in Stockport, Hyde and Oldham although coarse spinners in Bolton and Manchester also set up integrated mechanized weaving sheds. The vertical integration of the manufacturing processes continued during the 1840s and reached a peak during the next decade.[33] The application of steam power to spinning and weaving did not involve substantial amounts of capital investment. The financial burden for existing firms was not onerous because hand mules could be converted to power-driven self-actors by the replacement of the headstocks. Capacity could be increased by simply adding more spindles to each carriage. Higher costs were offset by the substantial economies which arose through increased running speeds while the additional power that these called for was met by either increasing the pressure of, or replacing, the boiler of the existing engine. New entrants were aided by the fall in machinery prices while the cost of mill building remained roughly constant between 1815 and 1835.[34]

It is generally assumed that firms in the industry grew during the second quarter of the nineteenth century, as previously, by the ploughback of profits. However, there are indications that profit rates were now declining. Profits at the Ashworths' New Eagley mill averaged 2.8% between 1832 and 1854 as opposed to 4.9% between 1818 and 1831. However, whether there was either a secular fall or profit rates had a greater variation over the course of the trade cycle is unclear. Margins in spinning fell from 1826 to 1833, with only a brief interruption in 1831, and remained at low levels until 1836. There was again heavy pressure on profits during the last years of the decade and the industry suffered a severe slump during the early 1840s. It was this fall in spinning margins which led many manufacturers to establish integrated weaving sheds. Output continued to expand because of the heavy burden of overheads, which made it imperative that they were spread as widely as possible. Investment in power weaving was not checked, because overall weaving capacity could be regulated through the amount of yarn either put-out or sold to 'domestic' weavers.[35]

Possibly indicative of a fall in profit margins are two new features of the finance of the industry during the second quarter of the nineteenth century. One was a growing practice of borrowing money from employees.[36] The other was an increased reliance on bank finance and possibly not just for credit but also for long-term funds. Many mills in the Manchester district were built during the boom of the first half of the 1820s through bank finance – usually by bills 'in dead advance' and more rarely by 'a dead loan upon the mortgage of a building'.[37] There was an even greater reliance on banking facilities during the 1830s boom of which a feature was the upsurge of joint stock bank formation in the North West. Eighteen out of the 79 banks established in England between 1834 and 1836 were set up either in Liverpool or in the textile area around Manchester.[38] Most were ill-managed concerns which relied heavily on rediscounting in London one-name bills to support their perilously low cash ratios. Their willingness to discount nearly all paper, whatever its quality, together with the highly illiquid nature of their assets made them ill-prepared to weather any financial stringency.[39] Eight of the new North Western banks failed during either the crisis of 1836 or the ensuing slump. Others suffered badly like the District Bank, which in 1837 had bad debts of £375,000 as a result of advances to textile firms in Saddleworth.[40]

Manchester representatives before the Select Committee on Banks of Issue directly linked new mill building and the expansion of credit caused by the aggressive loan policies of the new joint stock banks.[41] However, the main body of the evidence dealt with the connection between prices and the circulation and therefore indirectly with the question of profit margins. Here they blamed the 'lax' credit policy of the Bank of England as being the primary cause for the movement of prices during the 1830s boom and slump, though their contentions were challenged by S. J. Loyd.

The cotton industry in the late 1830s was still made up of small and medium-sized producers: 40% of the firms spinning and weaving cotton used less than 20 h.p., and 90% had less than 100 employees. Financial conditions may have played a part in producing this structure. The abundance of credit, especially in the 1830s, considerably eased the problem of entry into the industry. However, falling profits together with the difficulties of selling in the growing distant markets of India and South America meant that it was not easy to grow beyond a certain point. The few dozen giant firms, those which had over 100 h.p. units of production, were usually of long standing, had benefited considerably from the high profit decades before 1800, had mercantile connections, and had cultivated lines of credit in the metropolis. It was they who usually combined machine spinning and weaving under one roof while the small producers tended to be single-process firms.[42]

★

The dramatic growth of the mechanized cotton industry from the closing decades of the eighteenth century, which caught the attention of contemporaries and subsequently historians, has tended to overshadow the remarkable development of other branches of the textile industry, especially wool in the West Riding of Yorkshire. Both cotton and woollen manufacturing could be found on either side of the Pennines, while at the centre was the important source of carding and other machinery in the Calder valley. By 1800 there were about 200 woollen, worsted, cotton and flax mills in the West Riding,[43] but the dominant trade of the county was the production of woollen and worsted cloths. Yorkshire during the eighteenth century came to be the most important centre of woollen production, having in 1770 an output of worsted equal to that of the Norwich region.[44] The industry continued to expand and it has been estimated that the amount of fixed capital invested in wool textile mills in the West Riding increased from £245,000 to £2.3m. between 1800 and 1835. Worsted led, with a continued growth of fixed capital from the late 1790s until the early 1820s. Wool, from a base of fewer mills, grew more slowly and with greater fluctuation. There were peaks in wool investment in 1802 and 1816, major booms in the 1820s and mid-1830s, but checks in 1822 and between 1825 and 1827.[45] Actually the production of worsted and woollen cloths was organized on different bases, while the methods of production were transformed both at different stages of production and at different periods of time.

Mechanization in the worsted branch began in the 1780s with spinning, but initially at a slow pace. Adaptations of jennies, the water frame and mules were used, powered by hand, horse or water. Steam power, as in cotton, was introduced at the turn of the century and by the 1820s spinning had become a factory process. The availability of machine-spun yarn allowed the adoption of the flying shuttle in weaving but power weaving was not significant on any scale until the 1840s. The preparatory process, combing, was only mechanized successfully in the 1840s.[46] The adoption of mechanization may have been facilitated by the structure of the worsted industry, which in the 1800s consisted of specialized large firms, generally larger, wealthier and more enterprising than woollen clothiers. This difference in scale and attitudes may have been due, it has been suggested, to less 'historical inertia' within the worsted industry, because it had developed in the West Riding only during the eighteenth century.[47] However, firms in both wool and worsted were usually family partnerships which grew, as in cotton, through the ploughback of profits.

It was the preparatory processes in wool which were first mechanized and located in 'mills' alongside the fulling stocks. Both the flying shuttle and spinning jenny were in general use in the Leeds woollen industry by

1780 but unlike worsted these new devices were readily absorbed within the domestic system of manufacture and did not lead to a dramatic change in the mode of organization.[48] The first scribbling machines for carding wool, just as frames, jennies and mules in worsted, were worked by hand, horse or water, though the last was the most usual source of power.

Scribbling machines were erected either in existing fulling mills or adapted buildings, usually corn mills, but from the 1780s specific mills were built and steam power was applied from the 1790s.[49] A large number of scribbling–fulling mills after 1800 were built by joint stock companies comprised of 10 to 15 shareholders, usually domestic clothiers, and by 1844 this form of mill ownership was the norm rather than the exception.[50]

The woollen clothier, certainly in the Leeds area, by 1800 was essentially a weaver. Carding had been taken over by the scribbling mill, often owned by clothiers, while the cloth merchant was gaining control over the supervision of finishing, using the services of specialist dyers and dressers. Most clothiers owned jennies but yarn could be and was obtained either through putting-out or from a merchant. A few clothiers, such as James Walker, did push the domestic system of organization to its limits but they never became proto-factory masters. Walker owned a fulling and scribbling mill and 21 looms, he employed 100 workers on his own premises, and gave work to a further 30 domestic spinners and weavers.[51]

By the 1830s there were 11 woollen factories in Yorkshire, employing over 200 workers, and 204 worsted mills powered by 159 steam engines with an average employment of 80 per mill.[52] Until the 1830s the woollen and worsted industries of the West Riding appear to have been able to finance their growth without recourse to extra-regional supplies of finance. There were differences in the organization of the two trades but, in each, mechanization was generally a smooth, highly divisible process which did not strain the existing structure of credit and capital. Many of the early worsted mill builders were established capitalists in the domestic trade. Some mills, as in Keighley and Halifax, were rented, and in a few instances worsted mills were actually converted cotton concerns, the re-equipment costs having come from pre-1800 cotton profits. The woollen industry continued to consist of a large number of basically small domestic manufacturers who banded together to erect scribbling mills. Gradually woollen cloth production shifted into the factory even though substantial numbers of the machines employed continued to be powered by hand. Woollen mill building was financed through family income generated in other tades and mortgages raised through the services of local attorneys. Some domestic clothiers became factory masters by renting mills built by landowners and merchants.[53]

Generally credit terms in both wool and worsted were long during the first quarter of the nineteenth century and became shorter during the second. The first link in the credit chain was the woolstapler and usually he was the most important source of credit. He traded on his own capital or used bank credit. Normally the stapler was paid in bills, either four to eight months for German or Spanish wool or two to four months for English. As the worsted trade was more rigidly subdivided into specialized branches, credit played a greater role in the industry's finances than it did in wool. The length of credit in the cloth trade varied widely but one month had become common by the 1830s and 1840s. Credit terms within the industry changed as a result of its increasing reliance on colonial wool supplies from the 1840s.[54]

★

The industrialization of the British economy led to a general increase in the demand for coal. This was not simply due to the growing application of steam power and the substitution of coke for charcoal but because there was an across-the-board rise in the demand for energy inputs in all types of manufacturing. Coal had been an important fuel since the beginning of the seventeenth century and not only as a simple source of heat but also because a wide range of interlocking technologies had been built upon it.[55] Unfortunately there are not yet available estimates of fixed capital investment for the coal industry comparable to those which have been produced recently for the cotton and wool textile industries. Consequently there are no indicators of the volume of investment requiring finance which the growth of the coal industry generated. Any attempt to make such an estimate is fraught with difficulties. The industry even in 1800 was widely scattered and encompassed a wide range of production techniques varying from shallow undrained pits involving a capital of £50 to £100[56] to large deep mines whose sinking had absorbed at least £10,000.[57] This diversity was not simply between separate coalfields but was also current within fields. The other major problem in estimating the amount of capital absorbed by the industry arises from trying to define the exact extent of the industry. Capital was not only invested in 'winning' the mineral but also in transporting it to the market, and consequently estimates will vary greatly, depending on what is included: simply collieries, or their immediate transport networks, or waggonways, staithes and perhaps even coastal shipping.

The North East was the major area of production, probably contributing about 30% of national output in the 1780s and 24% in the mid-1850s. Large-scale investment in this field had taken place from the beginning of the eighteenth century, one indicator being the 137 Newcomen engines at work by 1778. Very deep mining had become common by the 1810s, involving shafts greater than 100 fathoms.[58] The rising trend of output involved the further absorption of resources, and Kenwood has estimated that £2.4m. had been invested in the Tyne and Wear areas alone by 1829. A quarter of a century later, possibly £14m. had been sunk in the north-east, with the largest wave of investment taking place during the second half of the 1830s.[59] A significant part of this process was the opening of pits made commercially viable following the construction of railways linking the interior of the region with the coast. This had begun in the Tees area in the early 1830s and continued throughout the rest of County Durham during the second half of the decade.[60] The Tees area became attractive as it was less expensive to work with its shallow seams and no underground water, while the development of good rail communications reduced the need to build extensive colliery lines.[61]

A contemporary estimate of the capital employed in the north-eastern field of 1843 reveals the industry's organization. It was still dominated by aristocratic and gentry coalowners. Lord Londonderry's trustees, the Countess of Durham's executors, and the 'Grand Allies' – Lord Ravensworth, Lord Wharncliffe and the Bowes family – each had investments in coal of £0.5m. These great partnerships of landed magnates constituted the top rung of the ladder marking out the scales of operations. Lord Londonderry was a 'heroic' aristocratic entrepreneurial figure, having built in the late 1820s Seaham harbour and opened up the adjacent part of the coalfield. Similarly the Earl of Durham in the 1830s owned six collieries, of which two were then working, that had absorbed £384,331, while their stocks and associated railways were valued at £156,364.[62] The second rung of coalmasters, those employing capitals of £200,000, was also made up of aristocratic owners but encompassed proprietors from the landed gentry who usually owned more than one colliery. Below them were single-colliery companies, of which concerns with capitals in the range £40–60,000 were common, although in the geologically more favourable Tees area, pits usually had smaller capitals, £8–25,000 being more typical.[63] In addition there were a number of joint stock companies, one of which, the Hetton Coal Company, was amongst the largest units on the field with its capital of over £0.5m. The investment boom of the 1830s had encouraged the formation of a number of other joint stock concerns but all proved to be speculative 'bubbles', failing within a year of formation.[64]

The other main coalfields in the mid-1850s were first Lancashire with an output two-thirds that of the North East, followed by Scotland, South Wales and Staffordshire which each had an output about half the size of the North East, and lastly the small Midland field. The main period of expansion in the output of these fields began in the 1840s, as generally prior to that poor communications had limited their market to the immediate locality in which they were situated. Before the coming of the railways there had been some large units of production on the West Cumbrian field, which served the Irish market, and in South Wales, where collieries were associated with metal works.[65] However, generally outside the North East the industry consisted of small family-based partnerships owning at the most two collieries,[66] usually with a low output. The growth of output in South Wales during the 1840s had been facilitated through the tappings of local savings accumulated by solicitors, mining engineers and shopkeepers. Welsh collieries were also assisted by medium-term bank finance.[67] Banks appear to have been important in the expansion of the Yorkshire field in the Barnsley area. For instance, Barker, Firth & Co., who worked two collieries, obtained credits from the local bank, usually without security, and in 1851 were allowed £2,000 when a shaft collapsed. The Barnsley Bank accommodated other colliery proprietors, particularly during the investment boom of the mid-1850s.[68] These regional variations apart, it would appear that most collieries grew on the basis of internally generated financial resources. The Butterley Company in the East Midlands, which had interests in ironworks and lime kilns as well as coal, expanded its capital from £30,000 in 1815 to £436,000 in 1858 simply by ploughing back profits. It did have the advantage that its collieries had a regular demand for their product as a result of the company's interests.

★

During the second half of the eighteenth century the iron industry adopted coal as a fuel, initially for producing pig iron and subsequently from the 1790s for the production of wrought iron.. These changes in techniques, especially puddling, resulted in both the industry shifting to the coalfields and the integration of the smelting and refining processes. By 1800 the coal and primary iron industries can be considered almost as one, since most ironmasters owned collieries while in some areas, like South Staffordshire, the surplus production of coal frequently led small coalowners jointly to establish ironworks.[69] There were a number of relatively large works in the industry, particularly in South Wales,[70] but the typical and representative unit at the turn of the century probably had a fixed capital of about £20,000.[71] For small and large firms alike, working capital was usually equal to, if not greater than, fixed assets employed.[72] Whatever their size, the erection and running of ironworks required a flow of investment that was generally beyond the resources of a single entrepreneur, and consequently most firms were partnerships. They were occasionally very complex in their structure, especially when more than one site was involved. Most of the successful English and Welsh ironmasters of the period 1780 to 1830 had moved into the primary industry from the secondary metal trades. Frequently they were non-conformists, with Quakers being dominant before 1750 joined by a growing number of Methodists thereafter.[73] Intermarriage was common within these religious groups and, before 1820, wedding settlements played an important part in the business and financial organization of the industry.

As with other industries, expansion appears to have been largely financed through the ploughing-back of profits. One of the critical factors affecting the profitability of a concern was the cost of its mineral rights, and a low mineral rent was usually a major factor affecting growth, especially before 1800. Loans were also important and were often provided by iron merchants in either Bristol or London and were sometimes secured on partnership shares. This was often one way by which merchants became sleeping partners in iron concerns. Banks became increasingly important sources of loan capital and, as in cotton, ironmasters frequently became bankers. A number of joint stock companies were established within the industry from the 1820s – there were ten in 1844, most of which were in South Wales – but none was very successful.[74] Investors had been lured into these companies, as with the coal flotations of the 1830s boom, by the rise in iron prices, but their expectations of substantial dividends evaporated during the slump of the late 1830s and early 1840s. Generally investment in both the coal and iron industries appears to have been a function of output prices. These were shaped by the short-run inelastic supply curves of the two industries and the cyclical volatility of the demand for their outputs.

The expansion of the Scottish section of the primary iron industry came with the adoption of the Neilson hot blast process in the 1830s which enabled the full exploitation of the black band ore. Within two decades Scotland became the most important area of iron production and the British economy's lowest-cost producer of pig iron. The epicentre of these developments was Coatbridge. This town's group of six firms came to dominate the whole of the Scottish industry through building plants throughout the region and by 1845 they accounted for between two-thirds and three-quarters of the Scottish make of pig. Coming from tenant-farming backgrounds, they had usually moved into iron-making via operating small collieries, with the profits derived from agriculture and coalmining providing them with the necessary finance. Nearly all the successful firms were either single proprietorship or small family partnerships and, as in England and Wales, the joint stock company made little headway. Like most of the larger iron concerns south of the border, most of the Scottish Coatbridge firms had close links with banks. In the 1840s the Baird family, the largest single producer of Scottish pig iron, had interests in the Union Bank of Scotland, the Clydesdale Bank, and the City of Glasgow Bank.[75]

There were two important aspects of Scottish bank finance. The first was the unique cash-credit system, introduced by the Royal Bank of Scotland in 1728, which consisted of limited advances, made on two securities and repayable on demand. They ranged usually from £200 to £1,000 with an average of £800, and in 1826 the Scottish banks had provided some £6m. in this form through some 11,000 individual transactions. This source of credit, which had no fixed duration, was an important source of funds for many Scottish ironmasters.[76] The other important feature was the readiness of Scottish banks to lend on iron warrants to within a few shillings of the current market price, which reduced considerably the burden of stockholding. Consequently Scottish ironmasters generally borrowed on the security of either iron scrip or iron warrants and refused to make use of bills of exchange.[77]

The secondary metal trades consisted mainly of workshops organized in some instances on a domestic basis. Birmingham, the Black Country, and the Sheffield region were the main centres of the industry. As yet there is little information on the finance of these various and diverse trades which turned wrought iron, brass and copper into a variety of artifacts ranging from nails to railway-waggon buffers and springs. There are some indications for the 1830s from the archive of the Birmingham branch of the Bank of England but the sample of firms is restricted in size and consists only of those which had sufficient standing to open an account.[78] The least capital-intensive were nailmakers, which had an average capital employed of £6,875 and a turnover of £17,500 per annum. Iron manufacturers had an average capital of £10,400 and an average turnover of £21,250, and gunmaking, button- and toymaking, and needle and jewellery production were similar.[79] The ratios of fixed to working capital of the order of 1:3 to 1:2 suggested by this sample probably applied to only the largest firms in these trades in the Birmingham area.

★

By the mid-nineteenth century the word 'factory' was still a synonym for a cotton-spinning plant. There were other capital-intensive units of production, especially in coalmining in the North East, in the primary iron industry, in copper smelting, in glassmaking,[80] and in brewing.[81] However, elsewhere in the economy the increase in output which marks the industrial revolution had taken place through a multiplication of existing modes of production. These were basically small-scale units of production, little more than 'shops' or sheds frequently not employing either water or steam power, and in some trades and industries this system of organization continued well into the last quarter of the nineteenth century. The general external demand for finance that the industrial revolution generated, whether it originated in either the factory or the 'shop', was for credit to allow stocks of raw materials, semi-finished goods, and finished goods to be carried and to meet the wage bill. The principal financial problem that many new entrants into the manu-facturing sector faced was to insert themselves into the structure of credit. Working capital could be obtained from other manufacturers supplying inputs, such as cotton yarn, from merchants and wholesalers and from the banking system which had developed from the mid-eighteenth century.

Despite the establishment of formal financial institutions and their integration into a national distributive mechanism for credit by the 1830s, there are indications that industrial growth may have been blunted by shortages of working capital. Until the 1870s there was a high demand for money within the economy and consequently banks in industrial areas were overlent, with ratios of advances-plus-discounts: deposits in excess of 100%.[82] This imbalance could only be met by rediscounting, not in itself a dangerous practice but one which, when coupled with immature management, led to heavy bank failures during periods of financial stringency. In addition such banking practices made the supply of industrial credit particularly sensitive to conditions in the London money market.

Credit conditions may have been aggravated by government legislation in the 1840s. The purpose of the Bank Charter Act of 1844 was to make the quantity of paper money in circulation behave in the same manner as specie, an intention which if it had been achieved could have resulted in the English economy entering a period of stagnation in the 1850s and 1860s. The monetary straitjacket tailored by the authors of the 1844 Bank Charter Act was not donned by the economy, because of the continued growth of bank deposits and an increase in the use of the bill of exchange. Whereas the share of bills within the total means of payment had been declining during the 1830s and early 1840s, thereafter it rose, increasing from approximately 34% in 1844 to 41% in 1855.[83] But the volume of bills in circulation did not behave in the manner presumed by the currency school, fluctuating directly, not inversely, with the level of interest rates, and hence they were an important destabilizing factor in cyclical fluctuations.[84]

While the further recourse to the long-established bill system, coupled with a further acceleration in the growth of bank deposits, frustrated the aims of the Bank Charter Act, future bank promotion was restricted by the Joint Stock Banking Act of 1844, the provisions of which were extended to Scotland and Ireland in 1845. This Act was an attempt to regulate joint stock banking following government enquiries in the late 1830s and early 1840s. It made future banking promotions exceedingly difficult by requiring new establishments to obtain a charter from the Board of Trade and to have a minimum capital of £100,000 divided into shares of at least £100. During the Act's lifetime only 12 banks were formed. It did not improve the quality of bank management, revealed as the main problem in the parliamentary investigations which had preceded it, and two of the banks formed under its conditions – the Royal British and the London and Eastern – failed in 1856 and 1857.[85] There were the same number of joint stock banks in 1860 as there had been two decades previously, about 100. Although joint stock banks had generally prospered from the mid-1840s, private concerns had dwindled in number with some 50 going out of business through bankruptcy between 1844 and 1857.[86] In 1863, at the beginning of a new boom in bank promotions, *The Economist* admitted that 'the banking of the country was...very much underdone'.[87]

Whereas by the mid-1830s a national, albeit volatile, market for credit existed, there was not a comparable group of institutions mobilizing capital, particularly capital for industry. In any case industry made little use of the joint stock company, despite the statutory recognition of the unincorporated enterprise in 1844, a type of organization that was equated in the contemporary mind with monopoly and speculation. It was generally held that a manufacturing concern could only be directed profitably if it was guided by those who were heavily financially committed to it rather than by a hired manager and a socially prestigious body of directors. The joint stock companies that were established in both the coal and iron industries were generally unsuccessful, while the scribbling mill companies in the woollen industry were more akin to large partnerships than corporate bodies. Non-ferrous metal mining was a case apart. It was becoming increasingly costly and risky as lodes and veins had to be followed down, and so semi-corporate forms of organization were used to raise the necessary capital. Elsewhere in extractive and manufacturing industry, either the single proprietorship or the private co-partnership was the normal mode of financial organization. Therefore the initial source of industry's capital was the social and economic backgrounds of its entrepreneurs. These were diverse in any particular industry but most manufacturers had some wealth and very few had artisan backgrounds. Usually the necessary finance to set up an enterprise was assembled through private, often family, connections though some significant amounts did come through trading links. Merchants provided loans and sometimes acted as 'sleeping' partners, investments which had a degree of regional mobility. London and Bristol merchants invested in the iron industry, especially in South Wales and Shropshire, with Barings financing for some time, although unsuccessfully, the Weardale works in the North East. However, generally industrial equity capital was raised privately from local pools of savings held by relations or co-religionists. Loan capital was more mobile but normally only at a local or regional level with attorneys playing an important role through arranging mortgages.

It is generally accepted that industrial firms expanded through the ploughback of profits, but this picture has been drawn mainly from business-history material composed mainly of firms which have survived in various ways until the third quarter of the twentieth century. However, longevity was the exception rather than the rule during the industrial revolution. Henry Burgess, the publicist for the country bankers, thought that 90% of large manufacturing units had changed hands between 1819 and 1836. Similarly R. Baker, a factory inspector, estimated that nearly half of the 318 firms in his district went out of existence during the late 1830s and early 1840s.[88] The high incidence of bankruptcy and failure may mean that a different picture of the financial problems of an industrial enterprise during this period should be portrayed. Generally in the early years of any enterprise profits were low, if they were generated at all, and conversely fixed assets loomed large in any balance sheet struck. In this situation finance was required for both stocks and plant and consequently the firm was highly susceptible to any tightening of monetary conditions. Entry into an industry may have been encouraged by the lure of high profits during a boom and assisted by a bank willing to discount any type of paper presented in order to obtain customers. The crucial factor was whether a firm could survive its first four or five years, which usually would have spanned the upper turning point of the trade cycle and some form of a credit crisis. This gives a rather different perspective to industrial problems than the one normally described of difficult early years and then almost steady growth financed by the ploughback of profits, and bank and other forms of credit. Unfortunately, short-lived firms which may have been more typical have left few traces of their existence.

Notes

(Place of publication is London unless otherwise stated)

1 S. D. Chapman, 'Fixed Capital Formation in the British Cotton Industry 1770–1815', *Economic History Review*, 2nd series, XXIII, 1970, p. 252.

2 M. M. Edwards, *The Growth of the British Cotton Trade,* Manchester, 1967, pp. 182–3.

3 S. D. Chapman, *The Early Factory Masters,* Newton Abbot, 1967, p. 143.

4 S. Shapiro, *Capital and the Cotton Industry in the Industrial Revolution,* Ithaca, New York, 1967, p. 157.

5 ibid., pp. 157, 162; Chapman, 'Fixed Capital', pp. 243–4.

6 Chapman, 'Fixed Capital', pp. 239–43.

7 S. Pollard, *The Genesis of Modern Management,* Harmondsworth, 1968, p. 112.

8 The above is drawn from Edwards, op. cit., pp. 182–90, 205–12.

9 R. Boyson, *The Ashworth Cotton Enterprise,* Oxford, 1970.

10 Chapman, 'Fixed Capital', p. 239.

11 S. D. Chapman, 'The Peels in the Early English Cotton Industry', *Business History,* XI, 1969, pp. 61–89.

12 C. H. Lee, *A Cotton Enterprise 1795–1840. A History of M'Connel and Kennedy, Fine Cotton Spinners,* Manchester, 1972, pp. 101, 103.

13 Chapman, 'Fixed Capital', p. 241.

14 Lee, op. cit., pp. 101, 105

15 Edwards, op. cit., p. 201.

16 Chapman, 'The Peels', p. 66.

17 Lee, op. cit., pp. 104–5.

18 F. Crouzet, 'Editor's Introduction. An Essay in Historiography' in Crouzet (ed.) *Capital Formation in the Industrial Revolution,* 1972, pp. 36–9; Edwards, op. cit., pp. 255–9.

19 Shapiro, op. cit., p. 137.

20 Edwards, op. cit., pp. 216–22.

21 Lee, op. cit., p. 106.

22 Boyson, op. cit., p. 59.

23 Lee, op. cit., pp. 106–7.

24 Boyson, op. cit., p. 59.

25 Edwards, op. cit., p. 228.

26 Lee, op. cit., pp. 106–7.

27 Boyson, op. cit., p. 59.

28 Lee, op. cit., pp. 102–3, 105, 108.

29 Boyson, op. cit., pp. 16–21, 29, 33.

30 A. J. Taylor, 'Concentration and Specialisation in the Lancashire Cotton Industry, 1825–1850', *Economic History Review*, 2nd series, I, 1948/9, pp. 114–16.

31 M. Blaug, 'The Productivity of Capital in the Lancashire Cotton Industry during the Nineteenth Century', *Economic History Review*, 2nd series, XIII, 1961, pp. 359–61.

32 Pollard, op. cit., pp. 113–15.

33 Taylor, op. cit., pp. 117–22.

34 Blaug, op. cit., pp. 365–7.

35 R. C. O. Matthews, *A Study in Trade-cycle History. Economic Fluctuations in Great Britain,* Cambridge, 1954, pp. 129–42.

36 R. E. Tyson, 'The Sun Mill Company Ltd.–a Study in Democratic Investment, 1858–1959', unpublished M.A. thesis, University of Manchester, 1962, p. 81; D. A. Farnie, 'The English Cotton Industry 1850–1896', unpublished M.A. thesis, University of Manchester, 1953, p. 275.

37 Farnie, op. cit., p. 436.

38 S. E. Thomas, *The Rise and Growth of Joint Stock Banking,* 1934, appendix M, pp. 657–61.

39 *Hints by Way of Encouraging the Formation of Joint-Stock Banks in London,* 1834, pp. 11–12.

40 Farnie, op. cit., p. 436; Matthews, op. cit., pp. 192–200.

41 *B.P.P.,* 1840, IV, *Select Committee on Banks of Issue,* evidence of J. B. Smith, director of the Bank of Manchester, q. 6; R. Cobden, calico printer, q. 546, and W. R. Wood, merchant, q. 623.

42 See V. A. C. Gatrell, 'Labour, Power, and the Size of Firms in Lancashire in the Second Quarter of the Nineteenth Century', *Economic History Review*, 2nd series, XXX, 1977; S. D. Chapman, 'The International Houses: the Continental Contribution to British Commerce 1800–1860', *Journal of European Economic History*, VI, 1977; S. D. Chapman, 'Financial Restraints on the Growth of Firms in the Cotton Industry', *Economic History Review*, forthcoming.

43 D. T. Jenkins, 'Early Factory Develop-

ment in the West Riding of Yorkshire' in N. B. Harte and K. G. Ponting (eds) *Textile History and Economic History,* Manchester, 1973.

44 E. M. Sigsworth, *Black Dyke Mills. A History,* Liverpool, 1958, p. 1.

45 D. T. Jenkins, 'The West Riding Wool Textile Industry, 1780–1835. A Study of Fixed Capital Formation', unpublished D.Phil. thesis, University of York, 1969, pp. 279, 288, 291, 320, 322.

46 Sigsworth, op. cit., pp. 2–7, 9–10, 30, 34.

47 R. M. Hartwell, 'The Yorkshire Woollen and Worsted Industries, 1800–1850', unpublished D.Phil. thesis, University of Oxford, 1955, pp. 291–2.

48 W. B. Crump, 'The Leeds Woollen Industry, 1780–1820. General Introduction' in Crump (ed.) *The Leeds Woollen Industry 1780–1820,* Thoresby Society, XXXII, Leeds, 1931.

49 Jenkins, op. cit., pp. 252–8.

50 Hartwell, op. cit., pp. 341–6.

51 Crump, op. cit., p. 28.

52 Pollard, op. cit., p. 116.

53 Jenkins, op. cit., pp. 343–60. See also R. G. Wilson, *Gentlemen Merchants. The Merchant Community in Leeds 1700–1830,* Manchester, 1971, pp. 92–5, 108, 111, 121–4.

54 A. J. Topham, 'The Credit Structure of the West Riding Wool-textile Industry in the Nineteenth Century', unpublished M.A. thesis, University of Leeds, 1953, pp. 37–69.

55 J. R. Harris, 'Industry and Technology in the Eighteenth Century: Britain and France', inaugural lecture, Birmingham, 1972.

56 A. R. Griffin, *Mining in the East Midlands 1550–1947,* 1971, p. 21.

57 A. R. Griffin, 'Fixed Capital Formation in the Coalmining Industry in the Early Nineteenth Century. A Discussion Paper', mimeographed paper, Midlands Economic Historians' Conference, University of Nottingham, 1974.

58 Pollard, op. cit., pp. 79–80.

59 A. G. Kenwood, 'Capital Investment in North Eastern England 1800–1913', unpublished Ph.D. thesis, University of London, 1962, pp. 79–80, 91–2.

60 Matthews, op. cit., pp. 155–6.

61 Kenwood, op. cit., p. 94.

62 D. Spring, 'English Landowners and Nineteenth Century Industrialisation' in J. T. Ward and R. G. Wilson (eds) *Land and Industry. The Landed Estate and the Industrial Revolution,* Newton Abbot, 1971, pp. 33–7, 48–50.

63 Griffin, op. cit., pp. 1–2; Kenwood, op. cit., pp. 93–4.

64 Matthews, op. cit., p. 156; Kenwood, op. cit., pp. 88–9.

65 Pollard, op. cit., pp. 80–4.

66 R. A. Ward, *A Treatise on Investments,* 2nd edn, 1852, p. 178; B. R. Mitchell, 'The Economic Development of the Inland Coalfields, 1870–1914', unpublished Ph.D. thesis, University of Cambridge, 1956, pp. 121–4.

67 J. H. Morris and L. J. Williams, *The South Wales Coal Industry 1841–1875,* Cardiff, 1958, pp. 143–9.

68 Midland Bank Archives, London; A14 Barnsley Banking Company, Loan Accounts Book 1844–1860, and see below, pp. 215–17.

69 A. Birch, *The Economic History of the British Iron and Steel Industry 1784–1879,* 1967, pp. 23–7, 197, 211. See also D. S. Landes, *The Unbound Prometheus,* Cambridge, 1969, pp. 88–94.

70 Pollard, op. cit., pp. 94, 97.

71 Birch, op. cit., p. 198.

72 S. Pollard, 'Fixed Capital in the Industrial Revolution in Britain', *Journal of Economic History,* XXIV, 1964.

73 T. S. Ashton, *Iron and Steel in the Industrial Revolution,* 3rd edn, Manchester, 1963, pp. 209–10, 211–13, 220–1. There are now a number of business histories of early firms, usually the 'giants': M. Flinn, *Men of Iron: The Crowleys in the Early Iron Industry,* Edinburgh, 1962; A. Raistrick, *Dynasty of Iron Founders. The Darbys and Coalbrookdale,* 1953; J. P. Addis, *The Crawshay Dynasty: Study in Industrial Organization and Development 1765–1867,* Cardiff, 1957; R. H. Campbell, *Carron Company,* 1961.

74 Ashton, op. cit.; Birch, op. cit., pp. 201–9.

75 I. F. Gibson, 'The Economic History of the Scottish Iron and Steel Industry, with Particular Reference to the Period 1830 to 1880', unpublished Ph.D. thesis, University of London, 1955, pp. 536–55.

76 As well as ibid., p. 97, see also R. Cameron, 'Scotland 1750–1845' in Cameron (ed.) *Banking in the Early Stages of Industrialisation*, 1967, pp. 75–80.

77 Gibson, op. cit., pp. 366–71, 558.

78 I am grateful to Miss Caroline Woodhead, a post graduate student at the London School of Economics: she is preparing a doctoral dissertation on the development of the Birmingham branch, the preliminary results of which she presented in a seminar paper at the Institute of Historical Research, London, in February 1975.

79 For a description of the organization of the Sheffield and Black Country trades, see J. H. Clapham, *An Economics History of Modern Britain*, I, *The Early Railway Age 1820–1850*, Cambridge, 2nd edn, reprinted 1964, pp. 172–8.

80 On glass and copper see T. C. Barker and J. R. Harris, *A Merseyside Town in the Industrial Revolution: St Helens, 1750–1900*, Liverpool, 1954; T. C. Barker, *Pilkington Brothers and the Glass Industry*, 1960.

81 On brewing see P. Mathias, *The Brewing Industry in England 1700–1830*, 1959.

82 S. Nishimura, *The Decline of Inland Bills of Exchange in the London Money Market 1855–1913*, Cambridge, 1971, pp. 57–61.

83 R. Cameron, 'England' in Cameron (ed.) *Banking*, op. cit., p. 47.

84 J. R. T. Hughes, *Fluctuations in Trade, Industry and Finance. A Study of British Economic Development 1850–1860*, Oxford, 1960.

85 K. S. Toft, 'A Mid-nineteenth Century Attempt at Banking Control', *Revue internationale d'historie de la banque*, III, 1970.

86 W. F. Crick and J. E. Wadsworth, *A Hundred Years of Joint Stock Banking*, 3rd edn, 1958, pp. 24–7.

87 *The Economist*, 24 September 1863, p. 1177.

88 R. M. Hartwell, 'Business Management in England during the Period of Early Industrialisation: Inducements and Obstacles' in Hartwell (ed.) *The Industrial Revolution*, Oxford, 1970, p. 31, n. 3.

3 The development of company law 1825–1914

Business firms came to be organized in three separate legal ways – the partnership, the unincorporated company, and the full corporation. Somewhat misleadingly all three types of enterprise could be known as a company and carry in their title the suffix 'and Co.' The partnership came under the law of contract, the unincorporated company under trust law, a branch of equity, and the corporation was subject to the state, either the Crown or Parliament, its formation being regulated initially by specific acts and charters but from the mid-nineteenth century by general statutes. The key legal difference was that a corporation had its own legal personality which was independent of that of its shareholders. In the case of a partnership, its rights and liabilities were simply the sum of those who constituted it. The unincorporated company was in a 'grey' area of the law, a consequence of being in some ways the product of opportunism – attempts to establish as close an approximation to a corporation or rather some of the attributes of a corporation without being subject to the scrutiny of the state.

A partnership was created by a contract, the articles of which laid down the enterprise's purpose and its method of management. It specified the capital of the entreprise and how it was to be subscribed but a 'share' in a partnership was only transferable with the unanimous consent of all the partners. Although a partnership's capital was jointly subscribed, each individual member of it was personally liable for all debts incurred by the partnership. He was as one Chief Justice explained 'liable to his last shilling and acre'. Creditors of partnerships could therefore proceed against both the stock of the partnership and its members' personal estates for the recovery of debts. This was not the situation in the case of a full corporation with limited liability as its shareholders were only liable for the debts of such a company to the extent of the nominal value of their holding in the company. Unlike a partnership, each shareholder could normally freely transfer his holding in a full corporation without any reference to other shareholders. Whereas the objects of a partnership were those which its partners may from time to time have chosen to undertake, in the case of a limited company from the mid-1850s its business was closely and specifically defined in the memorandum of association which constituted it. If its directors went beyond those objects, then they were open to an *ultra vires* action being brought by a shareholder. A company's memorandum of association could not be readily altered but its articles of association which governed its management could be changed freely with the consent of its shareholders.

Until the mid-1850s, it was extremely difficult to establish without the express consent of either Parliament or the Crown a full corporation, that is a joint stock company with limited liability. When either some long-term permanency was required, or the ability to mobilize greater amounts of capital than was possible within the confines of a partnership, then before 1855 resort was often made to the unincorporated company. The assets of such companies were vested in the supervision of trustees through a deed of settlement, a procedure which had grown out of land law. Although shareholders in such companies were called co-partners, attempts were made by the lawyers who drew up the trust deed to make the company's shares more or less freely transferable, like those of a full corporation. However each shareholder, as a partner, was fully liable for the debts of the company, but this was eased by clauses in the deed of settlement which laid down that no shareholder would be answerable for the debts of the company to a greater extent than the proportionate amount of his share. Consequently as long as all his fellow shareholders were solvent, no individual shareholder ran any major risk. England was unique in Western Europe in having the trust as well as the contractual obligation. In addition to the advantages that have been mentioned already, the trust device has others, all of which made it almost but not quite a pseudo-corporation. While not having a distinct legal personality of its own, an unincorporated company could act legally through its trustees rather than in terms of its total proprietary, at least in the Court of Chancery, and therefore came close to a corporation's ability to sue and be sued in its own name. Its property was kept intact because a creditor of an individual member could not obtain the latter's share in the company until dissolution had been agreed by all its members. During the eighteenth century partnership law, in terms of inter-partner obligations and the relationship of the partnership to third parties, was established and developed by cases in common law, particularly under Mansfield, while the Court of Chancery oversaw the legal development of the unincorporated business association.

Pressure for full incorporation began to develop at the end of the eighteenth century but initially the limited company found little general support. It was seen, drawing from the examples of the great trading corporations, as a bastion of monopoly power and as almost constituting a state within the state. Stress was now placed upon the superiority of private enterprise in which ownership and control were combined and where the profits and losses bore fully upon those responsible for their creation. The divorce of ownership and control which a joint stock company appeared to imply seemed to be a recipe for economic suicide, the possible inability of a limited company to meet its debts fully was regarded as immoral, while the creation of limited companies could always spark off the destructive whirlwind of speculation which could ultimately lead to the diminution of savings rather than the creation of productive capital. These views continued well into the nineteenth century even after full incorporation became freely available.

The pattern of the development of company law during the nineteenth century can be broken down into four phases. The first, running from the 1820s until the mid-1850s, was a period of gradual change which involved the statutory recognition of the unincorporated company and the removal of some of the barriers and difficulties to obtaining charters. There then occurred a series of Acts, beginning in 1855 and consolidated in 1862, which suddenly and totally transformed the law. After 1856 joint stock companies with limited liability could be formed for most purposes by the simple process of registering a memorandum of association signed by seven shareholders. The reasons for this dramatic change in the basis of company law are still in some part unclear and had little to do with the financial requirements of manufacturing industry. There had been three parliamentary inquiries into company law during the first half of the 1850s but these came to no clear conclusion about the desirability of allowing free incorporation. The only evidence they gathered which appears to have played a role in shaping the government's argument for totally liberalizing the law was the small but growing number of companies that were establishing themselves abroad in order to obtain the privilege of limited liability. England after 1856 had the most permissive commercial law in the whole of Europe and one of its distinguishing features was 'the facility for the formation of a company'.[1] Between the 1860s and the

1880s, the third phase in the development of the law, the consolidating Act of 1862 remained essentially unaltered but there was mounting criticism of it and pressure from various quarters for reform, initially in order to protect shareholders from unscrupulous company promoters and later to maintain the rights of company creditors. Finally from the late 1880s the government acknowledged that reform was required but then, as a result of opposing pressure from vested interests, found that it was difficult to enact.

★

During the first half of the nineteenth century the basis of company law was altered in three ways. First, some of the legal difficulties which bore upon the unincorporated company were lifted, while, second, its formation after 1844 was regulated by statute. Third, by a series of statutes, of which the most important was that of 1837, some of the privileges of incorporation were made more freely available. The starting point for these reforms was the repeal of the Bubble Act in 1825, which not only did away with the nebulous statute of 1720 but included provisions which empowered the Crown to prescribe henceforth to any extent the degree of a shareholder's responsibility in a 'corporation'. However, the exact legal position of a company established without the sanction of either the Crown or Parliament and which had more than seven partners and freely transferable shares, continued to remain undefined until legislation in 1844. The 'quasi-corporation' found no favour in the eyes of the judiciary despite the repeal: Lord Eldon maintained that to act as a corporation, without having been established either by private Act of Parliament or by Royal Charter, was an offence under common law and this opinion held sway in the courts until the early 1840s.[2] Industrialists for the most part were not affected by either the slow reform of the law or hostile legal doctrine, because manufacturing concerns continued to be organized as private partnerships. The still uncertain state of the law after 1825 affected mainly insurance companies, which during the first half of the nineteenth century constituted the largest single group of unincorporated companies. In 1844 there were about 970 unincorporated companies, of which 170 were in the field of insurance.[3] By the mid-1840s most of the latter had obtained the power to sue and be sued in the name of a chief officer through private Acts of Parliament, with nearly 100 such Acts being passed between 1800 and 1844. This legislation removed one difficulty of acting as an unincorporated company, while in addition insurance companies attempted strenuously to remove another, through clauses in both their deeds of settlement and the policies that they issued which limited the liability of their shareholders.[4]

The main area of the reform of the law in the 1830s affected the granting of charters establishing corporations. The ability of the Crown after 1825 to confer, by Letters Patent, corporate privileges was administered by the Board of Trade. Initially the principal corporate power conferred was the ability to sue and be sued in the name of an officer of the company. This in no way assisted a company to raise its capital but was an important aspect of the status of a corporation. In spite of the mainly administrative nature of the privilege – its main benefit was in legal cases – the Board of Trade considered favourably only applications from a narrowly defined range of companies, namely mines, public utilities, insurance companies, and charitable or educational bodies. These administrative rules, which were formulated following the repeal of the Bubble Act, remained unaltered even when the law was modified further in 1834 by the Trading Companies Act. This statute, together with the earlier legislation of 1825, was repealed in 1837 by an Act which enabled the Board of Trade, at its discretion, to confer on an applicant full corporate status, including the privilege of limited liability, by grant of either a charter or Letters Patent. Between 1837 and June 1854 there were 164 applications for charters, of which 93 were approved, a success rate somewhat higher than the impression given by either interested contemporaries or some subsequent commentators.[5] However, such charters were costly to obtain – one estimate is £402[6] – while the procedure involved did allow 'behind the scenes' pressure to be exerted to the detriment of the applicant's case. This can be seen in the case of an attempt to obtain a charter for a trans-Atlantic shipping line in the 1850s which was successfully blocked by the Cunard line, a private partnership. The opposition took the form of what apparently appeared to be a totally unconnected memorial to the Board of Trade from the shipowners, shipbuilders and merchants of Dumbarton, in which they objected generally to charters being granted to shipping companies. They argued that there was a lack of neither capital nor enterprise in the shipowning industry, and maintained that chartered concerns were unjust because, by their creation, private firms were disadvantaged, which checked free competition.[7] This written protest was followed up in the Commons by W. Brown, and its success led to the applicants' solicitor, E. W. Field, writing *Observations . . . on the right of the Public to form Limited Liability Partnerships . . .* , which subsequently has been considered to be one of the most effective statements by those who wished to reform the law in the mid-1850s.[8] Individual disgruntlement over the way charter applications were handled by the Board of Trade may have privately led the government to introduce legislation totally reforming the law in the mid-1850s, but it was not a main plank of the supporting argument advanced in the debate following the publication of the bill.

Despite the problems caused by both their uncertain legal status and the partiality of the Board of Trade, the number of unincorporated companies increased substantially during the second quarter of the nineteenth century. The combination of their growing numbers with the highly speculative nature of the booms in which they were promoted led eventually to legislation in 1844. The government had attempted to pass a general companies bill in 1838, following immediate criticism of the 1837 Act dealing with charters, but it was defeated in the Lords by opposition led by Lord Brougham. A Select Committee was established in 1841 to investigate insurance company frauds, but when it was reconvened in 1843, its terms of reference were widened to a general consideration of the position of joint stock companies. Its recommendations were the basis for the Joint Stock Companies Registration and Regulation Act of 1844.[9] This statute was one component of Peel's attempt to ensure general monetary and financial stability by legislation, the others being the Joint Stock Bank Act and the Bank Charter Act of the same year. The Companies Act required the registration of all non-banking partnerships which had more than 25 members and freely transferable shares and, unlike the Joint Stock Bank Act, this requirement applied to existing concerns as well as future formations. Companies so defined could carry on business as unlimited corporations once they had completed a two-stage registration process. This involved specified minimum levels of subscribed capital, a procedure intended to check the formation of bubble companies. Investors in these unlimited companies were further protected through publicity provisions that included half-yearly returns of shareholders and audited balance sheets, both of which were to be filed with the newly created office of Registrar of Joint Stock Companies. In terms of its requirements, the Act was to mark a high watershed in the development of English law, and many reformers in the 1870s and 1880s attempted to reintroduce its provisions, either in whole or in part.

Between 1844 and 1856, 910 unlimited companies formed in England and Wales were registered under the Act, of which the most important types were insurance (219), gas and water (211), markets and public halls (85), shipping (46), and petty lending (41).[10] The period when the Act was in force coincided with a substantial boom in the establishment of life insurance companies: by the early 1850s there were at least 150 life offices in existence, of which 80 had been set up between 1845 and 1852.[11] However, the belated full recognition of the unlimited company had very little effect upon the organization and finance of manufacturing industry.

Only 106 English and Welsh industrial companies were registered, of which the largest single group was 13 cotton companies.[12] Their formation marks the beginnings of the establishment in the cotton industry of a large number of corporate spinning concerns, and the seedbed of this development was a number of mutual and cooperative industrial societies.[13]

★

The reform of company law during the first half of the nineteenth century had been a slow and gradual process which had been checked by both the hostility of the courts and the inflexible attitude of the Board of Trade in interpreting legislation. Then suddenly in 1855 and 1856 the law was totally liberalized, and it is extremely difficult to account for this sharp and dramatic change. No single pressure group was responsible for all the various parliamentary committees which examined various aspects of the law between 1850 and 1854, although the Christian Socialists were an important force behind the inquiries of 1850 and 1851. Commercial and legal opinion was divided over the question of whether some form of limited liability should be freely available, but generally was hostile. As in the previous half-century, limited liability was associated with either monopoly power or speculation, and therefore was a privilege which should be bestowed only with extreme caution. The debate of the first half of the 1850s over limited liability, which took place not only in the hearings of the parliamentary committees but also through a large pamphlet literature and contributions to the various quarterly journals, will be examined by considering some of the interpretations which have subsequently been developed, and by looking at the views of both the various pressure groups operating, and informed and influential opinion.

The most important and influential historical interpretation is that put forward by Jeffreys, who placed the responsibility for the change in the law on the capitalists of the Home Counties, who, he maintains, were seeking fresh outlets for their accumulating savings. New openings for investment were required because of the diminution of savings possibilities in the 1850s. The National Debt was contracting with amortization, while there was a decline in the demand for capital by domestic railway companies. Consequently this section of society sought the general availability of limited liability in order to be able to invest in domestic manufacturing industry.[14] Although highly plausible, this interpretation is open to a number of objections. First, the growing number of studies of the flows of funds within the railway capital market of the second quarter of the nineteenth century does not reveal a dominance of south-eastern investment. While extra-regional flows of savings were important, purchases of securities by residents in Lancashire and the West Riding at times played a role equal to, if not greater than, that of the Home Counties.[15] Second, the low level of public issues of railway securities in the 1850s was due partly to the unwillingness of investors to subscribe. They were not prepared generally to purchase new railway shares, especially ordinary shares, because of the very low earning power of the majority of existing shares. Actually railway companies were still seeking funds during the decade, but as a result of the failure of public issues, were forced to develop other methods of raising money.[16]

To concentrate on domestic outlets for savings in the 1850s is likely to be misleading because it was precisely during this decade that Britain became a substantial exporter of capital. According to Imlah's estimates, the balance on current account rose sharply from £8m. per annum average during the first half of the decade to £26.2m. during the second,[17] and this was before the liberalization of the law in 1855 and 1856 could possibly have had an effect. It seems unlikely, therefore, that the mid-Victorian economy was running out of investment placements for its savings by the 1850s, but the volume of savings was such that the investor was confronted with the problem of a declining rate of return on low-risk securities. This was summarized at the time in the following way:

> The immense aggregate of accumulated money capital, for which no eligible channel of investment, combining the qualities of security and lucrativeness, can be found, is a perplexing feature in the social condition of England ... Persons who are dependent on the interest of small sums of money, say £2,000 or £3,000 find it a trying operation to maintain a family on the income which the investment of such sums in Consols will produce.[18]

The writer had his own solution in the form of American securities, but the case he was presenting in his advertising literature seems to have considerable solidity. Consols in the mid-1850s were yielding 3.4%, a return inflated by the impact of the Crimean War, and the solicitor who pointed this out maintained that:

> No one with common prudence can purchase railway shares ... In like manner let the reader consider the millions which have been thrown away in foreign loans, the numberless families whose property has been lost irretrievably in the attempt thus to obtain from a moderate capital means of subsistence, or to receive 5 or 6 per cent. for their spare capital.[19]

Another solicitor calculated that the annual return on land was 3%, on a first mortgage on real property 4%, and from ground rents $4\frac{1}{2}$%.[20] Whatever their immediate attractions, foreign securities and the shares of any limited companies could not be considered as simple replacements in a portfolio for either Consols or mortgages. While there may have been a problem in the 1850s of finding higher yielding but still reasonably secure investment outlets, it was not solved by the introduction of limited liability.

Whatever the designs of the capitalists of the Home Counties, manufacturers generally neither took immediate advantage of the change in the law nor complained about a shortage of capital. A report of the Society for Promoting the Amendment of the Law stated that:

> It cannot be said that large capitals are wanting in Great Britain for carrying on the usual undertakings in commerce and manufactures on the most expensive scale. But it may be alleged that in some kinds of business such as banking, mining, steam navigation, and others requiring a large outlay before adequate returns can be looked for, capital is not always ready to be advanced by respectable persons to a sufficient extent to answer the wants of our increasing enterprise at home and in our foreign dependancies.[21]

Such needs were indicated by others in the debate of the 1850s, but where it was acknowledged that capital was required, ways of raising finance outside the partnership had been developed in some cases since the beginning of the eighteenth century. Banks could be established as unlimited companies from 1825, following legislation, although their formation had been checked by Peel's Joint Stock Bank Act of 1844. The cost book company had become the basic unit of organization in non-ferrous metals mining from at least the 1750s, although by the 1850s there were complaints that the industry was beginning to suffer from a shortage of funds.[22] Steam shipping even in the 1850s was still in its infancy, but companies could be formed as either ship partnerships, unlimited companies or, after 1837, by charter. Between 1837 and 1854, thirteen chartered shipping companies had been founded, but not all applicants were so successful. It is difficult to establish both who exactly constituted the Society for Promoting the Amendment of the Law and the exact nature of its aims. James Stewart, a barrister, gave evidence on the Society's behalf to the 1851 parliamentary inquiry in which he made plain its reformist attitude. The Society's reasoning was very close to that of the Christian Socialists in that it saw limited liability, with workmen investing their savings with prescribed risk in their employers' concerns, as a way of reconciling the conflict between capital and labour. Stewart also highlighted the problem of the need to finance inventors who, he thought, were usually workmen.[23] William Hawes, a member of the Society's council, made the same general points but with some important qualifications in a pamphlet in 1854:

> It must be clear to everyone that working men are not deterred from uniting in co-operative associations from fear of unlimited liability, but I believe they are deterred from a distrust of themselves. The great bulk, certainly the more intelligent of them, know the different duties and responsibilities of master and men; and were the law of partnership so improved, that masters could give to all connected with their works an interest in their success, I am satisfied nothing would be heard from working men of co-operative societies; and whilst the profit of trade would thereby be decreased, the harmony and good feeling thus established between men and their masters would prevent the recurrence of those differences which ending in strikes are a disgrace to our age and to our laws.[24]

Hawes was probably provoked into publishing his views by the negative report of the Royal Commission on Mercantile Laws. However, unlike other members of the Society, he did not believe in total reform and his pamphlet was dedicated to Lord Brougham who had prevented the enactment of a general companies bill in 1838.

The discussion about working-class savings had been initiated by the Christian Socialists and their role, particularly that of their Parliamentary spokesman, Slaney, has been highlighted by Saville in his discussion of the reform of the law.[25] In May 1849 Slaney had tried to form a committee to consider measures for the social improvement of the working classes, including the safe investment of their savings. On this occasion he was unsuccessful, but in 1850 he did obtain, with government approval, the appointment of a Select Committee 'to consider and suggest means of removing obstacles and giving facilities to the safe investment for the savings of the middle and working classes'. This committee's report led to the setting up in 1851 of a Select Committee on the Law of Partnership. Both committees were chaired by Slaney, who although not a Christian Socialist, was influenced greatly by their ideas on co-operative production.[26] This phase of the debate was brought almost to an end[27] with the successful passage of Slaney's Industrial and Provident Societies bill which allowed such concerns to be formed on a trustee basis rather than as unlimited companies.[28]

One of the grounds for opposition to the introduction of any form of limited liability into company law was that it would increase speculation through the formation of 'bubble' companies. This concern was shared by the Registrar of Joint Stock Companies, who had submitted suggestions to the Board of Trade in February 1850 which, if implemented, would have further reduced the opportunity for speculative and fraudulent company promotion. The Registrar was purely an administrative officer, but in processing company registrations he became aware of the abuse of even the relatively tightly framed 1844 Act. He pointed out an instance where a promoter had absconded with the shareholders' deposits, and suggested that in future three promoters should sign the application for provisional registration. The rest of his proposals were in a similar vein.[29] Most of the 'bubbles' in the 1840s and early 1850s were insurance companies, and J. Hooper Hartnoll, the proprietor of *The Post Magazine,* the insurance trade journal, published in 1853 an open letter to the President of the Board of Trade. Hartnoll's main aim was the protection of the policy-holder, and he pointed out that while 291 companies had been proposed during the period 1844 to 1851, only 131 had been established of which 78 had subsequently failed.[30] Insurance companies were considered by a separate parliamentary committee in 1853 and as a result were excluded from the legislation of 1855 and 1856. It was not until company law was consolidated in 1862 that the privilege of limited liability was extended to insurance companies. However, the general protection of investors, desired by the Registrar, was not increased in the mid-1850s, but was done away with completely. To this extent the mid-1850s' legislation was a major retrograde step and the safeguards lost were never fully recovered.

If McCulloch represents the classical economists, then the profession was opposed to the general availability of limited liability. McCulloch followed Smith in advocating joint stock companies for public utilities, banks and insurance—concerns which worked on a 'routine system'—but was appalled at the prospect of 'all sorts of agricultural, and manufacturing, and commercial businesses' being organized in any form other than as partnerships.[31] Although he began his attack on reform by re-expounding Smithian doctrine, McCulloch extended his argument along lines common with other anti-reformers. Joint stock companies caused speculation, a conclusion he derived from the excesses of the promotional booms of the 1820s, 1830s, and 1840s, while he concluded that the general availability of limited liability would result in a greater incidence of bankruptcy. In his view public registration, introduced in 1844, was no safeguard because it did not involve any close scrutiny of the sources of a company's capital, and similarly he had little faith in other aspects of the 1844 Act such as either published or filed balance sheets. He maintained that limited companies would be able to obtain credit which their actual resources did not justify, but above all he was convinced of the superiority of individual enterprise which meant consequently that there was no profitable future for limited companies conducted on prudent lines:

> In ordinary business, that is, in all business for carrying on branches of agriculture, manufacture, or trade, partnerships with limited liabilities can be neither more nor less than unmixed nuisances. If honestly conducted they must fail in their competition with private parties, and if otherwise they will only add to the means, which are already sufficiently extensive, of wasting capital and fleecing the public.[32]

In his discussion, McCulloch was concerned primarily with the effects of the introduction of limited partnerships on the continental model (*société en commandite*) in which there were 'sleeping' limited partners and 'active' unlimited partners. This particular modification of the law had been mooted first in the 1820s and was the central point of debate from the late 1840s until the Report of the Royal Commission on Mercantile Laws in 1854.[33]

The momentum given to reform by Slaney, the Christian Socialists, and the Society for the Amendment of the Law had been dissipated by the time of the publication of the Report of the Royal Commission on Mercantile Laws. However, the pressure for liberalization was now continued in Parliament by a diverse group of 'free traders'. Cobden had been a member of Slaney's 1851 committee, but, as with other economic issues, Manchester was not a monolith with regard to changing the basis of company law. Manchester merchants led by T. Potter in the guise of 'Manchester Man' opposed the introduction of limited liability:

> I must confess, Sir, I wish the Board of Trade would explain a little more clearly, and define more exactly beyond this, for whose benefit these Bills are intended. Capitalists do not ask for them; the middle classes have knowledge sufficient to work their own capital successfully, and they have not asked for limited liability.[34]

Cobden,[35] Bright, and the Manchester Commercial Association favoured reform, while the Manchester Chamber of Commerce opposed firmly any change. There was a similar division in other northern industrial and commercial centres. The Leeds Chamber of Commerce came out against the general introduction of limited liability, a member writing:

> You know that a man of more than ordinary ability who gives his attention to business can soon place himself in a position to have plenty of capital to second his efforts. I approve of the Board of Trade giving a charter to charitable concerns or to projects for the

housing of the people. But I cannot agree with Limited Liability in general trade.[36]

Generally there was little provincial support for the reform of the law, though the degree of opposition did vary from city to city, and it was precisely this lack of a clear consensus that led the Royal Commission on Mercantile Laws to vote five to three against any change.

Instead of maintaining the existing law, the negative but confused Report of the Royal Commission led to a resolution in the Commons urging modification. It was introduced by Collier, the Attorney-General, and seconded by Viscount Goderich.

> That the law of partnership which renders every person who, though not an ostensible partner, shares the profits of a trading concern liable to the whole of its debts, is unsatisfactory and should be so far modified as to permit persons to contribute to the capital of such concerns on terms of sharing their profits, without incurring liability beyond a limited amount; and such modification is especially necessary in Ireland, regard being had to the peculiar social and industrial condition of that part of the United Kingdom.[37]

It would appear that what was being sought was the introduction of the continental limited sleeping partnership, while the special mention of Ireland was the result of an amendment during the debate. The resolution influenced the government to the extent that the Board of Trade refused to accept any further applications for charters on the grounds that the law was being considered. Bouverie, the Vice-President of the Board of Trade, moved in June 1855 the second reading of two bills, one to amend the law of partnership on the lines of the resolution while the other was to allow joint stock companies, excluding banks and insurance offices, to be formed with limited liability through an amendment to the 1844 Act. The provisions of the first bill allowed loans to be made to partnerships at a rate of interest varying with the profitability of the concern, without the lender incurring the liabilities of being a partner. This had been made possible by the repeal of the remaining parts of the usury laws the year before. It was thought that this would both allow widows to leave capital safely in their deceased husbands' firms and facilitate the supply of finance to small businesses and inventors. The bill lapsed at the end of the session and a subsequent bill in 1856 failed on a technical drafting point.

The limited liability bill did reach the statute book. Bouverie argued the case for it on the grounds that increasing numbers of companies were seeking incorporation under French and American laws so as to give their shareholders limited liability.[38] He drew his evidence of this practice from T. Barker's memorandum to the Royal Commission on Mercantile Laws and pointed out that 20 'English' companies had been formed in France during 1853/4.[39] Robert Lowe supported the measure, but as an advocate of complete economic freedom wished that it went further, and consequently attacked its clauses that specified a minimum capital of £20,000 and a minimum share value of £25. The bill, which received Royal Assent in August after being forced through the Lords, allowed companies to be formed with limited liability, but retained the stipulations of the 1844 Act regarding a two-stage process of registration, filed returns of shareholders, and filed balance sheets.[40]

Lowe replaced Bouverie at the Board of Trade and, not surprisingly, in 1856 introduced a joint stock companies bill based on his concept of economic freedom. In his view the only role that the state had was to ensure 'the greatest publicity to the affairs of such companies, that everyone may know on what grounds he is dealing',[41] but ironically all the publicity provisions contained in the 1844 Act were now abandoned, except annual returns of shareholders. Twenty years later in 1877, when Lowe sat on the second parliamentary committee to investigate the operations of the limited liability laws, he was to regret the radical nature of his 1856 bill, which was to survive basically unaltered until 1900. From 1856 the privilege of limited liability, which previously had been closely guarded, was made freely available; the only requirement made by the Act was the filing of a memorandum of association with the Registrar, signed by seven shareholders, who needed merely to have taken up one of the company's shares, for which there was no prescribed minimum value, and on which no money needed to have been subscribed.[42] English company law now became the most permissive in Europe.

In 1857 banks were partially assimilated into the new company code. Lowe argued that the 1844 Joint Stock Bank Act had put barriers in the way of establishing banks but had not prevented mismanagement and failure. He would have liked to have brought in insurance companies as well, but they continued to be excluded in deference to the wishes of the 1853 Select Committee which had asked for separate legislation. Unlike in his 1856 Limited Liability Act, Lowe did retain some vestiges of Peel's policy in his 1857 Banking Act, in particular a minimum share value of £100 and unlimited liability.[43] A further general amending Act was passed in 1857, but the alterations it introduced were 'in language not in principle': they allowed shares to be converted into stock, regulated more effectively the winding-up process by giving greater powers to the court, and facilitated company amalgamations. The Fraudulent Trustees Act of the same year did return to shareholders some of the protection that they had lost in 1856. It made issuing a fraudulent prospectus a criminal act, while company officers would be guilty of a misdemeanour if they took for their own use company funds or property, if they made false book entries, or if they altered the company's books.[44] However, there was no statutory requirement that a company should keep any specific books. During the same session a bill was officially introduced to extend limited liability to insurance companies, but it did not succeed.[45] The privilege of limited liability was extended to banking in 1858 as a result of Headlam's activities in the Commons.[46] The government in the next session contemplated introducing a general consolidating act with special regulations for insurance companies. A bill passed through the Lords, virtually without debate, but a change of ministry prevented it from being placed before the Commons.[47] It was reintroduced in 1860, passed through the Lords, where an amendment to reintroduce filed balance sheets was defeated, but was crowded out of the Commons' order paper. No bill was introduced in 1861, although one was expected by some members, and in a question, the Attorney-General blamed the Board of Trade for the delay.[48] The reformed law was consolidated finally by the Companies Act of 1862, which brought together the legislation of 1856 to 1858, repealed the last remaining fragments of Peel's Joint Stock Bank Act, and extended limited liability to insurance companies. Unfortunately the statute was imperfect as it did not give companies the power to reduce capital; this omission was an oversight–the necessary clause had been contained in the 1856 Act–but the failure to re-enact it was to lead to serious difficulties in the mid-1860s and the late 1870s. Worst, it was to bedevil the various attempts to reform the law by creating a second line of discussion. A separate statute, the Industrial and Provident Societies Act of 1862, allowed cooperative companies to be established with limited liability,[49] so that from November 1862, when the two statutes became operative, all types of concerns were placed on an equal footing before the law.

All the goals of the various groups in the 1850s who had sought to amend the law in one direction or another were finally achieved in the mid-1860s. Partnership law was amended in 1865 by an Act introduced by Milner Gibson that allowed loans to partnerships to enjoy a rate of interest which could vary with the rate of profit of the borrowing concern, without the lender becoming liable for the debts of the partnership beyond the extent of the loan.[50] The Act was abused, since lenders refused to remain passive and instead merged their loans with the equity of the active partners. The refusal of sleeping partners to remain dormant led to confusion as to their exact standing and by the early 1880s there was 'a strong demand in the country for some form of true limited partnership'.[51] The continental *société en commandite par actions*, involving unlimited directors and limited shareholders, was introduced into English law by the Companies Act of 1867, following a recommendation of the Select Committee on the Limited Liability Acts of the same year. However, it is doubtful whether any company had been established with unlimited directors and limited shareholders by the mid-1880s.[52]

The total reform of English company law during the years between 1855 and 1862 marks a sudden and sharp break; change both before and subsequently was a long drawn out, gradual process. Not only was the pace suddenly quickened, but the law itself was turned upside down, with all the barriers in the way of company formation being removed. This extreme degree of permissiveness was to become the hallmark of English law. The abuses to which it could lead when its full potential was explored by unscrupulous company promoters were very quickly revealed in the waves of company flotations which occurred in the 1860s and 1870s. But the resulting cries and pressure for reform made no impact, while many regarded any reintroduction of any forms as either at best worthless, or at worst as a totally retrograde step. It is highly likely that the extreme freedom that the law gave to company promoters led ironically to limited companies getting a 'bad name', with their formation being regarded with disfavour by manufacturers and industrialists. Registrations during the 1860s and the early 1870s varied generally with the conditions of the trade cycle, and the underlying trend in registrations did not turn up until the mid-1870s, when increasing numbers of companies were formed privately without the aid or otherwise of a promoter. Permissiveness in this way provided an unfavourable legal environment for the finance of industry and it was not until 1900 that any steps were taken to change it. Such conditions were in marked contrast to company law established in France and Germany during the third quarter of the nineteenth century.

★

In France, the *société en commandite par actions*, a 'halfway house' to the full limited company, had been available as a unit of business organization for entrepreneurs and promoters since 1807. However, in 1856 such a company was made subject to further regulation; in future, before one could begin business, all its shares had to be taken up and 25% of its nominal capital subscribed. Minimum share values were also stipulated: 100 francs (£4) where a company's capital did not exceed 200,000 francs (£8,000), and 500 francs (£20) above that level. The final part of the 1856 reforms made activities of the company's unlimited directors (*gérants*) subject to a committee of surveillance, consisting of some of the passive limited shareholders. These regulations, aimed at dampening down speculation and fraudulent promotion, were evaded by registering companies either in Belgium or, ironically, England, and the multinational problem was made more complex by the Franco–British Convention of 1862 which allowed British companies to operate in France. The liberalization of English law in the mid-1850s led consequently to a degree of reform in France in 1863 which allowed joint stock companies with full limited liability (*sociétés à responsabilité limitée*) to be established without a charter, provided that the capital involved did not exceed 20m. francs (£800,000).[53] This ceiling was removed in 1867 as it had been found that it was too onerous and made the law ineffective.

Company formation was further facilitated by waiving the 1856 stipulation that required all of a company's shares to have been subscribed before it could start business. French law then remained basically unchanged until 1893 when the requirements regarding minimum share values and subscription levels were altered. Small and large companies continued to be treated differently and, despite the fall in prices during the last quarter of the nineteenth century, the dividing line was maintained at a capital of 200,000 francs. However, the minimum share value of a small company was reduced to 25 francs (£1), but it was required that all its shares were to be subscribed and fully paid. The minimum share value of a large company was reduced to 100 francs (£4) and while all had to be subscribed, only 25% of the shares' value needed to be paid up before the company could begin operations.

Company law in the German states generally was similar to the French, being based either upon the Napoleonic code of 1807 or influenced by it, but such a generalization does mask some wide variations.[54] Free incorporation was not permitted in Prussia until 1870,[55] but 295 chartered companies, with a total capital of 2,405m. marks, had been established during the preceding twenty years. Although the majority were railway companies, mines together with foundries and salt works accounted for a tenth of the aggregate authorized capital. In France 408 chartered companies had been founded between 1855 and 1870, of which the largest single category, some 149 concerns, was insurance companies.[56] The reform of company law in Prussia was followed by a major boom in company formation, with 203 companies being established in 1871, 478 in 1872, and 162 in 1873. After the speculative excesses of the *Grunderjahre*, company promotion fell sharply and only 123 limited companies were formed in Prussia between 1874 and 1882.[57]

The Imperial German company code, enacted in 1884, strictly regulated limited company formation. It introduced a two-stage process of establishing a company: its constitution by its shareholders being followed by formal registration which gave incorporation. Normally companies had to have a minimum share value of 1,000 marks (£50), although this could be reduced to 200 marks (£10) with the consent of the Federal Council. Constitution involved a company's shareholders agreeing to its governing articles, appointing its managing board, and its board of supervision, while the whole of the company's shares had to be allotted and 25% of its capital subscribed. The last part of the first phase was a shareholders' meeting, called to receive satisfactory reports of the formation of the company. The position of the shareholders continued to be protected by the company's board of supervision, on which no company 'director' sat, and which examined and reported on the company's yearly accounts and had the power to convene general meetings. Registration consisted of filing certain documents signed by five shareholders, which stated whether the company's shares had been issued at premium, if any shares had preferential rights, how general meetings were to be convened, and how the company was to make public announcements. The promotion arrangements had to be specified in some detail; it being necessary to state whether certain shareholders had special advantages, whether any shares had been issued other than for cash, the particulars of the purchase of any property, and finally the nature of the promotional expenses. Generally most companies were formed under this code by a process known as 'simultaneous formation' in which the promoters subscribed for all of a company's shares and in so doing constituted the company; later, if desired, the shares could be sold off, either publicly or privately, the usual channel being a bank which had acted as one of the promoters. Publicity was ensured as the filed documents required for registration were open to inspection at a local court and extracts were published in the *Imperial Gazette*.[58]

Although company law was liberalized on the continent almost at the same time as in England, it developed subsequently in a different, more controlled way. Regulations generally ensured that companies could not be established with insufficient capital, while the activities of company promoters and directors were subject to a degree of supervision by shareholders and general publicity. In England, until the 1900s, there were no built-in safeguards whatsoever despite repeated campaigns for the reform of the law. The reformers often looked to continental law as a model for emulation in England, just as part of the campaign for the introduction of some form of limited liability into English law during the first half of the century had been the attempt to transplant the continental sleeping partnership.

★

There was a major boom in company promotion in England during the first half of the 1860s, in which all the weaknesses and defects of the new permissive legal code were revealed. It is significant that the Select Committee which followed the 1866 crisis did not investigate the Bank of England and the monetary and banking system as in 1847 and 1857, but instead was established to inquire into company law. Perhaps somewhat surprisingly, pressure for reform came initially from the London Stock Exchange, which submitted a series of proposals to the Registrar of Joint Stock Companies, who, in turn, passed them with annotation to the President of the Board of Trade on 2 February 1866, some months before the failure of Overend, Gurney, and the financial panic. The ten suggestions comprised substantially the reformer's case which was to be presented, and re-presented, with some difference in stress, during the next thirty years.

1 That before a Company is registered the Registrar should satisfy himself as to the status of the subscribers of the Memorandum of Association.
2 That Companies should be restricted from employing their funds in the purchase of or in advances upon, their own shares.
3 That they should also be restricted from borrowing money on debentures or on mortgage upon the general funds of the company.
4 That vendors should be enabled to enforce Registration of transfers by summary process before a Judge in chambers.
5 That any fraud, misrepresentation, or suppression of facts by Directors, or other officers of the Company should be made punishable as a misdemeanour.
6 That Companies should not in any case increase their Capital without the consent of the shareholders convened specially for the purpose . . .
7 The Subcommittee desire to call the attention of the Registrar to clauses 54 and 76 of Table A.
8 Before the Articles of Association are effective, they are to be examined and approved as in the case of a Benefit Society.
9 All deposits to be returned unless a specified amount of the nominal capital be applied for and allotted.
10 If half the proposed capital be not subscribed for and allotted bona fide within three months, the company shall not commence business but give notice to the Registrar who shall cancel the registration.[59]

Subsequently a further suggestion that each and every change and vacancy with regard to seats on company boards should be published in the *London Gazette* was added. The Registrar favoured the reform proposals and in certain cases amplified and extended them; for instance with regard to suggestion 7, he wanted discretionary powers to refuse a registration where he considered that there were valid objections to any of the articles of association.

The collapse of Overend, Gurney and the suspension of the Bank Charter Act in May 1866 temporarily diverted attention from company law. However, the pamphlet literature generated by the monetary and financial crisis, which was generally concerned with credit and the operation of the Bank Charter Act, did usually refer to the new companies in derogatory terms and not simply because most of them were either banks, discount houses, or finance companies.[60] Echoes of the 1850s debate were also heard. Howell, who had given evidence to the 1851 Select Committee and the 1854 Royal Commission, maintained that the limited partnership should have been introduced rather than the limited company with freely transferable shares.

> Limited Liability, which is, as I have always maintained, a principle of liberty and justice, comprehending the sacred right freely to labour and, if not immorally, freely to contract (a principle to the benefit of which every working man is entitled, be he artist, mechanic, or clerk), instead of becoming, as it might have been, the national support and an assistance to British industry in its new and sharp competition with foreigners under Cobden's tariff, has in England only opened a rich field to the gambler and fraudulent concocter of schemes; with its luring but deceptive flag, 'LIMITED', it has been a snare and a delusion, like the candle to the moth, or gunpowder in the hands of children.[61]

Howell's plea for the introduction of *en commandite* partnerships was supported by Levi, who regarded the subsequent amendment introduced by the 1867 Act as not going far enough. Levi sympathized with the Stock Exchange proposals, shook his head over the number of abortive companies, and desired that the registration process should not be purely nominal, by requiring that a company should have in future half of its shares allotted and 25% of their value subscribed before being allowed to begin operations.[62]

One aspect of the 1866 crisis was a sharp fall in share trading caused by what can be termed 'unlimited liability'. A large number of 'public' companies established during the 1860s boom, particularly financial concerns and some of the larger industrial companies, had been formed with shares of large denomination but on which only a small amount had been called up.[63] During the crisis such shares became unsaleable, mainly because buyers were not prepared to take on the potential liability that they involved. As has been pointed out already, the 1862 Act, unlike the 1856 Act, contained no provision whereby companies could either reduce their nominal capitals or subdivide their shares. In 1866 the only way open for a company affected by the problem was to go through the costly process of winding up, followed by reconstitution with a lower nominal capital and shares of a smaller denomination. Newmarch estimated that between £20m. and £30m. invested in company shares 'was in a state of suspended animation, in consequence of the unmarketable character of shares'.[64] The initiative to make the necessary amendments to the 1862 Act was taken by David Chadwick, an important company promoter,[65] and W. R. Drake, a solicitor who specialized in company matters and who was a company director.[66] Chadwick petitioned the President of the Board of Trade for an amending bill in November 1866,[67] and subsequently Milner Gibson introduced a measure which would have allowed companies to subdivide their shares, but not below a minimum value of £10. This passed the Commons but failed in the Lords as a result of the opposition of a peer who was strongly antagonistic to the general availability of limited liability.[68] The measure is of note because it was the only occasion after 1862 that the government attempted, legislatively, to introduce a minimum share value.

A fresh bill was prepared by Drake and it, together with the suggestions of the Stock Exchange, were considered by the Select Committee on the Limited Liability Acts which sat during the spring of 1867. Nearly all the witnesses who gave evidence supported the provisions of the bill which allowed both the reduction of nominal capital and the subdivision of shares to any extent.[69] However, most did not stop there, since they were asked about the Stock Exchange suggestions for reform, which led in replies to specific illustrations of abuse and fraud, together with proposals to remedy the situation. The reforms suggested varied widely, the most reactionary proposals coming from Swinton Boult, who reiterated the arguments of Adam Smith and McCulloch and consequently only favoured limited companies if they were restricted to the fields of banking, insurance, water supply, and internal transport.[70] The central pressure group of Chadwick, Drake and Newmarch, basically representatives of some shades of 'City' opinion, did favour further reforms, besides those for which they were pressing, but in this wider area their views varied considerably.

Newmarch did not support any general moves which would entail radical reform but wanted three specific changes: first, the ability to issue bearer shares, a proposal supported by Drake;[71] second, the circulation of a company's articles of association, either with its prospectus or at a subsequent date; and third, the circulation annually amongst a company's shareholders of a printed list of shareholders in the company. In addition, Newmarch strongly opposed companies being able to deal in their own shares and wanted the practice prohibited.[72] Chadwick, who was to lead the reform movement a decade later, in the mid-1860s wanted merely the Registrar of Joint Stock Companies to have the same powers as the Registrar of Friendly Societies and suggested that the model table of articles of association contained in the 1862 Act should be mandatory for all companies, on the basis of any desired deviations from it having to be justified to the Registrar.[73] This latter proposal was supported by some other witnesses.[74]

Most of the other witnesses were lawyers, amongst whom C. Wordsworth, Q.C., a writer on company law, made the most wide-ranging suggestions for radical reform. His basic intention was the resurrection of the 1844 Act but with limited liability, more or less the situation as it had been following Bouverie's Act in 1855. Consequently he wanted the reintroduction of minimum share values together with a stated minimum proportion paid up,[75] and this received support from two other witnesses, a bank director and an accountant, who suggested that between 25% and 75% of a company's issued capital should be subscribed.[76] Wordsworth's second main reform involved the signatories to a company's memorandum of association taking a minimum number of shares, which he coupled with the requirement that the promoters should take, in addition, a substantial number of a company's first 'public' issue of shares,[77] and here he received the support of the chief clerk of the Roll's Court.[78] His intentions were twofold: on the one hand, he wanted companies to be provided with the capital that they required in order to operate successfully, while on the other, by stipulating that the promoters provided some significant proportion of those funds, they were tied in a direct way to the company whose capital they were raising from the public. Other witnesses also favoured a greater regulation of the process of company formation and had similar aims to Wordsworth, but thought that they could be obtained through different statutory requirements. Henderson, an accountant like Chadwick, wanted a company's first directors to be appointed not by the promoter, but by the shareholders, with the directors so appointed validating the original prospectus.[79] However, Browne, a barrister, desired to return to the 1844 Act in that he wanted the Registrar to certify that a company's memorandum and articles were consistent with its prospectus.[80] While the Registrar in the early 1850s and in the mid-1860s had favoured further reform, the incumbent of the office in 1867 asked only for the registration of balance sheets and directors' names, and the full publication of the names of new

companies, together with those who failed to submit the statutory required returns.[81] However, at one extreme, the Master of the Rolls warned
that it would be dangerous to extend the Registrar's powers,[82] while at the
other, Wordsworth wished to go as far as giving the Registrar the
discretionary power to investigate a company's accounts.[83] There was some
consensus that a company's borrowing powers should be defined and
restricted;[84] the general feeling was that, as with railway companies, loan
capital should be no more than a third of the equity.[85] Wordsworth
maintained that mortgages ought to be registered and Browne favoured the
registration of debentures.[86]

Little of the factual evidence of the substantial incidence of abuse and
near-fraud during the 1860s financial boom made any impact upon
members of the Select Committee, who similarly took no heed of the
large number of calls for the tightening up of the law in order to protect
the investor. The committee merely supported the proposals of
Chadwick's pressure group regarding the ability to reduce nominal
capital, to subdivide shares, and to issue bearer shares. Consequently it
has been claimed with considerable justification that there was little
connection between the evidence that the committee heard and the
recommendations that it made.[87] The reason for such an outcome is not
difficult to establish. The committee contained a large 'City' contingent
amongst its membership, some of whom, in particular Goschen and G. G.
Glyn, either knew personally or had strong business connections with
Drake, Newmarch and Chadwick.[88] As a result they had similar aims in
wanting to remove the threat of 'unlimited liability' overhanging the
Stock Exchange, but were not prepared to go any further in the direction
of general reform, whatever the wishes of members of the Stock
Exchange. General reform would have been relatively easy in 1867, with
the 1862 Act having been operative for barely four years, but the
members of the committee seem to have had a view close to that of
Newmarch, who said before them:

> I would venture to say that I should think it very undesirable that any
> interference except of a limited character should take place with the
> phraseology and construction of the Act of 1862, because we have
> now had five years' litigation under that Act, and the meaning and
> bearing of the Act is in course of being very rigidly settled.[89]

The law was not as firmly established as Newmarch implied and for half a
decade following the 1866 crisis there were a series of important
judgments in Chancery.[90] Reform was both required and possible in
1867; a very persuasive case had been made out, backed by a substantial
body of evidence. However, the committee did not take the initiative, and

subsequently judicial decisions firmly established the law, which made reform more and more difficult.

The recommendations of the committee were adopted in an amending bill which contained clauses allowing companies to reduce both their nominal capitals and the value of their shares, and to issue bearer shares, if they were fully paid. The bill contained two other recommendations which had not come from the Chadwick group but which the committee had put forward. One was a limited gesture towards the protection of the shareholders by requiring a company general meeting within four months of registration, while the other was a response to a number of witnesses who had asked for the introduction of the continental *en commandite* form of company.[91] This was done by permitting companies to register, if they wished, with both limited and unlimited shareholders. The bill passed through both Houses without any debate and few changes. The only significant amendments were, first, the substitution of 'unlimited' directors for 'unlimited' shareholders,[92] an even closer approximation to the continental practice, and second, the insertion of a clause requiring that details of every contract made by a company, or its promoters, directors or trustees, should be disclosed in its prospectus or notice of share issue; if those details were omitted, then the prospectus was deemed to be fraudulent.[93] This attempt to protect the shareholders was added to the bill as a result of litigation arising out of the conversion of Overend, Gurney into a limited company, and its lack of precision, probably caused by hurried drafting, led subsequently to very great difficulties over what constituted a contract which was required to be disclosed.[94]

★

The campaign for a thorough reform of the law was taken up in the mid-1870s by Chadwick, one of the 1867 pressure group, who had entered Parliament in 1868. His first, successful, piece of legislation was an amendment to the Joint Stock Companies Arrangement Act of 1870 which dealt with winding-up procedure,[95] an area in which he had been involved considerably during the late 1860s. Six years later, Chadwick introduced his own bill to reform the law. His aim was to repeal the unsatisfactory clause of the 1867 Act dealing with disclosure and replace it by a far more wide-ranging but highly specific measure. Under his scheme the following was to be stated in the prospectus: the names, addresses and occupations of the vendors; the dates of, the names of the parties to, and the material contents of, every contract made before the issue of a prospectus; the memorandum of association and the name, address and occupation of anyone who was to receive fees for issuing the company's capital; and the minimum proportion of capital, not to be less than 50%, required to be subscribed before the company could begin operations. Coupled with this clause were other requirements, some similar to those suggested to the 1867 committee. These included a more rigorous allotment procedure, the immediate circulation after allotment of a printed list of shareholders, specified forms of balance sheets including profit and loss which were to be certified by a company's directors and accountants and filed with the Registrar, and the production of a printed annual report which was to be sent to every shareholder.[96] This bill had the backing of 160 Associated Chambers of Commerce, but was opposed in the Lords by the Lord Chancellor on the grounds of insufficient time due to the imminent end of the session. It received a second reading in the Lords when it was acknowledged that the subject required Parliament's attention.[97]

General reform in 1877, as ten years previously, was bedevilled by the question of the extent of a company's ability to reduce its nominal capital. The Master of the Rolls had decided, in a case affecting the Ebbw Vale Iron Company, a concern that Chadwick had promoted, that under the 1867 Act a company could only reduce the unpaid portion of its nominal capital. This decision raised immediate difficulties, particularly for over-capitalized iron and steel companies during the severe slump of the late 1870s. Consequently Chadwick, in the two bills that he introduced in 1877 as part of his reform campaign, sought the explicit power of reducing subscribed capital.[98] His first bill was withdrawn after its first reading, but the second was referred to a Select Committee after receiving a second reading in the Commons.[99] The government introduced its own bill to empower companies to reduce paid-up capital, following representations to the Board of Trade from both M.P.s and large northern coal, iron, and steel companies, many of which had been promoted by Chadwick.[100]

The Select Committee on the Companies Acts, which was chaired by Lowe, the architect of the 1856 Act, and of which Chadwick and a number of his industrialist friends were members, heard a similar range of evidence to that given to its predecessor ten years earlier. The only significant difference was that both members of, and witnesses before, the 1877 Committee paid greater attention to the procedures of winding up and liquidation. Most witnesses in 1877, including Newmarch, supported both Chadwick's disclosure procedures and giving a company the ability to reduce its subscribed capital.[101] A majority wanted company formation to have the greatest possible publicity and were inclined generally to favour the French practice of a minimum amount of capital being subscribed before a company could commence business.[102] Chadwick's first bill of 1877 had required 75% of a company's issued capital to be taken up before it could begin operations, but in the second bill this was reduced to 66%. Newmarch did point out that a deposit of capital at the registration stage could be meaningless 'as the money could be borrowed one day and repaid the next',[103] the device that railway bill promoters had adopted thirty years earlier to circumvent Parliamentary Standing Orders. Where the witnesses did divide was over the question of the registration and publication of balance sheets, some maintaining that such a requirement would put limited companies at a severe disadvantage because their competitors would be able to gauge their profitability.[104] The main opposition to Chadwick's bill came from the Rt Hon. George Jessel, the Master of the Rolls.

In its report the Committee recommended the abandonment of Chadwick's bill, but did try to put some reforming legislation in its place. Its main recommendation was that, as under the 1844 Act, registration should be a two-stage process, being completed only when the capital proposed in a company's prospectus had been taken up and the stipulated proportion subscribed. As a result of the Registrar's evidence that 5,500 companies had not made the required returns,[105] the Committee attempted to ensure that the statutorily required returns were made punctually. Lastly, it pointed out that it considered the existing methods of liquidation to be unsatisfactory. The Committee's Report was ignored in the most pointed way: none of its recommendations was embodied in the 1877 Companies Act which consisted of only six clauses, which merely enabled any type of share capital to be reduced.[106] Chadwick took no further part in the reform campaign, although his bills of the mid-1870s joined the 1844 Act and continental practice as models for amending legislation. He was unseated in 1880, ironically on an election petition which contained charges of bribery treating, undue influence, and personation.[107] However, his 1876 bill clauses were included in a consolidating bill[108] introduced in 1884 by a group led by Sir John Lubbock, but the measure was dropped after its first reading and as a result was never discussed in the House. A different group of reformers in 1887 revived Chadwick's suggestions, to which they added the 1877 Committee's proposal of double registration,[109] but, after being resubmitted in 1888, their bill was withdrawn[110] because the government introduced its own reforming measure.

★

It took the 'Great Depression' to persuade the government that company law required drastic wholesale reform. Limited liability and company law were considered carefully by the Royal Commission on the Depression of Trade and Industry, which sat during the mid-1880s. Most of the witnesses who appeared before it were asked specific, if not loaded, questions that led to the Commission collecting a considerable body of evidence, most of which favoured reform, generally on the lines which had been suggested in 1867 and 1877. As well as going over old ground in terms of proposals aimed at protecting the shareholder and preventing fraudulent promotion, some evidence indicated the growth of new problems which would have to be considered in any reform of the law. One was caused by the growing number of 'private' companies, formed without any public appeal for capital. Although this type of company had probably been in existence since the liberalization of the law in the mid-1850s,[111] it was only during the early 1880s that their existence was being recognized. The Registrar estimated that 560 'private' companies had been registered during the five years ending 31 December 1884.[112] It was argued strongly by many witnesses that 'private' companies should be treated differently from other companies and particularly with regard to disclosure provisions. Sir Lowthian Bell, on behalf of the iron trade, thought that it would be unreasonable to require either 'private' companies or companies which did not raise loan capital to publish their balance sheets and borrowing powers.[113] He was supported by J. Lee, the textile manufacturer, who, while in favour of reform, thought that it was undesirable for private family companies to have to publish their accounts.[114] The possible need to treat 'private' companies in a different way was one new problem. Another was fully outlined by Joshua Rawlinson, an accountant from Burnley, who presented to the Commission a most comprehensive scheme for reform, the aim of which was the protection of the company's creditors rather than its shareholders.[115] Only three witnesses were totally opposed to any change in the law, and they were R. H. Reade and J. T. Richardson, representatives of the Belfast linen trade, which by the 1880s consisted solely of limited companies,[116] and Sir Thomas Farrer, who had been Secretary to the Board of Trade.[117]

The majority Final Report of the Royal Commission made few definite recommendations for the reform of the law, instead preferring the whole matter to be considered by experts. However, amongst the large number of minority reports there were positive reform proposals, calling for capital to be taken up and subscribed before a company could commence business, reserve liability, restricted borrowing powers, and annual accounts to be filed with the Registrar.[118] The government now conceded that company law required serious attention and indicated in the Queen's Speech of 1888 that reforming legislation would be introduced. Unfortunately the measure did not reach the Lords until the end of June which meant, as with earlier reforming bills, that there was not sufficient time before the end of the session for it to go through the necessary stages of consideration. The bill was very wide ranging and tried to deal with most of the issues that had been raised before the Royal Commission. Its provisions called for the full disclosure in a prospectus of any arrangement which would benefit a promoter, with, in the case of default, the promoter being liable to a civil action for damages and criminal prosecution. The registration process was to be in two stages, as under the 1844 Act, and involved minimum subscription levels. Audited accounts were to be published and this requirement was to apply to all companies, both 'public' and 'private'. The bill introduced a totally new principle, that of directors' responsibility, by requiring directors to take 20% of all shares allotted and not less than ten shares each. This was coupled with a parallel requirement which laid down that any director's share qualification had to be set out clearly in the prospectus, together with the way in which it was acquired. This was in conjunction with a stipulation that a company was not to be allowed to make a further share issue within a year of its registration, except with court approval, while directors were required to take the same proportion of capital issued subsequently as in the initial issue.[119]

With the 1888 bill the government moved into the van of the reform movement, a position that it had not occupied since 1862, but the measure met with considerable hostility in the Lords, and consequently did not proceed beyond the committee stage. Both Bramwell and Herschell, who were judges and Law Lords, asked for a Select Committee to consider the bill,[120] a stratagem which was a definite blocking attempt and did not succeed. Their concern was mainly with the 'private' company but their hostility spread to encompass the whole of the bill. In the debate, Bramwell pointed out that the bill did not consider the position of the private company and maintained that published balance sheets would give secrets away to competitors, while Herschell thought that the proposed directors' responsibilities were so large that they would be shouldered only by 'those who had nothing to lose'. They received support from Thring, who considered the bill to be a retrograde step as it would reimpose burdens which had been lifted by legislation in 1856 and 1862. Such arguments had been voiced before the Royal Commission, and were positions which were taken up again and again during the next twenty years when further initiatives were taken to reform the law. In 1888, only Denman, a judge, besides the Lord Chancellor and Salisbury, supported the measure in the Lords.

Three bills did reach the statute book in 1890. The government had contemplated introducing a consolidating measure, but instead brought in two separate bills to reform specific parts of the law. The first, dealing with the memorandum of association, had been prepared by a joint committee under Lord Herschell, and its aim was to allow companies to alter their memoranda of association, but only with leave of a High Court.[121] The need for such legislation had arisen out of a decision by Lord Selborne in which he had ruled that a memorandum of association was the 'unalterable law' of a company.[122] Such a rigid situation, which did not take into account changes in either the company's circumstances or the economy in which it was operating, could be and was eased by the ingenuity of the draftsmen of the memorandum, but until the 1890 Act, with a limited number of exceptions, once framed a memorandum could not be altered except by the expensive process of obtaining parliamentary authority.[123]

The second bill was concerned with winding-up and attempted to place company liquidation on the same footing as bankruptcy and bring it within the jurisdiction of county and other local courts. The need for change came from the high cost of winding-up which was due to liquidators, who were often self-appointed, being paid by the amount of time that they spent, which led them to have an interest in keeping the process going on as long as possible. When Hicks Beach introduced the bill in the Commons, he pointed out that at the end of 1888 42% of all companies currently in liquidation had ceased active trading more than five years previously.[124] The bill ran into difficulties because initially it was poorly drafted and consequently appeared to be in conflict with the 1862 Act, the relevant sections of which it did not repeal. When it reached the statute book, it contained clauses which introduced a degree of directors' responsibility, the principle which the government bill of 1888 had first framed. Henceforth in a winding-up, directors could face a public examination when the Official Receiver reported a case as requiring investigation.[125] A further innovation was the establishment of committees of inspection consisting of shareholders and creditors to supervise the work of the liquidators. The Act also transferred the powers relating to compulsory winding-up from the High Court to the Board of Trade.[126]

The Directors' Liability bill, a private measure,[127] arose out of an Appeal decision made in 1889 which had laid down that there was no liability under common law for untrue statements made, although they were known to be technically untrue, unless there was dishonest intention.[128] The sponsors of the bill wanted to ensure that every person who was responsible for issuing a prospectus was bound by the statements it contained. The Attorney-General did not object to the bill receiving a second reading, but did not wish it to go any further thereafter.[129] However, the bill was sent to the Standing Committee on Trade and subsequently was considered alongside the government's winding-up measure.[130] When it received the Royal Assent, it established a civil liability for untrue statements in a prospectus on the part of directors and other persons who had authorized its issue, but it did contain a number of saving clauses which stated that there was no liability for statements believed to be true, if they were based upon either reports drawn up by accountants and other professional advisers, or if they were copies of official documents.

In 1894, after a lull in activity of four years, the government introduced a draft bill with the aim of thoroughly reforming the law and remedying all the defects which had been apparent since the second half of the 1860s. The bill, which consisted of a whole series of alternative clauses, was considered first by a Board of Trade departmental committee under Lord Davey and it then went to the House of Lords in 1896, where it remained for four years, during which it was considered by a Select Committee and a technical committee.[131] In this long-drawn-out process, the original bill containing the clauses recommended by the Davey Committee was emasculated, and one comment on the 1900 Companies Act, the end result of the series of deliberations, was: 'In a word, considering all the time spent upon it, it is a pity that the Act achieves so little.'[132] The considerable opposition that the bill ran into prevented both the 'prudent investor' and the 'careful and diligent director', characters which the Davey Committee had formulated on the basis of existing judicial decisions, from becoming recognized in an Act. The end result was little more than an unstructured series of miscellaneous clauses, although the 1900 Act did give legal sanction to underwriting and made auditors obligatory.

★

When the Davey Committee sat, there were three pressing problems which required legislation. The first had existed since company law had been liberalized in the mid-1850s and was frauds on shareholders carried out by unscrupulous company promoters. Typically this was done by loading the purchase price of the assets to be acquired by the embryonic company through, usually, a series of contracts made between the vendors, 'dummy' vendors, and finally the company, the price of the assets increasing with each contract. This type of fraud had not been stopped by the clause in the 1867 Act, which was far from clear as the result of hurried drafting, a defect revealed in subsequent court cases.[133] The second problem had become apparent in the 1880s when it was argued that any disclosure requirements introduced, particularly those relating to balance sheets, should not apply to 'private companies', the numbers of which were growing substantially. The last problem was relatively new in the mid-1890s and arose out of a new trend in frauds, directed at the creditors rather than the shareholders. Increasingly, failing partnerships were being converted into companies, with the vendors subscribing for the equity and being paid for the assets that they transferred in cash and debentures secured by a floating charge on the companies' assets. If the converted company failed, then its 'outside' creditors received little or nothing in settlement of their claims because the vendors' debentures had priority.

The Davey Committee considered the government's draft bill and looked back over every inquiry made into company law since 1867, taking into account earlier bills and proposals for reform and revision. The aims of the consequent *Report* were contained in its sixth and seventh sections:

> It may be a counsel of perfection and impossible of attainment to say that a prospectus shall disclose everything which could reasonably influence the mind of an investor of average prudence. But this in the opinion of your Committee is the ideal to be aimed at, and for this purpose to secure the utmost publicity is the end to which new legislation on the formation of companies should be directed.

And this was coupled with:

> a more efficient system of registration of mortgages and in particular of floating charges is demanded in the interests of creditors, and more stringent provisions respecting accounts, balance sheets and audits, and provisions for better securing the responsibility of directors.

With regard to private companies, the committee thought that they were difficult to define,[134] but at the same time implicitly recognized them to a degree by not requiring its disclosure provisions for the prospectus to apply to circulars and notices inviting private subscription.[135]

The Davey Report recommended that every prospectus for a public issue of either shares or debentures should contain the following information: the names and addresses of the company's directors, together with the number of shares that they had taken up, and the names and addresses of its auditors. The minimum quantity of share applications on which the directors were prepared to proceed to allotment, which was to be prescribed in the company's memorandum or articles, was also to be indicated in the prospectus. Lastly, with regard to the prospectus, the purchase money paid to the real vendor was to be given, as were the payments made to every promoter or intermediate purchaser, together with any underwriting commission. By such recommendations, the committee wished to make it obligatory for every company to have auditors, and give legal sanction to underwriting which previously, with regard to shares, had been held to be illegal as it involved issuing a company's capital at a discount.[136] The issue of debentures or the arrangement of mortgages which were secured on either unpaid calls or by a floating charge was not opposed, but the committee recommended a public register of certain types of mortgage, including all charges on uncalled or unpaid capital and all floating charges. Increased protection for creditors was sought through other recommendations which involved enlarging the grounds for winding-up and making directors, in certain instances, liable personally for debts to unsecured creditors.[137]

One of the main intentions of the committee was to define clearly the duties, responsibilities and liabilities of directors and promoters, especially with regard to the promotion of a company and the issue of its prospectus. Here they wished merely to codify the state of the law as represented by court decisions. Consequently the committee thought that directors should exercise 'reasonable care and prudence', and if this requirement went beyond any judicial decision, it was nevertheless recommended as being 'right in principle'.[138]

The committee did not accept all the proposals that reformers had made in the past. It considered that the advantages gained by a company's 'general' shareholders of requiring the subscribers to its memorandum of association to take collectively a minimum proportion of the share capital and individually a minimum amount were plausible but illusory. Similarly it opposed the introduction of any form of double registration, arguing that this would remove the hallmark of English law — the ease of forming a company. The committee saw greater safeguards arising from transforming a company's first statutory meeting into a more active occasion. Accordingly it recommended that seven days before this meeting, which was to be held within one month of formation, each shareholder should receive a full statement of the board's views regarding the position and prospects of the company, in which the directors were to indicate clearly any reasons for now doubting statements made in the prospectus. This statement was to be certified by at least two directors and, as to certain financial matters, by the auditors. At the meeting the shareholders could, if they wished, appoint a committee of inquiry and withdraw from contracts on specified legal grounds. Here the committee appear to have been influenced greatly by the Imperial German code of 1884 and its subsequent working. The Davey Committee did pay heed to earlier English proposals regarding the composition of both a company's shareholders and its capital, by proposing that companies should file with the Registrar, within seven days of allotment, a return of all shares allotted and, with regard to those not paid for in cash, a statement of the extent to which they were paid up and the consideration for which they were allotted. Such information was also to be given in a company's subsequent annual returns and in its balance sheet, while the annual return was also to include the amount due on mortgages requiring registration, and the names and addresses of directors.[139]

The final area of concern to the committee was company accounting, and it laid down that 'proper books of account' should be kept, and recommended that auditors should be made obligatory. Unlike earlier reformers, it did not propose that balance sheets should be filed publicly, but instead asked that they be issued annually to shareholders together with a report from the directors and a full auditors' report. The committee did specify that certain items should be contained in the balance sheet. Additionally, and in order to generate increased care and attention on the part of directors, it recommended the annual production of an internal balance sheet. This was to be supplied to the auditors by the directors and was to be the document on which the shareholders' balance sheet was founded. It was to be certified by the auditors.[140]

The draft bill which the Davey Committee produced was criticized considerably by the witnesses who gave evidence to the House of Lords Select Committee chaired by Lord Halsbury. The opposition took two forms, direct and indirect, and in many cases the latter was more effective. Witnesses frequently stated that they were in favour of reform, but not as specified precisely in the bill. A reply often made was, 'It is the form of the clause I object to', but this was seldom followed by a suggestion of an alternative in a concrete form. Another form of indirect opposition was comments maintaining that the wording of the bill was too vague, particularly with regard to specified duties, whereas the penalties attached were too harsh. Many witnesses expressed considerable surprise at the Davey Committee's view of judicial decisions with regard to the role of the director.

The Davey concept of the 'careful and prudent director' perhaps aroused the greatest amount of hostility, and the proposed position of the director continued to be considered too onerous even after Lord Davey substituted 'diligence' for 'prudence' at the first session of the Select Committee.[141] A fellow member of the committee, Lord Kimberly, summarized the witnesses' position as being:

That at present a large number of directors are not very clear as to what the law is, and if you put in black and white in a statute precisely your opinion, the statutory opinion I mean, of what the law

is you would terrify directors, and consequently you would prevent
prudent men from accepting that office.[142]

Many pointed out that directors' duties were regarded as being
deliberative and advisory and accordingly their fees were small, usually
being of the order of £200 to £300 per annum.[143] Next to the position of
the director, the greatest controversy and opposition was aroused over the
recommended provisions of the balance sheet, and the failure to recognize
overtly the private company and exempt it from all the provisions of the
bill. One body of opinion, located in Belfast, the views of which were
aired by J. W. Budd, the President of the Incorporated Law Society,
wanted none of the provisions to apply to the private company, a concern
he defined as one which did 'not invite subscriptions from the public' and
consequently did not need to publish accounts.[144] While specific
proposals did lead to considerable antagonism, the opposition to the bill
during the five years that it was considered in the Lords was total to the
extent that witnesses even maintained that the disclosure of the amount
paid in underwriting commissions would stop the public subscribing.[145]
As a result the 1900 Companies Act[146] was only a pale shadow of the
original Davey bill.

The Act concentrated upon company formation and endeavoured to
tighten up the process, removing the possible area for abuse. Despite the
attitude of the Davey Committee, following the Act company creation
became essentially a two-stage process, because before a 'public' company
could commence business, certain specified conditions with regard to its
capital had to be fulfilled. The Act isolated the allotment process as the
main area for increased regulation. Accordingly the conditions for the
allotment of shares were clearly defined. No allotment could take place
unless the minimum amount of share applications specified in a
company's memorandum of association had been received, exclusive of
any shares payable otherwise than in cash. The specified minimum level
was left to the promoter to decide, but if none was laid down, then the
whole share capital had to be applied for before allotment could take
place. In addition each applicant was required to pay 5% of the nominal
value of each share on subscription, and this requirement also applied to
any subsequent share issue by the company. Such regulations were
designed essentially to prevent companies in future being formed with
insufficient capital, and only once they had been fulfilled, and a
declaration to that effect had been filed with the Registrar, could a
company commence business. This was because it was only at this stage,
rather than at registration, that any contracts into which the company had
entered became binding. This two-stage process did not apply to

companies which did not issue a prospectus, hence the Act, as Davey had done, implicitly recognized the 'private' company, but all companies had to file, within one month, details of their share allotments. In cases where shares were allotted other than for cash, as frequently happened with vendors' holdings, then a written contract had to be filed with the Registrar giving details of the consideration.

The Act contained no 'Davey' concept of either a 'prudent' or 'diligent' director but the mode of qualifying to be and appointing a director was specified. In the first place, a director had to send his formal consent to act as such to the Registrar. Second, if he was required by the company's articles to hold a certain number of shares in order to act as a director, then in the case of a 'public' company's first issue of shares, the director had either to sign the company's memorandum of association for the specified number of shares or to file a contract with the Registrar to take up and pay for his qualification shares. Third, a director had to obtain his share qualifications within two months of being appointed.

The regulation of the allotment process was coupled with a close specification of the contents of the prospectus. Every prospectus had to be dated, signed by every director, and filed with the Registrar before it could be issued. It had to specify the directors' share qualifications, if any, the remuneration of the board, and the minimum number of share applications required before allotment could take place, if it was less than the total share capital. The particulars of material contracts and of places where they could be inspected had to be stated, together with the amount of shares or debentures being issued other than for cash, and the names of the vendors with the amount being paid to them and the mode of payment. Finally, the amount of underwriting commission, if any, the amount of preliminary expenses, fees to promoters, and the names of the company's auditors had to be given. These conditions more or less followed the recommendations of the Davey Committee. While the Act legalized share underwriting, to a certain extent it also made it redundant, because it laid down for public flotations a minimum subscription payment and called for a specified minimum level of shares to be applied for before allotment could take place.

As the emphasis of the Act lay upon the allotment procedure, it is understandable that the Davey recommendations for the first statutory meeting were not adopted. However, the statute did call for a meeting to be held within three months of a company commencing business. Where Davey was followed was in requiring mortgages and charges to be registered, with the total amount involved specified in a company's annual return of its capital to the Registrar. Similarly, shares issued other than for cash had to be distinguished from shares issued for cash in the annual return. Lastly the Act did adhere to the Davey recommendations in requiring companies to have auditors: they were to be appointed at every annual general meeting.[147]

It is clear from the description given of its contents that the main burden of the 1900 Act dealt with the problem of frauds on shareholders by promoters, especially those involving the loading of the purchase price. In addition the Act attempted to ensure that 'public' companies started with an adequate capital, while by requiring the registration of mortgages it also went some way towards diminishing the possibility of frauds on unsecured creditors. The 1900 Act, like the Davey Committee, was ambiguous with regard to the private company; on the one hand, it did not define it, while on the other, most of the provisions dealing with company formation did not apply to companies which did not publicly issue a prospectus. The original Davey bill had had 49 sections: the 1900 Act contained only 36. A considerable amount of valuable provisions had been lost, particularly as the duties and liabilities of directors and promoters had been erased, together with clauses dealing with the nature and contents of the balance sheet.

Although the 1900 Act was a very much watered-down version of the Davey bill, because of the opposition that the latter had encountered in the Lords committees, its provisions were regarded generally as being too restrictive. The marked fall in company registrations which took place during the opening years of the twentieth century was attributed to the increased regulation of the 1900 Act.[148] It was in this atmosphere of concern that the Loreburn Committee was established in 1906[149] to review yet again the state of company law. Its findings led to the 1907 Companies Act,[150] which made three main changes to the law. First, the private company was recognized explicitly and defined legally on the basis of three criteria, namely it did not raise capital from the public, it had no more than 50 shareholders, and its articles of association restricted the right to transfer the company's shares. Private companies so defined were excluded from most disclosure and publicity requirements, the goal of so many since the mid-1880s. Second, every public company which did not issue a prospectus was required to file a statement with the Registrar containing the particulars which would have been required if a prospectus had been issued. This requirement had to be fulfilled before either shares or debentures were allotted. Third, every public company was to file in its annual summary returned to the Registrar an audited balance sheet, disclosing the general nature of the company's liabilities and assets. In 1908 existing legislation was consolidated, with no important additions or amendments.[151]

★

The legislation of 1900 to 1908 went some way to meeting the case that had been made out by reformers since the mid-1860s, but English company law still remained unsatisfactory. The attitude of the state in this area had varied considerably during the nineteenth century. Peel's Act of 1844 was interventionist, an attempt to regulate company formation so as to reduce speculation – a measure in the public interest. However, when limited liability became generally available following the legislation of 1855 to 1862, Peel's controls and publicity provisions were swept away. On the one hand, the new company law could be seen as emancipatory since it removed barriers blocking the mobility of capital, but on the other, no satisfactory limited partnership legislation was introduced until the end of the century. Government then stepped back and left the permissive company law, consolidated in 1862, untouched in its essentials until the 1890s. Pressure for reform grew within four years of the liberalization of the law but made no headway in the face of indifference on the part of the state and open hostility from the judiciary. The state's inaction in the 1860s and 1870s may be explained by the relatively small size of the problem as the volume of company registrations did not become sizeable until the late 1870s and early 1880s. It would appear that government only became convinced of the need for reforming legislation following the report of the Royal Commission on the Depression of Trade and Industry. However, by then strong interest groups had developed, mainly centring on the private company, which wished to maintain the liberal 1862 code. Consequently the reforms which did reach the statute book were but pale reflections of those which had been proposed.

Notes

(Place of publication is London unless otherwise stated)

1 B.P.P., 1895, LXXXVIII, *Report of the Departmental Committee Appointed by the Board of Trade* (Davey Committee), c. 7779, paras 11, 24.

2 See B. C. Hunt, *The Development of the Business Corporation in England, 1800–1867*, Cambridge, Mass., 1936, pp. 14–15, 17, 19, 20, 41–3.

3 B.P.P., 1845, XLVII, *Return of all Joint Stock Companies registered as having been in Existence before the passing of 7 & 8 Vict. c. 110*. Not all the concerns listed in this return were strictly unincorporated companies: a few, like the Royal Mail Steam Packet Company, had been formed by either a Royal Charter or a private Act of Parliament.

4 B. Supple, *The Royal Exchange Assurance. A History of British Insurance 1720–1970*, Cambridge, 1970, pp. 118–19.

5 B.P.P., 1854, LXV, *Returns of all Applications referred by Her Majesty to the Board of Trade, praying for Grants of Charters with Limited Liability under the Act 1 Vict. c. 73*. There is an element of double counting which inflates the success rate, because some companies applied for additional charters either to modify or extend their existing charters. The Pacific Navigation Company, for instance, obtained

an additional charter in 1845 simply to allow its directors to hold company meetings in England and Wales.

6 E. W. Field, *Observations of a Solicitor on the right of the Public to form Limited Liability Partnerships and on the Theory, Practice and Cost of Commercial Charters*, 1854, pp. 51–73.

7 P. R. O., BTI/498/1938/52.

8 J. Saville, 'Sleeping Partnership and Limited Liability 1850–1856', *Economic History Review*, 2nd series, VIII, 1955.

9 Hunt, op. cit., pp. 84, 92, 94.

10 See H. A. Shannon, 'The First Five Thousand Limited Companies and their Duration', *Economic History*, II, 1930–3.

11 Supple, op. cit., p. 111.

12 Shannon, op. cit., p. 420.

13 D. A. Farnie, 'The English Cotton Industry, 1850–1896', unpublished M.A. thesis, University of Manchester, 1953, pp. 231–5, 275–6; and see below, p. 107.

14 J. B. Jeffreys, 'Trends in Business Organisation in Great Britain since 1856...', Ph.D. thesis, University of London, 1938.

15 See S. A. Broadbridge, *Studies in Railway Expansion and the Capital Market in England 1825–1873*, 1970; J. R. Killick and W. A. Thomas, 'The Provincial Stock Exchanges, 1830–1870', *Economic History Review*, 2nd series, XXIII, 1970; M. C. Reed, *Investment in Railways in Britain 1820–1844*, 1975.

16 See P. L. Cottrell, 'Railway Finance and the Crisis of 1866: Contractors' Bills of Exchange and the Finance Companies', *Journal of Transport History*, new series, III, 1975.

17 A. M. Imlah, *Economic Elements in the Pax Britannica*, New York, reprinted 1969, pp. 72–3.

18 Anglo-American, *American Securities*, 2nd edn, 1860, p. 13.

19 E. Moss, *Remarks on the Act of Parliament, 18 & 19 Vict. c. 133 for the Formation of Companies with Limited Liability*, 1856, pp. 9–10.

20 R. A. Ward, *A Treatise on Investment*, 2nd edn, 1852, pp. 6, 61, 209.

21 Society for Promoting the Amendment of the Law, *Report of the Committee on the Law of Partnership on the Liability of Partners*, 1849, p. 25.

22 J. H. Murchinson, *British Mines considered as a means of Investment*, 1856, pp. 17–18.

23 B.P.P., 1851, VIII, *Select Committee on the Law of Partnership*, qq. 315, 318.

24 W. Hawes, *Observations on Unlimited and Limited Liability; and Suggestions for the Improvement of the Law of Partnership*, 1854.

25 Saville, op. cit., p. 419.

26 ibid., pp. 419–21.

27 For the main contemporary literature, see A. Scratchley, *Industrial Investment and Emigration*, 1851, pp. vii–viii; J. Lalor, *Money and Morals*, 1852, pp. 199–207; W. R. Grey, *Investment for the Working Classes*, 1852, a reprint of an article which first appeared in *The Edinburgh Review*, CCIV, 1852.

28 R. E. Tyson, 'The Sun Mill Company Ltd. – Study in Democratic Investment 1858–1959', unpublished M.A. thesis, University of Manchester, 1962, p. 20.

29 P.R.O., BT1/447/431/50.

30 J. Hooper Hartnoll, *A Letter to the Right Hon. E. Cardwell...on the Inoperative Character of the Joint Stock Companies Registration Act, as a means of preventing the formation of Bubble Assurance Companies*, 1853, p. 6.

31 J. R. McCulloch, *Considerations on Partnerships with Limited Liability*, 1856, p. 4.

32 ibid.

33 Saville, op. cit., p. 422.

34 A Manchester Man [T. Potter], *The Law of Partnership*, 1855; see also his 'On Jurisprudence in Relation to Commerce', *Transactions of the Manchester Statistical Society*, 1858–9; and A. Redford, *Manchester Merchants and Foreign Trade*, II, *1850–1939*, Manchester, 1956.

35 Even Cobden's position as a reformer varied: see W. S. Lindsay and R. Cobden, *Remarks on the Law of Partnership and Limited Liability*, 1856.

36 Quoted in M. W. Beresford, *The Leeds Chamber of Commerce*, Leeds, 1951, p. 40. There was a strong body of opinion in Liverpool against the introduction of limited liability: see S. Boult, *Trade and Partnership*, 1855.

37 Hansard, CXXXIX, 1855, p. 311.

38 ibid., p. 321.
39 ibid., p. 323; see also P. L. Cottrell, 'Anglo-French Financial Co-operation 1850–1880', *Journal of European Economic History*, III, 1974, pp. 62–5.
40 D. Gibbons, *Limited Liability Act, 18 & 19 Vict. c. 133*, 1855.
41 Quoted in Hunt, op. cit.
42 The 1856 Act required all partnerships of more than 20 members to register as joint stock companies, whereas the 1844 Act had applied to partnerships of more than 25 members.
43 The 1857 Banking Act increased the maximum permissible number of partners in a private bank from six to ten.
44 H. Thring, *Joint Stock Companies Acts 1857*, 1858; see also Society for Promoting the Amendment of the Law, *Report of Special Committee on Partnership*, ?1857.
45 Shannon, op. cit., p. 399, n. 1.
46 *The Bankers' Magazine*, 1858, pp. 209–13.
47 C. Walford, *The Insurance Year Book*, 1870, p. 16; Shannon, op. cit., p. 399, n. 1.
48 Shannon, ibid.
49 Tyson, op. cit., p. 37.
50 *The Economist*, 18 March 1865, p. 308.
51 F. Pollock, 'The Law of Partnership in England with Special Reference to Proposed Codification and Amendement', *Journal of the Institute of Bankers*, I, 1880, pp. 721–30. See also M. D. Malleson, 'The Law of Partnership in England', ibid., V, 1884, pp. 1–10; and *The Economist*, 9 December 1876, pp. 14, 29–30.
52 Pollock, op. cit., p. 724; see also *B.P.P.*, 1877, VIII, *Select Committee on the Companies Acts, 1862 and 1867*, evidence of Sir George Jessel, Master of the Rolls.
53 Davey Committee, 1895, para. 10, and appendix by Edouard Chinet; C. E. Freedman, 'Joint Stock Business Organisation in France, 1807–1867', *Business History Review*, XXXIX, 1960, p. 197; R. E. Cameron, *France and the Economic Development of Europe*, Princeton, N. J., 1961, p. 198.
54 D. S. Landes, 'The Structure of Enterprise in the Nineteenth Century. The Cases of Britain and Germany', *XIe Congrès Internationale des Sciences His-*

toriques, Rapports, V, *Histoire contemporaine*, Uppsala, 1960, p. 116.
55 D. S. Landes, *The Unbound Prometheus*, Cambridge, 1969, p. 198.
56 L. Levi, 'On Joint Stock Companies', *Journal of the Statistical Society*, XXXIII, 1870, p. 15.
57 J. Riesser, *The Great German Banks*, Washington, D. C., 1911, pp. 47–8.
58 Davey Committee, 1895, Memorandum by E. Schuster.
59 P.R.O., BT13/1 E284, E295.
60 See F. W. Fetter, *Development of British Monetary Orthodoxy, 1797–1875*, Cambridge, Mass., 1965, pp. 237–41; P. L. Cottrell, 'Investment Banking in England 1856–1882: Case Study of the International Financial Society', unpublished Ph.D. thesis, University of Hull, I, pp. 497–502.
61 J. Howell, *Partnership Law Legislation and Limited Liability Reviewed in their relation to the Panic of 1866*, 1869, p. 10.
62 Levi, op. cit., pp. 16, 22–3.
63 See below, pp. 81–2, 118.
64 *Select Committee on Limited Liability Acts*, 1867, evidence of W. Newmarch, q. 528; see also q. 954.
65 See below, p. 113.
66 See Cottrell, op. cit., p. 918.
67 *Select Committee on Limited Liability Acts*, 1867, evidence of D. Chadwick, q. 850.
68 ibid., Drake, q. 536.
69 The only major exception was H. Thring, a writer on company law.
70 ibid., q. 1734.
71 ibid., qq. 630–1.
72 ibid., qq. 523, 547–8, 550, 586–9, 959, 1037.
73 ibid., qq. 844, 848, 895.
74 ibid., q. 819.
75 ibid., qq. 295–7.
76 ibid., evidence of M. H. Chaytor, a director of a number of banks, q. 2163, and W. K. Henderson, an accountant, q. 929.
77 ibid., qq. 295, 298, 428.
78 ibid., evidence of Boyle Church, chief clerk of the Rolls' Court, q. 1510.
79 ibid., q. 927.
80 ibid., q. 1113.
81 ibid., q. 83.
82 ibid., q. 1374.
83 ibid., q. 359.

84 ibid., q. 301.
85 ibid., Browne, qq. 1133–4.
86 ibid., qq. 346, 1198.
87 M. Rix, 'An Economic Analysis of Existing English Legislation concerning the Limited Liability Company', unpublished M.Sc. (Econ.) thesis, University of London, 1936, p. 10.
88 Cottrell, op. cit.
89 *Select Committee on Limited Liability Acts,* 1867, q. 1057.
90 See Cottrell, op. cit.
91 *Select Committee on Limited Liability Acts,* 1867, evidence of Webster, qq. 784–90; J. Howell, q. 2007.
92 30 & 31 Vict. c. 131, s. 4.
93 ibid., s. 38.
94 Rix, op. cit., pp. 21–2.
95 Hansard, CCIII, 1870, pp. 1569–70; 33 & 34 Vict. c. 104, s. 2.
96 *B.P.P.,* 1876, 1, *Bill No. 211.*
97 Hansard, CCXXX, index; CCXXXI, pp. 1065, 1068.
98 *B.P.P.,* 1877. I, *Bill No. 45* and *Bill No. 109.*
99 Hansard, CCXXII (1877) Index, CCXXXIII (1877) Index, CCXXXIV (1877) Index.
100 ibid., p. 1293.
101 *B.P.P.,* 1877, VII, *Select Committee on the Companies Acts, 1862 and 1867,* evidence of W. Newmarch, qq. 248, 262, 687, 762; W.Turquand, President of the Institute of Accountants, qq. 462–3, 484; J. Morris, solicitor, qq. 818, 829, 879.
102 ibid., Turquand, q. 438.
103 ibid., q. 337.
104 ibid., Morris, q. 967.
105 ibid., q. 54.
106 40 & 41 Vict. c. 26, s. 3.
107 *Macclesfield Courier,* 1 May 1880, p. 5; 26 June 1880, p. 3.
108 *B.P.P.,* 1884, II, *Bill No. 38.*
109 *B.P.P.,* 1887, I, *Bill No. 218.*
110 See Rix, op. cit., p. 36.
111 See below, p. 80.
112 *B.P.P.,* 1886, XXI, *First Report of the Royal Commission on the Depression of Trade and Industry,* c-4721, q. 668.
113 ibid., 1886, XXII, *Second Report of the Royal Commission on the Depression of Trade and Industry,* c-4715, q. 3682.
114 ibid., 1886, XXIII, *Third Report of the Royal Commission on the Depression of Trade and Industry,* c-4797, q. 8052.
115 *Second Report of the Royal Commission on the Depression of Trade and Industry,* q. 5869.
116 ibid., qq. 7030–1.
117 ibid., 1886, XXIII, *Final Report of the Royal Commission on the Depression of Trade and Industry,* c-4893, qq. 15, 136–45.
118 ibid., paras 68, 105, and minority reports signed by G. A. Jamieson, R. H. I. Palgrave, T. Birtwistle, J. P. Corry, Lord Dunraven, W. F. Ecroyd, P. A. Muntz, and N. Lubbock.
119 See Rix, op. cit., pp. 37–9.
120 Hansard, CCCXXVII, 1888, p. 1514; CCCXXVIII, 1888, p. 1502.
121 ibid., CCXLI, 1890, p. 848.
122 T. B. Napier, 'The History of Joint Stock and Limited Liability Companies', *A Century of Law Reform,* 1901, p. 396.
123 Hansard, CCCXLIV, 1890, p. 428.
124 ibid., CCCXLI, 1890, p. 397.
125 Rix, op. cit., p. 41.
126 A. Essex-Crosby, 'Joint Stock Companies in Great Britain, 1890–1913', unpublished M.Comm. thesis, University of London, 1938, p. 78.
127 Hansard, CCCXLII, 1890, p. 173.
128 *Derry v. Peek:* see Rix, op. cit., pp. 38–40.
129 Hansard, CCCXLII, 1890, p. 1116.
130 ibid., CCCXLIV, 1890, p. 1609; CCCXLV, 1890, pp. 607, 1245–90, 1881–906.
131 *B.P.P.,* 1896, IX; 1897, X; 1899, VIII.
132 M. Barlow, 'The New Companies Act, 1900', *Economic Journal,* XI, 1901, p. 192.
133 The leading case was and still is *Twycross* v. *Grant* (1877), the argument being over who exactly constituted the vendors and what was a material contract.
134 Davey Committee, 1895, op. cit., para. 63.
135 ibid., para. 38.
136 ibid., paras 36, 53; see also *Select Committee of the House of Lords on the Companies bill,* evidence of J. W. Budd, qq. 190–1, 196–7.
137 Davey Committee, op. cit., paras 33, 44, 45, 49.
138 ibid., paras 21, 30, 32.
139 ibid., paras 25, 39, 57, 58.
140 ibid., paras 51, 52, 53, 55.
141 *Select Committee of the House of Lords*

on the Companies Bill (1896), op. cit., evidence of J. W. Budd, q. 218.

142 ibid., evidence of J. H. Tritton, q. 932.

143 ibid., Budd. qq. 22, 226.

144 ibid., qq. 7, 8.

145 ibid., qq. 183, 198; for a fuller account of the opposition to the Davey bill, see Rix, op. cit., pp. 42–76.

146 63 & 64 Vict. c. 48.

147 See Rix, op. cit., pp. 78–82; Barlow, op. cit., pp. 187–92.

148 4,444 new limited companies were registered in England in 1899; registrations then fell each year, reaching 3,421 in 1904, before recovering. See below, p. 162.

149 The Company Law Amendment Committee; for its report and the evidence presented to it, see *B.P.P.*, 1906, XCVIII.

150 7 Edw. VII c. 50.

151 8 Edw. VII c. 69.

4 Shares and shareholders of early limited companies

Between the mid-1850s and the mid-1880s, following the liberalization of company law, a substantial number of limited companies were established. During the decades after Lowe's Act of 1856, 5,310 such concerns were formed in the United Kingdom, of which by far the greatest number, 4,859, were registered in London. Most attention has been paid to London registrations,[1] because of their dominance, and the analysis in this chapter will be restricted to such concerns. Throughout the 30-year period being considered, there was an upward movement in the secular trend of London registrations, with 6,111 during the period 1866 to 1874 and 9,551 between 1875 and 1883. Not all of these registrations resulted in a company subsequently raising capital and commencing business: 36% of registrations made between 1856 and 1865 were abortive, and 31% during the following decade. In addition, not all of the companies which managed to proceed beyond the registration stage raised capital publicly. Although the private company was not recognized legally until 1900 and not defined legally until 1907, a significant proportion of registrations, even before 1885, were made to establish private companies. Shannon states that 14.5% of registrations which took place between 1875 and 1883 were for private companies, and suggests that the registrations of 1866–1874 'contain a fair number of private companies'.[2] It is highly probable that the private company was in existence from the liberalization of company law in 1855/6. Before examining the impact of free incorporation upon the organization and finance of manufacturing industry, this chapter will consist of a general consideration of some of the features of corporate finance. Attention will be paid in particular to, first, the type of shares that the new limited concerns used and, second, the geographical and social composition of the investors who took up the shares. These two aspects are linked because the character and denomination of the issued shares will to a certain extent determine the nature of the investor prepared to subscribe for them.

Both Shannon and Jeffreys[3] have concluded in general that share values were initially high but then fell from the mid-1860s, with the result that the £10 share was typical in the 1870s and the £1 share was almost commonplace in the 1880s. According to Jeffreys, large share values were used initially both because of the tradition established by the canal and railway companies and as a deterrent to speculation. A somewhat different trend is portrayed in tables 4.1 and 4.2, which are based upon an annual 10% random sample of abstracts of company registrations contained in Parliamentary returns produced by the Registrar on almost an annual basis from 1864.[4] The mean share value of the sample fluctuates considerably over time and with a cyclical pattern; higher share values going hand in hand with booms and lower share values being characteristic of slumps. However, the large value of the standard deviation in every year indicates a considerable variance in the annual sample around its mean. The actual distribution of share values of the sampled companies is shown, in terms of percentages, in table 4.2. While there is a wide scattering of share values used in every year throughout the period, a high proportion of companies each year had share values of £10 or less, namely 79%. From 1874, shares of £5 or less were used on average each year by 55% of the companies in the sample, while after 1877 £1 shares became more common, being used annually on average by 29% of the companies in the sample. There was therefore a secular change in the size of share denominations but it was not a dramatic one. Instead shares of £10 or less were used by nearly all companies throughout the period, but there was an increasing use of shares of £5 or less from the mid-1870s and £1 or less from the late 1870s.

What appears to have led to the view of Shannon[5] and Jeffreys was the use of large shares during the boom of 1863–6 compared with the growing use of shares of £5 or less from the mid-1870s, together with the sharp increase in the use of £1 shares from about 1877. The high use of large share values during the 1860s boom can be attributed largely to the dominance of banks, discount houses, and finance companies in company registrations, especially in the public flotations of joint stock companies.[6] Nearly all financial concerns used large shares, not so much because of the practice of the canal and railway companies, but rather owing to a

Table 4.1 Mean share value 1856–82

Year	Mean £	Standard deviation
1856	12.35	17.27
1857	7.20	13.96
1858	5.62	8.08
1859	6.72	7.69
1860	7.5	13.20
1861	8.34	11.70
1862	13.90	22.79
1863	20.39	27.13
1864	17.17	21.39
1865	14.10	19.89
1866	16.33	24.01
1867	16.31	23.28
1868	10.65	20.66
1869	15.90	25.41
1870	12.12	19.94
1871	11.55	20.25
1872	13.16	22.11
1873	12.43	20.65
1874	10.46	18.18
1875	10.92	18.77
1876	14.70	23.66
1877	7.48	14.67
1878	14.13	23.35
1879	8.47	15.31
1880	12.36	21.02
1881	9.78	18.27
1882	13.31	23.16

Source: See text.

different precedent, that set by joint banks formed during the 1830s. It was only for this type of company that a norm in terms of share denomination had been established by previous practice. However, it should be pointed out that there is a bias in the data presented here, caused by the way in which they have been computed, and this bias is present also in Jeffreys' and Shannon's data. The volume of share denominations is aggregated by the number of companies instead of in terms of the amount of capital issued. This tends to deflate the proportion

Table 4.2 Share denominations 1856–82

Year	Size of sample	0–£1		£1+–£5		£5+–£10		£10+–£25		£25+–£50		£50+	
		no.	%	no.	%	no.	%	no.	%	no.	%	no.	%
1856	21	1	4.8	3	14.3	13	61.9	2	9.5	1	4.8	1	4.8
1857	34	13	38.2	7	20.6	9	26.5	4	11.8			1	2.9
1858	28	9	32.1	11	39.3	4	14.3	3	10.7	1	3.6		
1859	29	6	20.7	9	31.0	10	34.5	3	10.3	1	3.4		
1860	36	5	13.9	15	41.7	12	33.3	3	8.3			1	2.8
1861	42	11	26.2	15	35.7	8	19.0	3	7.1	5	11.9		
1862	44	8	18.2	16	36.4	8	18.2	6	13.6	2	4.5	5	9.1
1863	69	7	10.1	17	24.6	24	34.8	2	2.9	9	13.0	10	14.5
1864	90	8	8.9	18	20.0	29	32.2	17	18.9	11	12.2	7	7.8
1865	90	5	5.5	28	31.1	31	34.1	14	15.4	6	6.6	6	6.6
1866	66	7	10.6	19	28.8	22	33.3	6	9.1	5	7.6	7	10.6
1867	41	3	7.3	15	36.6	9	21.9	7	17.0	3	7.3	4	9.7
1868	40	8	20.0	19	47.5	5	12.5	5	12.5			3	7.5
1869	43	11	25.6	12	37.9	8	18.6	4	9.3	3	6.9	5	11.6
1870	52	7	13.5	24	46.1	10	19.2	3	5.8	5	9.6	3	5.8
1871	69	9	13.0	20	28.9	32	46.4	1	1.44	2	2.9	5	8.7
1872	92	16	17.4	26	28.3	33	35.9	5	5.43	4	4.3	8	8.7
1873	106	20	18.9	26	24.5	38	35.8	11	10.4	3	2.8	8	7.5
1874	107	16	14.9	39	36.4	33	30.8	11	10.3	2	1.9	6	5.6
1875	105	16	15.2	43	40.9	25	23.8	11	10.5	4	3.8	6	5.7
1876	89	12	13.5	35	39.3	20	22.5	8	8.9	5	5.6	9	10.1
1877	84	23	27.4	24	28.6	29	34.5	5	5.9			3	3.6
1878	76	20	26.3	24	31.6	19	25.0	1	1.3	3	3.9	9	11.8
1879	95	29	30.5	27	28.4	24	25.3	8	8.4	4	4.2	3	3.1
1880	109	29	26.6	26	23.8	31	28.4	9	8.2	6	5.5	8	7.5
1881	138	51	36.9	30	21.7	32	23.2	12	8.7	6	4.3	7	5.1
1882	145	37	25.5	45	31.0	30	20.7	14	9.6	5	3.4	14	9.6

Source: See text.

of large shares used and conversely inflates the proportion of small shares, because large denomination shares generally tended to be used for large capital issues, or rather by companies which had large nominal capitals. However, this bias has to be discounted because large shares, and similarly large nominal capitals, were seldom, if ever, fully paid up. Banks, in particular, used the large unpaid element in their share capital, which was often of the order of 75–80%, as a form of extra security for their depositors. Some of the variance around the mean share value given in table 4.1, therefore, can be accounted for by certain types of company, with an already established share denomination, tending to dominate company registrations at particular points of time. During the first half of the 1860s the bank promotion boom led to an increase in the use of large shares, £20, £50 or more, while the boom in 'worker' cotton company formations between 1859 and 1861 caused a contrary movement, with their use of small shares, £5 or less, a tradition for these companies set by previous mutual and cooperative concerns.

Throughout the period being considered, given that most companies issued shares of £10 or less, the size of shares would not appear to have been a major barrier preventing any person with some means from investing in a joint stock company, though there were a limited number of exceptions, as in the case of bank shares. However, denomination alone *does* not provide a sufficient indicator of type of investor; instead it has to be considered in conjunction with the amount of capital called up on a share. Small calls would mean that there was no barrier at all to investment but the subscriber, unwittingly or not, in such a situation did incur a large degree of potential liability as the result of the extent of unpaid capital. Shannon,[7] and Jeffreys to some extent, both basing their interpretation on evidence drawn mainly from the experience of banks and financial companies in the 1860s, argue that initially shares were issued with a high proportion unpaid, but following the events of the 1866 crisis there was a general tendency to issue fully paid-up shares. Jeffreys does point out, however, that there was a wide variation in practice between different types of company. Such a break in trend, following the 1866 crisis, cannot be established from the evidence given in the Parliamentary returns which is laid out in table 4.3. The basis of this table is not a 10% random sample of the abstracts of returns, as was used for tables 4.1 and 4.2, but instead it is all abstracts of returns where details of both nominal and paid-up capital were given. From the data it is evident that there was a wide variation between companies with regard to the proportion called up, but on average after 1866 until 1882 companies called up initially only 25% of their nominal capital. The proportion called up during the 1860s boom was lower, averaging 18.9%

Table 4.3 The relationship of paid-up
capital to nominal capital 1856–82
Annual average of all complete returns

Year	$\dfrac{Paid\text{-}up\ capital}{Nominal\ capital} \times 100$
1856	38.48%
1857	32.29
1858	57.81
1859	54.73
1860	39.25
1861	27.78
1862	27.87
1863	13.50
r1864	21.20
1865	25.80
r1866	15.20
r1867	23.20
r1868	31.20
r1869	13.30
r1870	25.40
r1871	37.00
r1872	27.70
1873	31.20
r1874	25.72
r1875	15.56
r1876	23.23
r1877	24.00
r1878	15.27
1879	25.05
r1880	39.99
r1881	24.77
r1882	20.55

r = Parliamentary   return   (retrospective)
made during that year.

Source: See text.

per annum, and this is due mainly, as with higher share denominations at
that time, to the weight of bank and financial promotions during these
years.

The data derived for the period 1856 to 1862 is somewhat difficult to interpret because the first Parliamentary return, although retrospective, was not made until 1864. It is not evident from this return whether the Registrar in compiling it used either a company's first annual summary of capital or its current summary in 1864. The considerably higher proportions of nominal capital paid-up shown for the late 1850s and early 1860s depend upon the material assembled by the Registrar. They may reflect either, if the Registrar used the first annual summary, that early companies called up initially greater proportions of their capital than subsequent companies or, if the Registrar in 1864 used the current returns, that they called up progressively more capital during the years after their foundation. The continuing generally low levels of paid-up capital in relationship to nominal capital during the early 1880s, in the case of public companies, is confirmed to a degree by Essex-Crosby's analysis of companies quoted on the London Stock Exchange. Using *Burdetts Official Stock Exchange Intelligence* for 1885, he found that the average unpaid liability was 38.5%, with a higher proportion unpaid in the case of banking, insurance and financial companies.[8] This evidence would indicate also that companies did call up capital progressively after their establishment.

Nearly all securities issued before 1885 were ordinary shares. This is confirmed by the data in table 4.4 where every issue other than of ordinary shares as indicated in the Parliamentary returns has been aggregated annually. However, it would appear that there was some implicit differentiation in the case of ordinary shares, because quite frequently companies would appear to have called up different amounts of money on the ordinary shares that they issued. This practice is indicated in the table by the annual series titled differential calls. Primarily this arose out of the practice of paying vendors in either fully paid-up or partly paid-up shares of the companies to which they were selling their businesses. Very gradually from the early 1870s this became formalized with the creation and issue of either vendors' shares or deferred shares. There would appear to be no significant difference from the general pattern of issuing solely ordinary shares in the case of public companies because only 12.2% of company securities quoted on the London Stock Exchange in 1885 were preference shares, the majority of which had been issued by overseas railways and financial companies.[9] It would appear that generally very few companies during the 1860s and early 1870s made use of loan capital. The exact position is difficult to quantify because until 1900 there was no legal requirement to make annual returns of loan capital. Financial companies did make some use of debentures and other types of loan instrument during the 1860s boom,[10] while some of the coal, iron, and steel companies formed during the early 1870s, used debentures

Table 4.4 Character of shares 1856–82

Number of issues

Year	Differential calls	Preference shares	Deferred shares	Vendors	Founders	Others
1856	19	1	–	–	–	1
1857	12	4	–	–	–	11
1858	32	1	–	–	–	4
1859	18	–	–	–	–	2
1860	27	1	–	–	–	2
1861	28	1	–	–	–	1
1862	41	–	–	–	–	2
1863	15	–	–	–	–	–
1864	51	–	–	–	–	–
1865	20	–	–	–	–	–
1866	3	–	–	–	–	–
1867	9	–	–	–	–	–
1868	5	–	–	1	–	–
1869	15	–	–	–	–	–
1870	16	–	–	–	–	–
1871	41	1	–	7	1	11
1872	49	3	–	16	–	15
1873	51	4	–	17	–	9
1874	113	3	–	25	–	12
1875	90	–	–	6	1	4
1876	31	7	5	15	–	6
1877	62	7	1	7	2	10
1878	41	9	6	10	7	13
1879	55	20	5	18	7	11
1880	97	8	3	17	2	21
1881	125	–	–	14	3	2
1882	152	1	–	3	–	–

Source: See text.

as well as fully paid-up shares in order to pay vendors for their property.[11] In nearly all cases before the mid-1870s, debentures were issued for a limited term, seven years being common, and so in nature were analogous to those issued by the domestic railway companies from the late 1830s until the mid-1860s. The practice of issuing debentures, and other fixed loans of longer maturity, grew steadily from the mid-

1870s so that by 1885, in the case of companies quoted on the London Stock Exchange, such loan capital in aggregate amounted to 26% of the companies' aggregate paid-up capital.[12] However, this debt had been created primarily by overseas railway companies and finance, land and investment companies and trusts, with the latter group making issues under the Mortgage Debenture Act of 1865.[13]

The bulk of securities issued between the mid-1850s and the early 1880s consisted of ordinary shares that had a value of £10 or less on which initially on average 25% was called up. Smaller share values became more common from the mid-1870s, with first an increasing use of £5 shares, while from the late 1870s the £1 share was used more widely. This fall in share denominations was slightly offset by a parallel fall in the price level which was of the order of 17% between 1870–2 and 1880–2.[14] By the early 1880s there were more public issues of preference shares and debentures, and payments in securities to vendors were sometimes being formalized through creation of specific vendors' shares instead of using, as previously, ordinary shares credited with a proportion paid-up. Broad generalizations obscure wide variations in practice between companies, the most distinctive exception being financial institutions, which throughout the period used large share denominations, on which a small proportion was called, even when the concern had been in existence for some time, and which also relied heavily on loan capital of some form. Accordingly, there was no democratization of the market brought about by a sharp fall in the size of share denominations from the 1860s to the 1880s; instead, for most types of company, because of the widespread use of shares of £10 or less throughout the period, potential subscribers to their securities could come from nearly all walks of life where there was an income sufficient to give rise to savings. The problems that such potential investors faced were twofold. First, as securities were nearly always ordinary shares, they carried a considerable element of risk, particularly in terms of potential return. Second, the persistent practice of only calling up a small proportion initially could lead to investors incurring a considerable element of unpaid liability. Therefore ordinary, only partly paid, shares were by their nature highly risky securities to hold, which could restrict considerably the type of investor to which they appealed.

★

In order to try and determine the general social and geographical composition of shareholders in early limited companies, the first annual summary of capital of a 10% random sample of companies was analysed for two benchmark years, 1860 and 1885. The companies were identified from the parliamentary returns for the two benchmark years, and details of their shareholders were taken from the actual summaries of capital that they sent to the Registrar.[15] Accordingly 37 company files were examined for 1860, and 115 for 1885. Political clubs were not included in the sample because the object was to analyse purely profit-orientated concerns. These were the only companies excluded. Some of the basic characteristics of the companies in both samples are given in table 4.5.

Table 4.5 Characteristics of the sampled population of companies 1860–85

	1860	1885
Number of companies	37	115
Number of abortive companies	13 (35.13%)	37 (32.17%)
Number of live companies	24	78
50% of the companies survived for	29 years	3 years
25% of the companies survived for	51 years	13 years
Duration of last surviving company	81 years	39 years
Number of reconstructions	4	9
Composition of live companies		
Colliery	1	–
Slate quarrying	2	–
Non-ferrous metals mining	1	3
Overseas mining	1	6
Cotton spinning and manufacturing	5	–
Manufacturing	3	19
Waggon	1	–
Patent	1	–
Shipping	1	9
Other transport	–	1
Foreign railway	–	2
Financial	–	10
Commercial	1	17
Other service-sector companies	2	–
Building and property	2	8
Gas	3	3
Number quoted on London Stock Exchange	1	9
Paid-up capital as % of aggregate	3.12%	30.23%
Number with London Registered Offices	8	39
Paid-up capital as % of aggregate	54.91%	78.31%

In each sample a number of companies were abortive, that is they did not proceed beyond the stage of registering a memorandum of association. The incidence of abortion, about one company in three in both samples, agrees with the overall company mortality statistics established by Shannon.[16] Usually, abortive companies went informally out of existence and consequently cluttered the company register until 1880 when the powers of Registrar, with regard to companies not making statutory returns, were augmented. It was the practice of the Registrar's office to ask companies for returns which they had not made, giving a warning of the statutory fine. The issued notices were usually returned by the Post Office marked either 'not known' or 'gone away'. Occasionally a notice from the Registrar did elicit a response and in both samples there are some such replies. Generally they indicate that the embryonic company was unable to raise sufficient capital with which to begin business. The two replies contained in the 1860 sample are in that vein, namely: 'A few shares only being taken',[17] and 'The Company has not made sufficient progress to justify them in proceeding with its business, in fact there have been only 7 shares allotted since the filing of the Memorandum of Association and the Articles of Association'.[18] There were four replies in the 1885 sample, three of which were similar to the two of 1860, but with interesting differences in the case of two of these. They both reveal the use of formal intermediation in the company's creation: in one case a broker,[19] and in the other the publication of a prospectus.[20] This is very slender evidence but it is indicative of a greater use of the more formalized machinery in company flotations by the mid-1880s. The only other reply contained in the 1885 sample gives an entirely different reason for the company's failure to commence business: 'borings for water unsatisfactory and expended company's funds'.[21]

The incidence of abortion left 24 companies in the 1860 sample and 78 in the 1885 sample to be considered. The type composition and the survival rates of these live companies are given in table 4.5, and the 1860 data can be compared with the data computed by Shannon for all London registrations. The dominance of cotton and gas companies in the sample agrees closely with Shannon's material, which reveals that these two groups of companies were the most numerous amongst those established during 1860, with 45 cotton-manufacturing companies and 39 gas and water companies out of a total of 246 effective registrations.[22] The survival rates of the 1860 sample are difficult to compare exactly with the Shannon data but would appear to be in general agreement, if gas companies are removed from the sample, as Shannon does for the overall population.[23]

Most of the 'live' companies in the two samples would appear to have raised capital privately without the help, or otherwise, of formal financial institutions. The shares of only one company in the 1860 sample and nine in the 1885 sample were quoted subsequently on the London Stock Exchange. However, the nine in the 1885 sample account for 30.23% of the aggregate paid-up capital of the sampled companies and were generally the larger companies, in terms of paid-up capital, within the sample. This use of the London Stock Exchange by generally only large joint stock companies agrees with the evidence of Essex-Crosby who found that in 1885, 1,585 joint stock companies had their shares on the London list, only 17.7% of the number then registered in England and Scotland, but with an aggregate paid-up capital of £332m. they accounted for 69.9% of the total paid-up capital of all registered companies.[24] The company files do not indicate generally how the companies actually raised their initial share capital; the proportion of shares held by solicitors, particularly in the case of the 1860 sample (see table 4.7), may indicate that they acted as company midwives. Most of the larger companies, in terms of paid-up capital both in 1860 and 1885, had their registered offices in London and appear to have used London legal and accounting firms for the process of registration. By the late 1870s there existed in London company agents, who were either licensed vendors of stamps or law stationers, and they were responsible for a substantial number of all registrations, but according to the Registrar they had 'nothing to do with the actual formation and promotion of the company, as a rule'.[25]

The geographical and social composition of the initial shareholders of the companies in the two samples can be seen in tables 4.6 and 4.7. It should be noted at the outset that the method used in compiling both tables does produce a bias, in that the proprietary of the larger companies, in terms of paid-up capital, does dominate, and this has to be remembered in any interpretation. The geographical sources of capital were established by measuring the distance between a company's registered office and the address given by each shareholder:[26] the only items of information contained in a company file. There is some ambiguity about both these pieces of information. First, when comparing 1860 and 1885 there would appear to have been a growing use of registered offices in London, and these were probably nearly always not connected with the site of the 'works' of the companies involved. This development is probably primarily due to an increasing practice of the registered office being located at either the premises of the solicitor involved in the company's formation or even the offices of a company agent or promoter. Second, it is probable that a significant number of shareholders had more than one address, especially where either a London address was given or if the address would appear to be that of

Table 4.6 Geographical sources of funds invested in limited joint stock companies registered in London 1860 and 1885

Distance from the companies' registered offices (miles)	Percentage of total funds subscribed	
	1860	1885
0–10	75.91	46.67
11–20	3.55	1.38
21–30	2.04	1.08
31–40	1.49	4.13
41–50	0.56	0.12
51–60	0.65	3.36
61–70	1.28	0.70
71–80	0.24	0.99
81–90	0.41	0.26
91–100	—	0.43
101–110	0.78	1.42
111–120	0.26	0.57
121–130	0.33	0.88
131–140	0.21	0.84
141–150	0.05	0.41
151–160	1.17	0.98
161–170	1.11	0.71
171–180	0.05	0.16
181–190	0.99	1.04
191–200	1.08	1.96
201–210	0.03	0.28
211–220	0.41	0.18
221–230	—	0.15
231–240	0.52	0.15
241–250	1.14	0.10
251–260	0.37	0.26
261–270	0.16	0.04
271–280	—	0.03
281–290	—	0.11
291–300	—	0.01
301–310	—	0.08
311–320	—	—
321–330	—	—
331–340	—	0.01

Table 4.6 Cont.

	1860	1885
341–350	—	0.02
351–360	—	—
361–370	—	—
371–380	—	1.16
381–390	—	0.75
391–400	2.67	1.63
401–410	0.01	0.04
411–420	0.03	0.27
421–430	—	0.08
431–440	—	—
441–450	—	0.01
451–460	—	—
461–470	—	—
471–480	—	—
481–490	—	—
491–500	1.54	0.91
501–510	—	—
511–520	—	—
521–530	—	—
531–540	—	0.01
541–550	—	0.01
551–560	—	—
561–570	—	—
571–580	—	—
581–590	—	—
591–600	—	0.02
Irish	1.11	1.06
Foreign	0.80	24.18
Unknown	0.01	0.12

business premises. However, in the case both of the site of the registered office and of the shareholder's place of residence, it is practically impossible to improve greatly upon the information given in the company files. Accordingly table 4.6 must be treated as only an impression of the catchment area of the companies' capital.

The 1860 sample portrays a picture of a very localized capital market with over 75 % of the funds subscribed coming from an area within a ten-mile radius of the companies' registered offices. In fact the table understates the parochial nature of company finance because 28.5 % came from within a one-mile radius and 67.9 % from within a five-mile radius. While nearly three-quarters of funds subscribed came from either local or regional addresses, just under a fifth (17.01 %) was contributed by shareholders who gave an address which was more than 50 miles away from the companies' registered offices. While local finance can be easily and logically explained, it is difficult, without other information, to account for the dispersed nature of the sources of nearly a fifth of the capital subscribed in the 1860 sample other than through personal or intra-industry and trade links. The 1885 sample would appear to show an entirely different pattern of geographical sources of funds subscribed, with only 46.67 % coming from addresses within a radius of ten miles of the companies' registered offices. However this apparent shift away from a heavy reliance on local and regional funds may be spurious for two reasons. First, 24.18 % of the aggregate paid-up capital came from abroad, primarily in connection with six overseas mining companies and an American patent fire extinguisher company, and in some senses these subscriptions could be classified as regional if not local. Accordingly, if it is added to the amount coming from within the 10-mile radius, then the resulting proportion, 70.85 %, is not too dissimilar from the 1860 sample. Second, 39 companies in the 1885 sample had London registered offices, and they account for 78.31 % of the sample companies' aggregate paid-up capital. If foreign subscriptions are ignored, then 61.55 % of British domestically subscribed capital came from within a ten-mile radius of the companies' registered offices but, given that a majority of the latter, in terms of paid-up capital, were located in London, it is difficult to estimate the role of extra-regional finances as the greater London area in 1885 was both one of the most populated districts in Great Britain[27] and probably one of the most wealthy as well. While any conclusions about the precise role of regional and local finance with regard to the 1885 sample are fraught with difficulty due to foreign subscribed capital in connection with certain types of company, and the dominance of companies with London registered offices within the sample, it would appear that the sources of finance were becoming slowly more 'perfect' between 1860 and 1885. If foreign and Irish subscriptions are ignored, while 22.61 % of subscribed capital came from addresses outside a radius of ten miles of the companies' registered offices in 1860, the proportion with regard to the 1885 sample is 37.53 %. This is not a dramatic change and one that must not be over-emphasized, given that it is between two benchmark years only, one of which consists statistically of a very small sample indeed.

The social composition of the shareholders in the companies contained within the two samples is given in table 4.7. The classification is based upon the occupations that the shareholders gave themselves and therefore has to be treated with some caution. Self-classification probably introduces an 'upward' bias in the sense that some significant proportion chose to describe themselves either as 'gentlemen' or 'merchants' for reasons of social prestige. However, despite this bias, it would seem that both in 1860 and 1885 the two main sources of subscriptions were trade and people who described themselves as not being gainfully employed, with the professions being the next most important group. Some of the minor differences between the two samples are due to the weights of different types of company within each sample. The relatively large share of industrial skilled and semi-skilled workers in 1860 (4.62%) is simply a reflection of the large numbers of 'worker' cotton companies established at that time and of which the sample contains five. Similarly the share of shipowners in the 1885 sample (3.69%) can be accounted for by the nine shipping companies contained within it, which again is a fair reflection of contemporary national trends in company formation.

The two benchmark samples depict a capital market which was highly localized and dependent mainly upon subscriptions from three social groups, the unoccupied, trade and the professions. By 1885 there would appear to have been a slight increase in the role of extra-regional funds while subscriptions from industrialists may have become more important, but both these changes would appear to have been small. At present, there is very little other similar evidence with which to compare these conclusions. An analysis of the proprietors in some joint stock banks in Liverpool in the early 1860s showed that in the case of two newly formed concerns, most of their shares were held locally and predominantly by either merchants and shipowners or the 'unoccupied', which supports the conclusions drawn here.[28] A similar picture was established in the case of the Australian Mortgage & Finance Co. Ltd formed in London in 1863; the majority of its initial shareholders were gentlemen, merchants, military officers, clergymen, and younger sons of wealthy landed families. Most were Londoners, though a significant number lived in the provinces.[29]

The domestic railway capital market in its formative period before 1844 displays a slightly different pattern of investment from that being portrayed here for the early limited companies. A common characteristic was that both relied considerably on subscriptions from investors involved in trade but, in the case of the railway companies, share purchases by 'gentlemen' and 'women' were not important initially; rather this group of investors only bought shares of established

Table 4.7 Social composition of investors in limited joint stock companies registered in London 1860 and 1885

	Percentage of aggregate subscribed capital			
	1860		1885	
Unoccupied				
Male	27.46		16.14	
Female	3.04		2.65	
Subtotal		30.50		18.79
Land		2.12		0.55
Professions				
Solicitors	7.08		2.58	
Bankers	0.87		0.49	
Accountants	0.53		0.86	
Stockbrokers	0.63		1.03	
Other professions	8.39		10.29	
Subtotal		17.49		15.28
Commerce				
Merchants	10.17		25.09	
Middlemen and agents	5.60		2.81	
Retailers	6.05		1.25	
Subtotal		21.82		29.17
Industrial				
Secondary agrarian and port industries	2.12		0.37	
Manufacturing industry	5.42		10.99	
Subtotal		7.54		11.36
Service Industries				
Shipowners	0.01		3.69	
Construction and inland transport	0.96		0.33	
Other service industries	0.58		3.45	
Subtotal		1.55		—
Non-industrial skilled and semi-skilled artisans and workers				
Employees		2.37		1.37
Directors	—		0.21	
Managers	0.09		0.43	
Subtotal		0.09		0.64
Industrial skilled and semi-skilled workers	4.62		0.07	
Service workers	2.13		0.64	
Master mariners	—		0.18	
Unskilled workers	0.29		0.04	
Institutional and corporate holdings		—		2.45
Unknown and bearer shares		8.24		11.90

companies. In the case of early railway companies, non-local sources of finance were important from the beginning, whereas the early limited companies appear to have relied mainly on local and regional savings, though this.pattern may have been changing slightly by the mid-1880s.[30] However, very close parallels in the characteristics of these two markets should not be expected, for many reasons. From their inception, issues of railway company securities were considerable and their sheer volume gave them a marketability which, in general, joint stock company securities did not have even in 1914. Exact comparisons are difficult but whereas railway companies by 1842 were the largest single group of joint stock companies quoted on the London market, the 'new' limited companies accounted for only 4.5% of the nominal value of all securities quoted on the London Stock Exchange in 1883.[31]

Appendix

1860 SAMPLE

Company name	File number
London and Mediterranean Steam Navigation	BT31/444/1716
Hertford Building	446/1727
Birtle Spinning	449/1737
Great Moelwyn Slate	452/1747
Lower Park Mining	455/1758
Dover Gas Light & Coke	458/1768
Coingafar & Trelodan Slate	461/1779
Plymouth Improved Dwellings Association	14312/1789
Exeter & West of England Wagon	465/1799
Tipton Moat Colliery	467/1809
Patent Machine-Cut Firewood	469/1819
Sowerby Bridge New Market	472/1830
Manchester Cotton Mill	473/1840
European Wine Growers Association	475/1852
Wem Gas Light & Coke	477/1862
Carreg Fawr Slate & Mineral	479/1872
Patent Machine Brick & Tile	481/1883
British & Foreign Cork	482 III/1894
Pachua Silver Mining	483/1904
Palladium Annuity & Advance	485/1915
Tonge Manufacturing	487/1925

Company name	File number
Anglo-French Artificial Marble	491/1936
Todmorden & Cornholme Bobbin Manufacturing & Commercial	493/1946
Anglo-French Agricultural Trading	494/1957
Western Waggon	497/1968
British Ebontine	500/1979
Devon County School Association	502/1990
Bolton & District Cotton Spinning	504/2000
London Omnibus Tramway	506/2010
Hurstpierpoint Gas	14319/2020
Hide and Leather Factors	510/2030
Rifleman Newspaper	512/2040
Grindleton Industrial Association	514/2050
Ship Raising	516/2060
London & Provincial Turkish Bath	30704/2070
Redbourn Gas	520/2080
Hargreaves Street Manufacturing	31741/2090

1885 SAMPLE

Company name	File number
Coryton Manganese	BT31/3428/20639
The London Assets Purchase Association	3430/20659
The Contractors' Conveyance	3431/20669
Imported Meat	3432/20680
Sailing Ship 'Otterspool'	3433/20691
Barrett Gold Mining	3433/20701
London Mont-de-Piete	3434/20711
The South Eastern Railway of Spain	3435/20721
London & Rotterdam Steamship	3437/20731
The House Purchase	3439/20742
Thomas Lunn	3441/20763
Oldham Aerated Water	3442/20774
British Velveteen	3443/20786
Electric Manufacturing	3444/20797
Midland Corn Supply Association	3446/20809
Vale of Evesham Seed Growers	3447/20820
Pure Bred Welsh Cattle	3448/20831

Company name	File number
South London Steam Laundries	3449/20841
Eastbourne Omnibus & Carriage	3450/20861
'Fawn' Steamship	3454/20891
British Press	3457/20912
Gold Amalgamated Syndicate	3459/20923
John Horrocks	3460/20933
Manchester Skip	3461/20943
The Derby Patent Hobby Horse	3462/20954
International Electric Railway Syndicate	3463/20964
Derby Sanitary Dairy	3466/20986
Poulton-le-Fylde Gas, Coal, Lime & Coke	3468/20996
'San Antonio' Shipowning	3469/21006
Gwern-y-Mynydd Lead	3471/21017
Hornachos Silver Lead Mining	3474/21047
London & Spanish	3475/21057
Carn Marth Fire Brick & Clay	3476/21067
The Salop & North Wales Gaseous Fuel	3476/21077
Great Las Nieves	3477/21087
Cottenham Water	3478/21097
Leiple Manufacturing	3479/21107
W. W. Fyfe	3483/21139
Manchester Financial Association	3484/21149
Bognor Assembly Rooms	3485/21160
Bull, Bevan	3486/21170
Victoria Pier	3487/21180
Trojes United Mining & Smelting	3489/21200
Willans, Arnold	3490/21211
Improved Martins Anchor	3491/21221
Ship Share & Insurance	3492/21231
Rugby & Bilton Cement	3493/21237
Charles S. Windorer	3494/21241
The Supper Club	3495/21252
Ladies Store	3499/21283
Tunstall Coffee House	3500/21294
The Excelsior Temperance Club	3500/21304
Youard & Co.	3501/21314
St Helens Union Loan, Discount & Deposit	3502/21324
The 'Eureka' Salt Manufacturing	3504/21335

Company name	File number
National News	3508/21357
Oxford Artistic Monumental & Terra Cotta Manufacturing	3510/21368
Penarth (Cardiff) Pier	3511/21379
The Gorsedd & Sinclair United Mines	3512/21389
Alliance Printing & Publishing	3514/21399
J. H. Houghton & Co.	3515/21410
The Theatrical Syndicate	3517/21430
Gold & Silver Ore Treating	3519/21441
The Club	3520/21451
Llangorse Steam Boat	3521/21462
Seaton Beach & Clarence Hotels	3522/21472
Cromwell Gardens Hotel	3523/21482
Cornbrook Brewery	3524/21492
Wharton & Co.	3525/21501
British Emery	3527/21512
Lewis Hand Fire Extinguisher	3528/21522
Wingham Gas	3529/21532
Imperial Club & Residential Chambers	3530/21542
Guildford & District Club	3534/21562
M. Nadin	3535/21572
Iguana Gold Syndicate	3536/21582
Garw Water & Light	3537/21592
Paragon Annouce	3540/21602
London Sailing Club Boat House	3541/21613
Talybont Silver Lead	3542/21623
Home Industries Association	3543/21633
Steamship 'Chelydon'	3544/21643
City of Para Tramways	3546/21653
Wigan Junior Club	3541/21663
Ruddiman Johnston	3548/21673
Armstrong & Co.	3549/21683
Wyoming Coal & Coke	3550/21693
Steamship 'Heliades'	3551/21703
Knight of St John Steamship	3551/21713
Wratten, Fallowfield, Morgan & Kidd	3554/21724
The Twerton-on-Avon Water Works	3555/21734

Company name	File number
The Birmingham Freehold and Leasehold Property Association	3556/21744
Hanley Bowling and Recreation Club	3557/21754
The Pure Bread	3558/21764
Hull & Grimsby Bill Posting & Advertising	3561/21784
The Economic Gas Lighting & Heating	3562/21796
Tarbutt's Liquid Fuel	3563/21806
The Elthorne Mineral Water	3564/21816
Bull River Phosphate	3564/21827
Wigton Bay Granite Quarries	3566/21837
Transparent Wire Wove Roofing	3567/21847
Steamship 'African Prince'	3567/21857
Don Sheet Iron & Steel	3569/21867
City & Provincial Contract Corporation	3570/21877
The Egyptian Cigarette and French Government Tobacco	3571/21887
The Ventonwyn Tin Mining	3573/21897
The Direct Meat Supply	3574/21907
The Liverpool Athletic Grounds	3576/21918
The Iron Sailing Ship 'Balmoral'	3576/21928
The Walsall Central Arcade	3577/21938
The Congo Railway Syndicate	3579/21948
The Landed Estates Agency	3579/21958
'Pictorial World'	3580/21969

Notes

(Place of publication is London unless otherwise stated)

1 The other places of registration were Edinburgh (Scotland), Dublin (Ireland), and for mining companies Truro (the Stannaries); Welsh registrations were normally made with the London office of the Registrar of Joint Stock Companies. On Scottish companies see P. L. Payne, *The Early Scottish Limited Companies, 1856–1895: an Historical and Analytical Survey,* Social Science Working Paper Number 222, California Institute of Technology, Pasadena, 1977.

2 H. A. Shannon, 'The First Five Thousand Limited Companies and their Duration' *Economic History,* II, 1931, hereafter cited as Shannon, 'First Five Thousand'; and Shannon, 'The Limited Companies of 1866 and 1883', *Economic History Review,* IV, 1932–3, hereafter cited as Shannon, 'Limited Companies, 1866–83'. It should be noted that Shannon's overall abortion rate is a slight overestimate of the incidence of companies failing to proceed beyond the registration stage, be-

cause he includes in his numerator 'small' companies – those with an average paid-up capital of under £300.

3 J. B. Jeffreys, 'Trends in Business Organisation in Great Britain since 1856, with Special Reference to the Financial Structure of Companies, the Mechanism of Investment and the Relations between the Shareholder and the Company', unpublished Ph.D. thesis, University of London, 1938, part II, chapter IV; and see Jeffreys, 'The Denomination and Character of Shares, 1855–1885', *Economic History Review*, XVI, 1946.

4 *B.P.P.*, 'Return of the names, objects, places of business, date of registration, nominal capital, number of shares, etc. of all joint stock companies formed or registered...': 1864, LVIII; 1866, LXVI; 1867, LXIV; 1867–8, LIV; 1874, LXII; 1875, LXXI; 1876, LXVIII; 1877, LXXVI; 1878, LXVIII; 1880, LXVII; 1881, LXXXIII; 1882, LXIV; 1883, LXIV.

5 The results from the sample used here are not significantly different from those given in Shannon, 'Limited Companies 1866–83'.

1863–5

Shannon	(%)	Above sample	(%)
£1	7	.£1	8.0
£5	19	£1+–£5	25.3
£10	31	£5+–£10	33.7
£10–£25	19	£10+–£25	13.25
£25+	18	£25+	19.7

1873–5

Shannon	(%)	Above sample	(%)
£1	12.5	£1	16.5
£5	29	£1+–£5	33.0
£10	32.5	£5+–£10	30.1
£10–£25	7	£10+–£25	10.8
£25+	11	£25+	10.0

6 See Shannon, 'First Five Thousand'; Jeffreys, op. cit.; P. L. Cottrell, 'Investment Banking in England 1856–1882. Case Study of the International Financial Society', unpublished Ph.D. thesis, University of Hull, 1974, I, pp. 126–35.

7 Shannon, 'First Five Thousand', pp. 407–9; Jeffreys, op. cit.

8 A. Essex-Crosby, 'Joint Stock Companies in Great Britain, 1890–1930', unpublished M.Comm. thesis, University of London, 1938, p. 26.

9 ibid.

10 Cottrell, op. cit., pp. 213–15.

11 Jeffreys, op. cit., chapter VI; and see below, p. 128, 132.

12 Essex-Crosby, op. cit., pp. 26, 31.

13 Jefferys, op. cit.

14 Calculated from the Rousseaux overall price index, as published in B. R. Mitchell with P. Deane, *Abstract of British Historical Statistics*, Cambridge, 1971, pp. 471–3.

15 The annual returns in the case of dead companies are contained in the series BT31 held by the Public Record Office, London; live companies in Company House; for a full list of the companies and source material see the appendix at the end of this chapter.

16 See Shannon, 'First Five Thousand'; Shannon, 'Limited Companies 1866–83'.

17 Dover Gas Light and Coke Company: P.R.O., BT31/458/1768.

18 Coingafar and Trelodan Slate Company: P.R.O., BT31/461/1779.

19 Ventonwyn Tin Mining Company: P.R.O., BT31/3573/21897.

20 'Pictorial World' Company: P.R.O., BT31/3580/21969.

21 Cottenham Water Company; for other factors responsible for the high incidence of abortion, see Shannon, 'First Five Thousand'; Shannon, 'Limited Companies, 1866–83'; Cottrell, op. cit.

22 Shannon, 'Limited Companies, 1866–83', p. 312.

23 Shannon, 'First Five Thousand', pp. 404, 423. On company survival rates see also D. H. Macgregor, 'Joint Stock Companies and the Risk Factor', *Economic Journal*, XXXIX, 1929; G. Todd, 'Some Aspects of Joint Stock Compan-

ies, 1844–1900', *Economic History Review*, IV, 1932–4.

24 Essex-Crosby, op. cit., p. 25.

25 *B.P.P.*, 1877, VIII, *Report of the Select Committee on the Companies Acts of 1862 and 1867*, Evidence of W. H. Cousins, the Registrar of Joint Stock Companies, qq. 11, 25, 49, 51.

26 Each distance was measured by using either Ordnance Survey maps at scales of one inch to the mile and 2½ inches to the mile, or mileage charts published in *The Reader's Digest AA Book of the Road*. Therefore local distances are in terms of straight-line measurement, while longer distances are in terms of the shortest distance on classified routes, using car ferries where necessary!

27 In 1881 Greater London had a population of 4,770,000, about 16% of the total population of Great Britain: calculated from Mitchell with Deane, op. cit., pp. 6, 19. Some of the conclusions suggested by the data analysed here are supported by the recently published work of W. D. Rubinstein: see 'The Victorian Middle Classes: Wealth, Occupation and Geography', *Economic History Review*, 2nd series, XXX, 1977.

28 B. L. Anderson and P. L. Cottrell, 'Another Victorian Capital Market: a Study of Banking and Bank Investors on Merseyside', *Economic History Review*, 2nd series, XXVIII, 1975.

29 J. D. Bailey, *A Hundred Years of Pastoral Banking. A History of the Australian Mercantile Land and Finance Company*, Oxford, 1966, pp. 12–13.

30 See M. C. Reed, *Investment in Railways in Britain, 1820–1844. A Study in the Development of the Capital Market*, 1975, pp. 193–203.

31 Calculated from E. V. Morgan and W. A. Thomas, *The Stock Exchange, its History and Functions*, 1962, table V, pp. 280–1.

5 Cotton and iron: the provinces and the metropolis 1855–85

Manufacturing, processing, and extractive industry accounted for 44% of all effective London company registrations between 1856 and 1883. The volume of effective registrations of this group displays the same general cyclical movement as other types of company but with possibly some leads and lags at upper and lower turning points. Industrial effective registrations peaked in 1865, 1874 and 1883 with corresponding troughs in 1863, 1868 and 1878, whereas other effective registrations peaked in 1864, 1873 and 1881 with troughs in 1858, 1867 and 1878. There is some dissimilarity during the late 1850s and early 1860s with a minor peak in industrial effective registrations in 1861/2 whereas other effective registrations rose smoothly from a trough in 1858 to a major cyclical peak in 1864. The highest cyclical peak in industrial effective registrations was 1874 with 450 registrations, 57.8% of all effective registrations in that year; the 1883 peak, though higher than the 1865 cyclical upper turning point, is lower than that of 1874 and this may be explained by some underlying secular fluctuation in the effective industrial company registrations. Other registrations do not have this secular pattern, each subsequent cyclical peak being higher, though the upswings of the mid-1860s and early 1870s have a similar amplitude while that of the early 1880s was very much greater.

Shannon has broken down effective registrations for the period 1875–83 in terms of public and private companies, and industrial companies make up the bulk of the latter, accounting for 61.3% of all private effective registrations during the period. It would seem that private industrial registrations, though displaying a cyclical movement with a trough in 1876 and a peak in 1883, predominated, in terms of their share of all private effective registrations, during the mid- and late-1870s depression.

The volume of effective company registrations is a guide to the extent of the use of the limited company as a form of business organization both by the economy as a whole and by different branches of industry. On this basis it would appear that by the mid-1880s the limited company was becoming more widespread in the following areas: coal and iron-ore mining, non-ferrous metals mining, iron manufacture and general engineering, the production of bricks, tiles and cement, cotton manufacture, the production of household goods, and the food-processing industries. Certain new industries, such as the electrical trades, were from their inception organized almost entirely on the basis of the limited company.[1] In other trades and industries the limited company made hardly any headway, as in the cases of shipbuilding, non-ferrous metals manufacture, coal by-products and woollens and worsted production. With regard to most industry groups, nearly 40% of all effective registrations between 1875 and 1883 were to establish private companies, but in the areas of non-ferrous metals mining, railway equipment, shipbuilding, the electrical trades, coal by-products, food and provisions, and breweries and flour mills, effective registrations tended to be predominantly for the establishment of public companies.[2]

This picture of the changes in business organization within manufacturing industry during the 30 years following the general availability of limited liability is broadly confirmed by the survey undertaken by the Royal Commission on the Depression of Trade and Industry during the mid-1880s. It found that the limited company dominated the Oldham spinning section of the Lancashire cotton industry but elsewhere within the industry the private partnership remained the unit of organization. There were hardly any limited companies in Preston, while there were only five public and two private companies in Burnley.[3] The only other part of the textile industries where the limited company had the same hold as in Oldham was the Irish linen trade.[4] It was reported that there were no limited companies in the silk industry,[5] very few in the woollen trade,[6] and none in the worsted trade.[7] With regard to jute, there were no limited companies in Dundee, the Scottish centre of the industry, one in Aberdeen, and one in Barrow.[8] However, in the case of the London clothing trade, by the early 1880s a large number of concerns had been converted into limited companies.[9] Outside the textile industries, the Royal Commission did not collect a comparable body of comprehensive evidence concerning the impact of limited liability. It received the impression that the larger iron and steel companies were limited concerns,[10] and was told that in the Birmingham engineering district there was a long list of limited companies such as Nettlefold Screw, Tangye's, Patent Bolt and Nut, Muntz's Metal, Elliot's Metal, and Perry & Co., most of which were old private firms converted into limited companies.[11] However, there were only a few limited companies in the Sheffield cutlery trade.[12] The only other industry on which evidence was collected was papermaking, the representative of which stated that limited liability had been adopted in Manchester by a number of large manufacturers and elsewhere for a number of new mills.[13]

Very few of the witnesses before the Royal Commission gave reasons for the adoption of limited liability, which, outside the Oldham cotton district, was primarily a case of converting existing private companies. R. P. Harding, the chief receiver in bankruptcy, thought many companies had been formed to enable 'a family to divide a concern'.[14] The Birmingham representatives said that conversions had occurred in the engineering trades because the firms concerned were 'getting unmanageable and too large for private undertakings'. They went on to point out that the limited companies had more capital, larger works, and greater production than the private firms.[15] Vickers stated that though his steel firm was now a limited company and had consequently greater resources, no other limited iron and steel companies 'have been arranged like ours has, where we are enabled to work as individual partners'.[16] However, in the case of London limited clothing companies, conversion had not enlarged their resources but instead had enabled them to be worked with smaller capitals.[17] It is difficult to generalize in any way from this small and diverse body of evidence.

There are no other general bodies of contemporary evidence similar to that collected by the Royal Commission on the Depression of Trade and Industry which can be placed alongside the data on 'effective' registrations assembled by Shannon. However, there are a limited number of historical studies of the coal industry which can be used to extend the range of the Royal Commission evidence for one area at least. In an analysis of the economic development of the inland coalfields during the last quarter of the nineteenth century, Mitchell found that collieries owned by joint stock companies made up a small but significant proportion of the industry in 1870 in a number of fields. Public colliery companies in Lancashire, North Staffordshire, and the East Midlands owned about 10% of the mines in each field, and in Yorkshire 6%. Private colliery companies were unimportant except in North Wales, where they owned 21% of mines, in North Staffordshire (9%),

Lancashire (8%), East Midlands (7%) and Yorkshire (6%). The picture is complicated because in many of the coal fields, mines were owned by either iron companies or brick and fire-brick producers. Public joint stock iron companies were important owners of collieries in Yorkshire, Lancashire and the East Midlands, where 30% of all mines were owned by iron firms in 1870.[18]

A view across the coal industry in 1870 understates the role of the limited company because most of the effective colliery registrations occurred between 1871 and 1876.[19] This wave of successful company formation changed the organizational structure of the coal industry in South Wales, where by 1874 over 25% of sale-coal collieries were owned by limited companies. When mines controlled by public iron companies are included as well, the share owned by limited companies in this area increases to 50%.[20] On the basis of the experience of the South Wales field, it is probable that there was a sharp increase in the ownership of the mines by joint stock companies during the first half of the 1870s in other fields, with the exception possibly of the north-east.[21]

It would appear that the limited company made its greatest impact upon the structure of business organization and finance before 1885 in cotton spinning and in iron, steel and coal. These two areas will now be examined in greater detail in order to see why the limited company made such headway and from what sources it raised finance.

★

Companies had been established for cotton spinning before 1855 but after the liberalization of company law their numbers increased dramatically. Between 1856 and 1867, 162 cotton companies were registered of which 108 were formed during two single years, 1860 and 1861. There were further sharp bursts of company formation between 1873 and 1876, and 1883 and 1884.[22] The origin of this growth was the establishment of cooperative production concerns in Lancashire and the West Riding during the first half of the 1850s. These were usually in weaving, which needed less capital than spinning, and they were often twinned with cooperative retail societies. At the end of 1860 there were 28 cooperative production companies in Lancashire, with total nominal capital of £1m. Most by this time were limited joint stock companies as this reduced considerably the risk incurred by their proprietors. A representative of this type of concern is the Oldham Building and Manufacturing Co. Ltd, which was formed in 1858, subsequently became the Sun Mill Co. Ltd in 1867, and as such was to be the inspiration and model for the various 'Oldham Limiteds' formed during the 1870s and 1880s. The Oldham

Building Co. came out of the Oldham Industrial Co-operative Society and was formed by skilled engineers, who were mainly liberal in their political outlook, and as such were typical of promoters of cooperative cotton mills. They accepted the capitalist society but sought to gain a greater equality of income and wealth. With this essentially passive outlook they came close to the mode of reconciling capital and labour proposed by some of the Christian Socialists in their campaign for the reform of company law during the first half of the 1850s. The Oldham Building Company had initially shares of £1 but these were soon raised to £5 when the capital of the company was increased. However, the denomination of cooperative joint stock company shares varied widely.[23]

The wave of cotton company promotions at the beginning of the 1860s affected the whole of the English industry, including areas such as Holywell and Greenfield on the North Wales coast. Most of the new companies were the conversion of existing concerns but about a quarter formed in both years were established to build new mills. Unlike the subsequent formations of the 1870s these companies encompassed the whole of the manufacturing process with roughly equal numbers being spinning firms, combined firms, and weaving firms.[24] A substantial number of these companies were 'worker' concerns, similar in nature to those that had been established during the previous decade, This major boom in the formation of cotton companies accounts for the minor cyclical peak in effective industrial registrations in 1861/2. Most of the companies appear to have relied on local subscriptions, and no prospectuses issued by their promoters were noted by either *The Economist* or *The Bankers' Magazine*. Their formation came at the end of a wave of substantial investment in the industry which had got underway in 1858, and had been generated by the growth of the eastern export market and assisted by favourable raw cotton supply conditions.[25] Further investment and company promotion was first checked and then totally stopped by the outbreak of the American Civil War and the consequent cotton famine. Many of the new limited concerns failed during the 1860s; of the 162 formed between 1856 and 1867, 77 had gone by 1871 and only 49 were left in Lancashire and the West Riding in 1882, most of which had been established before 1861.[26]

The cyclical depression after 1866 was, as one Manchester banker commented, 'somewhat longer in duration than usual...and...the features proper to it have shown an exaggerated and exceptional intensity'. The cotton industry seems to have been affected as a result of 'the low tone of commercial feeling characteristic of the period...strengthened and perpetuated by such a continuous chronicle of failure amongst spinners, manufacturers, agents, and shippers, as will be ever memorable to Lancashire'.[27] The cotton famine and then the slump of the second half of the 1860s acted as a winnow, removing the chaff – the companies formed during the euphoria of 1860 and 1861. However, the effects of the famine must not be overemphasized, because the decline of the Scottish industry from the early 1870s would appear to have been caused more by haemorrhage of enterprise, first from spinning and then from weaving.[28]

Recovery came in the early 1870s and was followed, as in the late 1850s, by a company promotion boom which had two aspects, the setting-up of mill building companies in Oldham and the conversion of existing concerns. During the mid-1870s 31 concerns were turned into private limited companies, the boom conditions providing an ideal time to turn a failing business, possibly being pursued by a creditor, into a company, while other private conversions seem to have been due to the death of the senior partner. An equal number of firms were converted into public companies during the mid-1870s, with 33 flotations, but most were burdened by the exactions of their promoters.[29] These companies were mainly locally promoted and locally financed, with only a very limited amount of subscriptions coming either from London or abroad. Shares were taken up by Friendly Societies, banks and bankers, engineers and mill architects, Manchester merchants, and some Liverpool cotton brokers. In the case of Preston and West Riding companies, landowners, farmers and agricultural labourers were shareholders.[30]

The companies which made a real mark upon the industry and were a matter of local and national debate in the mid-1880s were the 'Oldham Limiteds'. Whereas the need to spread overheads during the second quarter of the nineteenth century had led to vertical integration within the industry, producing the combined firm, from the 1860s this process went into reverse. Overhead costs still remained the force which shaped the firm, but from the 1860s they were offset by increasing the size of the unit of production. This increase in size was assisted by both factory legislation, which favoured the larger employer, and the establishment of plants in the suburbs, where the land was cheaper. The other responsible factor was the end of major technical change in the industry. The self-acting mule was fully developed by the 1860s, a situation which, it was claimed later, made spinning 'simpler' and therefore suitable for corporate management. Two mill building companies were set up in Oldham in 1873 and they were followed by 31 others in the next two years. Most were for spinning coarse counts and by contemporary standards were large units of production: 10 companies had 43,000 to 50,000 spindles each, and 15 companies 56,000 to 72,000 spindles each.[31] The promoters of these concerns came from extremely varied back-grounds and fall into no definite single social or occupational category, but generally they had some knowledge of, and expertise in, cotton spinning. The companies generally had shares of £5 denomination, on which only a small proportion was called, with initial deposits being as low as one shilling, and the unpaid portion was used as security for loan capital. Most of the shares were taken up locally, and during the promotion boom of 1873–4 over 75% of the shareholders were wage-earning manual labourers.[32] After 1873 the proportion of shares held by the working classes fell, for two reasons. First, the success of the established companies led to local retail tradespeople and private cotton spinners becoming shareholders, with the result that by 1877 each of these two groups held 25% of the shares of the 'Oldham Limiteds'. Second, the depression of the late 1870s forced many of the companies to call up further equity capital, calls which working-class shareholders were unable to meet.[33]

These broad conclusions are supported by Smith's analysis of the share registers of four particular Oldham companies dated variously 1874, 1876, 1881 and 1884. In each case more than 50% of the shares were held by Oldham residents, with most of the remaining shareholders living in either the Manchester area or the Lancashire seaside retirement towns of Southport and St Annes-on-Sea. Nearly all the individual holdings were small, being generally less than 100 shares, while most of the capital came from manufacturers, merchants and local traders.[34] It should be noted that the later companies, namely those promoted in the boom of 1883–4, did have a somewhat different character, being established and owned by mill building groups of land companies, architects, contractors, and machine builders, together with private spinners, Manchester manufacturers and merchants, sharebrokers and a number of Liverpool cotton brokers.[35]

A secondary market in mill shares developed almost simultaneously in Oldham with the promotion of mill companies. By early 1874 stock-brokers were publishing share lists in the local press and it is estimated that some 40 sharebrokers were active between 1874 and 1887. They, like the mill promoters, came from wide-ranging backgrounds. Until the late 1870s there were four loosely organized markets, located in public houses, which were also the places where mill promotion meetings were held. It was not until 1880 that a formal association of sharebrokers was established and it did not have its own premises until 1883.[36]

The Oldham cotton mill companies' capitals consisted of loan finance as well as equity subscriptions, with, in the case of nearly every company, the former being equal to the latter. This heavy reliance on loan capital was not a particular feature of the Oldham mill-building companies but was a general characteristic of all joint stock companies formed in the Lancashire cotton industry since 1844. Its origins lie in the use by private cotton spinners of small loans from workers and others which had

developed from the 1830s. In the case of the 46 mill-building companies
and 18 converted companies in the Oldham area in 1879, their aggregate
share capital was £2,299,304 while their aggregate loan capital amounted
to £2,249,050.[37] The loan capital consisted of small sums, which were
withdrawable on demand, placed by small shopkeepers, publicans,
lodgekeepers, overlookers and mechanics and employees of local machine-
making firms. The rate of interest paid on these 'deposits' was 5% to 6%
in the mid- and late 1870s but fell to 4% during the first half of the
1880s.[38] The mill companies acted almost as savings banks – they issued
pass books – and they did drain money away from the Oldham savings
banks and local cooperative societies, which paid a lower rate of interest
on deposits.[39] The decline in the working-class ownership of shares from
the mid-1870s was to some extent counteracted by their preponderance as
deposit-holders. The high gearing of the Oldham companies augmented
considerably their dividend-paying capacity during trade booms but, of
course, it had an adverse effect during slumps. In August 1880, 39 out of
the 75 Oldham companies were not paying a dividend and consequently
their shares were being quoted at a discount. The other 36 companies
were paying dividends, ranging from 2% to 25% but only eight
companies' shares were being quoted at a premium, and five at their
nominal value.[40]

There was a further wave of promotions across the industry during the
trade upswing of the early 1880s; 23 companies were projected in 1880,
25 in 1881, 24 in both 1882 and 1883, and 45 in 1884. Whereas a
substantial number of the companies formed in 1873 and 1874,
particularly outside the Oldham area, had been conversions, most during
the first half of the 1880s were new concerns formed by promotional
groups consisting of a promoter, an architect, a builder and a machine
builder.[41] Building in the 1880s was encouraged by both the high
dividends distributed by the established companies and a fall in costs.
The Oldham mill-building companies of 1871 to 1874 had erected their
concerns at an approximate cost of £1 15s. a spindle for fireproof mills,
but by the mid-1880s building costs had fallen to £1 1s. a spindle. The
new mills of the mid-1880s were more dependent than their forerunners
on loan capital: four new mill companies in the mid-1880s had an
aggregate share capital of only £117,219 as opposed to a combined loan
capital of £307,250.[42] By 1886 there were 90 limited mills in the Oldham
district; they had a combined share capital of £3,498,667, had issued
962,099 shares, and had £3,396,378 on loan. The total balance-sheet
value of these mills was £5,723,306, and with 3,360,010 twist spindles
and 2,520,810 weft spindles, the average cost per spindle was 19s. 5½d.
The spindleage of the industry, including doubling spindles, had hardly

increased between 1878 and 1887, rising from 44,206,690 to 44,348,921, but during that period Oldham had gained 2 million spindles. Over a longer period, from 1870 to 1887, the number of spindles in Lancashire had increased by 6.75 millions, of which 4.5 millions had been set up in the Oldham area.[43]

The Oldham companies came under attack during the trade depression of the mid-1880s. It was alleged that they were responsible for an undue increase in the number of spindles and that as limited companies they were able to bear greater losses than private traders.[44] In fact, as has been shown, the overall capacity of the industry had stabilized from the late 1870s although Oldham's share of it had increased. It was pointed out that the general availability of limited liability had been only one factor among many, including profits, capital accumulation and banking facilities, that had been responsible for the increase in production.[45] Representatives of both spinners and operatives argued that the new mills had been built by speculators, strangers, ignorant shareholders from all over England and the continent, who, by establishing non-resident corporations, were destroying the resident body of employers, and by overstocking the market in a depression and introducing new machinery were causing a 'greater want of employment and a greater absence of profit'.[46] While the companies of the 1880s boom were promoted by non-locals, their shareholders still came mainly from either Manchester or other parts of South Lancashire. Smith has found only a few instances of French and German cotton spinners investing in Oldham companies.[47] Where both supporters and critics of the Oldham companies agreed was that the unlimited borrowing powers of the companies should be controlled.[48] The heavy and growing reliance of the companies on loan capital was the characteristic which most galled the private spinners. One complained that the private spinner sought 'for loans in vain' and 'a mortgage at 5 per cent amounting to one-third the value of his mill property' was 'the most he will obtain, and that liable to be withdrawn in one solid lump at any moment'.[49] The real problem caused by the Oldham companies was their competitive edge: these new mills were conduced on 'new principles' by the 'best talent' using 'first class machinery'.[50] However, although 'there [were] in [Oldham] more important joint stock companies than in any other place in the kingdom in proportion to its size',[51] the Oldham mill companies, even taken together with the other public and private converted companies, still in 1886 did not dominate overwhelmingly the cotton industry, only coarse spinning. Fine spinning was still mainly in the hands of private firms, while joint stock companies were only just appearing as a permanent feature of the weaving branch of the industry in the mid-1880s.[52]

★

Most of the important iron, coal and steel company promotions of the 1860s and 1870s were undertaken by the accounting firm of Chadwicks, Adamson and Collier of Manchester and London. The principal partner of this firm was David Chadwick and, through him, savings generated in the North West, especially in Manchester and the surrounding cotton towns, were placed in the shares of industrial companies which he converted. In the case of ten companies converted between 1863 and 1868, on average 63.45% of their shares were taken up by shareholders residing in the North West, with the averages for Manchester and the cotton towns being 43.53% and 14.97%, respectively. If north-western companies, like the Ashbury Railway Carriage Company, are excluded, the North West remained the most important regional source of subscribers, accounting for 40.73% of the companies' shares, with the contributions of Manchester and the cotton towns being 26.32% and 12.55%, respectively. The precise occupational breakdown of shareholders is more difficult to establish but it would seem that shareholders who described themselves as being involved in either the cotton industry or the cotton trade took up at least 10% of the companies' shares, and this level of subscriptions should be regarded as a minimum.[53]

Apparently Chadwick established his connections with potential investors in the North West during the period when he was the Treasurer to the Corporation of Salford. He was elected to this post in 1844 at the age of 22 and held it until 1860 when he became a consulting accountant. His early education had been limited: he left school at 11 after which he began work in a warehouse. He remedied this lack of formal education by evening classes, a factor which led to his subsequent interest in the development of Working Men's Colleges, Mechanics' Institutes,[54] and free public libraries.[55] His decision to become an accountant in 1843 may have been due to his father, John, who has been described as an accountant.[56] David Chadwick had wide-ranging interests besides his profession, including engineering and statistics. His first pamphlet published in 1849 consisted of 5 pages of text and 21 pages of statistical tables.[57] His main published work in the 1850s was a series of pamphlets concerned with the physical and social condition of towns and their inhabitants.[58] The statistical expertise revealed in his quantification of the sanitary question, together with some pamphlets on the economics of life insurance, resulted in him being asked to become the local agent for the Globe Insurance Company,[59] a position which may have led him to an established circle of clients in the Manchester area with savings for which they sought investment outlets. It also brought him into contact with

William Newmarch, the future manager of Glyn, Mills,[60] who later invested in Chadwick's promotions and assisted him in bringing pressure to bear for the reform of company law.[61]

It was Chadwick's interest in the engineering aspects of sanitary reform which led to his first company promotion. In 1854 he had taken out jointly with the Borough Surveyor of Salford a patent for a stench-trap grid. During the same year he read a technical paper on water meters to the Institute of Civil Engineers, which was reprinted subsequently as a pamphlet[62] and for which he was awarded a Council of the Institute of Civil Engineers Premium. Chadwick, together with Herbert Frost, patented their device and in 1860 sold their rights to a company, the Manchester Water Meter Company, which Chadwick established. Among the signatories to its memorandum of association were Robert Rumney, a manufacturing chemist, Thomas Chadwick, an estate agent, E. R. Langworthy, a merchant and sometime Mayor of Salford, and H. D. Pochin, a manufacturing chemist and a future Mayor of Salford,[63] all of whom subsequently assisted Chadwick in his conversions during the 1860s and 1870s. Chadwick retained an interest in the water meter company until the late 1870s, while the concern continued in its original form until 1899 when it was reconstituted by Frost's son.

In 1860 Chadwick began to practise as an accountant in Manchester and by 1863 was in partnership with Alexander Hathorne.[64] During the following year he established a new partnership with John Adamson and either then or in the next year opened an office in London.[65] In the mid-1860s the partnership was styled Chadwick, Adamson, McKenna & Co.,[66] and W. C. McKenna, a London financial agent who was related to J. N. McKenna, a director of the National Bank and company promoter, was probably a partner.[67] In all, Chadwick was to have ten partners between 1860 and 1892, and from seven he was separated by law suits. In one obituary it was commented that he 'found excitement in litigious-ness'.[68] Although the London office may have brought him into greater contact with the institutions of 'the City' and extended his circle of investing clients, it would appear that Chadwick's connections with Manchester and the North West remained the more important in his promotional activities. Between 1862 and 1874 he was involved in the establishment of at least 47 limited companies, most of which were the conversion of family-owned industrial concerns. Generally this was a private activity, although less so in the 1870s, with Chadwick acting as an intermediary between industrialists who wished to turn their partnerships into limited companies, and savers who were willing to invest in industrial shares.

From 1862 to 1868 Chadwick undertook at least 18 conversions, of which ten were iron, steel and coal concerns,[69] four were engineering companies,[70] and two were cotton-manufacturing enterprises.[71] In 1867 he stated that over the previous seven years he had aided in the formation of perhaps 40 companies and had been involved in the investment of £40m. in the capital of limited companies.[72] This amount he scaled down later to £20m.[73] However, it would appear that even with this smaller figure Chadwick was exaggerating his own importance; on the basis of his firm's own list, only 18 companies were promoted up to 1867 and their aggregate nominal capital amounted to only £15,905,000. Some of the difference may be due to Chadwick including in his figures the capital of a number of banks which he reorganized following their failure in the 1866 crisis.

In 1877 he gave greater details of how his firm went about converting a concern; generally they acted for the vendors, charging a 1% commission and 'a mere trifling cost...incurred for expenses'.[74] As a result he claimed that he was not a promoter but an agent, acting between the investing public and those who had property to sell.[75] He regarded the promoters as being the seven signatories to a company's memorandum of association, who were normally the vendor, 'who...we never allow to take his hands off the property', the vendor's friends, and some of Chadwick's friends.[76] During the 1860s, by his own definition, Chadwick was a promoter in the case of three companies – Ebbw Vale, Yorkshire Engine, and Palmers. Despite his evidence, it would appear that the vendors did not always sign the memorandum of association, as was the case with the following companies: Charles Cammell, Patent Nut and Bolt, Ebbw Vale, Manchester Carriage, and Palmers. But certainly Chadwick had a group of people, Mancunians, who acted with him in his conversions, the most prominent members being: J. Ashbury, the carriage and waggon builder; J. Holden, a merchant; H. J. Leppoc, a merchant; H. E. Leo, a merchant; H. D. Pochin, a manufacturing chemist; Benjamin Whitworth, a merchant and cotton manufacturer; T. Vickers, a manufacturing chemist; and G. Wood, a merchant and cotton dealer. As these people normally became directors of the concerns that they 'promoted', they formed a major interlocking management block in the iron, steel, coal and engineering industries in the 1860s.

The property for sale was valued by a professional, appointed by the 'promoters', though occasionally, where the vendor had had the assets to be transferred valued already, then Chadwick insisted on a second, independent valuation. In both cases the costs incurred were borne jointly by the vendor and the company.[77] It seems that a substantial number of the valuations for sale were made by W. Armstrong of Durham,[78] but sometimes a number of reports were made; in the case of Bolckow,

Vaughan, a separate valuation was carried out by T. McKenzie of Glasgow,[79] while in the Palmer conversion there were three reports, one by Fuller and Horsey, a second by W. W. Hulse, the Manchester engineer, and the third by J. T. Coleman, the London accountant.[80] However, in the 1860s the valuation process appears to have been more haphazard and less independent, because Chadwick stated in 1867 that 'the vendors estimated the amount too heavily' and 'the companies were compelled to be formed before the valuations were made upon which the price was settled'. While a valuer was used for the Bolckow, Vaughan conversion, the company's nominal capital was based upon the vendor's estimate of a selling price of £1.8m., but as a result of subsequent negotiations, this was reduced to £0.8m. Accordingly the company was registered with a nominal capital of £2.5m., while in practice only £1.5m. would have been sufficient.[81] Valuations continued to give rise to problems in the 1870s, and in one case led to a protracted law suit.

The vendors were paid in a number of ways: cash, partly paid-up shares, and debentures. There is some evidence of the method of payment in the case of six conversions during the 1860s. In nearly all instances the vendors received a substantial proportion of the selling price in shares which were either fully or partly paid up, with, in the latter case, the proportion credited as paid ranging from 100% to 50% of the nominal value of the share. With regard to the Manchester Carriage conversion, shares specifically called vendors' shares were used, while the vendor in the Ashbury Railway Carriage conversion, who received £50,000 in 500 paid-up shares, agreed not to dispose of more than 50 within one year.[82] As a result of these payments in shares, the vendors became major shareholders in the new companies, with a mean holding in the case of seven companies of 22.88% of the issued shares (s. 9.09). Any remaining balance of the purchase price due was normally paid in cash over a period of time, which could be as long as a year,[83] and sometimes interest was paid on the cash instalments.[84] Although vendors in the 1860s do not appear to have always signed the memorandum of association of the new concern, their large shareholdings were at least one way of making sure that they did not take their 'hands off the property', especially if there were restrictions on sales of shares held by them.

Chadwick maintained that the directors of the companies were also among 'the largest shareholders' and 'no such thing as fraudulently and dishonestly giving a director a qualification or anything approaching a qualification has ever been entertained or thought of'.[85] This claim would appear to be well founded. The directors, excluding any vendors' shares, held 22.23% of the shares of Park Gate Iron, 19.66% of the shares of Yorkshire Engine, and 10.75% of the shares of Charles Cammell. In most instances the vendors became directors, as did members of Chadwick's Manchester circle, and, in the case of the Yorkshire Engine Company, Chadwick went on to the board. Given that the vendors held a substantial proportion of their converted concerns' shares, and became directors, members of the companies' boards, though not holding a majority of the issued shares, had usually a substantial holding, in some instances as much as 40%. While the Chadwick method of conversion did introduce to the boards of these companies Manchester men who were without past direct experience of management in the iron, steel or coal industries, they were conversant with the problems of business, through being either merchants or manufacturers. Erickson in her study of British industrialists has corrected the somewhat negative picture painted by Burn of the effect of these conversions upon the management of the steel industry. If there was a backward step in management through public conversion, according to Erickson it came in the 1890s and the first quarter of the twentieth century,[86] and not in the 1860s and 1870s as a consequence of Chadwick's activities.

Chadwick stated that the companies' shares were offered to his firm's 'friends',[87] through either a private circular or a prospectus, though in the 1860s a public prospectus was drawn up in the case of the conversions of Ebbw Vale[88] and Bolckow, Vaughan.[89] Even where only a private circular was issued, occasionally it received comment in the national press, and the following conversions were noted in the money market daily article in *The Times*: John Brown, Sheepbridge Coal and Iron, Manchester Carriage, Yorkshire Engine, and Palmers, with usually the statement that all the shares had been subscribed.[90] When a public prospectus was used by Chadwick in the 1860s, it was for his largest conversions. The Ebbw Vale company had a nominal capital of £4m., and in 1865 the company's shares were in 482 holdings; similarly, Bolckow, Vaughan had a nominal capital of £2.5m., held in 1865 in 419 holdings. At the other end of the spectrum there were a number of companies with relatively small nominal capitals held in a few holdings. The Globe Cotton Company had a nominal capital of £200,000 with 25 shareholders, Yorkshire Engine £200,000 in 36 holdings, Ancoats Vale Rubber £100,000 in 21 holdings, and Birchills Estate, an iron company, had a nominal capital of £40,000 with 14 shareholdings. It is evident that these companies were 'private' concerns, while in the cases of Globe, Yorkshire Engine and Birchills Estate the first two were totally new concerns and the last was a private take-over through incorporation by the Knowles family of existing assets. The most intimate conversion was that of Vickers, where the shares were held initially by Edward Vickers, his four sons, W. Whitehead, an employee, and E. L. S. Benzon, the merchanting partner.[90a] Formations which were neither public issues nor 'private' conversions had generally nominal capitals in the range £0.3m. to £1m. held in holdings ranging from 52 to 316. In the Chadwick fomations of the 1860s there would appear to be a fairly strong positive correlation between the number of shareholdings and both nominal capital[91] and subscribed capital.[92]

All of Chadwick's companies in the 1860s had large share denominations; only three had £20 shares, while four had £50 shares and 11 had £100 shares. A small proportion, on average 26.22%, was called initially on the shares issued to the 'public' in the case of conversions undertaken before the 1866 crisis, with the result that their holders incurred a large degree of unpaid liability. As such the equity capital structure of the Chadwick companies was very similar to that of most of the banks and finance companies formed during the 1860s boom, and consequently their shares were practically unsaleable following the 1866 crisis. This was the main reason why Chadwick and his associates attempted to modify the law following the crisis.[93] 'The holder of shares in those companies finds himself with an uncalled liability much greater than the amount paid, and in the public estimation, that is a very great defect. People will not, after the late crisis, invest their money in the purchase of shares even in sound trading companies having so large a margin of capital unpaid.' Chadwick went on to state that 'within the circle of our own acquaintance and clients, which extends all over the country, many millions of money are held in reserve on that account'.[94] Although the Chadwick companies were affected badly by the 1866 crisis through the unmarketability of their shares, the 'public' shareholders in some of these conversions were assured of a return on their investment; for instance a dividend of 10% was guaranteed to 'other' shareholders by Bolckow and Vaughan, who agreed not to receive dividends until 10% had been paid on the other shares for five years.[95] This form of vendors' guarantee on dividend distributions was used again by Chadwick in the 1870s.

The first annual returns of shareholders for 13 of the industrial companies formed by Chadwick in the 1860s were analysed to discover their geographical and occupational composition, and the results are given in tables 5.1 and 5.2.[96] Comment has already been made on the high proportion of shares held by people in the North West, particularly in Manchester and the cotton towns, even when the concern converted was situated outside the region. The other important regional sources of subscriptions were the South East, the West Midlands, the North, and Yorkshire and Humberside. However, when extra-regional flows are considered by excluding 'native' conversions,[97] then the South East and the West Midlands were the main sources of funds besides the North

Table 5.1 Chadwick industrial promotions in the 1860s: regional distribution of shareholdings*

	Ashbury Railway Carriage & Iron 30.4.1863	Charles Cammell 13.4.1865	Parkgate Iron 12.4.1865	Patent Nut & Bolt 27.5.1865	Ebbw Vale 27.6.1865	Bolckow, Vaughan 1865	Globe Cotton Spinning 2.1.1865	Manchester Carriage 1.3.1865	Yorkshire Engine 9.9.1865	Samuel Dewhurst 5.1865	Palmers Shipbuilding & Iron 30.6.1866	Ancoats Vale Rubber 10.6.1866	Birchills Estate 8.11.1869	$\bar{x}$	s
North†		0.27			0.03	35.66					45.76			6.28	14.81
Yorks & Humberside	1.27	28.11	34.83	0.17	1.00	1.8		0.3	26.4		0.56			4.56	10.09
North West	96.17	54.6	8.83	25.46	17.66	48.25	97.34	99.15	47.75	95.99	23.82	95.00	88.88	63.45	31.23
East Midlands		0.16		4.33	0.3	1.95		0.15			0.47	5.00		1.63	2.75
West Midlands		2.19		66.92	13.3	1.04					2.68		8.33	7.26	18.37
East Anglia					0.05						0.55			0.04	0.14
South East	2.55	11.35	54.00	2.13	53.4	6.94	2.64		22.47	4.00	20.38		2.77	14.04	19.01
South West		0.20	1.66		2.65	0.28					0.47			0.40	0.81
Wales		0.70			6.74						1.13			0.65	1.86
Scotland		1.96			0.14	0.48			2.8		0.86			0.48	0.89
Ireland, C.I. & I.o.M.		0.06	0.33	0.30	1.79	2.68		0.38			2.74			0.63	1.03
Foreign		0.15			2.85	0.03			0.56		0.50			0.31	0.78
Unknown	0.23					0.88					0.01			0.08	0.24
Manchester	73.95	42.82	30.33	20.94	11.16	34.19	64.02	76.2	39.32	63.22	17.94	78.00	13.88	43.53	24.76
Lancs cotton towns	16.02	9.8	2.16	3.81	1.9	10.22	30.73	22.33	5.61	25.79	3.15	2.00	61.11	14.97	16.95
Area of works (73.95)		20.68	50.66	65.25	6.5	32.99	2.64				42.55		2.77		
London		8.15	1.42	1.42	48.3	5.85					16.74				

* Percentage by region of total number of shares issued as per first return to the Registrar of Joint Stock Companies.
† Standard regions of England and Wales: see Office of Population Censuses and Surveys, *Census 1971 England and Wales Preliminary Report*, 1971, appendix A.
Source: Company returns, see appendix to this chapter.

Table 5.2 Chadwick industrial promotions in the 1860s: occupational distribution of shareholdings*

	Ashbury Railway Carriage & Iron 30.4.1863	Charles Cammell 13.4.1865	Patent Nut & Bolt 27.5.1865	Ebbw Vale 27.6.1865	Globe Cotton Spinning 2.1.1865	Manchester Carriage 1.3.1865	Samuel Dewhurst 5.1865	Palmers Shipbuilding & Iron 30.6.1866	Ancoats Vale Rubber 10.6.1866	Birchills Estate 8.11.1869	$\bar{x}$	s
Unoccupied												
Male	2.73	12.19	24.45	11.40	8.24	8.55		14.82	10.00	2.77	9.51	7.04
Female	0.36	0.35	1.14	1.88				1.25	1.50		0.64	0.72
Subtotal	3.09	12.54	25.59	13.28	8.24	8.55		16.07	11.50	2.77	10.16	7.48
Land			0.40	0.11				0.26			0.07	0.14
Professions	19.67	11.51	9.65	19.87	0.86	4.07	3.34	17.48		8.33	9.47	7.54
Commerce												
Merchants	16.75	16.48	13.01	17.36	30.72	29.15	57.23	12.49	41.50		23.46	16.53
Middlemen and agents	2.55	8.36	0.43	7.08	31.58	6.15	0.88	9.40	10.00	6.94	8.33	8.84
Retailers	3.64	0.90		0.30		0.15	0.88	1.36			0.72	1.13
Subtotal	22.94	25.74	13.44	24.74	62.30	35.45	58.99	23.25	51.50	6.94	32.52	19.02
Industrial												
Manufacturers	49.72	36.66	44.43	25.84	24.31	7.61	33.63	39.57	22.00	69.44	35.32	17.10
Secondary agrarian and port industries		0.80		0.21		0.30					0.13	0.25
Handicraft				0.08		0.23					0.03	0.07
Subtotal	49.72	37.46	44.43	26.1	24.31	8.14	33.63	39.57	22.00	69.44	31.48	17.00

Service industries

	1	2	3	4	5	6	7	8	9	10	11
Construction and inland transport	3.64			1.20	4.27	25.46		0.05		3.46	7.89
Other service		1.20		1.39		0.15		0.07		0.28	0.53
Subtotal	3.64	1.20		1.59	4.27	25.61		0.12		3.64	7.87
Employees											
Managers		2.15	0.21	0.33		4.61	1.93	1.05	5.00	1.69	1.93
Service workers		3.25	0.34	0.30		1.23	1.93	1.92		0.89	1.13
Ind. skilled		0.13		0.02		0.30		0.05		0.05	0.09
Unskilled							0.14		12.50	0.01	0.04
Unknown	0.91	5.98	5.89	12.55		10.78		0.18	10.00	5.14	5.08
Vendors	18.21	19.61	26.52	18.83		9.23		35.62	17.00		
Cotton	27.32	12.58	4.00	0.80	24.31	2.46		1.10			
Iron	5.46	7.18	16.00	15.94				1.42			

*Percentage by occupation of total number of shares issued as per first return to the Registrar of Joint Stock Companies.
Source: As for table 5.1.

West, with mean subscriptions of 14.04% (s. 19.01), 1.74% (s. 3.95) and 40.73% (s. 19.23) respectively. The pattern of subscription flows, therefore, is a mixture of local finance, which is partly accounted for by vendors' shares, and extra-regional sources of subscriptions, mainly from the North West and the South East, the regions in which Chadwick had an office. While there are these common elements, the high variance around the means indicates that each particular company had its own unique geographical pattern, as Pochin stated in 1867: 'In Bolckow, Vaughan & Co., the shares are held to a very large extent in Manchester . . . but in the case of Palmer's company . . . the shares are held all over the country'.[98]

Chadwick had some intuitive guidelines about the type of person who should invest in his conversions. In 1870 his *Circular* carried the following advice: 'we never recommend clergymen, ladies, or others having limited fixed incomes to invest in bank or trading companies' shares, however eligible. All such investors should be content with a return of 4 to 5%, from guaranteed investments, or those which are free from all ordinary commercial risk'.[99] On the other hand, Chadwick did try to get workmen to take an interest in the share capitals of the companies that employed them, 'but with no substantial success', although 'some of the managers, clerks and foremen in each case took shares and some even borrowed money to do so'.[100] The occupational structure of the shareholdings would seem to bear this out. Female shareholders without occupation had a mean holding of only 0.64% (s. 0.72), industrial skilled and semi-skilled workers 0.05% (s. 0.09), and unskilled workers 0.01% (s. 0.04), while managers and service workers, the latter being mainly clerks, had mean holdings of 1.69% (s. 1.93) and 0.89% (s. 1.13), respectively. The most important occupational sources were, in declining order, manufacturers, merchants, males who gave no occupation, professional people, and middlemen and agents. The proportion held by industrialists is inflated considerably by vendors' holdings. However, even when this factor is allowed for, manufacturers were still the second most important source of subscriptions, and this is due in part to two factors: first, intra-industry and trade investment both in the case of iron and cotton conversions; and second, subscriptions by cotton manufacturers to iron conversions. There is some limited evidence that cotton manufacturers were investing outside of their industry from as early as the 1820s. M'Connel and Kennedy at this date were buying land and shares of insurance and water companies with funds arising out of profits.[101] Similarly, but much later during the 1860s and 1870s, Henry Ashworth, the owner of New Eagley Mill, invested excess capital which built up in his bank account in shares.[102]

Chadwick's industrial promotions in the 1860s can be divided into two distinct groups, first the conversion of twelve iron, steel, and coal concerns which were either large or rapidly growing, and second the conversion of five Manchester firms involved in varying industries. Why were these firms converted and why by Chadwick in particular? These are two questions which cannot be completely answered, either in general or in particular terms, but a number of factors can be put forward. First, financial conditions during the mid-1860s were favourable for flotations; between 1863 and 1866, £35.6m. was subscribed to public new issues of securities,[103] excluding foreign-government loan flotations, a new issue boom which had begun in the summer of 1862[104] and which may have been sparked off by cheap money.[105] Second, the boom in real output in the 1860s was the result of a number of factors, with the initiating stimulus appearing to have had a domestic origin. Estimates of domestic investment show an increase of 105% between 1859 and 1865, with the share of railway investment rising from 21.9% in 1859 to 28.9% in 1865.[106] The number and tonnage of steamships also increased over the same period, with the annual volume of steam tonnage launched rising by 372.6%.[107] These increases in investment in turn affected the iron, steel and coal industries. In these sectors, recent previous investment had taken place mainly during the first half of the 1850s but had then been depressed by the 1857 crisis and, in the case of the iron industry, by the high level of inventories held thereafter. It seems likely that by the beginning of the 1860s stocks had been run down and industrial capacity created during the 1850s was beginning to be fully utilized, as a result especially of the major upturn in domestic railway construction. In such a situation, given the short-run inelastic nature of the supply curve of the heavy industries, further increases in demand would result in rising product prices which, in turn, would lead to entrepreneurs contemplating and embarking upon new investment.

Exports, by value, fell from 1860 to 1862 and then rose, increasing by 52.3% between 1862 and 1866, and by 1866 they were 38.9% above their previous peak level (1860).[108] In the case of the iron industry, any expansion plans arising from this new external increase in demand was coupled with the decision whether to take up the Bessemer process, which from 1860 was a practical proposition. Hughes has found that during the 1850s investment in coal and iron was related mainly to long-period price movements. Available price data for coal and iron in the 1860s are scanty but both the Sauerbeck London price index and the export coal price series display rises from 1864, while Scottish pig iron prices rose from 1862.[109] Such data, allowing for timelags, point to new investment influenced by product price taking place from 1863/4, but Hughes states that new investment took place in coal and iron from 1862,[110] at least a year earlier and before exports started to rise. The general background conditions against which the conversions took place was, therefore, a substantial new issue boom coupled with rising investment in certain industries following increases in, first, domestic demand from 1859 and, second, foreign demand from 1862.

The geographical centre of Chadwick's iron, steel, and coal conversions in the 1860s was Sheffield, its immediate locality and the North Midlands, an area which had closer links with Manchester to the west, than Leeds to the north-east. Between 1863 and 1867 Chadwick established the following as limited companies: Staveley Coal and Iron, John Brown, Charles Cammell, Parkgate Iron, Sheepbridge Coal and Iron, Yorkshire Engine (which was actually not a conversion but a new venture), and Vickers, Sons & Co. Some business history evidence allows a closer examination of the possible reasons why some of these concerns elected to become limited companies in the mid-1860s. Browns, Cammells and Vickers began as small partnerships in the steel trade of Sheffield in the 1830s. Both Browns and Cammells shifted into the production of railway material in the 1840s, with Charles Cammell establishing the Cyclops works in 1845 and John Brown opening the Atlas Steel and Spring works in 1856, following the success of his patent conical spring buffer. Vickers, however, do not appear to have begun making rolling-stock parts until the 1860s, and instead continued to concentrate on steel bars and sheets for tool manufacture, a substantial proportion of which was exported to America. The Brown plant was enlarged considerably between 1859 and 1861, while Vickers built a new works in 1863. Both Browns and Cammells began to manufacture armour plate, which led in the case of Browns to the opening of a new armour-plate plant with a 2,000-ton press, an investment of £250,000. At the same time both firms took up the Bessemer process, Brown being a friend of the inventor. No definite reasons can be given for the conversion of these two firms, but following their establishment as limited companies they continued to make substantial investments in new plant. Cammells acquired the Yorkshire Steel and Iron works at Penistone in 1864, and erected works for manufacturing armour at Grimesthorpe, which opened in 1865, while in the previous year a system of forging steel ingots by hydraulic pressure had been introduced. Browns, which had grown rapidly in the early 1860s and had a turnover of £1m. in 1864 with a workforce of 3-4,000, enlarged their Bessemer plant in 1865 and began the manufacture of weldless steel railway tyres. It would seem therefore in the case of Browns and Cammells that it was the need to finance expansion which led to their conversion. Vickers also had invested heavily in the 1860s, but the reason why this firm went limited was 'financial distress'. It was badly shaken by the 1866 crisis and as a result became in effect a 'limited partnership'. Chadwick may have been used to establish the company because Benzon, one of the partners, had become a director of John Brown when it was incorporated in 1864.[111]

The Park Gate Iron Company at the time of its conversion was in the hands of the Beale and Geach families,[112] who had taken over the works in 1842. Charles Geach, a Midlands banker–ironmaker, had considerable connections with the railways and it was his decision to commence the production of iron rails. He owned already the Patent Shaft and Axlebox Company, which was later incorporated, and became subsequently a director of two domestic railway companies and the concessionaire for a number of foreign lines. In the mid-1850s, as a result of the Crimean War, the Park Gate works, like Browns and Cammells, began producing rolled armour plates, the company having gained the necessary experience through fabricating plates for the *Great Eastern*. However, unlike the urban Sheffield companies, large-scale steel manufacture at Park Gate was not embarked upon until the late 1880s.[113] Beale, with others, and through Chadwick, established in 1865 the Yorkshire Engine Company, a new concern which set up its works near Sheffield with the aim of producing 300 to 400 locomotives per annum. It was, like Vickers, essentially a private company; the minimum subscription was announced as 50 £100 shares with no shares to be transferred either within 12 months of its formation, or afterwards, except with the special consent of the board.[114] Actually a number of the initial shareholders, six out of 36, held less than 50 shares.[115] Production of locomotives began in 1866, and although the company gained a reputation for building colliery and quarry haulage engines, it never achieved its ambitious annual production target.[116]

Either the reputation that Chadwick gained, or the contacts in the iron, steel, coal and engineering industries that he established through his successful Sheffield conversions and promotions, may have been responsible for his other formations in these industries during the 1860s. The concerns were scattered widely, one in Manchester, two on the north-east coast, two in the West Midlands, and one in South Wales. Patent Nut and Bolt was his first conversion outside of the Manchester and Sheffield regions and was one of five that he undertook between April and June 1864, the height of the 1860s new issue boom. It was the incorporation of Watkin's and Keen's London works, Smethwick, and the new company took over subsequently in 1865 the Stour Valley Works, West Bromwich, owned by Weston and Grice.[117] The other Midlands conversion was Birchills Estate Company Limited, undertaken in 1868, in which the vendor appears to have been William Hatton, the general manager of the newly formed Staffordshire Joint Stock Bank.[118] It is highly probable, given evidence of the position of similar works in the locality, that the Birchills Ironworks and Collieries had failed in the 1866 crisis with a large debt to the bank. In the conversion, which established a private company with only 14 shareholders, the assets were taken over in effect by the Knowles family, Lancashire colliery proprietors.[119]

Ebbw Vale was the only Welsh conversion carried out by Chadwick in the 1860s and it was the first time that he issued a public prospectus. The concern had been taken over by Abraham Darby IV and Thomas Brown, the son of an Ebbw Vale ironworker, in the late 1840s,[120] but by the mid-1860s, Darby's partners appear to have been H. Dickinson, a Coalbrook-dale ironmaker, W. Tothill, an ironmaker of Bristol who had banking connections through his son, and J. Robinson, the London representative. Ebbw Vale was a large concern when it was converted, with, according to the prospectus, 23 blast furnaces, of which 16 were in blast, producing 90,000 tons of rails and finished iron, collieries yielding 850,000 tons per annum, and ironstone mines in Somerset providing 280,000 tons of ore.[121] The company was given a nominal capital of £4m. consisting of 80,000 £50 shares on which initially £10 was called. The share issue was nearly wrecked by the long running dispute between the company and Bessemer over its possible infringement of the latter's patent. Following a visit to Chadwick by Bessemer, who through overhearing a conversation in a railway carriage had learnt of the conversion, a settlement was reached.[122] The aim of the conversion, according to Erickson, was the full introduction of the Bessemer process or at least the Ebbw Vale variant of it, and according to the prospectus 'considerable extension'. In all 79,814 shares were taken up, but the company was over-capitalized, although this was not realized until the 1866 crisis, when its high denomination shares with 80% unpaid were rendered unmarketable. As a result a new company was formed in 1868, the Ebbw Vale Steel, Iron and Coal Company, with a more realistic capital structure of a nominal capital of £2,383,000 divided into 74,475 £32 shares.[123]

The other large public issue carried out by Chadwick in the 1860s was Bolckow, Vaughan, a concern which had been started in 1839 by a German corn merchant and the son of a Worcester ironworker.[124] The original aim was to manufacture bar iron and make ships' engines, using Fife pig iron and Durham coal.[125] In 1846 they established their own primary iron plant and then, following the discovery of Cleveland ore by Vaughan, set up works at Middlesbrough in 1851, aided by the Peases. The firm was in the van of technical innovation, building high, large-volume furnaces in order to make the low-grade Cleveland ore economic to use, and it expanded considerably: 13 of the 45 furnaces built in the area in the 1850s were erected by the firm.[126] However, it did not make the decision to take up the Bessemer process until 1871.[127] As with Ebbw Vale, the firm was converted in the spring of 1864, its shares were issued by public prospectus, and all were taken up. Its new board interlocked with that of Browns.[128] Palmers was the other north-east conversion, the reason the vendor gave being 'alone, as it were, and having such large undertakings on my hands, I felt it not only due to myself, to my family, and to the whole district of the North of England, and, I may also say, to the nation, that such a gigantic concern should be placed upon a broader basis than depends upon one individual'.[129] The immediate origin of the firm, 'the largest vertically integrated concern in the country in 1865', was Palmer's partnership in the Marley Hill Collieries with John Bowes which was established in 1846, the profits from which he used to take over 18 collieries from the 'Grand Allies'. In the 1850s he started to build iron-screw steam colliers, which he owned through an unlimited company, in order to sustain the London coal trade in the face of railway competition, and developed an existing shipyard and an ironworks with his brother, first leasing, then owning the iron mines. As with Browns, Cammells, and Park Gate Iron, he began making rolled plates for armour, the first warship being *Terror* of 1856.[130] Palmers was one of the few successful conversions of a shipbuilding concern in a wave of such formations in the 1860s, with 17 being registered between 1863 and 1865.[131] While Palmers was converted by Chadwicks, a significant minority of the shareholders appear to have come into the company through its London bankers, Glyn, Mills, and some of the bank's associates, such as L. M. Rate, sat on its board.

Chadwick's other industrial conversions of the 1860s were Manchester companies, and most appear to have been private concerns, involving only a small number of shareholders. The first, the Ashbury Railway Carriage, converted in 1862, through its intra-industry connections may have brought the Manchester accountant into contact with such Sheffield firms as John Brown and Charles Cammell which produced rolling-stock parts and may have supplied them to the Ashbury company. Two of the 'Manchester conversions' were cotton companies – Globe Cotton Spinning and Manufacturing,[132] the conversion of the Lower Heyes Cotton Mill and Samuel Dewhurst, again an integrated firm owned previously by two partners, Dewhurst and Henry Sugar, who both described themselves as merchants. The remaining formations were Manchester Carriage, which involved the fusion of three partnerships and integrated a firm of coachbuilders with omnibus proprietors, and Ancoats Rubber.

Following the 1866 crisis, Chadwick's activities turned to other but related areas and, apart from Birchill's Estate, he does not appear to have been involved in company promotion until the end of the decade. Instead, his energies were taken up in dealing with the effects of the crisis and, in particular, rescuing his own and other companies which either had been embarrassed or had failed as a result of the events of 1866. His successful efforts to alter the law so as to allow companies to reduce their nominal capitals and the denomination of their shares has been discussed already. However, strangely, only three of his concerns took advantage of the 1867 Act – Palmers, Yorkshire Engine, and Samuel Dewhurst, and the latter two in the mid-1870s[133] – while in the case of Ebbw Vale, a completely new company was formed. Although Chadwick had made great play about the position of Bolckow, Vaughan before the 1867 Select Committee, this company continued with a nominal capital of £2.5m. divided into £100 shares. At the same time as pressing for the modification of company law, Chadwick's firm involved itself in the attempted resuscitation of four banks which had failed during the crisis, the Agra and Masterman's, the Bank of London, the Consolidated Bank, and the Preston Bank.[134]

★

Chadwick began converting and promoting companies again in April 1869, when the economy had begun to pull out of the post-1866 slump both with regard to real and financial activity. However, it was not until the autumn of 1871 that he once again brought domestic industrial shares and debentures to the attention of his clients and friends. These securities took two forms, issues arising out of conversions, and further capital issues for firms which had been converted in the 1860s. Between 1871 and 1874 the firm converted a further 15 industrial companies, raised £400,000 in 6% debentures for Vickers and Llandore–Siemens, and issued 8,000 5% £20 preference shares for Bolckow Vaughan, the latter issue probably being connected with the company commencing to produce Bessemer steel. By 1871 Chadwick's investment activities covered the whole spectrum of the market: his firm was an agent for American railroad securities[135] and land sales, and had established a number of overseas mining, telegraph and tramway companies as well as domestic commercial and public utility companies.

Chadwick appears to have followed the same method of conversion during the first half of the 1870s as in the mid-1860s. In the case of Earles' Shipbuilding and Engineering Company, converted in 1871, Chadwick's commission amounted to £3,000, 1% of the company's nominal capital, while other charges including the costs of the valuation amounted to £2,057, a total of £5,057,[136] being 1.68% of the nominal capital involved and 8.44% of the subscribed capital. The same group of 'promoters' aided Chadwick, with for instance, B. Whitworth, J. Holden and H. J. Leppoc acting in the case of Silkstone and Dodworth Coal and Iron,[137] but there were a greater number of occasions during the 1870s when either Chadwick or one of the partners of his firm was involved directly in the actual transfer of the assets.[138] Valuations had, on Chadwick's own admission, given rise to problems during the 1860s and the difficulties involved were made greater by the 'coal famine' of the early 1870s when the price of coal rose from 9s. 8d. per ton to 20s. 6d. between 1871 and 1873.[139] Pig iron prices, naturally, also rose, with Scottish pig rising from 58s 11d. to 117s. 3d., and Cleveland No. 3 from 47s. 2d. to 98s. 5d. over the same period.[140] Burn has claimed that most of the iron and steel promotions of the 1870s acquired overvalued assets and that 'Chadwick's worst practice', although legal, was 'unscrupulous and improper', but allowing that there was 'pardonable failure to forecast the change of price trend in the seventies'. He concludes that the experience of the flotations of the 1870s 'checked the pace and changed the direction of industrial investment in Great Britain'.[141]

Burn's argument is based on only one limited secondary source dealing with one conversion only, the Blochairn Iron Company, which took place in 1873 and led to considerable litigation at the end of the decade. In the case of this company, Chadwick had been approached initially in 1871 by Messrs. Hannay & Sons, the vendors, through Mr Brogden, M.P., who owned the Tondu Ironworks which were converted successfully by Chadwick in 1872. He declined the proposal because the Scottish ironworks did not have collieries, but in 1873 was asked once more to convert the concern following Hannay's purchase of a suitable colliery. Hannay's valuation of the assets was £400,000 while Hulse valued the ironworks at £277,000 and Armstrong valued the collieries at £24,000, a total of £301,000, and the assets were purchased subsequently for £300,000. The prospectus was issued in May 1873, just as the London money market was beginning to be troubled by the Viennese *krach*. It stated that the purchase money was payable two-thirds in cash, in instalments over 18 months and one-third in shares of the company, which were to be retained in hand as a guarantee that the net profits for the next five years were to be not less than 10% per annum – Chadwick's normal practice established in the 1860s. However, the prospectus was either misleading or fictitious in four areas. It named a Mr Grieve as a director, who, although he had been approached, had not agreed to join the board; it omitted to state that interest was to be paid on the instalments of cash, which were being paid through bills; it overstated considerably the then turnover and output of the works at £1m. per annum; and it understated the area of land taken over by the company at 17 acres, whereas it was actually 20 acres.

The flotation was not successful, with only two-thirds of the shares being taken, including those credited to the vendors, but the Hannays pressed to go on and an allotment was made. Although the company did not get off to a good start financially, its difficulties were compounded by errors of management and what may have been insanity. The managing director made 'great alterations' in the works' new rolling mills, and the chairman, Robert Hannay II, purchased large quantities of pig iron at the peak in its price. These latter transactions led to a loss of £100,000 and the bankruptcy of the Hannay family, following which Hannay II 'suffered aberrations of the mind, absented himself from the works, and was found dead'.

Consequently the company was not successful and went into liquidation in 1874. Legal actions were started in January 1876 by Edmund Wilson, a Leeds solicitor, who had sent circulars to shareholders in Manchester, and in May 1876 issued 78 writs against Chadwick, alleging misrepresentation in the prospectus and *Circular*. A test case, *Robinson* v. *Chadwick* was arranged, but the plaintiff declined to open it and judgment was given in Chadwick's favour with costs. Three years later in 1881, a new test action, *Smith* v. *Chadwick*, was brought, in which four of the 15 objections were allowed against the statement in the prospectus. Chadwick appealed in 1882 and, as a result, the earlier decision was reversed and the action dismissed with costs and costs of the appeal.[142] The Blochairn litigation occurred during the slump of the 1870s and was one of many law suits in which the ashes of the flotation booms of both the 1860s and 1870s were raked over. Along with these proceedings, there were three parliamentary committees, the Select Committee on Foreign Loans (1875), the Select Committee on the Companies Acts (1877), and the Royal Commission on the Stock Exchange (1878), which also considered the financial events, both foreign and domestic, of the past 15 years. This places the Blochairn case in its true perspective, that of general disgust on the part of investors with foreign and domestic securities. However *Smith* v. *Chadwick* did highlight the most serious fault of the Manchester accountant – overdressing the prospectus – which had also occurred with regard to the Ebbw Vale and Yorkshire Engine promotions in the 1860s. But unlike most other company promoters, Chadwick did employ professional valuers when he converted companies, and did not inflate the price of the transferred assets by having them sold in the first instance to 'dummy' vendors. When the West Cumberland Iron and Steel Company was formed in 1872, 'Sigma' wrote to *The Times* asking, with other questions, 'What is the actual final net sum to be paid to the original owners of the works named, after all deductions for commissions, syndicate, financial agencies, division of profits between actual and advertised sale price (if any) are made?' To which Chadwick, Adamson, & Co. replied: 'The net amount to be paid to the owners is £485,000 as stated in the prospectus. The financial agents and promoters act simply as brokers, and their total charge is a commission of 1 per cent. There is no difference between the price of purchase and the price of sale, and consequently no profit to go to the Directors.'[143] Neither did Chadwick manipulate the stock market price of the securities that he was issuing, in order to attract subscribers – the premium dodge, which was used by many others both for foreign and domestic securities.

In terms of standards, Chadwick represented the best of company promoters in the 1870s: his level of commission was low, not the usual 5% to 6%, occasionally rising to 50%,[144] and he did not load the contract price. In stark contrast are the activities of Albert Grant.[145] Through the use of double contracts and dummy vendors, and despite the amendment passed in the 1867 Companies Act,[146] he mulcted the companies that he promoted, the examples that went to court being the Canadian Oil Wells Company, and the Lisbon and Cunetra Tramways Company.[147]

As in the 1860s the vendors in Chadwick's conversions received part of their purchase price in shares credited with a proportion paid up. It would appear that the mean holding of vendors in the 1870s was higher than in the 1860s – 30.69% of issued shares (s. 7.7) in the case of five companies, as opposed to 22.88% (s. 9.09). This higher level of vendors' holdings was accompanied in the 1870s by a greater use by Chadwick of the public prospectus, with five being issued for iron, steel and coal firms.[148] In all these instances, the 'public' shareholders were guaranteed a level of return, in the range of 10% to 15%, usually for five years.[149] The greater use of both the public prospectus and guaranteeing a return may indicate that Chadwick found it more difficult to attract his friends and private clients to take up his conversions in the 1870s, although he still managed to convert 'privately' a number of firms with large capitals such as Pelsall Coal and Iron, which had a nominal capital of £240,000, and Andrew Knowles and Sons (Limited), which had a nominal capital of £1,250,000. In the case of the 1870s conversions there appears to have been the same strongly positive relationship between the number of shareholdings and a company's nominal capital, as with the conversions of the 1860s,[150] but the correlation between the number of shareholdings and paid-up capital, while positive, was less strong.[151]

The events of the 1866 crisis had some effect upon the capital structure of the firms that Chadwick converted in the 1870s, in that their nominal capitals were not as large as those of the companies converted in the

1860s. However, Chadwick continued to use generally large share denominations: in the case of twelve conversions, one had £100 shares, seven had £50 shares, two had £20 shares, and only one had £10 shares. But on these large shares, a higher proportion was called initially from 'public' subscribers; the mean for the 12 conversions being 39.4% (s. 28.24) as opposed to a mean of 26.2% for the conversions of the 1860s. Consequently the shares that Chadwick issued in the 1870s still carried a high proportion of unpaid liability but not as great as those floated before the 1866 crisis.

As with the 1860s conversions, the first annual returns of shareholders for 10 industrial companies were examined to establish their geographical and occupational composition, and the results are given in tables 5.3 and 5.4.[152] Despite the greater use by Chadwick of the public prospectus in the 1870s, the North West, in particular Manchester and the cotton towns, was still the most important regional source of subscribers, but its dominance was not as great as it had been in the 1860s. The South East, the West Midlands, the North, and Yorkshire and Humberside, continued to be the other most important regions of subscriptions, but at the same time there was, admittedly to a very limited extent, a greater geographical spread of subscriptions, with Wales and Scotland in particular playing a greater role. The same is evident when extra-regional flows are considered. This greater geographical spread in the pattern of subscriptions as compared with the 1860s is probably due to two factors. First was Chadwick's own use of the public prospectus; but second, the public flotation of industrial companies was a general feature of the 1870s' new issue boom unlike in the 1860s, and consequently investors were therefore more aware of, and probably more prepared to subscribe to, such securities. However, the greater geographical spread of subscriptions should not be overstressed, because the basic underlying pattern was very similar to that of the 1860s, namely a mixture of local finance (partly accounted for by vendors' shares), and two particular extra regional sources, Manchester and London. The 1870s occupational data has to be treated with some caution because of the high proportion of shares (a mean of 11.7%) where the subscriber did not give the relevant information. The same five groups as in the 1860s were the most important subscribers, but there was a change in their order of importance. In the 1870s the professions were the most important single group, whereas they had only ranked fourth in the 1860s, their share then being less than that of manufacturers, merchants, and gentlemen who gave no occupation. The other important change is that the individual shares of the leading three most important groups of subscribers in the 1870s were more comparable in size than they had been in the 1860s, namely 22.3% (professions), 19.95% (manufacturers), and 15.80%

Table 5.3 Chadwick industrial promotions in the 1870s: regional distribution of shareholdings

	Glanmore Mining 13.6.1873	Earle's Shipbuilding and Engineering 25.1.1872	Llynvi, Tondu & Ogmore Coal & Iron 18.9.1872	West Cumberland Iron & Steel 23.1.1873	John Wood & Bros. 13.9.1873	Pelsall Coal & Iron 28.7.1873	Silkstone & Dodworth Coal & Iron 22.7.1874	Laurie & Marner 14.11.1873	Bouch & Co. Ltd., 31.12.1873	Stour Valley Coal & Iron 14.3.1874	$\bar{x}$	s
North		1.16	6.8	38.52	2.08	1.66	0.99			0.49	5.17	11.89
Yorks & Humberside	44.28	36.83	1.66	8.33	95.83	4.99	4.82	0.82		4.86	6.23	11.11
North West		21.08	29.21	13.43		33.59	70.46	4.34	97.4	88.12	49.77	35.29
East Midlands		5.64	1.00	0.57		0.68	1.53		2.6	0.72	1.27	1.73
West Midlands	26.0	1.66	1.58	13.11		42.50	0.34	4.10		0.30	8.95	14.92
East Anglia		0.08	0.94	0.79		0.19		0.82		0.1	0.29	0.39
South East	18.85	31.03	39.02	12.36	2.08	11.06	14.7	87.25		4.13	22.04	26.04
South West		1.41	0.73	0.5		0.63	0.08	2.62			0.59	0.84
Wales	1.14		16.55			1.02	0.08				1.87	5.17
Scotland	9.16	0.58	1.47	11.33		0.93	0.61			0.30	2.43	4.17
Ireland, C.I. & I.o.M.	0.28	0.33	0.32	0.87		2.3	4.12			0.75	0.89	1.32
Foreign		0.16	0.04			0.09	1.7				0.19	0.53
Unknown			0.62			0.29	0.43			0.20	0.15	0.22
Manchester	27.14	16.48	16.45	5.64	8.33	15.73	53.67	1.47	61.4	65.11	25.21	22.66
Lancs cotton towns	5.55	1.26	3.01	3.38	12.50	7.39	5.57	1.23	4.0	10.66	5.45	3.22
Area of works		8.68	15.62		37.50	22.72		84.38			33.78	30.23
London	16.00	28.86	31.13	10.33	2.08	5.53	10.61	84.38		3.88	19.28	25.23

Source: As for table 5.1.

Table 5.4 Chadwick industrial promotions in the 1870s: occupational distribution of shareholdings

	Glanmore Mining 13.6.1873	Earle's Shipbuilding & Engineering 25.1.1872	Llynvi, Tondu & Ogmore Coal & Iron 18.9.1872	West Cumberland Iron & Steel 23.1.1873	John Wood & Bros. 13.9.1873	Pelsall Coal & Iron 28.7.1873	Silkstone & Dodworth Coal & Iron 22.7.1874	Bouch & Co. Ltd. 31.12.1873	Stour Valley Coal & Iron 14.3.1874	$\bar{x}$	s
Unoccupied											
Male		11.17	52.13	5.75	57.29	6.07	12.88		2.80	16.45	22.16
Female		1.10	1.93	1.05		1.78	5.86	2.00	1.39	1.67	1.73
Subtotal		12.27	54.06	6.80	57.29	7.85	18.74	2.00	4.19	18.13	20.75
Land		0.58	0.33	0.51		0.48	0.77		0.60	0.36	0.29
Professions	17.35	26.13	25.76	22.35	4.16	15.74	14.55	31.00	43.73	22.3	11.28
Merchants	31.47	22.66	6.94	10.61	18.75	15.32	21.71	1.30	13.45	15.8	9.06
Middlemen and agents	19.7	2.93	4.32	1.87	2.08	2.45	3.20	11.50	3.72	5.75	5.99
Retailers	3.23	2.52	0.97	1.00		1.66	1.64		1.20	1.35	1.06
Subtotal	54.4	28.11	12.23	13.84	20.83	19.43	26.55	12.80	18.37	22.96	13.07
Manufacturers	2.94	12.29	4.29	41.37	17.70	35.74	18.85	26.40	20.05	19.95	12.98
Secondary agrarian and port industries	2.94	0.10	0.28	1.02		0.88	1.03			0.58	0.96
Handicraft		0.41	0.11	0.39		0.34				0.25	0.34
Subtotal	5.88	12.80	4.68	42.78	17.70	36.96	19.88	26.40	20.05	20.79	12.9

Service industries											
Construction and inland transport	2.05	0.92	0.05	0.62		1.24	1.38			0.36	0.57
Other Service			0.34	0.41		0.58	0.64			0.39	0.33
Subtotal		0.92	0.39	1.03		1.82	2.02		0.65	0.72	0.69
Employees											
Directors & Mgrs.		2.51	0.57	0.87		0.24	2.21	2.50	0.70	1.06	1.05
Service Workers		2.36	0.66	0.99		1.48	4.11	2.30	1.56	1.72	1.18
Industrial skilled and semiskilled			0.05	0.02		1.04	0.06		0.15	0.14	0.33
Unskilled			0.02	0.01						0.003	0.007
Unknown	20.29	14.27	1.17	11.09		14.88	11.03	23.00	9.60	11.7	7.67
Vendors			34.89	36.00	37.50	20.07	17.90		25.00	30.69	7.70
Cotton		2.98	3.11	2.42	13.54	4.16			11.90	8.00	6.31
Iron		20.51	4.73	27.49	2.08	31.84	4.84		6.45	15.6	12.85

Source: As for Table 5.1.

(merchants). It would appear also that intra-industry investment played a very minor role in the iron and steel conversions in the 1870s in comparison with the 1860s. However, investment by the cotton industry and trade, both in cotton and iron conversions in the 1870s, seems to have been approximately at the same level as in the 1860s. These changes in occupational sources together with the slightly greater spread of regional sources of subscriptions in the 1870s may indicate that Chadwick was tapping a wider geographical range of sources of savings and in so doing was involving more 'blind' investors in industrial finance.[153]

The general economic and financial background against which the Chadwick conversions of the 1870s took place was similar to that of the 1860s, with a boom in both economic and financial activity. However the upswing of the early 1870s was probably the most vigorous of any nineteenth-century trade cycle. It got underway during the last quarter of 1869, faltered in 1870 because of the uncertainty caused by the outbreak of the Franco–Prussian war,[154] and then went on to reach a peak in 1873. Although there were crises in Vienna in the spring and in New York in the autumn of 1873, there was no major panic in London at the upper turning point as there had been in 1866. Instead, economic and financial activity turned down slowly in a form of progressive collapse, mainly in response to foreign events but with a minor domestic crisis in 1875.[155] Unlike the 1860s the initiating stimulus would appear to have been foreign demand; between 1868 and 1872 the value of exports at current prices increased by 42.6%,[156] with most of this expansion being caused by a development boom in the United States and the trade-creating effects of the European system of 'most favoured nation' trade treaties built up during the 1860s. Domestic investment at current prices did not pick up until 1870 but then rose to a peak in 1876,[157] not being affected immediately by the fall in export values after 1873. Coal prices moved up sharply in 1872, reached a 'famine' peak in 1873 and continued to remain above the slump levels of the late 1860s until 1878. Iron prices show a similar upward movement but led coal prices downwards in the second half of the 1870s.[158] As in the 1860s investment in the capital goods industries appears to have been strongly determined by these price movements, which were the product of inelastic short-run supply curves. For instance, capital expenditures on new plant by five north-eastern iron and steel companies, with the overall pattern being dominated by Bolckow, Vaughan, from a trough of £21,700 in 1869 rose sharply during the following two years, and reached a peak for the decade of £286,900 in 1872. Annual expenditure continued to remain above £200,000 until 1878, when it fell quickly and suddenly to £74,800, a trough for the decade.[159] Share prices recovered with exports, but the Stock Exchange in 1870 was affected seriously for a short period by the Franco–Prussian War. Most of the 90 'public' companies which issued their shares by prospectus in 1870 were formed during the first half of the year before the outbreak of the war, and the financial boom did not get underway fully until a year later.[160] Issues by manufacturing, trading and mining companies played a substantial role in the new issue boom of the early 1870s. Manufacturing and trading companies accounted for 27.9% of capital offered publicly for subscription by all new companies, including foreign railways, and 27.19% of deposits paid in 1872. In the following year 35 new colliery companies were introduced to the market, 'the effect of the high price of coal', and accounted for 7.84% of the capital offered and 10.67% of deposits paid. The overall volume of new issues fell in 1874 but industrial companies continued to be an all-important feature of flotations, their volume of created securities not declining as rapidly as other types of company, particularly foreign railways.[161]

Chadwick was one of a considerable number of industrial promoters acting in the provinces and the metropolis in the 1870s but in contrast to most of his competitors he had an established position and could point to the success of his earlier conversions, like the Park Gate Iron Company which distributed a dividend of 10% at the end of 1870/1.[162] Chadwick's industrial promotions in the 1870s began in the autumn of 1871 with the conversion of Earle's Shipbuilding Company and the formation of the Bilbao Iron Ore Company, and continued until 1874. As in the 1860s they consisted of a number of Manchester firms, covering a wide range of industries, together with iron, steel and coal incorporations. These latter companies were scattered all over the country, there being no central geographical core, like that of the Sheffield conversions of the 1860s. A few were converted as a result of illness of the existing partners, this being the case with Earles, and Laurie and Marner,[163] the latter a London carriage building firm. Some arose from Chadwick's firm now being the trustees and auditors of the Bessemer royalties; while others were due to Chadwick's Manchester connections.

On the north-west coast, Chadwick set up the West Cumberland Iron and Steel Company, a reformation of the West Cumberland Hematite Iron Company, which had been established in 1860 by a local coal-owning family, the Fletchers. It had begun pig iron production in 1862, wrought iron manufacture in 1867, and in the early 1870s it adopted the Bessemer process.[164] The company was to run into considerable difficulties in the late 1870s and 1880s,[165] despite its coastal position and local supplies of ore and coal. Chadwick's Welsh promotion, the Llynfi, Ogmore and Tondu Iron and Coal Company, like the Cumberland concern, was a reformation rather than a straightforward conversion. The

Tondu Iron works had been bought in a derelict condition by the Brogden family of Manchester in the early 1850s, while the Llynfi and Maesteg works had been amalgamated as a joint stock company in the first half of the 1860s.[166] In order to reduce competition between these works, Brogden arranged a further amalgamation in 1872 and its shares were floated by Chadwick. On the three sites in 1872 there were nine blast furnaces, 59 puddling furnaces and seven rolling mills – small in scale compared with the major South Wales producers further to the east. In the early 1870s the main output was railway iron for the booming market in the United States. The new combine raised further capital in 1873 in the form of £100,000 6% debentures issued through Chadwick, but in the mid-1870s it made losses and went into liquidation in 1878. After writing off its loan debt it carried on as the Llynfi and Tondu Coal and Iron Company, but it stopped being a fully vertically integrated concern when it abandoned ironworking in the mid-1880s. Ebbw Vale, one of Chadwick's earlier conversions, also ran into financial difficulties in the late 1870s, with losses from 1875 on, which amounted to £670,000 by 1877.[167] An attempt to reduce the firm's subscribed capital, as opposed to its nominal capital, was stopped by the Master of the Rolls, a decision which led to the Select Committee on Company Law of 1877.[168]

Most of the iron conversions of the 1870s were family malleable-iron businesses,[169] but those undertaken by Chadwick acquired long lists of proprietors. Two West Midland conversions, Pelsall Coal and Iron, and Stour Valley Coal and Iron, fall into this category, the incentive to convert them being probably the district's growing lack of competitiveness due to high transport costs and dwindling local supplies of coal and iron. *The Times* commented in 1873 that 'a noticeable feature of the South Staffordshire iron trade just now is the absorption of private concerns by joint stock companies'.[170] Although Chadwick's valuers may have erred considerably with regard to the Blochairn conversion, in the case of Stour Valley a conservative reckoning was made.

> The valuation on which the purchase has been made is based on the moderate calculation of 1s 6d and 2s per ton profit on the coal and 5s per ton on the pig iron actually produced, and reckoning interest at 16 per cent for the capital employed. This principle and basis of valuation present a strong contrast to data given in some recent cases of colliery purchases.[171]

On the north-east coast in 1874 Chadwick converted Thomas Richardson & Sons' works into the West Hartlepool Iron Company.[172] A year before, in South Yorkshire, he established privately the Silkstone and Dodworth

Coal and Iron Company, an issue which was oversubscribed by a factor of five by his private clients.[173] The Knowles conversion, which took place privately in December 1873, was also oversubscribed, but not to the same extent. This formation involved the property of Andrew Knowles and Sons, the businesses of Knowles and Hall, and Knowles and Stott, and included their private railway rolling stock, the whole being valued at £1m.[174] Lastly in the 1870s Chadwick undertook two Scottish iron and coal conversions, the ill-fated Blochairn Company, which has been mentioned already, and the Benhar Coal Company, incorporated in January 1872.[175]

Besides these conversions, a disparate range of other industrial companies were promoted by the London and Manchester firm. These consisted of the Glandmore Mining Company, an Irish venture, John Wood and Brothers Ltd, a conversion of an integrated Glossop cotton partnership,[176] Laurie and Marner, a London carriage-building concern, John A. Bouck & Co., an old-established Manchester chemical firm,[177] and John Fish Ltd, a Blackburn cotton company with two mills.[178] In addition, in 1874 Chadwick issued 5,400 $100 shares and 400 $1,000 bonds for the Joliet Iron & Steel Company of Chicago.[179] The very last concern with which he appears to have been associated was the Railway Lighting Company, a small private patent concern, established in February 1874.[180]

The last copy of the *Investment Circular* appeared in August 1875 and it contained fittingly a list of the principal companies which had obtained their capital through Chadwick. Although he ceased to be a company promoter in the mid-1870s, it was at this point that he began his major campaign for the reform of company law, with the particular aim of preventing fraudulent formations.[181] His career in the late 1870s and early 1880s was blighted by the Blochairn litigation and his loss of a seat in the House of Commons.[182] In 1883 his firm was split into three,[183] and when he died in 1895 his business was taken over by Mellors Basden, chartered accountants of London and Nottingham.[184] They acquired the assets and book debts for £75 and agreed to pay Chadwick's widow 12½% of the net receipts arising out of any transferred business.

Chadwick's activities do mark an advance, but a small advance, in the development of a national market for the securities of joint stock companies. Although he did act as a channel by which extra-local sources of savings flowed into industrial securities, the dimensions of this conduit were very small indeed. This has been demonstrated in the regional analysis of the initial shareholders' places of residence, which shows that Chadwick acted primarily for a group of East Lancashire investors with whom he probably became acquainted when he was the Treasurer of

Salford and an agent of Globe Insurance Company. In some respects a direct comparison can be made between these investments and the early railway capital market of the 1830s, in which Lancashire, particularly Manchester during the second half of the decade, was the main source of extra-regional funds.[185] While the flows of funds involved are in no way comparable, Chadwick's Manchester circle of friends and clients became an important management group in the nascent steel industry, and their presence in some cases continued until the third generation. Despite his increased use of the public prospectus in the 1870s boom, Chadwick's activities remained essentially private and, overall, mark no real change in the mobilization of savings for domestic industrial investment. Compared with a meeting in an Oldham public house, called to interest workers and others in the securities of a new cotton mill, Chadwick's role, though important in terms of the companies that he converted and promoted, heralds no advance in the form of a permanent institutionalization of intermediation in the primary market for securities. He began as, and substantially remained, an interface between a private commercial and industrial 'grapevine' with funds to invest, essentially Mancunian, and a group of industrialists who wished for various reasons to take advantage of the recent liberalization of company law. 'Outsiders' were drawn in, but not to any great extent, and so Chadwick's firm continued to be primarily an accounting practice, although one which gave investment advice to its clients. Despite having offices in Manchester and London from the early 1860s, Chadwick did not establish a permanent bridge between the provincial, local, unstructured capital markets which had developed with industrialization, and the formal machinery of the metropolis which had grown from the 1830s with the financing of domestic railway construction and the export of capital.

Other iron, steel and coal companies were converted in the 1860s and 1870s by a range of agencies, both provincial and metropolitan. In the north-east a local solicitor, Joseph Dodds, acted as a promoter, being connected in the 1860s with Stevenson, Jacques & Co., and in the early 1870s with the Acklam Ironworks at Middlesbrough.[186] Other examples are difficult to gather and perilous to generalize from, but in the 1870s boom it would appear that a number of London agencies were prepared to act as company midwives. In the case of the South Staffordshire Iron Works, the company was promoted by Jay & Co. of Throgmorton Street, who charged £10,000 for their services in forming a company with a nominal capital of £70,000 although the firm agreed to take up 500 out of the 5,000 shares. The vendors obtained £14,000 in cash, £9,000 in acceptances at four months, £9,000 in acceptances at eight months, and £12,000 on a seven-year mortgage at 5% for their fixed assets and up to

£15,000 for stock, which was to be paid by three bills at four, eight and twelve months.[187] Thus only £1,000 of the company's nominal capital was left free in any way. This wave of conversion activity in the iron industry which peaked in the early 1870s, resulted in the limited company being by the 1880s 'an integral part of the [iron and steel] industry's financial structure'.[188] Jeffreys has estimated that in 1882, 41% of firms working blast furnaces were limited companies, with most of them located either in the North East or the Sheffield region.[189] According to Essex-Crosby, from an analysis based on *Burdett's Official Stock Exchange Intelligence,* there were in 1885 102 quoted coal, iron and steel companies which had an aggregate paid-up capital of £36.9m., consisting mainly of ordinary shares.[190]

★

What role did London play? In the metropolis by the 1870s there was a well-established capital market but it was geared to handling primarily large issues, generally government bonds and railway securities; each issue being large in volume compared with that generated by most domestic joint stock flotations of the 1860s and 1870s. Home securities were traded on the London Stock Exchange but they consisted mainly of the National Debt, managed by the Bank of England and the government broker, and with amortization declining in volume, and railway securities, floated to a large degree by the companies themselves. Apart from bank shares,[191] other domestic securities traded on the market were lumped together under a single heading, 'miscellaneous'. The liberalization of company law did lead to some developments in the institutional structure of the London capital market but generally they reinforced the market's already established bias towards relatively large issues.[192] After 1855 it became easier to establish a foreign bank or railway because instead of having to obtain a charter, the concession could be speedily and cheaply incorporated as a company by the almost nominal process of registration.

During the 1860s boom, a new form of issuing house did appear in the metropolis – the finance company, an English version of the continental investment bank. Most of these concerns had a life as brief as the financial boom of which they were products, with only five surviving the 1866 crisis. Generally they were involved in duplicating themselves, exporting capital abroad, and privately financing domestic railway construction. The most important were established by merchant bankers, railway contractors and directors, and financiers, while a host of imitative concerns were formed by all sorts of individuals on the periphery of the 'City'. The five premier concerns were the London Financial Association, the General Credit and Finance, and the International Financial Society, all set up in 1863, together with the less reputable Credit Foncier and Mobilier of England and the Imperial Mercantile Credit Association, which were established during the following year and were the results of mergers.

The International Financial Society, whose board consisted largely of merchant bankers, exhibited little interest in domestic industrial promotions during the 1860s boom. Its secretary entered into discussions with Messrs Newton, Keates & Co., brass founders of Liverpool, in March 1865 with a view to the sale of the partnership but, when he found that the net profit would give a return of $7\frac{1}{2}\%$ to 8% on the capital required, he informed Keates that 'the matter was not one which the international could take up'.[193] Similarly the International declined to promote a number of other concerns, including the Oil Seed Crushing Company,[194] and after a serious examination of the proposition, the Pembrey Copperworks.[195] However, it did invest some small amounts of its own funds in proving trials for inventions, in one case for 'the manufacture of iron' jointly with Messrs Guest,[196] and gave the Regents Canal Ironworks a loan of £8,000 for six months at 5% interest with a commission of 5% on the security of a promissory note and £10,000 debentures.[197] Lastly, during the 1866 crisis, the International established the Portland Stone Company, encouraged by the doubling in consumption of stone which had taken place during the first half of the 1860s. The company was the conversion of a partnership which had been quarrying 30,000 tons a year on a capital of £15,000 on which it had been making profits of £7,500. However, the 1866 crisis cut the demand for stone by 40%, while it was discovered that the quarry required a mineral railway and sawmill for efficient working, which involved an outlay of £17,000 that had not been envisaged. By 1871 it was the second largest producer amongst the four firms in the trade,[198] and the International held the majority of its shares until the mid-1880s when two stone-merchants took over the company.[199]

The only other front-rank finance company to undertake a domestic industrial promotion during the 1860s boom was the London Financial Association, which issued the prospectus of the Clyde Engineering and Iron Ship Building Company[200] in April 1864.[201] This was the conversion of the partnership of Smith and Rodger, owners of the Glasgow Middleton Yard, which was taken over initially by two London merchants for £125,000. During the same month, the Credit Mobilier together with the Mercantile Credit Association floated the capital of the Humber Ironworks and Shipbuilding Company,[202] which went into liquidation within two years of its conversion,[203] following some dubious financial dealings during its birth as a limited company.[204] Two other shipbuilding concerns were floated by finance companies. The London Engineering and Iron Shipbuilding Co., which survived until 1871, was brought out in July 1864 by the Oriental Financial Corporation, which took 400 of the company's 10,000 £50 shares.[205] In April 1865 the International Contract Company attempted to float the Plymouth Shipbuilding, Dock and Ironworks Co., but it 'fell through in forming'.[206] To this group of companies should be added the Millwall Ironworks and Shipbuilding Company formed in 1863 by Peto and Betts, Brassey and some partners of Overend, Gurney & Co.[207] It was reformed in 1864, although without any major change in ownership, and survived until 1874 despite its connection with the discount house to which it owed £422,565, a debt considered a total loss at the time of Overend's conversion into a limited company in 1865.[208]

Most of these shipbuilding concerns were converted in the spring of 1864, the crest of the financial boom of the 1860s, and it may be that the favourable financial conditions induced their transformation into limited companies. None was located on Tyneside, the developing focus of the English shipbuilding industry, and their conversion may either have been attempts to arrest a growing lack of competitiveness by an injection of capital, or the result of the various partners involved seeking to realize their assets while they were still marketable. The London and Glasgow stands apart as it was the only company to survive for any appreciable length of time; in September 1912 it became a private company and by 1914 the majority of its shares were held by Harland and Wolff. Its viability was probably a function of the growth of shipbuilding on the Clyde, because its other centre, the Thames, experienced a sharp contraction in construction activity during the second half of the nineteenth century.

A number of other domestic industrial flotations were carried out by second-rank finance companies during the 1860s boom. The Financial Corporation attempted to issue the capital of two ironworks, the Aberaman, the conversion of Crawshay, Bailey, and the Graysbrook; but the former, despite a statement in its prospectus claiming that half of its 10,000 £50 shares had been subscribed, never came into active existence.[209] The Financial Corporation was also responsible for floating the Shireoaks Colliery Company, which had been formed by J. N. Daniell, chairman of both the Alliance Bank and the Bank of Wales.[210] The only other industrial enterprise with which the finance companies were involved was the South Devon Slab and Slate Quarry Co., whose capital was issued publicly by Credit Mobilier in July 1864. This quarrying concern had been established six months earlier by a group of Exeter tradesmen and professional people in conjunction with a London

barrister and it was probably through him that the company's capital
came to be issued by a finance company.

Most of the second-rank finance companies failed during the 1866
crisis, while the five main houses were crippled, their assets having
become extremely illiquid. As late as January 1875, 48.9% of the assets of
the International Financial Society were still unsaleable, and these 'lock-
ups' restricted greatly the institution's ability to function as an investment
bank. Consequently it played only a very minor role during the boom of
the early 1870s. In 1871 the International did purchase, jointly with
George Elliot, the Cinderhill Colliery in order to convert it into a limited
company.[211] A similar venture, the Talk Hill Colliery and Ironworks,
Staffordshire, despite a favourable engineer's field report and an
agreement with the vendor, came to nothing because the International's
associates found that they had insufficient time and capital with which to
back the venture.[212] By the early 1880s the International's assets were at last
liquid but the Society was now but a pale reflection of what it had been
in the 1860s boom. Even in the 1880s its interests were mainly overseas
securities and, while it received a number of domestic industrial proposals,
mainly through its brokers, P. Cazenove, including the purchase of
the engineering works of Messrs May and Mountain of Birmingham,
generally it declined them. In the early 1880s three of the other remaining finance companies either went into liquidation or became moribund,
while following the 1866 crisis the General Credit had become a discount
house, a transformation that was not completed until the late 1870s.

The heyday of the finance companies was the 1860s boom, and most of
the flotations that they undertook were foreign. The first-class houses
appear to have had little contact with the domestic industrial economy
and even when they received proposals for the conversion of industrial
concerns, they did not actively pursue them. The smaller second-rank
houses were involved to a great degree in domestic flotations but their
main aim would appear to have been to maximize the profits of flotations
through manipulating the market in the securities of the companies to
which they were acting as midwives. The position was summarized by a
Mr King, a shareholder in the Mercantile Credit Association and the
Humber Ironworks. He complained that the prospectus of the ironworks
had spoken of a return of 20% from contracts of £300,000 which the
limited company was taking over, but instead they had resulted in a loss
of £40,000 and caused the company's shares, with £15 paid, to fall to a
price of 5s. He thought that:

It was the duty of a financial company like the present scrupulously
to investigate matters before they issued a prospectus because it was

on the faith of such a prospectus that the shares were subscribed for, and it could not be denied that the result of bringing out schemes in which all the promises were falsified would, in the end, be most injurious to the financial companies which brought them out.[213]

No London institution was to play such a role before 1914, but the need was recognized as early as the slump of the 1860s.[214]

Company promotion in the metropolis, particularly for domestic industrial concerns, after 1866 until 1914 remained primarily in the hands of financial agents, self-styled company promoters, and *ad hoc* syndicates. A few joint stock banks had entered the new issue market in the 1860s alongside, and sometimes in conjunction with, financial companies. Mainly they were involved with foreign ventures, but the English Joint Stock Bank brought out the Phosphate of Lime Company and the National Bank sponsored the Lundy Island Granite Company. These activities soon brought forth a rebuke from *The Economist*:

> Attention has been directed to the introduction of new projects by the joint stock banks. It is suggested that operations of this nature are beyond the province of bankers; that the latter might easily be induced to uphold the new companies fostered by themselves at the expense of their clients, and that in time their resources might become embarrassed in the way we have already seen brought about by a too close connection between bankers and trading or speculative companies, who are naturally exposed to a greater risk than that a banker should voluntarily encounter.[215]

This lesson was learnt the hard way during the 1866 crisis, and bankers generally thereafter for at least 20 years remained aloof from the London new issue market.

★

After 1866 company promotion in London was undertaken by a diverse group of people which contained a core of self-professed financial agents. In 1869 there were four firms so listed, and in 1873 and 1874 nine, including Chadwicks, Adamson, Collier.[216] Most had their offices in the vicinity of the Stock Exchange; some were probably 'outside' brokers, and others 'sworn' brokers who had paid a £5 admission fee to the Corporation of London. Unlike the Stock Exchange firms, 'outside' brokers, of which there were 143 in the early 1880s,[217] could advertise. Members of the Stock Exchange were not allowed to undertake 'extra-mural' activities but company promotion was a blurred area. During the

1870s it was maintained that 'as a rule Stock Exchange men are certainly not promoters and very few of them are directors of these new companies'.[218]

The Stock Exchange and the 'outside brokers' formed essentially a secondary market, dealing in securities which had already been issued, and so allowed investors to adjust their portfolios. However, the Stock Exchange was not entirely separated from the new issue market, because it did deal in securities which were in the process of being created, and company promoters, both of foreign and domestic concerns, did take advantage of this situation. The advent of a new company was heralded by the publication of its prospectus, a well-established device by the middle decades of the nineteenth century. However, a regular, specialist, financial daily press did not develop until the 1880s and then initially was only concerned with overseas mining affairs.[219] As a result the main way of spreading news of the advent of a new company was through the advertising columns of both the London daily newspapers, which had carried financial news since the mid-1820s, and weekly journals such as *The Economist,* which in 1865 set up an offshoot, *The Investor's Monthly Manual.* The daily papers were heavily dependent on advertising revenue and as a result a prospectus in the advertising section was often accompanied by a somewhat laudatory note in the financial column. By the 1870s it had become an established practice to circularize prospectuses to known shareholders, with share and advertising brokers having suitable compiled lists which they sold 'at so much per hundred'. Even religious papers were considered to be fit places in which to advertise prospectuses,[220] while circulars were often sent at the weekend 'so that they may come to hand on the Sabbath morning, when it is assumed the recipients in the country have leisure to read and study them'.[221]

Prospectuses, advertisements, circulars and newspaper comment were ways of attracting attention to a new company but they did not guarantee by themselves that the issue would be successful, especially as 'all householders and shareholders, as well as postmen, know the influx of prospectuses when a floating mania is on'.[222] The only way of ensuring a reasonable flow of subscriptions was to make sure that the company's shares were dealt in on the Stock Exchange at a premium, that is at a price above their par value. Such tactics were necessary until 1900 because the underwriting of share, but not debenture, issues was forbidden as the courts took the view that the provisions of the Companies Act of 1862 implied that a company could not issue shares at a discount which the payment of an underwriting commission involved.[223] The need to create a premium on shares about to be issued, in order to induce 'well-to-do tradesmen, clergymen, females of independent means and so forth' to subscribe, was known as early as 1860: 'Promoters of public companies – a class of person whose province is now as clearly defined as that of election agents – are well aware that no project will float unless the shares are at a premium.'[224]

The premium was created by the promoter placing immediate orders for shares with a number of brokers, including the one acting for the company. As no shares actually existed before allotment, their price rose rapidly above their par value. It was estimated in the late 1870s that artificial premium creation had been a feature of 75% of all public company formation.[225] The result was that the public came to expect all new shares to rise to a premium and consequently were unable to distinguish between viable and non-viable projects on the basis of their market price.[226] The public were informed of the premium through the press, although formally a company's shares did not enter the Stock Exchange Official List until after they had been allotted and their quotation had been approved by the Committee of General Purposes.[227]

It might be argued that these doubtful manoeuvrings were necessary because promoters were prevented from recourse to underwriting. However, a substantial number of promoters regarded premium creation as one of their major sources of financial gain arising from company creation. At allotment, shares needed only to be entered up in the names of the brokers with whom the original buying orders had been placed, so as to allow them to cover their positions, and the rest could remain with the promoter and his friends. Thus the market in the shares remained 'tight' and the premium sustained, which allowed the promoters to sell off their holdings at the enhanced price. Such tactics could be and were defended on the grounds that many applicants were either known 'stags' or 'guinea pigs' covering for 'stags'. In the cases where there were rival projects, issuing battles could develop with the price of a company's shares seesawing as its promoters bought shares which were not yet obtainable, while projectors of a rival concern sold shares which they had not got[228] to force their price down and so bring the rival company into disfavour.

Investors laid special emphasis on companies which received a special settlement and quotation on the Stock Exchange. With a special settlement, transactions in a company's shares became part of the normal fortnightly account system of the house's dealings, enforced by the rules with penalties for defaulters. A company's broker would apply for a special settlement as soon as a company's shares were known to be ready for delivery.[229] The Stock Exchange Committee had in the broker, someone over whom they held sway and who they could make responsible for the documents – the prospectus, the articles of association, the share applications and the allotment book – which he was required to produce.[230] However, the Committee was not interested in guaranteeing either the solvency or the soundness of a company but merely its technical origins. Sometimes fellow partners of a broking firm were both members of the Committee and involved in introducing companies to it. The Committee did not look out for fraud but rather waited to be informed of it;[231] however, the general public held the granting of a special settlement to be something entirely different: 'the public twist the grant of a settlement by the Committee of the Stock Exchange into some kind of certificate or voucher of what the Committee have no possibility of knowing'.[232] A special settlement, instead of being regarded as a technical process necessary in order to allow regularized dealings in a company's shares, was taken rather as a hallmark, and an even greater guarantee was associated with a quotation, an entry in the Stock Exchange Official List.

> In practice, people do not like to invest in securities which are not brought under their notice. They would choose those securities by preference in which they saw transactions recorded in the list. That is a matter of every day experience, I am sure, in every brokers' office. The client says, 'I do not like to touch that security, I never see it noticed in the list'.[233]

The rules for a quotation were more demanding than for a special settlement: two-thirds of a company's shares had to have been applied for by the public, its articles of association had to prevent its directors from buying the company's shares, and no further issues were to be made within one year.[234] In addition the company had to be of 'sufficient magnitude', a condition which ruled out many domestic industrial concerns as well as other companies.[235]

At the height of the 1860s new issue boom in March 1864, the Stock Exchange attempted to tighten up its rules. In future, share dealings were only to be recognized if the company involved had issued unconditionally at least half of its nominal capital, of which 10% had been paid up.[236] This was a move to thrash out the speculative chaff of the boom and it was followed by a memorial to the committee asking that dealings in shares before their allotment should no longer be recognized; the necessary alteration was made on 7 April 1864.[237] Promoters side-skipped the rule by using the 'outside' market and getting dealings there quoted in the press,[238] while brokers, sometimes to their cost, continued to accept business in shares before allotment. Samuelson, the vendor of the Humber Ironworks Company, bought 10,000 of its shares before allotment, through several brokers, which raised their price to a premium and was quoted in the press. When sufficient subscribers had come forward to guarantee the success of the issue, he repudiated his buying contracts on the grounds that they were not recognized.[239] The rule, a vain attempt to prevent the Stock Exchange from being used to create a false market in embryonic securities, lasted a year. In 1878 the Royal Commission on the Stock Exchange in its majority report condemned dealings before allotment and recommended that the investigations carried out before either a special settlement or a quotation was granted should be undertaken by some public functionary and enforced by law. Its views were upheld by *The Bankers' Magazine*[240] but opposed by *The Economist*, which in the 1860s had argued against the changes made in the house's rules:

> The more this market is left to itself the better for the dealers in it, for each will then be responsible for his own acts only. And the better for the public too, for then it will, not, as now, be misled by trust in unreal help, and by belief that as someone else is taking care of them, they need take the less care of themselves.[241]

The government was certainly not prepared to intervene in this area, in the same way that it did not countenance any reform of company law before the late 1880s. Goschen, the Chancellor, had put an end to any possible action arising from the proposed Royal Commission even before it was established, believing that no good would come out of it, while 'it would be exceedingly necessary to be very careful indeed as to the mode in which Parliament dealt with the inquiry'.[242] He did not want 'to encourage in the public mind the notion that the legislative could protect them'.

Artificial premium creation and the inability of small issues, both foreign and domestic, to obtain a London Stock Exchange quotation, conditions which continued until 1914, were factors which both militated against domestic industrial issues succeeding on the London market and reinforced any latent tendencies that led industrialists to seek finance either privately or locally. These conditions in turn were augmented by the way in which securities of moderate volume were dealt with once they had been admitted to the Official List. With regard to a summary of the Official List of 19 October 1877, a broker indicated that 1,082 out of the 1,367 securities which had a quotation were unmarketable, giving as examples National Provincial Bank of England shares, East and West India Dock stock, and the shares of water companies, gas companies and insurance companies, the total value of which he placed at £562.8m.[243] In the case of these securities, jobbers would not quote buying and selling prices but would only deal in them by negotiation, involving of course a much larger 'turn'. One dealer stated that he would not sell such shares unless he knew where he could obtain them,[244] and in this situation the broker had to reveal from the beginning of a transaction whether he was a potential buyer or seller. There was a noticeboard in the house whereby brokers who had an interest in unmarketable securities could get in touch with one another in theory, but in practice it was unworkable. In the late 1870s, the London Stock Exchange consisted of nine or ten separate markets with joint stock company securities spread over nearly all of them, and with no firms of jobbers or dealers specializing in them.[245] It was simply too risky to run a book in their securities, the supply of which was extremely limited, let alone attempt to balance transactions in them at the end of a day's trading.

This gap in the secondary market of the Stock Exchange was covered to a very limited extent outside the house. Sworn brokers, unattached to the Stock Exchange, dealt in 'unmarketable' securities, usually by keeping a register, a practice which continued at least until the 1890s.[246] Also, there were ephemeral rival institutions which hoped, by specializing in dealing in these securities, to sustain themselves. They were a feature of both financial boom and slump. In April 1863 the formation of the Commercial Institute and General Share Exchange was announced and it included in its aims: 'Arrangements...for the sale and purchase of shares in joint stock companies...by a system of free registration, which presents unequalled facilities for transfer alike in town and country and saves the present heavy charge of the dealers or "turn of the market" on both sides'.[247] Two years later, a similar company, the Investment and Finance Agency, was established.[248] After Black Friday the situation for holders of these securities became crucial; as *The Economist* put it:

> At the present time when so many securities are thrown upon the market, it is very desirable that the best possible means of selling should be used.... There is no single centre for these 'small quantity' securities, where an intended purchaser can be sure of meeting with the things he wants, and an intended seller of meeting with the money he wants.[249]

The London Stock and Share Company aimed to meet this need; it had evolved out of an agency established by George Templeton & Co., which also published annual directories for joint stock companies. By using a circular 'devoted more especially to the interests of shareholders in companies not officially quoted', of which part was a register for the sale of non-current stocks, and holding auctions, the company attempted to render these securities marketable. It lasted for less than six months.[250] The Report of the Royal Commission on the Stock Exchange gave further publicity to the problem, and in the early 1880s a number of similar institutions were formed,[251] to the extent that *The Statist* commented:

> The Stock Exchange had better look out. The frequent sales of stocks and shares by auction are attracting more and more attention. If this goes on we shall soon find the leading auctioneers competing with the Stock Exchange as 'sworn brokers' now do. The competition may even be more effectual. The 'sworn broker' has to do most of his business indirectly, through members of the Stock Exchange, who get some commission upon it. But the auctioneers will pay no commission to the Stock Exchange, and if they are careful to make good rules for the protection of the buyer and seller, they might run the Stock Exchange very hard. The public, it may be hoped, will be gainers by the competition.[252]

The outside market was always a cause of trouble and concern to the Stock Exchange but never supplanted it.[253]

With a highly imperfect secondary market for small issues in London, coupled with the dubious nature of the way that they were introduced, it is understandable why investors generally fought shy of them. They were advised even by 'outside' brokers never to invest in such companies, namely any with a capital of less than £100,000. Stock Exchange brokers were cautioned in the house rules 'against giving the sanction of their names to the bringing out of any company without due enquiry as to the bona fides of its objects, the character of its promoters, Directors and concessionaries, and of the other persons connected therewith',[254] a regulation which at least a few at Capel Court chose to ignore. As a result over the long term, except at the speculative feverish heights of financial booms, investors with no particular knowledge or connections, as a result either of warnings or bitter experience generally placed their savings in large issues, which meant apart from railway securities, foreign issues. This conclusion, based primarily on qualitative evidence, has been confirmed by the work of Edelstein. He found that in their preferences investors were to some degree biased towards large-scale issues and before the 1890s favoured somewhat non-domestic issues.[255]

London's practices, unsuited to small and modest issues, reinforced the provincial and parochial nature of domestic industrial company formation before the 1890s. The local, at most regional, nature of subscriptions led to a resurgence of the principal stock exchanges, most of which had contracted to a considerable degree following the collapse of the railway mania. Some new ones appeared, as at Oldham, Newcastle and Dundee in the 1870s, although the last was connected with Scottish investment in

America, as was the expansion of the Edinburgh exchange. There was not
an overall pattern of growth in the membership of the exchanges as
table 5.5 shows.

Table 5.5 Membership of the provincial stock exchanges.[256]

	1852	1853	1873/4	1878	1881/2	1887
Aberdeen			8		10	17(3)
Birmingham	13	12	14		18	19(6)
Bristol	15	13	20		12	15(4)
Dublin	45	47	34		65	60
Dundee					8(2)	15
Edinburgh	21	15	15		43	48
Glasgow	42	45	31	101	124(8)	122
Hull	17	12	(7)		(7)	
Leeds	30	36	12		13(6)	13
Liverpool	159	156	90	130	151(8)	157
Manchester	83	85	57	75	69(8)	73(8)
Newcastle			(4)		8	
Sheffield	14	14	18		31	29(3)
Oldham					25	
York	15	11	(5)		(5)	

The figures given in brackets are the number of brokers outside the organized stock
exchange.

The membership of the London Exchange grew far more rapidly,
rising in nearly every year from 1,067 in 1852 to 2,408 in 1881/2 with the
rate of growth accelerating in the 1870s. London, through the telegraph,
the growth in the number of country brokers, and the increasing
preparedness of banks and solicitors to buy and sell shares for their
customers through halving the commission with a London broker, was
drawing more and more business from ever-widening areas. In 1873/4
there were approximately 143 country stockbrokers in the United
Kingdom, who like banks and solicitors dealt essentially through a
London broker; by 1881/2 their numbers had more than doubled,
reaching 323. Provincial brokers associated with local exchanges also
passed business, on a shared commission basis, on to London. For some
securities they were forced to, because of institutional factors; they were
more or less barred from dealing in 'the funds' since there were no

registration facilities for the transfer of Consols outside London and Dublin, despite the existence of provincial branches of the Bank of England.

Provincial stock exchanges found in local industrial shares, over which they held almost a monopoly, a major new source of business. These securities were held by investors within the vicinity of the exchange, while the exchange's dealings in them prevented them from acquiring a wider distribution outside the area served by the town or city in which the exchange was located. As one London broker commented, the Leeds Exchange dealt in 50 securities in the 1870s which were totally unknown in London.[257] Different provincial exchanges came to specialize in different types of shares. Manchester and Sheffield, partly as a result of Chadwick's activities, became the chief centres for iron company shares, while railway carriage and waggon works companies were quoted mainly at Birmingham, Sheffield and Bristol. Some of the larger industrial concerns, such as Ebbw Vale and Bolckow, Vaughan, were quoted on the London Exchange, but the main market in their shares remained Manchester.[258] The marketability of these securities was not just a function of their local availability but also the mode of trading on the provincial exchanges. London was unique in having a market created by jobbers and dealers; in the provinces all members of the exchanges were brokers. Transactions were carried out by an auction call-over system – the secretary of the exchange reading out at least once a day the list of securities dealt in on the exchange, with business in them taking place between brokers when they were named. In this way something of an active market in each security was maintained.[259] At some of the larger exchanges, such as Liverpool and Manchester, some broking firms did act also as jobbers, and others, once the telegraph linked markets from the late 1870s, acted as shunters, specializing in arbitrage business between markets, but this mainly involved domestic railway securities.[260]

Where a share did not have a local quotation, then it was more or less unmarketable. In some cases the company secretary provided a medium through which transactions could take place, a situation which apparently was found to be satisfactory:

> This medium is, in fact, sufficient for all the purposes of buying and selling the shares of small companies; and in the case of well-established and profitable concerns, there will generally be found a certain number of persons waiting to purchase shares as soon as any shall be offered.[261]

★

The joint stock company form of organization was adopted rapidly in only a few areas of industry before 1885, namely cotton spinning and iron, steel, and coal. Most companies, except with regard to cotton spinning, resulted from either the public or private conversions of existing partnerships. The reasons for turning a concern into a limited company are not easy to discern but in not a few instances the main motivation would appear to have been to stave off bankruptcy in some way or another. In the cotton industry the incorporated company form was adopted to establish large and efficient, by contemporary standards, new spinning mills, while in iron it provided a way to raise extra finance required for new investment, including the introduction of the Bessemer process. Most flotations were the products of either local or regional capital markets in which formal financial institutions played very little part. Firms did become limited concerns, but in the case of all private conversions their equity continued to be held by the original partners, while with most public formations the shares were usually held by the vendors and members of the local middle class. The only major exception was Chadwick's conversions, where a block of Mancunian capital was introduced into the finance of the iron, steel and coal industry and Manchester men took over the management of the firms involved, usually in conjunction with the vendors. The institutions of the metropolis would appear to have played not merely a passive but a negative role by allowing unscrupulous company promoters to have free rein. The ability of promoters to prey upon the companies which they were floating was assisted also by the permissive nature of company law and the government's unwillingness to intervene. As a result a successful company promotion tended to be generally a local affair, the product of interested parties, with the shares of the company remaining subsequently in local hands. This is the picture that the analysis in chapter 4 gives; it seems to be portrayed also in the promotion of the Oldham spinning companies; while in the case of Chadwick's conversions, the underlying process was a mixture of local finance, and the introduction of Mancunian capital and management, together with some extra-regional investment, usually from London and the West Midlands.

Appendix: Company files analysed in tables 5.1–4

Ashbury Railway Carriage and Iron	BT31/670/2846
Charles Cammell	930/1166c
Parkgate Iron	14355/1179c

Patent Nut and Bolt	958/1311c
Ebbw Vale	970/1386c
Bolckow, Vaughan	30734/1705c
Globe Cotton Spinning	30735/1796c
Manchester Carriage	1068/1932c
Yorkshire Engine	1101/2124c
Samuel Dewhurst	1114/2200c
Palmers Shipbuilding and Iron	31744/2298c
Ancoats Vale Rubber	1255/3028
Birchills Estate	14406/4155
Glandmore Mining	1571/5135
Earle's Shipbuilding and Engineering	1646/5695
Llynri, Tondu and Ogmore Coal and Iron	1718/6258
West Cumberland Iron and Steel	1766/6618
John Wood and Bros.	14445/6621
Pelsall Coal and Iron	1834/7152
Silkstone and Dodworth Coal and Iron	1848/7246
Laurie and Marner	1873/7435
Bouck and Co.	1891/7589
Stour Valley Coal and Iron	1907/7757

Notes

(Place of publication is London unless otherwise stated)

1 See I. C. R. Byatt, 'The British Electrical Industry, 1875–1914', unpublished D.Phil. thesis, University of Oxford, 1962.

2 The above is based upon an analysis of H. A. Shannon, 'The Limited Companies of 1866 and 1883', *Economic History Review*, IV, 1932–3.

3 *B.P.P.*, XXII, 1886, *Second Report of the Royal Commission on the Depression of Trade and Industry*, c-4715, evidence of S. Andrew, secretary of the Oldham Master Cotton Spinners Association, and S. Taylor, mill-owner, qq. 4330, 4580; A. Simpson, spinner, manufacturer and merchant, Preston, q. 5595; and J. Rawlinson, chartered accountant, Burnley, qq. 5798, 5895.

4 ibid., evidence of R. M. Reade, company director, and T. J. Richardson, qq. 7025, 7028.

5 ibid., evidence of W. C. Brocklehurst, silk manufacturer, Macclesfield, q. 7231.

6 ibid., evidence of C. E. Bonsfield, woollen manufacturer, Leeds, q. 6331.

7 ibid., evidence of Sir J. Behrens, q. 6791.

8 ibid., evidence of J. H. Walker, J. J. Weinberg and A. Henderson, the President of the Dundee Chamber of Commerce, q. 6207.

9 ibid., evidence of G. Gribble of Messrs Cook, Sons & Co., London, q. 4100.

10 ibid., see the evidence of Sir Lowthian Bell, President of the Iron Trade Association of Great Briatin, and T. E. Vickers of Vickers, Sons & Co. Ltd.

11 ibid., evidence of H. L. Muller of the Birmingham Chamber of Commerce, and W. Wyley Lond, both general merchants and exporters, qq. 1519–21, 1525.

12 ibid., evidence of S. Uttley, filesmith, R. Holmshaw, scissor grinder, W. F. Wardley, table knife blade forger, representatives of the Sheffield Trades Council, q. 1205.

13 *B.P.P.*, XXIII, 1886, *Final Report of the Royal Commission on the Depression of Trade and Industry*, c-4893, evidence of G. Chater, qq. 14, 407–8, 14495–7.

14 *B.P.P.*, XXI, 1886, *First Report of the Royal Commission on the Depression of Trade and Industry*, c-4621, q. 529.

15 *Second Report*, evidence of Muller and Lond, qq. 1678, 1827–8.

16 ibid., evidence of Vickers, qq. 3440–1; and see below, p. 125.

17 ibid., evidence of Gribble, q. 4101.

18 B. R. Mitchell, 'The Economic Development of the Inland Coalfields, 1870–1914', unpublished Ph.D. thesis, University of Cambridge, 1956, pp. 121–7.

19 Shannon, 'Limited Companies, 1866–83'.

20 J. H. Morris and L. J. Williams, '*The South Wales Coal Industry 1841–1875*, Cardiff, 1958, pp. 150–3.

21 See below, p. 137.

22 D. A. Farnie, 'The English Cotton Industry, 1850–1896', unpublished Ph.D. thesis, University of Manchester, 1953, pp. 231, 266–8.

23 R. E. Tyson, 'The Sun Mill Company Limited – a Study in Democratic Investment 1858–1959', unpublished M.A. thesis, University of Manchester, 1962, pp. 29–38, 64–85.

24 Data supplied to the author by D. A. Farnie, superceding the material in Farnie, op. cit.

25 J. R. T. Hughes, *Fluctuations in Trade, Industry and Finance. A Study of British Economic Development 1850–1860*, Oxford, 1960, pp. 99–100. On the minor cycle of 1858 to 1860, see W. W. Rostow, *British Economy of the Nineteenth Century*, 1948, pp. 36–9.

26 Farnie, op. cit., p. 235.

27 J. Mills, 'On the Post-Panic Period, 1866–70', *Transactions of the Manchester Statistical Society*, 1870/1, pp. 92, 94–5.

28 See A. J. Robertson, 'The Decline of the Scottish Cotton Industry, 1860–1914', *Business History*, XII, 1970.

29 Farnie, op. cit., pp. 267–334.

30 ibid., pp. 301–8.

31 ibid., pp. 191–4, 266.

32 ibid., pp. 255, 260–1, 274, 280.

33 ibid., pp. 262–3.

34 R. Smith, 'A History of the Lancashire Cotton Industry between the Years 1873 and 1896', unpublished Ph.D. thesis, University of Birmingham, 1954, pp. 185–91. See also R. Smith, 'An Oldham Limited Liability Company, 1875–1896', *Business History* IV, 1961.

35 Farnie, op. cit., p. 268.

36 W. A. Thomas, *The Provincial Stock Exchanges*, 1973, pp. 148–52.

37 *The Statist*, III, 1st March 1879, pp. 7–8.

38 Farnie, op. cit., pp. 274–7.

39 Smith, op. cit., pp. 147–8.

40 *The Statist*, IV, 28th August 1880.

41 T. Ellison, *The Cotton Trade of Great Britain*, 1886, pp. 303–4.

42 J. C. A., *Limited Liability and Cotton Spinning*. 'A Paper read…Before the Blackburn Mule Overlookers' Society, August 10th 1886' (?Blackburn, 1886), pp. 5–8. J. C. A. was a private spinner.

43 S. Andrew, Secretary to the Oldham Master Cotton Spinners and Manufacturers, *50 Years' Cotton Trade* (paper read before the Economic Section of the British Association, Manchester 1887; reprinted from the *Oldham Standard* of September 1887), Oldham, 1887, pp. 6–7.

44 *Second Report of the Royal Commission on the Depression of Trade and Industry*, evidence of S. Andrew and S. Taylor, qq. 4328–9, 4502.

45 ibid., evidence of G. Lord, q. 5271.

46 ibid., evidence of James Mawdsley, representative of the Amalgamated Association of Operative Cotton Spinners, qq. 5041–6, 5072–3, 5117; and A. Simpson, qq. 5506–8, 5590–1, 5609.

47 Smith, op. cit., p. 187.

48 *Second Report of the Royal Commission on the Depression of Trade and Industry*, evidence of Andrew and Taylor, qq. 4388, 4396, 4433, 4581; Mawdsley, q. 5047; Lord, q. 5274; Simpson, qq. 5514–5, 5556; J. Rawlinson, Chartered

Accountant, Burnley, q. 5813. *Third Report*, evidence of J. Lee of Tootal, Broadhurst, Lee & Co., q. 8012. See also *The Accountant*, 16th September 1886, pp. 579–80.

49 J. C. A., op. cit., p. 10.

50 *Second Report of the Royal Commission on the Depression of Trade and Industry*, evidence of Andrew, q. 4497.

51 *The Accountant* 16th October 1886, p. 579.

52 Farnie, op. cit., p. 322.

53 This is because it is difficult to establish an occupational structure of shareholdings with any certainty, and with regard to the point being made it is highly likely that some 'cotton' subscriptions are lost under 'merchant' and 'gentlemen' headings (see tables 5.2 and 5.4).

54 Obituary, Institute of Civil Engineers, *Minutes of Proceedings*, CXXIII, p. 449.

55 D. Chadwick, *Free Public Libraries and Museums*, 1857; *Working Men's Colleges*, 1859.

56 *A History of Cooper Brothers & Co. 1854 to 1954*, ?1954, p. 45.

57 D. Chadwick, *Poor Rates – Principles of Rating*, ?Salford, 1849.

58 D. Chadwick, *Public Baths and Wash-Houses*, Salford, 1854; *The Financial Aspect of the Sanitary Question*, Manchester, 1855; *On the Rate of Wages in 200 Trades and Branches of Labour in Manchester . . .*, 1860, originally read to the Statistical Society of London, 1859; *On the Best Means of Obtaining and Recording the Vital Statistics of Towns*, Manchester, 1861, originally read to the Manchester Statistical Society, 1861; *On the Progress of Manchester during the Twenty Years from 1840 to 1860*, Manchester, 1861, originally read to the Statistical Section of the British Association for the Advancement of Science, Manchester, 1861; *On the Social and Educational Statistics of Manchester and Salford*, Manchester, 1862, reprinted from the *Transactions of the Manchester Statistical Society*.

59 Obituary, *Manchester Guardian*, 20th September 1895, p. 6.

60 Obituary, I. C. E., *Minutes*, op. cit., p. 449.

61 See above, 59–64.

62 *On Water Meters*, 1854.

63 P. R. O., BT31/471/1829.

64 *History of Cooper Brothers*, op. cit., pp. 45–6.

65 D. Chadwick, *Inaugural Presidential Address*, Manchester Institute of Accountants, Manchester, 1871, p. 4.

66 See *The Times*, 16th August 1864, p. 4; 26th January 1865, p. 6.

67 On the MacKennas, see Sir M. Slattery, 'Troubled Time', *The Three Banks Review*, no. 95, 1972.

68 Obituary, I. C. E., *Minutes*, op. cit., p. 450.

69 Staveley Coal and Iron; John Brown; Charles Cammell; Parkgate Iron; Ebbw Vale; Sheepbridge Coal and Iron; Bolckow, Vaughan; Palmers Shipbuilding; Vickers, Son & Co.; and Birchills Estate.

70 Ashbury Railway Carriage; Patent Nut and Bolt; Manchester Carriage; and Yorkshire Engine.

71 Globe Cotton; and Samuel Dewhurst.

72 B.P.P., 1867, X, *Select Committee on Limited Liability Acts*, evidence of D. Chadwick, q. 838.

73 B.P.P., 1877, VIII, *Select Committee on the Companies Acts, 1862 and 1867*, evidence of D. Chadwick, q. 1994.

74 ibid., qq. 1972, 1973.

75 ibid., q. 1973.

76 ibid., qq. 2048–52, 2057–9, 2074.

77 ibid., qq. 2085, 2088, 2100, 2107.

78 P.R.O., BT31/30734/1705c; *The Times*, 22nd September 1872, p. 5.

79 P. R. O., BT31/30734/1705c.

80 P. R. O., BT31/31744/2298c.

81 *Select Committee on the Limited Liability Acts*, 1867, evidence of D. Chadwick, q. 2130.

82 P. R. O., BT31/670/2846.

83 Ashbury Railway Carriage.

84 In the case of Park Gate Iron, 5%.

85 *Select Committee on the Companies Acts*, 1877, evidence of D. Chadwick, q. 1998.

86 C. Erickson, *British Industrialists. Steel and Hosiery 1850–1950*, 1959, pp. 196–7.

87 B. P. P., 1877 VIII, *Select Committee on the Companies Acts, 1862 and 1867*, evidence of D. Chadwick, q. 2041.

88 *The Times*, 29th June 1864, p. 12.

89 *The Economist*, 27th August 1864.

90 *The Times*, 20th February 1864, p. 10; 16th August 1864, p. 4; 26th January

1865, p. 6; 20th May 1865, p. 10; 20th July 1865, p. 7.

90a J. D. Scott, *Vickers A History*, 1962, p. 16.

91 Number of shareholdings =
    39.27 + 0.0001 nominal capital
    r = 0.8299;   r² = 0.6888
    16 observations.

92 Number of shareholdings =
    29.6414 + 0.0005 subscribed capital
    r = 0.9650;   r² = 0.9312
    12 observations.

93 See above, pp. 59–61; in addition to Chadwick and Newmarch, H. D. Pochin also gave evidence to the 1867 Select Committee.

94 *Select Committee on Limited Liability Acts*, 1867, qq. 858, 868.

95 A. Birch, *Economic History of the British Iron and Steel Industry 1784–1879*, 1967, p. 207.

96 It was only possible to look at the occupational composition of shareholders in the case of ten companies.

97 e.g. Patent Nut and Bolt in the case of the West Midlands, Bolckow Vaughan and Palmer in the case of the North, Charles Cammell and Yorkshire Engine with regard to Yorkshire and Humberside.

98 *Select Committee on the Limited Liability Acts*, 1867, evidence of H. D. Pochin, q. 2342.

99 *Chadwick's Investment Circular*, 3rd September 1870, p. 7.

100 D. Chadwick, *Is Profit-Sharing Desirable? In What Trades is it Practicable?*, paper read at a meeting of the Dulwich Eclectic Club, 1890, p. 7.

101 C. H. Lee, *A Cotton Enterprise 1795–1840. A History of M'Connel & Kennedy, Fine Cotton Spinners*, Manchester, 1972, p. 108.

102 R. Boyson, *The Ashworth Cotton Enterprise*, Oxford, 1970.

103 See the Spackman lists of new issues, published in the *Commercial History and Review*, 1863–6, supplements to *The Economist*, 20th February 1864; 11th March 1865; 10th March 1866; 9th March 1867.

104 *The Bankers' Magazine*, 1862, p. 537.

105 On the 1860s financial boom, see P. L. Cottrell, 'Investment Banking in England 1856–1882. Case Study of the International Financial Society', un-

published Ph.D. thesis, University of Hull, 1974, pp. 122–7.

106 G. R. Hawke, *Railways and Economic Growth in England and Wales, 1840–1870*, 1970, pp. 220–1, 209.

107 B. R. Mitchell with P. Deane, *Abstract of British Historical Statistics*, Cambridge, 1971, pp. 220–2.

108 Calculated from ibid., p. 283.

109 ibid., pp. 483, 493.

110 Hughes, op. cit., p. 141.

111 Charles Cammell & Co. Ltd, *Cyclops Steel and Iron Works, Sheffield England*, Sheffield, 1899, pp. 1–7; Thomas Firth & John Brown Ltd., *100 Years in Steel. Firth-Brown Centenary 1837–1937*, Sheffield, 1937, pp. 6, 30, 43; Birch, op. cit., pp. 310, 312–13, 327; Erickson, op. cit., pp. 144–5, 162–3; Scott, op. cit., pp. 11, 13, 16–17.

112 P. R. O., BT31/14355/1179C.

113 *Engineering*, 1890, p. 174; 'The Story of the Park Gate Iron & Steel Co. Ltd., 1823–1966', *British Industry and Commerce*, Sheffield edition, 1966, pp. 4–5.

114 *The Times*, 20th May 1865.

115 P. R. O., BT31/1101/2124C.

116 J. W. Lowe, *British Steam Locomotive Builders*, 1972.

117 P. R. O., BT31/958/1311C.

118 W. F. Crick and J. E. Wadsworth, *A Hundred Years of Joint Stock Banking*, 3rd edn, 1958, pp. 76–7.

119 P. R. O., BT31/14406/4155. The company had been hit badly by the post-1857 slump, while other Black Country works failed in the early 1860s and after the 1866 crisis. See Birch, op. cit., p. 156.

120 A. Raistrick, *Dynasty of Iron Founders. The Darbys and Coalbrookdale*, 1958, p. 274; Erickson, op. cit., pp. 13, 150–1.

121 *The Times*, 29th June 1864, p. 12.

122 Sir H. Bessemer, *An Autobiography*, 1905, pp. 296–302. On details of the dispute see Birch, op. cit., p. 326; Erickson, op. cit., p. 142.

123 BT31/33755/3956C; see also Erickson, op. cit., p. 151.

124 ibid., pp. 13, 154–5.

125 Birch, op. cit., pp. 332–3.

126 Hughes, op. cit., p. 154.

127 Birch, op. cit., p. 335; D. L. Burn, *The Economic History of Steelmaking 1867–1939*, Cambridge, 1940, reprinted 1961, p. 23.

128 Erickson, op. cit., pp. 154–5.
129 Speech by C. M. Palmer, First Annual General Meeting of Shareholders, quoted in *Fortunes Made in Business*.
130 D. Dougan, *The History of North East Shipbuilding*, 1968, p. 41; S. Pollard, *The Economic History of Shipbuilding 1870–1914*, unpublished Ph.D. thesis, University of London, 1951, pp. 80–1.
131 Pollard, op. cit., pp. 63–4; see above, pp. 142–3.
132 Farnie states that this company was promoted and financed by the Manchester Stock Exchange (op. cit., p. 234), but an examination of its initial shareholders does not support this (see P.R.O., BT31/303735/17960).
133 *Select Committee on Companies Acts, 1862 and 1867*, 1877, appendix 1.
134 *The Bankers' Magazine*, 1866, pp. 1324–5; *The Economist*, 26th January 1867; *Chadwick's Investment Circular*, 3rd August 1870, p. 2, and 5th September 1873, p. 210; *The Times*, 18th August 1873, p. 6. On the Bank of London and the Consolidated Bank, see T. E. Gregory, *The Westminister Bank through a Century*, 1936, II, pp. 51–3, 58–62; on the Preston Bank see Crick and Wadsworth, op. cit., pp. 150–1; neither of these two secondary sources mention Chadwick's role. The position of the Preston Bank is duscussed below.
135 *The Economist*, 9th August 1870, p. 472.
136 J. M. Bellamy, 'A Hull Shipbuilding Firm. The History of C. & W. Earle and Earle's Shipbuilding and Engineering Co. Ltd.', *Business History*, VI, 1963, p. 32.
137 P.R.O., BT31/1848/7246.
138 e.g. Llynri, Tondu and Ogmore Coal and Iron; West Cumberland Iron and Steel; John Wood and Brothers; Pelsall Coal and Iron; Bouck & Co. Ltd.; and Stour Valley Coal and Iron.
139 A. R. Griffin, *Mining in the East Midlands 1550–1947*, 1971, p. 100.
140 Mitchell with Deane, op. cit., p. 493.
141 Burn, op. cit., pp. 255–6.
142 D. Chadwick, *Blochairn Iron Company, Limited, Smith v. Chadwick Three Reports on this Case*, n.d., ?Manchester, 1882. For details of the prospectus, see *The Times*, 27th May 1873, p. 12, and *Chadwick's Investment Circular*, June 1873, p. 200.

143 *The Times*, 21st September 1872, p. 6.
144 A. K. Cairncross, *Home and Foreign Investment 1870–1913*, 1953, p. 100.
145 See Cottrell, op. cit.
146 30 & 31 Vict. c. 131, s. 38; see above, p. 62.
147 See W. F. Finlason, *Liabilities of Promoters of Companies, Report of Twycross v. Grant*, 1877; *Twycross v. Grant and others Speech of Albert Grant Esq.*, 1876.
148 Benhar Coal Co.; Llynri, Tondu & Ogmore Coal and Iron; West Cumberland Iron and Steel; Silkstone and Dodworth Coal and Iron; Blochairn Iron.
149 See *The Times*, 19th January 1872, p. 7; 10th May 1872, p. 12; 21st September 1872, p. 6; 29th April 1873, p. 11; 27th May 1873, p. 12.
150 Number of shareholdings =
    $19.56 + 0.0005$ nominal capital
    $r = 0.8524$; $r^2 = 0.7266$
    10 observations.
151 Number of shareholdings =
    $113.26 + 0.0002$ paid-up capital
    $r = 0.7409$; $r^2 = 0.5489$
    10 observations.
152 It was only possible to look at the occupational composition of the shareholders of nine companies.
153 While this tentative conclusion has considerable supporting evidence, it is not borne out by the regression evidence which itself is contradictory, with shareholding rising in the 1870s at less than half the rate (with respect to subscribed capital) accorded for the 1860s.
154 *Commercial History and Review of 1870*, p. 1, supplement to *The Economist*, 11th March 1871.
155 See R. Giffen, *Essays in Finance, First Series*, reprinted 1880, pp. 109–10.
156 Mitchell with Deane, op. cit., pp. 315–26.
157 C. H. Feinstein, *National Income, Expenditure and Output of the United Kingdom 1855–1965*, Cambridge, 1972, table 85.
158 Mitchell with Deane, op. cit., pp. 483–93.
159 A. G. Kenwood, 'Capital Investment in North Eastern England, 1800–1913', unpublished Ph.D. thesis, University of London, 1962, p. 448.
160 *Commercial History and Review of 1870*.

p. 43, and *The Economist*, 15th July 1871, p. 837.

161 See *The Times*, 30th December 1871, p. 4; 30th December 1872, p. 5; 31st December 1873, p. 4; 31st December 1874, p. 6.

162 ibid., 17th May 1871, p. 10.

163 *Chadwick's Investment Circular*, June 1873, p. 198; November 1873, p. 220.

164 Birch, op. cit., p. 343; Erickson, op. cit., pp. 17, 153.

165 See below, pp. 223–8.

166 Birch, op. cit., p. 169.

167 J. P. Addis, 'The Heavy Iron and Steel Industry in South Wales 1870–1950', unpublished Ph.D. thesis, University of Wales, Aberystwyth, 1957, pp. 7–8, 37, appendix E; Burn, op. cit., p. 29, n. 5.

168 See above, p. 63.

169 Burns, op. cit., p. 253.

170 *The Times*, 10th March 1873, p. 6.

171 ibid., 3rd November 1873, p. 6.

172 *Chadwick's Investment Circular*, June 1874, p. 248.

173 ibid., May 1875, p. 196; see also *The Times*, 29th April 1873, p. 7.

174 *The Times*, 20th December 1873, p. 6.

175 ibid., 19th January 1872, p. 7.

176 ibid., 23rd September 1872, p. 5.

177 ibid., 12th September 1873, p. 7.

178 *Chadwick's Investment Circular*, 8th August 1874, p. 255.

179 ibid., 9th March 1874.

180 ibid., 23rd February 1875.

181 See above, p. 62.

182 See above, pp. 64, 129–30.

183 *History of Cooper Brothers*, op. cit., p. 46.

184 Mellors Basden papers, Indenture (microfilm copy, Library, University of Hull).

185 See M. C. Reed, *Investment in Railways in Britain, 1820–1844*, 1975.

186 Kenwood, op. cit., p. 211.

187 Staffordshire County Record Office, Stafford, D695/8/12/1.

188 Birch, op. cit., p. 208.

189 J. B. Jeffreys, 'Trends in Business Organisation in Great Britain since 1856 . . .', unpublished Ph.D. thesis, University of London, 1938, p. 75.

190 A. Essex-Crosby, 'Joint Stock Companies in Great Britain, 1890–1930', unpublished M.Comm. thesis, University of London, 1938, p. 220.

191 See B. L. Anderson and P. L. Cottrell, 'Another Victorian Capital Market: a Study of Banking and Bank Investors on Merseyside', *Economic History Review*, 2nd series, XXVIII, 1975.

192 See below, p. 181.

193 University of Hull Library: International Financial Society, Minutes of Committee Meetings (hereafter referred to as I. C.), 27th March 1865.

194 University of Hull Library: International Financial Society, Minutes of Board Meetings, (hereafter referred to as I. B.), 21st July 1863.

195 ibid., 3rd March 1864.

196 ibid., 15th July 1864.

197 ibid., 27th July 1865.

198 ibid., 10th October 1872.

199 P. R. O., BT31/1268/3223.

200 Subsequently the London and Glasgow Engineering and Iron Ship Company; see P.R.O., BT31/1935b/1207c.

201 *The Economist*, 2nd April 1864, p. 424.

202 *The Economist*, 30th April 1864, p. 552; see also Bellamy, op. cit., p. 29.

203 P. R. O., BT31/945/1249C.

204 See below, p. 149.

205 BT31/988/1489C.

206 BT31/1092/2073C; *The Economist*, 29th April 1865, p. 524.

207 BT31/725/151C.

208 *The Economist*, 24th November 1866, p. 1361.

209 *The Economist*, 20th August 1864, p. 1057; 28th August 1864, p. 1104; *The Bankers' Magazine*, 1865, p. 202; P. R. O., BT31/1000/1551C.

210 *The Economist*, 30th April 1864, p. 563; *The Bankers' Magazine*, 1865, pp. 308m, 351; P. R. O., BT31/942/1232C.

211 I. B., 16th November 1871.

212 ibid. 20th March 1873; 1st May 1873; I. C., 5th May 1873.

213 *The Bankers' Magazine*, 1865, p. 966.

214 See W. P. Smith (ed.), *The Railway, Banking, Mining, Insurance and Commercial Almanack for 1867*, 1867, p. 85; *The Investors' Guardian Almanack for 1869*, 1869, p. 14.

215 *The Economist*, 17th June 1865, p. 726.

216 *The London Banks, Credit, Discount and Finance Companies*, 1869, p. 40; *The Banking Almanac . . . for 1873*, p. 154; *The Banking Almanac . . . for 1874*, p. 224.

217 *United Kingdom Stock and Share-brokers' Directory 1881/2*, p. 92.

218 *B. P. P.*, 1878, *Royal Commission on the Stock Exchange*, q. 2038.
219 See O. R. Hobson, 'The Financial Press', *Lloyds Bank Limited Monthly Review*, January 1934, pp. 3–4; N. J. Grieser, 'The British Investor and his Sources of information', unpublished M.Sc.(Econ.) thesis, University of London, 1940, pp. 119–27.
220 Jaycee, *Public Companies from the Cradle to the Grave*, 1883, pp. 19, 25.
221 A. Packer, *How the Public are Plundered by Promoters of Companies, Foreign States, Syndicates and Money-Lenders . . .*, 1878, pp. 16–17.
222 Jaycee, op. cit., p. 19.
223 See above, p. 70, and D. Finnie, *Capital Underwriting*, 1934, p. 7.
224 *The Bankers' Magazine*, 1860, p. 27.
225 *Royal Commission on the Stock Exchange*, 1878, q. 4022.
226 ibid., q. 4017.
227 ibid., q. 4041.
228 See the cases of the City of Moscow Gas Company and the Australian and Eastern Navigation Company as given in evidence to the *Royal Commission on the Stock Exchange*, 1878.
229 ibid., q. 2866.
230 ibid., qq. 1351, 1449.
231 ibid., qq. 1955, 2058, 7132, 7139, 7167.
232 ibid., q. 2866.
233 ibid., q. 2494.
234 *Fenn on the Funds*, 1867, p. 126, Rules 122, 123.
235 E. C. Maddison, *On the Stock Exchange*, 1877, p. 236.
236 *The Bankers' Magazine*, 1864, p. 309.
237 *Royal Commission on the Stock Exchange*, 1878, appendix V, p. 368.
238 ibid., q. 4862.
239 ibid., q. 1526.
240 *The Bankers' Magazine*, 1878, p. 837.
241 *The Economist*, 8th March 1877.
242 Hansard, 3rd series, CCXXXII, 1877, p. 236.
243 *Royal Commission on the Stock Exchange*, 1878, qq. 3436, 4783.
244 ibid., q. 3454.
245 ibid., qq. 495, 501, 1187, 2817.
246 W. Gutteridge & Co., Sworn Brokers, *Speculation and Investment in Stocks and Shares with a Minimum Risk*, 1882, p. 4; W. W. Duncan & Co., *Duncan on Investment and Speculation in Stocks and Shares*, 1894.
247 *The Investment Journal*, May 1863, p. 64.
248 *The Economist*, 6th April 1865.
249 ibid., 6th October 1866, p. 1164.
250 *The Joint Stock Monthly Record*.
251 *The Economist*, 10th January 1880, p. 42; 24th January 1880, p. 98; 14th February 1880, p. 188; *The Statist*, 8th May 1880, p. 220.
252 *The Statist*, 5th July 1879, p. 395.
253 E. V. Morgan and W. A. Thomas, *The Stock Exchange. Its History and Functions*, 1962, pp. 140–1.
254 Frances Levien, Secretary to the Committee for General Purposes, *Rules and Regulations for the Conduct of Business on the Stock Exchange*, 1888, p. 63, Rule 124.
255 M. Edelstein, 'Rigidity and Bias in the British Capital Market 1870–1913' in D. N. McCloskey (ed.) *Essays on a Mature Economy. Britain after 1840*, 1971.
256 The table is compiled from *Ralph's Stock and Share Brokers' Dictionary*, 1852/3; *Stockbrokers' Directory of Great Britain and Ireland*, 1873/4; Minutes of Evidence, *Royal Commission*, 1878, qq. 8095, 7882, 8017; *United Kingdom Stock and Sharebrokers' Directory*, 1881/2; and *Phillips' Investors' Annual*.
257 *Royal Commission on the Stock Exchange*, 1878, q. 2968.
258 Thomas, op. cit., pp. 122–4.
259 *Royal Commission on the Stock Exchange*, 1878, qq. 7891–2; q. 8022; q. 811.
260 Thomas, op. cit., pp. 73–4, 88–90.
261 Maddison, op. cit., pp. 235–6.

6 Private companies and public combines 1885–1914

The annual number of new limited companies registered in England increased secularly at a faster rate from the 1880s.[1] It is difficult to establish when this new trend set in because of institutional factors, since both the trend during the 1890s and the 1900s and the cyclical deviations from it were distorted to a significant degree by the impending major reform of company law. It was evident to those who sought to establish new companies in the 1890s that company formations in future would be more strictly regulated once the law was reformed. This was clear from the government bills of 1888 and 1895 and the considerations of both the Davey Committee of 1895 and the House of Lords Committees of the second half of the 1890s which reviewed the latter bill.[2] Consequently there was a widespread attempt during the 1890s to take advantage of the permissive legislation of 1862 while it was still available. Such forestalling registrations magnified both the cyclical upswing in registrations of the 1890s and the following cyclical downswing of the 1900s. This distorted the cyclical movement to such an extent that the pattern of regular fluctuations in annual registrations, each with a length of eight to nine years, was broken after the 1890s. The next cyclical peak in company registrations following the upper turning point of 1898 did not occur in 1906 but in 1910.

One of the main reasons for the faster growth in the annual number of new company registrations was the substantial increase in the number of private company formations, concerns which wished to limit their liability rather than raise funds from the public. Between a third and a fifth of all companies registered in 1890 were private and by 1914 the proportion had increased to nearly four-fifths.[3] As a result 46,428 out of the 63,969 limited companies on the register in 1915 were private concerns. The main driving force was the growing realization of the dangers of unlimited liability. These had been revealed spectacularly in the crash of the City of Glasgow bank in 1878, and the lessons learnt then were reinforced by the experience of the severe cyclical slumps of the mid-1880s and the early 1890s. One of the effects of the 'Great Depression' of the last quarter of the nineteenth century was the general acceptance of the limited company as the unit of business organization. This was aided by the very belated legal recognition of the existence of the private limited company in the legislation of 1900 and 1907. The spread of the take-up of the private limited company as the method of constituting firms is revealed in two trends in the capital structure of new registrations of limited companies. First was the growth in small companies, those with capital of less than £5,000; these constituted 20% of registrations in 1897 and 33% of registrations by 1901.[4] Consequently the average nominal capital of all existing companies fell from £54,000 in 1885 to £40,744 in 1915.[5] Second was the increasing proportion of the paid-up capital of newly registered companies which went to their vendors: the percentage rose from an annual average of 43.2% (1885–9) to 69.8% (1900–4) but fell back to 58.8% (1910–14).[6]

While the growing spread in the use of limited liability during the thirty years before the First World War was essentially due to private partnerships turning themselves quietly into private limited companies, the number of public companies did increase. However, the growth in their numbers was not comparable with the overall increase in the number of limited companies. The number of public companies, defined as those listed in *Burdett*, increased by a multiple of only 3.36 between 1885 and 1915, whereas all companies increased by a multiple of 7.16. One significant change in the type of public company established was the appearance from the late 1880s of multi-unit companies, often the product of the simultaneous conversion of a number of private companies into one public company. These multi-firm mergers occurred mainly in the finishing branches of the textile industry and some sections of the chemical industry, particularly salt production and the manufacture of alkalis by the Leblanc process.[7] Generally these companies were formed as defensive attempts by producers to restrict competition, in order to shore up prices and make excess capacity within their industries profitable. As such, part of the motive behind the creation of some public companies was similar to that which spurred the formation of private limited concerns. Both types of new limited companies were passive, if not negative responses to the increasing winds of competition, both at home and overseas, which blew with greater and greater force after the 1870s.

Although the number of public companies grew, this development did not lead to 'outside' shareholders gaining control of their assets. The equity, which carried voting rights, remained generally in the hands of their vendors whereas extra funds were raised at the time of conversions, or subsequently, by the issues of either preference shares or debentures. Such securities suited both the 'outside' investor and the management group behind the public company. The investor gained through having a guaranteed return and had, in the case of the debenture, a security, the principal value of which appreciated with the fall in prices, a marked feature of the last 30 years of the nineteenth century. These gains can be shown clearly if one considers what would have happened had the investor taken up ordinary shares. First, he would not have had a cyclical stable return on his investment, because the level of dividends would have fluctuated generally over the course of the trade cycle. Investors came to realize the dangers of the situation as a result of their experience with the ordinary shares of industrial companies which they had bought during the boom of the first half of the 1870s. They were simply very risky securities to hold.[8] Second, the situation for the holders of ordinary shares was made worse with the long-term decline in the profitability of English industry between the mid-1870s and the mid-1890s. However, with a preference share, particularly a cumulative preference share, the holder had a definite claim to a prescribed level of any profits that a company made. By issuing such non-voting securities to 'outside' investors, the management group of a converted company gained an advantage because they could continue to control it in an unfettered way and thus were in the same position as the shareholders of a private limited company. Management groups of public companies had an additional benefit in that loan capital and preference shares to a certain extent introduced an element of gearing into the capital structure of the companies from which the management groups, as the holders of the ordinary shares, benefited during periods of prosperity. However, during slumps the burden of fixed charges, incurred through the creation of such securities, could be onerous. In 1895 preference shares constituted 22.46% of the aggregate paid-up share capital of all companies listed in *Burdett*, while the value of debentures was equal to 40.58% of the aggregate paid-up share capital; in 1915 the respective percentages were 30.08% and 40.74%.[9] Debentures grew in importance during the period of falling prices in the 1880s and 1890s whereas, once inflationary forces set in from the mid-1890s, there was an overall shift in new public issues from debentures to preference shares.

Debentures were not a 'new' instrument with which to raise capital in the 1880s and 1890s; the 'general' investor had become accustomed to them during the first half of the nineteenth century as a result of issues by first the canal and then the railway companies. In the 1860s and 1870s they had been floated by financial concerns and, to a limited extent, by some of the converted iron, steel, and coal companies in order, in the case of the last, both to pay vendors and raise additional 'outside' capital. In the 1880s, borrowing through debentures became popular with all types of companies and they had a number of advantages over other types of securities. First, unlike shares, they could be issued legally at a discount and flotations consequently could be underwritten. Second, they were more secure and cheaper than advances from a bank, while in the long run they could either be liquidated or renewed, possibly on more favourable terms. Third, debentures were more flexible instruments than mortgages since they could be secured on a floating charge on even future assets and were easier to transfer.

The term of debentures lengthened from the late 1860s, a move to longer maturities which arose initially out of the financial difficulties faced by the domestic railway companies after the 1866 crisis.[10] With lengthening maturities, debentures came to be ranked alongside other long dated or perpetual fixed stock such as Consols, but especially colonial government bonds and domestic local authority stock. The yields on all these bonds fell during the 1870s and 1880s as their price rose, a consequence of such securities being bought not only by 'rentier' investors but also by insurance companies, banks and trustees who were seeking outlets that gave a greater income than either Consols or mortgages.[11] Nash commented in 1880, looking back over the past decade:

> In ten years ... Colonial Debentures have, not only as a class, but individually and without exception yielded a handsome return to all investors therein. But, at the same time, they had at length arrived at a position in the market which we can safely affirm will preclude them from yielding any such percentage of profit in future ... Still, similar diminutions of prospective profits can be urged in respect to Consols, railway debentures and preference stocks, and in almost all other classes of investments with fixed guaranteed dividends ... Foreign Government stocks and Colonial Government Debentures have, as has been shown, gradually increased with age in market estimation, but in Home Railways the bound has been surprising.[12]

Capital appreciation reduced yields, and advantage was taken of this situation in the 1880s by the government to reduce 3% Consols to $2\frac{1}{2}\%$. High-class debentures and other stocks were creamed off the market by financial institutions as they diversified their portfolios, and the yield on them fell as they appreciated. By the mid-1880s the yield on railway debenture stock had fallen to below $3\frac{1}{2}\%$ while from 1881 the prices of the various Consols rose and remained above par.[13] Yields continued to fall throughout the rest of the 1880s, through the 1890s, and did not start rising on railway debentures until after the turn of the century. This market situation pushed investors towards issues of other types of debentures which were more speculative, such as those made by investment trusts[14] and industrial companies.

The use of debentures fell away after 1900 as the yields on nearly comparable securities, particularly domestic railway ordinary stocks, rose. The growing lack of a market edge was not the only reason for the decline in the issue of industrial debentures. It became evident by the turn of the century to both investors and company directors that there were limits to the extent to which debentures could be issued. Brewery companies, in particular, were faced with a heavy burden of fixed charges as a result of debenture issues. Added to this was a growing distrust amongst the public of debentures secured on floating charges and taken up in the main by vendors of both public and private companies in order to remove assets out of the reach of creditors.[15]

Public issues of debentures were replaced gradually by issues of preference shares from the mid-1890s, although there had been a steady increase in the use of preference shares from the mid-1880s. Alongside preference shares appeared founders' shares. These were issued from the mid-1880s, initially to inventors and patentees but increasingly to promoters and underwriters. Whereas preference shares were used to attract 'rentier' savings, founders' shares, which enjoyed a high deferred dividend, came to be used to pay those who aided company flotations and company managers. Preference shares, as with debentures, had been issued earlier by the railway and canal companies, but with industrial concerns they were transformed into cumulative and participating shares. Their main use, as with debentures, was to ensure for both public and private companies that control was retained by the holders of the ordinary shares, usually the vendors and their associates. Founders' shares were a new innovation and led to a considerable amount of resentment because they received dividends out of all proportion to any 'work' done by their holders. This hostility caused them to be renamed as deferred shares in the years before the First World War, but their purpose was not altered: they remained a device to reward very generously specific groups of individuals, usually either company midwives or management employees.[16]

Whereas debentures and preference shares were used to raise 'outside' capital and were aimed in particular to attract 'rentier' savings, public issues of ordinary shares were generally infrequent. The £1 ordinary share became very common in the 1890s, and shares of even lower denomination appeared, usually issued by speculative concerns such as mining companies. Older companies took advantage of the 1867 Act to subdivide £10 and £20 shares, into £1 or £5 shares, especially during the 1890s.[17] Both ordinary and preference shares from the 1890s were issued in a fully paid-up form. In 1895 the average unpaid liability on shares listed in *Burdett* was still 33.2% but by 1915 unpaid liability, except in the case of financial and insurance shares, had ceased to exist.[18]

The type of securities issued by public companies changed completely during the 30 years before the First World War. In 1884 only 227 out of the 1,585 public companies listed in *Burdett* had more than one class of capital but by 1915, 75% of all public coal, iron, and steel companies had issued both preference shares and debentures, 75% of 'other' public commercial and industrial companies had issued preference capital, and 50% of this latter group had issued debentures.[19] In the years before 1914 domestic public joint stock companies issued more than 75% of their new capital in fixed-charge securities. With these issues, working capital and additional capital for development were raised from the public, particularly from investors who desired a stable return on their investments. Ordinary shares remained generally with the original proprietors, who took them in payment for the fixed assets and goodwill that they made over to the new limited concerns. Essex-Crosby has estimated that in 1915 the ordinary share capital of 42 out of 348 brewery companies, 25 out of 342 coal, iron and steel companies, and 142 out of 1,922 other commercial and industrial concerns listed in *Burdett*, was still entirely in private hands, and this was despite a growth in the average capital of the public company between 1885 and 1915.[20]

★

While the limited company had become almost the normal form of enterprise in English manufacturing industry by 1914, it is only possible, at present, to trace and delineate the spread of the public company after 1885.[21] Although all new company registrations have a marked cyclical pattern, the successful formation of public companies was particularly dependent upon general economic and financial conditions. Only an outstanding concern could be floated to the public during the downswing phase of the trade cycle, whereas during booms there could be competing claims for subscriptions[22] and in the late 1880s and after 1906 domestic issues had to contest with overseas flotations for subscriptions from the public. However, the Baring crisis of 1890, the Wall Street panic of 1893, and the end of the land boom in Australia were a series of shocks of sufficient magnitude to shake confidence in nearly all foreign securities for over a decade and as a result overseas lending fell from a peak in 1889/90. Consequently, only foreign concerns such as very speculative South African and Western Australian mining companies were able to elicit any interest from the most adventurous of investors in the financial boom of the second half of the 1890s, with the result that domestic issues during this decade had almost a complete monopoly of the market. This was one factor which was responsible for the dominance of domestic issues in the London, as well as the provincial markets, during the late 1890s. But for some types of issues, particularly those of brewery companies, the origins of their increased appeals to the public for funds lay in the second half of the 1880s, a period of high overseas lending.

In 1860 there were about 12 limited breweries, of which about half had their shares quoted on the London Stock Exchange.[23] The number of quoted breweries had increased to 18 by 1885 but then, following the public flotation of Arthur Guinness in October 1886, there was a major wave of brewery conversions which continued until the early 1900s, so that by 1906 307 brewery companies were listed in *Burdett*.[24] Breweries became public limited companies for two main reasons. First, with the work of Pasteur and Hansen in the 1870s, brewing became a more scientific process, which increased the optimum size of the brewery as did the development of bottling in the 1880s. However, although changes in technology may have required greater inputs of capital, beyond the internal resources of firms, the most acute problem that breweries faced from the 1870s was the need for assured market outlets. In 1869 the control of licences was returned to the local magistrates and, with the growth of the temperance movement during the 1870s, this led to a restriction in the availability of public houses. Between 1886 and 1914 the number of 'on'-licences in England and Wales fell from 104,792 to 88,445 and such onerous regulation increased the brewers' concern for, and financial involvement with, the retail trade. The growing shortage of licences resulted in sharply rising values of public houses. This increase in property values made it more difficult for publicans to buy houses without financial assistance from brewers. When given, such aid usually meant that the publican sold only the products of the brewery which was accommodating him, and the further expansion of tied houses from the

1870s led other breweries, which did not have assured outlets, to buy retail property in order to prevent their exclusion from the market. It has been established that tied property as a percentage of total licences increased from 70% in 1886 to 95% in 1913. Some of this property was acquired through either local amalgamations or metropolitan brewers taking over small country breweries.[25] It was the expansion in the number of tied houses which led to most brewers (except Guinness) coming to the capital market in order to finance their property buying through issues of debentures and preference shares.

The Guinness flotation was very large, £6m., comparable to any overseas issue, it was handled by a premier merchant bank, Barings, and it was oversubscribed many times.[26] The success of the issue was like the firing of a starting pistol; by November 1890, 86 other brewery companies had appealed to the public for funds. Most of these were very large concerns, like the Burton breweries of Bass; Ind Coope, and Allsopps Meux, Whitbread; and Truman Hanbury Buxton, the conversions of which generated securities comparable in volume to overseas flotations. Allsopps had faced difficulties in selling beer because of the further growth of tied houses, while the conversion of Whitbreads, which had 60 licensed houses, may have been prompted in 1889 by the death of one of its senior partners, Viscount Eversley.[27] Generally when breweries went public, both in the 1880s and the 1890s, the ordinary shares were held by the original family proprietors. In the case of Truman Hanbury Buxton, the 12 partners, representing the three families involved, took up all the ordinary capital of £1.215m. and £0.4m. of the debentures, with only the balance of the latter, £0.8m., being issued to the public.[28]

Glyn, Mills, the London private bank, which had become a joint stock concern in 1885 and which had undertaken investment business since the 1860s,[29] played a significant role in brewery flotations of the 1880s. Glyns carried out the registration and transfer of the Guinness stock for a commission of £250 per £m. except that none was charged on the £0.8m. out of the £6m. held by Sir E. C. Guinness.[30] In the cases of the Reid and Bass flotations, Glyns acted as the issuing house, though for Bass issue in conjunction with S. W. S. Scott & Co., bankers, and both the issues were made by tender. The Reid brewery was incorporated with a capital of £2m.; the 700 ordinary shares of £1,000 each were taken by the former partners, while £0.5m. out of £700,000 5% preference stock and £0.5m. out of £600,000 4% mortgage debenture stock was issued to the public. The flotation was a major success with applications for £1,197,000 debentures and £1,706,000 preference stock being received from the public. In the case of the debentures, tenders at and above £103 11s. per £100 were allotted in full, while those at £103 10s. received a third of the amount applied for; the average issue price being £103 13s. 7d. An even higher average price was obtained for the preference stock, £112 15s. 0d., with tenders above £112 1s. being allotted in full. As a result of the considerable public over-subscription, Reids received a premium of £63,970. Glyns charged a commission of 1% of the tender price of the stock allotted, plus ¼% on the nominal amount of the stock, but paid the expenses of printing and brokerage.[31] Bass had become a private limited company in 1880, and in 1888 Glyns issued their debenture stock, recommending that a flotation of preference shares be delayed because

> at present the recent issue of Preferred shares of Breweries such as Combe & Reid are partly in the hands of dealers. When they have been absorbed by the public it is probable that the price will rise as has been the case with Guinness & Co., and that would be a suitable time to offer your stock *by tender*, as there would then be a bona fide public demand for it.[32]

Prices did rise, the par value of the issued shares of all breweries being about £50m. in November 1890, while their market valuation was over £70m.[33]

The second wave of brewery flotations, most of which were amalgamated smaller concerns such as Barclay & Co., occurred during the home boom of the 1890s. Between 1890 and 1899 £86m. of brewery debentures and preference shares was offered to the public.[34] The public absorption of such securities began in 1894; new issues for breweries and distilleries in that year amounted to £4,297,000, with about the same volume being issued the following year. In 1896, with the financial boom well underway, issues shot up to £18,162,000 and stayed at that level for two years before falling to £8.5m. in 1899.[35] The Watney, Combe, Reid amalgamation accounted for £15m. of the brewery securities issued in 1898, with its authorized share capital of £9m., of which £8,710,820 was issued in 5% preference shares, 4% preferred ordinary shares, and deferred ordinary shares, together with £6m. in 3½% debenture stock. Combes and Watneys had been associated since the late 1880s and when Combes began to negotiate a merger with Reid, Vernon Watney asked to join, the result being the establishment of the largest London brewing firm.[36] Like most of the public brewery conversions of the 1890s, as opposed to those of the late 1880s, the assets were overvalued, being based on inflated tied house prices, and the Watney merger involved an increase in capital of £6m. over the combined value of the separate three businesses. Brewery conversions in the 1890s remained a London business; 'provincial only' breweries, of which there were about 30, had a total paid up capital of only £11.7m. in 1897 and their securities were dealt in mainly on the Manchester, Birmingham, Bristol and Leeds stock exchanges.[37]

The problems of watered capital and fixed debt charges arose for one brewery company after another from 1900, when the consumption of beer began to fall. As a result dividends were passed and capital had to be written down, the most affected companies being those who had bought property unwisely and had financed such transactions through fixed-interest securities. Consequently, as a result of this changed financial atmosphere, new brewery flotations came to an end and the ordinary share values of existing companies collapsed. The result of the waves of brewery conversions of the late 1880s and the second half of the 1890s was that by 1900 the limited public brewery had come to dominate London and most of the other cities and larger towns of England and Wales. As Clapham has pointed out, there were still in 1901 some private firms in some large towns but they were now mainly a feature of 'the lesser towns and big villages of rural England'.[38]

★

There were some other domestic industrial flotations alongside the brewery issues during the late 1880s. Some of the mining companies floated were home issues, and such iron and coal concerns accounted for £8m. of the £34m. issued by this group of companies in 1887.[39] Comparable in size to the brewing flotations were the issues of capital by two chemical cartels, the Salt Union, established in 1888, and the United Alkali Company, which was formed in 1890 and went 'public' in 1891. Both giant concerns were founded for the same reason, the growing lack of competitiveness of the British Leblanc alkali trade. The two companies were formed in each case following the failure of private agreements to restrict competition. The price of salt had been falling since the 1870s and an attempt at a private combination in the trade in 1885 had had little effect.[40] In 1888 a London syndicate, probably in conjunction with McDowell, the owner of Nicholas Ashton & Sons' salt works at Northwich, after a meeting of the trade at Liverpool, established the Salt Union, which took over initially 64 salt works.[41] The company was given a capital of £4m. consisting of 200,000 £10 ordinary shares, 100,000 7% £10 preference shares and £1m. 4½% first mortgage debentures. The properties that it took over were paid for two-thirds in cash and one-third in £10 ordinary shares, so that only 110,000 ordinary shares were issued to the public. Valuations were made by Thomas Ward, a respected member of the salt trade, but the promoters watered down considerably the company's capital by paying valuations in excess of Ward's estimates, which in any case were probably generous. This can be seen with regard to seven companies which were valued by Ward at £703,500 but were acquired for the Union at £1,085,400.[42] These overvaluations, together with high promotion charges, contributed to the Union's subsequent stagnation from the late 1890s. Its capital was issued by Morton, Rose & Co.,[43] a London Anglo-American merchant bank,[44] and initially the Union appeared to be successful as salt prices rose during the first year of its existence.

The Salt Union's apparent ability to restore the profitability of the salt trade led the Leblanc soda makers to follow the same course. Like the salt producers, these alkali manufacturers had attempted to band together voluntarily with an agreement in 1884, but in addition had modernized their equipment and diversified their range of products. However, competition from users of the newer and more economic Solvay method proved to be too strong and in 1889 the voluntary scheme for controlling the production of caustic soda and bleaching powder collapsed. In 1890 a large merger scheme, like that of the Salt Union, was talked about and in September 100 alkali manufacturers met at Liverpool and agreed to establish jointly the United Alkali Company. A public flotation was prevented by the Baring crisis, while there was considerable opposition to a 'Chemical Ring' in the press, especially *The Times*. Consequently the company was formed privately, taking over initially only 48 firms. A special committee was set up to manage the process and it was more judicious than the promoters of the Salt Union; the initial capital of £7.2m. did not include any allowances either for good will or promotion expenses. Some capital, £1.3m., was issued to the public in 1891 when security markets were calmer, and it consisted of 30,000 7% £10 preference shares, 66,000 £10 ordinary shares, and £372,000 5% mortgage debenture stock redeemable at £110[45].

The Salt Union was forced to write off £1.6m. of its capital in 1902, after failing to pay a dividend since 1897 but even then only managed to pay 5%, not 7%, on its preference shares. Leblanc product prices rose for four years after the formation of United Alkali Company but then started falling again. Consequently, and despite the company's surer financial base than the Salt Union, the United Alkali Company missed a dividend in 1894 and paid no dividends at all after 1896.[46] Such performance hardly boosted investors' confidence in domestic industrial securities, even when they were available in some volume and were issued by reputable London houses.

★

Public flotations of all types of securities dried up in the wake of the Baring crisis. 'During three years [after the Baring crisis] investors refused to put their money into any but the most absolutely secure stocks, with the result that the prices of such stocks unduly inflated.'[47] The main securities in demand were domestic railway stocks, which in 1889 had been admitted to the trustee list,[48] and their only competitors were domestic municipal corporation stocks, which had first appeared on the market in the 1870s, and some colonial government bonds. By the summer of 1894, investors began to be more adventurous and, though not prepared to consider foreign securities, were taking up fixed-charge securities such as gas, water, tramway, telegraph and brewery debentures.[49] The pressure was the decline in yields on 'safe' securities; whereas domestic railway debentures had been giving a return of 3% in 1891, by 1894 the yield had fallen to 2.77%.[50] Money was extraordinarily cheap. Call money was getting only 0.38%, three months bank bills were being discounted at 0.65% and six months bank bills at 1.01% in July 1894.[51] Anything which gave a higher yield and seemed reasonably safe, such as a preference share or a mortgage debenture, was being used to elicit the attention of investors. Company promoters had in the wings 'a great number of companies ... ready for bringing out', and 'there are signs that the public is getting ready to abandon its ultracautious attitude and go for second and third rate securities giving a comparatively large yield'.[52] Colliery debentures were offering yields in the range of 5.125% to 10.937%, although most were not quoted on the London market, while shipbuilding, engineering and metal fabricators' shares were returning over 5%.[53] As investors began to place their savings in these securities, so prospectuses of new companies appeared.

The financial boom took off in 1895 and continued until the turn of the century, with domestic issues rising from £39.7m. in 1895 to £132.3m. in 1900. A large proportion of these home issues consisted of railway securities and municipal stock but a substantial element was made up of securities floated for domestic industry: £8.4m. in 1895, £48.1m. in 1896, £46m. in 1897, £39.7m. in 1898 and £32.7m. in 1899.[54] These issues took place on both the London and the provincial markets, and dominant in them were those by breweries, which have already been considered, cycle companies, and the nascent automobile industry.

The modern cycle industry developed during the second half of the 1880s, following important technological breakthroughs, and as a result the number of manufacturers increased from about 30 in the late 1870s to something of the order of 280 in the early 1890s and 830 by the end of the decade.[55] The conversion of these concerns, some no more than back-street sheds employing only a handful of people, took place between 1893 and 1897 and coincided with a cycling craze amongst the public. The number of limited companies registered fluctuated between 30 and 50 a year between 1893 and 1895, but then rose to 312 in 1896. Public issues took place in 1893, 1896 and 1897, with £17.2m. and £7.2m. being offered in the last two years, mostly in the form of £1 shares. There were basically three types of public company, cycle manufacturers, tyre and rim companies, and sales concerns and, except for the Dunlop flotation in 1896, most companies had very small capitals, the average nominal capital being about £48,000. The cycle conversion boom was part of a general wave of issues for proprietary and patent companies which had got underway in the late 1880s, paused following the Baring crisis, but then continued until the turn of the century and, besides cycles, included automatic machine companies, gas-mantle companies, and motor car concerns.

The first cycle promotion boom, that of 1893, centred surprisingly on Dublin, where 50 concerns were floated. As the public demand for cycles increased, promoters switched their attention to Birmingham, where most of the issues of 1896 and the early months of 1897 took place at a rate of about four a week. The two main promoters were E. T. Hooley and H. J. Lawson, the former a Nottingham lace manufacturer who in three years promoted 26 companies, not all of which were cycle concerns, before going bankrupt.[56] Both Hooley and Lawson watered heavily the capital of the concerns that they issued, their general margin being about a third. However, many companies were placed in a dilemma about their future when the public demand for cycles increased in the mid-1890s. A member of the board of Humber wrote in September 1895:

> Humber & Co.'s business has been steadily growing and it is therefore proposed by my colleagues that a new company should be formed (to be called) say 'Humber Supply Co.' for which a capital should be raised of £100,000 cash (total capital £150,000) and that it should take over all the trading part of Humber & Co.'s business, so leaving the present Co. unfettered to give its attention to manufacturing solely. Further the Humber Supply Co. to acquire from Hooley the business of Marriott & Cooper, Humber's original partners, who have the right to sell machines under the style of 'The Humber Machine'. This competition is irritating to us, but they do not do a great deal of business and there is great doubt as to whether their right to use the style named is assignable. If not there can be no competing purchasers. My Co-Directors do not seem inclined to support my desire that Marriott & Cooper's rights to assign should be thoroughly sifted before we decide on this question of purchasing and the price.

It is proposed that the Humber Supply Co. should be managed by the same Managing Director and the same Board . . .

It is fair to assume that the Managing Director does not intend to act in that capacity for two companies, for one remuneration; while the Directors would also be drawing two remunerations.

The present Humber C. had no capital to spare during the busy season this year, but I am not clear that we should not have ample for probable growth of business, if the £200,000 which was locked up in Raleigh is available. We have got payment by *a bill* for this now, through my exerting very great pressure, but the Bill has yet to be met.

My strongest objections at the moment are:—

1. That principle introduced involves a fixing of prices, which the present company should charge the new company for machines, which prices are sure to be more beneficial to one company than the other. Conflicting interests would thus be created between shareholders and it further seems to me,

2. That a double organization as suggested would materially increase expenses, while the power of administration and control would not be strengthened because the management is limited to the same brain-force.

Also with Humber shares at 200% premium I contend it is unwarrantable to pay promoters and underwriters the amount which they would get, to form a New Company to help us conduct, or relieve us of part of our profitable business instead of adopting the simple process of increasing our capital, if necessary.[57]

Despite this director's attempts and qualms, Hooley became involved with the Humber company and overcapitalized it, as he did the Beeston Tyre Company and the new Beeston Cycle Company. In the speculative market of 1896 Beeston Tyre £1 shares rose from 2s. in January to £8 in May, with 35 new companies being floated in that month alone. The market broke in early 1897, and 28 out of 108 cycle firms quoted on the Birmingham exchange were in the hands of liquidators within a year. The market collapsed for many reasons: vendors and promoters unloaded their holdings as soon as prices began to fall, which depressed them further; while the industry's output overshot demand, which led to a price war and low or no dividends.[58] *The Engineer* estimated that £40m. had been invested in the cycle industry and steel tube production in 1896, but only a fraction of this sum could have been financed by public issues, given both the high promotion charges involved and that most issues were conversions, not involving any creation of new physical assets.[59]

Car company flotations during the mid-1890s were very much an appendage to the cycle boom and, like their two-wheel counterparts, were centred in Birmingham. Lawson bought out the Daimler company in 1896, his British Motor Syndicate having acquired the patent a year earlier and made £40,000 profit on the transfer. Most of the 25 companies formed in 1896, as with the cycle concerns, had very small capitals and few survived into the twentieth century. In all, 59 companies were established before 1900, of which only 21 were in existence in 1914. Although Lawson had been able to raise £100,000 in ordinary shares for Daimler before any motor car had been produced commercially in the British Isles, the company with its watered stock was virtually bankrupt in 1901 and had to be reconstructed in 1904. Other Lawson creations, Rover and Humber, survived by financial reconstruction and the introduction of new management. The most successful firms were those which started as private concerns and then, once established, came to the market. There were further flurries of market activity in the 1900s with motor- and cycle-manufacturing issues taking place in some volume in 1902, 1905–7 and 1911–13.[60]

★

Cycles and cars, and the former rather than the latter, were one feature of the financial activity of the home boom of the 1890s. The second main strand, apart from breweries, was appeals to finance merger activity. Between 1888 and 1914 an average of 67 firms each year disappeared as the result of mergers, but in the peak years of 1898 to 1900 650 firms valued at £42m. were absorbed in 198 separate mergers. In the case of heavy chemicals it has been argued already that the formation of giant holding companies was due to the obsolescence of British technology based on the Leblanc process, whereas mergers in brewing were the consequence of the era of restricted licensing after 1869. In other industries, especially tobacco, wallpaper, flour, soap, sewing cotton and linoleum, Hannah has argued convincingly that mergers were the result of important shifts in both the technical basis of production and the nature of market demand which gave rise to economies of scale. Mergers were not the inevitable outcome of these forces but to most businessmen they were preferable to the alternatives of either cut-throat competition, from which few would survive, or some form of collusion which was unstable in the medium term. While mergers arose out of real economic forces – the production function and demand – their timing would appear to have been determined by the availability of outside finance. Hannah has found a very strong correlation during the period 1880 to 1918 between share prices and mergers.[61]

Merger issues in bulk were the last phase of the home boom of the 1890s following the appreciation of existing industrial securities in 1894 and 1895 and the flotation of cycle and brewery companies in 1896. The provincial markets played a considerable role in the financing of merger activity. Manchester gained from the establishment of combines in the textile preparatory and finishing trades. These companies were generally soundly based, the valuations of the assets being made by local accountants, of which the Manchester firm of Jones, Crewdson & Yorath was the most important. As with the breweries, the public were generally offered preference shares and debentures, the vendors taking most of the ordinary shares. This was also the case with the formation of Imperial Tobacco. Most of the publicly issued securities were taken up by local investors in the West Country and, through the flotation, activity on the Bristol Stock Exchange was revived to the extent that it became the centre for tobacco shares.[62]

Not all of the plans for the creation of large combines were realized in their original form. Lever appears to have thought of establishing a large company in the soap industry by the exchange of shares in 1901–2 to overcome a deceleration in the growth of the market coupled with rising raw material prices. His plans were put off until the summer of 1906, when there was a very sudden and large rise in raw material prices. All previous agreements to fix prices had failed, while some had not been applicable to Lever's own entrepreneurial ideas of a national branded market. In July 1906 some of the large northern firms met Lever to find a solution to 'exploded agreements' but the proposed combine was defeated by press attacks. Lever then achieved his aim in a different way – through piecemeal take-overs financed by the issue of £6.5m. of capital. By 1913 his firm controlled over a third of the home market, a share much smaller than that achieved by some of the combines formed in the late 1890s.[63]

The combination movement also affected the coal, iron and steel industries. On the north-east coalfield there were a number of amalgamations: in 1896 Sir James Jocey & Co. took over Lord Durham's collieries, steamers, and plant for £1m.; in 1899 the Ashington Coal Company was established; and in the following year Horden Collieries Ltd. was formed, but only £45,000 of its £250,000 issued capital was raised from the public.[64] Earlier, in South Wales D. A. Thomas had formed the Cambrian Collieries, with a capital of £400,000, and nine years later in 1904 the United Collieries were established, which owned 23 collieries on the Scottish field. However, Sir George Elliot, despite his wide interests in the industry, was unable to get off the ground his plan for a national coal company.[65] More important in the organization of the industry was the growing number, especially after 1900, of public companies. They were to be found mainly in Yorkshire and the East Midlands, where the pace of investment and the costs of sinking had outrun internal finance in the form of retained profits. Some of these companies in the Midlands were formed to establish entirely new collieries but they attracted capital largely from professional coalowners. Concurrent with this increase in the number of public companies was the conversion of most other collieries of any size into private joint stock concerns.[66]

In iron and steel, amalgamations occurred in the opening years of the twentieth century, mainly amongst metal-users, and around 1910 amongst steelmakers.[67] Prior to this, there had been in the late 1890s a movement amongst steel armament firms to take over shipbuilding concerns in order to control the market for their products, spurred by the greatly increased naval estimates of 1899. These acquisitions established in this section of industry a number of large vertically integrated concerns, together with a number of jointly controlled subsidiaries, and by 1914 interpenetration also took the form of a large number of interlocking directorships, some of which had their origins in the Chadwick–Manchester group of promoters of the 1860s and 1870s.[68] By 1900 the joint stock company was the normal form of industrial unit in iron and steel making, with five-sixths of all blast furnaces in the British Isles being owned by such concerns.

After reaching a peak in 1900, domestic industrial new issues fell away sharply in 1901 and remained generally at a very low level until 1912.[69] Between 1904 and 1906, the main calls were made by motor car manufacturers, while the rise in the volume of issues immediately before the First World War was due primarily to the needs of armament manufacturers and the heavy industries which supported them.[70] Even domestic railway companies found it difficult to raise capital during most of this period. A major issue by the North Eastern in 1901 was badly undersubscribed, and its inability to raise finance, either on terms or in amounts to which it was accustomed, led to a growing deficit on its capital account from 1904. This company was not alone in facing such conditions: the Great Western, Great Central, and Great Northern in 1906 and 1907 all found that fresh borrowing could only take place at very high costs relative to past experience.[71] Foreign securities of all types proved to be more attractive to investors than either domestic industrial or railway securities from the mid-1900s. Edwardian investors wanted higher earnings and, with rising prices and interest rates, regarded a yield of 5% or more as the target to aim at. Such earnings could generally be obtained only on foreign securities and such issues rose from a low ebb to almost colossal proportions between 1900 and 1910. If higher yields were the pull, then the difficulties faced by the breweries in meeting their fixed borrowing charges, and the problems of companies with watered stock provided the push that propelled investors into foreign securities. The overall trend of domestic industrial share prices from the late 1890s until 1909 was downwards. The only exception was textiles, which recovered from 1904, and it was mainly Lancashire's export boom in the years around 1910 that pushed the overall index upwards during the years before the First World War.[72] Dividends followed a similar course, although in the case of iron, steel and coal, they were above average in the years around 1907.[73] In the quarter of a century before 1914, the boom of the 1890s proved to be a halcyon period for domestic industrial issues.

★

From the discussion in this chapter and its immediate predecessor, it is apparent that British industry raised finance through either local or the metropolitan capital markets in amounts which were relatively substantial during only a limited number of years – the booms of the early 1870s and the second half of the 1890s. Is this an indication that the manufacturing sector was ill-served by the machinery of the new issues market? This question has been posed since at least the 1910s, while during the on-going debate over the performance of the late-Victorian economy it has been claimed that an inadequate supply of finance was a critical deleterious factor. At the outset of any examination it should be pointed out that the overall volume of savings within the economy has always been held by commentators to have been adequate to meet investment needs; what has been questioned is the areas in which those savings were placed, namely whether some of the £4,082m. put in foreign securities between 1865 and 1914 should have been directed towards the domestic manufacturing sector. This has focused the debate initially on the behaviour of institutions in the capital market, in the sense of whether they were biased towards foreign as opposed to domestic securities, and more recently on the preference of investors. It is evident from this rather compressed description of the elements of the controversy that it has essentially been, and has remained, a supply-orientated debate. Those that have damned in one way or another the financial institutions involved have assumed, or asserted, that an increase in the volume of funds available for investment at home would have allowed a frustrated demand to have been fulfilled, which in turn would have led to an increase in the British rate of economic growth, possibly coupled with beneficial structural change.

The earliest commentators pointed out that before 1914 there were no domestic issuing houses comparable either in size or in reputation to those which handled overseas issues. The contrast was a sharp one; on the one hand there were houses like Rothschilds, Barings and others, on the other there were mainly private individuals, collectively called promoters. A further comparison made was between the respective sizes of flotations and their costs; overseas issues being generally large, on which costs of legal fees, underwriting, etc., bore proportionally less. Together, such conditions were likely to make domestic issues both difficult and relatively costly and to subject them to the depredations of unscrupulous individuals, whose activities before 1900 were largely unfettered by company law.[74] The conclusion drawn was that 'while it may be admitted that the market is most efficient in supplying large quantities of capital to reputable bodies, it must be recognized that its wastefulness in meeting the needs of smaller ventures might be largely remedied by the development of strong intermediary organizations'.[75] Historians in the 1960s have restated this criticism in equally forceful terms.[76] However, blanket observations conceal the segmented nature of the market for home industrials. Actually, as Lavington has shown, it consisted by the 1900s of roughly three compartments: flotations by existing, usually large companies, some of which were rights issues and which generally faced no difficulties; private flotations, as in the cotton industry, where the funds were subscribed by directors and their friends, with remaining sums being obtained through informal channels; and lastly, public, generally small or medium-size, issues made either on the provincial exchanges or the London market. It is the market conditions that these latter issues faced on which the debate has turned.

It is difficult to estimate the relative sizes of these three segments of the new issue market for home industrials. Lavington, from *The Times* series of prospectuses, thought that in the years 1912 to 1913 about half of the new issues were made by existing companies.[77] These were years of relatively low activity for home issues, while the use of the prospectus had been affected by the reform of the law in 1900 and 1907. Before 1900 two-thirds of new issues on the London market had been by prospectus but in 1902, following the provisions of the 1900 Act, two-thirds of issues were being made by private introduction. The 1907 Act required that where a prospectus was not used, a statement had to be filed, making the same disclosures as required in a full prospectus. In 1909 275 out of 383 applications for entry to the London Stock Exchange, the *secondary* market, were made by companies which had issued prospectuses.[78] Local private issues cannot be gauged from available data, while the size of the provincial markets is also doubtful. Thomas has estimated that of the £9.5m. raised from the public by companies which issued prospectuses during 1911–13, £2m. to £3m. came from the provinces. However, during the home boom of the 1890s, individual markets easily exceeded this volume, Manchester alone raising £7m. between 1896 and 1897. Therefore he has concluded that on average £4m. to £5m. a year was probably the provincial contribution during the early years of the twentieth century.[79]

Issuing facilities grew and matured in London as a result of overseas flotations.[80] Although domestic securities were always the largest component of the stock of outstanding long-term securities held in the United Kingdom before 1914, most of them were floated by machinery outside the London market. The National Debt was handled by the Bank of England, while the railway companies generally issued their own capital unaided. Consequently, formal institutions grew up only to handle overseas issues and by the 1870s, when the long-term securities of domestic concerns other than railways made up only around 4% of the nominal value of securities held,[81] this sector of the market had considerable maturity. However, it did not handle all foreign issues, being concerned primarily with large flotations on which there were significant issuing economies. Generally, untried foreign borrowers, even where they required finance in large amounts, were not catered for by 'reputable' major merchant banks in London. Their issues were handled instead by 'ad hoc' syndicates, and speculative foreign mining companies faced the same difficulties as home industrial concerns.[82] The London merchant banks and their associated institutions were the main elements in the development of issuing facilities on the London market from the 1850s and they became accustomed to retailing a more or less standardized commodity, namely fixed-interest securities, each issue of which was of considerable volume and very similar in nature, being made usually on behalf of a foreign government or railway. After the mid-1880s domestic industrial issues could occasionally be tailored to fit the developed 'mass production' techniques of these issuing houses, as with the Guinness flotation carried out by Barings, the Salt Union issue undertaken by Morton, Rose, and the Hotchkiss issue made by Anthony Gibbs & Sons. It may be concluded therefore that the first-class issuing houses in London were considerably biased in their activities, but not so much to foreign issues, as to undertaking large issues which yielded economies on cost. Before 1914 there were very few domestic industrial issues which met the criteria of such houses.

Generally foreign securities met the desires not only of the first-class London issuing houses but also of the investor. They gave a greater yield. From a sample of first- and second-class quoted securities, Edelstein has found that between 1870 and 1913 the geometric mean price-deflated rate of return on overseas assets was 5.72% as opposed to 4.6% on domestic securities. Although he established that a number of home industrial equities did generate returns equal to non-domestic equity assets, generally, as has been shown earlier, domestic industrial equity was not issued to the 'investing public'. Public domestic industrial issues after the mid-1880s consisted mainly of preference shares and debentures and, in the case of these assets, the yields on various home and overseas assets by type were not comparable. Domestic *industrial preference shares* gave returns equal to those generated by *foreign debentures*, the latter a less risky asset, while the returns on domestic manufacturing debentures were 'well below' those of the 'highest overseas debenture returns'.[83]

Over time, as the supply of both home and overseas assets increased, the rate of return on them fell, but in this secular pattern there were fluctuations – long swings – which were out of phase. Long swings in domestic returns peaked in 1895 and 1911, while the peaks in overseas returns were in 1879 and 1905, but 'the absolute difference between home and overseas returns was smaller during 1870 to 1876, 1887 to 1897, and 1910 to 1913, the periods of home dominance, than 1877 to 1886 and 1897 to 1909, the periods of overseas dominance'.[84] Investors, then, behaved rationally in buying higher-yielding overseas securities, while during periods of domestic dominance in the capital market, the market edge of home securities was less than that of overseas securities during periods of foreign dominance. Domestic securities' hold on investors, in terms of yield, was simply weaker.

There were other considerations, besides realized rates of return, of importance to an investor, primarily the liquidity of a security once it had been bought. High-yielding domestic industrial securities, if they could not be traded on the secondary market, could only form a small proportion, with safety, of the portfolio of any 'general' investor who was not prepared to assume any form of entrepreneurial risk. It was pointed out in the last chapter that securities arising from small issues were generally unmarketable on the London Stock Exchange during the 1870s and no evidence has come forward to show that their marketability increased subsequently. It was argued that the provincial exchanges with their different method of trading – 'the call-over' – gave local stocks a greater marketability but there are indications that this may have declined during the last two decades of the nineteenth century. The conversion of industrial companies gave the provincial exchanges new life and consequently they tried to prevent their lists from becoming cluttered. In 1890 Liverpool decided that it would no longer provide a quotation for companies with share capitals of less than £50,000, and similarly Manchester resolved to reject quotations of small companies whose shares were 'insufficiently in the public hands'.[85] After 1890, with the increase in activity, provincial brokers chose to follow the London pattern of business, that of concentrating on securities which were not difficult to obtain and in which there was generally a high turnover. Such decisions, although understandable, first eroded further the liquidity of some industrial shares and, second, made the comparison of the price of newly issued securities with those of existing counterparts very difficult. Liquidity came only with large issues which, for domestic industrial securities, meant mainly preference shares and debentures, which normally gave a lower return than foreign securities of the same type. Liquidity was even more important for institutional investors than their 'private' counterparts as the securities that insurance companies and commercial banks bought went into their reserves to be used in times of crisis or panic. While such institutions became more adventurous in their reserve investment policies, with the insurance companies taking up foreign bonds from the 1870s, followed by the banks in the 1890s, they did not move into domestic industrials before 1914,[86] with perhaps the exception of small holdings of brewery debentures.[87] Consequently there was no institutional floor in the domestic industrial sector of the secondary market.

Kennedy has argued with some force that the risk preference of British investors – their appetite for relatively low-yielding foreign stocks and bonds – had the serious effect of constricting the volume of financial resources flowing into inherently profitable but risky domestic ventures. This pattern of behaviour led to a reduction of aggregate capital formation when foreign investment was out of favour, maintained a pattern of demand which discouraged structural change, and acted to increase the cost of domestic capital formation.[88] During periods of domestic investment, the total investment rate fell to levels below those current during overseas lending booms; the average rates for 1881–9 and 1903–13 being 13.5% and 15.2% of G. N. P., respectively, while in the 1890s it was only 11.38% (1891–8 average).[89] Kennedy infers from such evidence that the domestic economy alone was unable to absorb productively the level of savings generated within it, with domestic securities not being regarded by investors as close substitutes for overseas assets. In the 1890s domestic financial instruments were taken up, but not in sufficient numbers to push up investment rates to the levels pertaining during overseas lending booms. The nature of overseas lending, the largest single component of which was the finance of railway construction, maintained the domestic economy's reliance on the production of railway iron and rolling stock for export long after this sector had ceased to be the most rapidly growing part of international trade.

Continued foreign lending in a fixed pattern was both sustaining an increasingly outmoded domestic export sector and blunting the impact upon it of major changes in overseas demand. The late Victorians worried over export performance and the growth of competitors, especially Germany, but they did not diagnose the beginnings of a structural imbalance within the domestic economy. It was to take a major world war, which accelerated underlying trends, and a decade of high unemployment to turn people's attention to the nature of the beast that was the British economy.

It is now necessary to look at perhaps the most crucial question: was structural change before 1914 retarded by factors in the capital market, in particular the cost of raising long-term finance? So far in the discussion, it has been argued that issuing facilities of a high reputation developed in response to the overseas demand for capital in the form of large issues which offered economies in the costs of flotation. These issues had a market edge in the form of a higher yield, while their size ensured generally their liquidity in the secondary market. As such they were highly acceptable to both 'private' and institutional investors. Institutional development with regard to domestic industrial issues was far slower because until the late 1880s such flotations, with the exception of some iron and steel issues in the mid-1860s and early 1870s, were made either privately or locally. Generally, before the last decade or so of the nineteenth century, informal machinery and knowledgeable pools of local savings were sufficient to satisfy the demands of industry. The situation changed with the appearance of large domestic industrial and commercial issues, in particular those arising out of some brewery conversions and large-scale mergers in other sections of industry.

It has been claimed that by the 1890s there existed professional promoters for domestic issues, and one commentator has maintained that their presence was one of the factors which made possible the merger issues of that decade.[90] Payne has argued that with the professional promoter having become a major figure in the capital market by the mid-1880s and with the growing practice of underwriting shares, the necessary evolutionary financial changes had taken place to allow the possibility of setting up giant companies in Great Britain. He also admits that the range of integrity amongst such promoters was wide, while underwriting was of dubious legality until 1900. The critical change identified in his argument would appear to have been that promoters in the 1890s 'provided the initiative [to convert companies] and [unlike Chadwick in the 1860s and 1870s] were no longer content to act merely as the servants of the vendors'.[91] How efficient were these new men in the market and how much did their services cost? Except for those who landed in court because of their activities, such as Bottomley and Hooley, it is difficult, if not impossible, to establish who they were and how they undertook their business: their 'names have not even survived, hovering on the fringes of the financial scene, coalescing into groups to promote one or two schemes and then splitting up and disappearing into obscurity'.[92] There is one exception, H. Osbourne O'Hagan, who wrote his autobiography; he appears to have been a man of some probity, and therefore provides a measuring rod of best practice with regard to promotion techniques in the 1880s and 1890s.

O'Hagan's education was limited and he had no formal training in either law or accountancy. However, he gained his early experience as a clerk to a tramway promoter in the 1860s, when he established contacts and got to know the provinces. In the 1870s he set up in partnership with his brother, an engineer, and began to promote tramways on his own behalf. The partnership was turned into a company, the City of London Contract Corporation, in 1882 and O'Hagan remained active as a financier through it until the early 1900s. His main domestic concerns appear to have been breweries, some coal companies, and the cement combine. He obtained promotional proposals through his own private contacts, from solicitors acting on behalf of vendors, and occasionally via stockbrokers. O'Hagan was associated with one London broking firm, Panmure Gordon, which provided him with business contacts and 'a greatly increased underwriting connection'. In his autobiography he claims to have been responsible for the development of underwriting of share issues, which was mainly undertaken by private individuals, trusts and investment companies. In order not to contravene the law, which before 1900 prevented companies issuing shares at a discount, the underwriting contracts were with the vendor not the embryonic company. On two occasions, he specified his charges. With regard to the Stanhope Main Colliery, he was paid £5,000 for preparing the company's memorandum of association, articles of association, and the necessary agreements between the vendor and the company. The company's capital of £200,000 was raised by the vendor himself during the course of a market day in Barnsley. Even O'Hagan appears to acknowledge that this was a large fee for the services that he rendered, because he went on to point out that he negotiated the company's subsequent merger with a neighbouring concern, Newton Chambers & Co., without rendering an account for his services. The other company of interest is the Plymouth Brewery, where O'Hagan's brother's charges along with legal fees amounted to £40,000 for £320,000 of capital. So it would appear from these two isolated incidences that the range of charges made by the O'Hagan company was of the order of 2.5 to 12.5%.[93] This fits closely with one estimate of provincial issuing costs of the order of 10% in the cases of flotations of £250,000.[94] O'Hagan justified his charges on two accounts: first, that he rejected two out of every three companies that he investigated and, second, that his charges on larger transactions were no more than 'the profits enjoyed by a firm of estate agents'. He attributed his personal fortune to profits arising from a large turnover, claiming 'at a very busy time' to have been handling five companies a month.[95] Whatever their justification, the apparent upper bound of his charges was very close to the average yield on private gross domestic capital stock, 11.3%, during the years before the First World War (1910–14).[96] Individual marginal yields may have, of course, been much higher but on a very simple comparison of issuing costs and average yields, there was not much incentive to raise new finance through such professional promoters. Only in the case of large issues, made by the merchant banks and similar institutions, did issuing costs fall to levels of 1% to 5%.

O'Hagan appears to have had the same attitude to the nature of company promotion that Chadwick had had two decades earlier. He investigated closely proposals that he obtained; certainly in the case of breweries, he required that the vendors and other management personnel remained with the company and continued to have a financial interest in it, and he frowned upon the Stock Exchange practice of dealings before allotment. The critical differences appear in their scale of charges and O'Hagan's development of underwriting, a procedure which he regarded as necessary in order to protect the vendor if the public issue should fail. There were probably other promoters like him in the 1880s and the 1890s but how many it is difficult to judge. Bottomley, Hooley and Lawson were certainly of a different ilk, in that they tried to maximize their profits by all sorts of devices, usually at the expense of the companies that they established. They were at one end of the spectrum but acting like O'Hagan as financiers, while during the 1890s boom, as in other previous issuing booms, a variety of other individuals from all walks of life were prepared to try their hand at promotion. In the case of breweries, O'Hagan retreated from the field in the face of competition from bankers, brokers, solicitors and others who, he claimed, in their struggle to get their hands on what appeared to be 'a good thing', pushed up brewery prices to ridiculous heights. Consequently it is difficult to detect any important qualitative shift during the last quarter of the nineteenth century in the mechanics of promotion of small and medium issues except perhaps a greater development of underwriting. In the 1890s, as in the 1860s and 1870s, domestic company promotion was handled by a variety of agencies, some good, but most apparently bad, judging by the backwash of watered companies' capitals they left in their wake.

Perhaps the real problem that a 'professional promoter' faced was the lack of a foundation in the form of day-to-day less risky business. Chadwick had had his accountancy practice, while the merchant banks were heavily involved in the provision of acceptance credits for international trade and undertook private short- and medium-term finance for their clients. There were no such outlets for the professional promoter: some continuity could be maintained by handling both domestic and overseas issues but this widened the scope of knowledge and contacts required. There are very few instances where the promoter developed a client relationship with any of his offspring. These factors taken together often meant that each promotion had to be regarded as a major 'killing', to be milked to the limit, for there was no certainty of what tomorrow had in store. Such situations could lead a firm to wonder seriously whether it was worth taking the risk of using the services of a 'London professional promoter' if capital could not be obtained either privately or locally. Such a speculation has some solidity, because O'Hagan did come across some vendors who were prepared to sell only if their concerns were *not* going to be converted into public companies.

What is extremely difficult to establish is whether the barriers to the successful flotation of small and medium-sized domestic issues, namely high costs and frequently unscrupulous promoters, were real or not. Did they lead to a frustrated demand for capital, a demand that was not prepared to make its presence felt, which in turn severely limited structural change in the real sector and perhaps also in the financial sector? The available evidence is patchy and conflicting. Burn, in a masterly study of the iron and steel industry, has diagnosed its pre-1914 failings as being due to a number of factors, of which one was the inability to raise finance for restructuring.[97] However, on the one hand, other work has stressed other debilitating factors, in particular inadequate entrepreneurship and restricted market growth resulting from the imposition of tariffs,[98] while on the other an entirely different picture has been painted in which American and British productivities in 1913 were virtually indistinguishable and the cessation of British productivity growth 'was a reflex of the exhaustion of available technology, not slower growing demand'.[99] In any case, by the 1890s iron and steel issues were generally of some size and consequently did not face the specified market barriers. The coal industry had a different organizational structure, consisting primarily of a multitude of small companies each owning at most two or three collieries, but recent studies have found that inadequate financial resources were not a constraint on the introduction of mechanized mining.[100] In commercial shipbuilding, there was an increase in the amount of capital per worker from the 1890s through the introduction of electric, hydraulic and pneumatic power-transmission and a new range of machine tools. Consequently the capital required for a 'fair sized shipbuilding yard' increased from a range of £0.25m.–£0.5m. to £0.3m.–£1m. between 1900 and 1914, but no firms seem to have run into any difficulties in financing their growth.[101] The Lancashire cotton industry appears to have been able to finance its long-term capital requirements almost entirely from local sources.

A similar conflicting picture arises out of any view of the development of the so-called 'new' industries before 1914, though the contrasts here are somewhat sharper, which may allow rather firmer conclusions to be drawn. The story of the development of artificial fibres would have heartened those supporters of company law liberalization in the mid-1850s who sought to assist the inventor. The discovery and development of the manufacture of artificial silk was a pan-European process in which British inventors hit upon the right solution. Cross and Bevan, and later Cross and Stearn, the chemists responsible, worked in the 1890s through two private limited companies, the Viscose Syndicate and the Viscose Spinning Syndicate, whose shares were taken up by both British and German manufacturers, some of whom were closely associated with the industrial scientists. Their patent rights in Britain were bought by S. Courtauld & Co., a decision which appears to have been stimulated by the commercial success of a French process, together with the lower input costs that the British viscose method appeared to offer. Courtaulds were not only attracted to the new technology by the gains that it apparently offered, but were also pushed by the decline in profitability of the company's traditional crêpe trade, even though new variants had been developed. Almost at the same time as Courtaulds considered embarking upon the new venture, the concern was made into a public company, which provided £100,000 in cash. These financial resources, together with some limited transfers of reserves, met the initial cost of the new investment which after a four-year gestation period brought in profits sufficient to pay dividends of 20% or more, increased both the company's reserve fund and its holdings of cash tenfold, quadrupled its investment holdings, and in 1912 paid commissions to the firm's salaried managing directors, which in total were equal to a quarter of the firm's gross trading profits.[102] Here the limited liability legislation and the pre-1914 capital market would appear to have played the role which its most stringent critics have subsequently demanded, but ironically no mention of the new process was made in the prospectus for the public appeal for capital.

The development of electrical engineering and car production does not reveal the same matching of financial resources with risk and enterprise. The early British automobile industry has already been considered and, as

Kennedy has recently demonstrated, the pattern that occurred of early and calamitous issues crippling medium-term development was more or less a repetition of the previous experience of the nascent electrical industry in the 1880s and 1890s.[103] The conclusion that emerges is that promoters, the stock exchanges, and investors were prepared to support in some measure 'mania' waves of flotations. But once fingers had been burnt with watered stocks and shares, and worthless patents, then surviving firms, even those with good profit records, found it difficult to raise finance in either sufficient quantity or of the right type, namely equities as opposed to debentures by which the firm immediately incurred fixed interest charges. This meant that subsequent booms in product demand could not be satisfied, management became apathetic and the field was left open to either foreign imports or direct investment.[104] 'Manias' were a feature of issuing booms, foreign and domestic alike, and generally led to single spurts of investment which resulted, in the case of the domestic manufacturing sector, in the appearance of a multitude of small firms, most of which were crippled by watered capitals. If fewer firms had been promoted, after more careful investigation, and if most of the capital raised had gone into their own bank accounts and not those of their promoters, then, of course, the story might have been different. In their early stages, most new technologies do involve many blind alleys; but was it just unfortunate that each blind alley offered another promoter a chance to get in on the current issuing 'mania', which in turn satisfied those investors who had been unable as yet to obtain any of the current 'highly prized' 'mania' securities? This was the case with electricity, for which £7m. was raised in 1882, but where in the early 1890s Cromptons were totally unable to raise even debenture finance, with only £10,000 of a £25,000 bond issue made in the summer of 1890 being sold by March 1891.

There were therefore some important barriers in the formal long-term capital market which militated against small and medium-size issues, both domestic and overseas. In the case of the nascent car and electrical industries, they limited severely the subsequent growth of the respective industries. However, long-term securities of domestic non-railway enterprises did rise from about 4% of the stock of all securities held in the United Kingdom in 1870 to 19% by 1913.[105] But this change needs to be put into perspective: most firms continued to rely on either internal sources of funds or bank finance to finance their expansion until 1914 and later. One early estimate, which is still probably of the right order of magnitude, suggests that in 1907 no more than 10% of domestic industrial development was financed by public offers of securities.[106] The institutional structure of the formal capital and investors' preferences primarily affected new concerns such as car and electrical machinery manufacturers; of far greater importance to most industrial companies was their own profitability and the terms and availability of bank finance.

Notes

(Place of publication is London unless otherwise stated)

1 Trend of the annual number of London registrations of limited companies, 1856–84 (Y/1,000; 1870 = 0)
$$= 0.76 + 0.03t.$$
Trend of the annual number of London registrations of limited companies, 1885–1914 (Y/1,000; 1899 = 0)
$$= 3.79 + 0.16t.$$

2 See above, pp. 66–72.

3 J. B. Jeffreys, 'Trends in Business Organisation since 1856...', unpublished Ph.D. thesis, University of London, 1938, chapter III.

4 A. Essex-Crosby, 'Joint Stock Companies in Great Britain, 1890–1930', unpublished M.Comm. thesis, University of London, 1938, p. 51.

5 ibid., tables I, III.

6 Jeffreys, op. cit.

7 See M. A. Utton, 'Some Features of the Early Merger Movements in British Manufacturing Industry', *Business History*, XIV, 1972, p. 53, table 1.

8 See R. L. Nash, *A Short Inquiry into the Profitable Nature of Our Investments*, 1880, pp. 102–3.

9 Essex-Crosby, op. cit., pp. 31, 60.

10 P. L. Cottrell, 'Investment Banking in England 1856–1882 + Case Study of the International Financial Society'. unpublished Ph.D. thesis University of Hull, 1974, pp. 506–11.

11 B. Supple, *The Royal Exchange. A History of British Insurance 1720–1970*, Cambridge, 1970, pp. 342–8; C. A. E. Goodhart, *The Business of Banking, 1891–1914*, 1972, pp. 134–5.

12 Nash, op. cit., pp. 10, 11, 34.

13 See C. K. Harley, 'Goschen's Conversion of the National Debt and the Yield on Consols', *Economic History Review*, 2nd series, XXIX, 1976.

14 A. R. Hall, *The London Capital Market and Australia 1870–1914*, Canberra, 1963, p. 54.

15 Much of the above section is based upon Jeffreys, op. cit., chapter VI. See also Essex-Crosby, op. cit., pp. 181–2; and above, p. 69.

16 See Jeffreys, op. cit., chapter V.; also Essex-Crosby, op. cit., pp. 127–9.

17 Jeffreys, op. cit., chapter IV.

18 Essex-Crosby, op. cit., pp. 32, 61.

19 ibid., pp. 122–3.

20 ibid., p. 210.

21 As yet no-one has analysed, in the way that Shannon has done for the period 1856 to 1883, the annual registrations of new limited companies after 1883. The task would be prodigious because of the substantial rise in registrations from the mid-1880s and the splitting, since Shannon undertook his work, of company files between the Public Record Office and the Company Registration Office.

22 J. Blackman and E. M. Sigsworth, 'The Home Boom of the 1890s', *Yorkshire Bulletin of Economic and Social Research*, XVII, 1965, pp. 92–3.

23 J. Vaizey, *The Brewing Industry 1886–1951*, 1960, p. 3.

24 H. W. Macrosty, *The Trust Movement in British Industry*, 1907, p. 241.

25 Vaizey, op. cit., pp. 4–17.

26 ibid., p. 8.

27 *The Story of Whitbreads*, 3rd edn, 1964, pp. 30–1.

28 *Trumans: The Brewers*, 1966, pp. 44–5.

29 See below, p. 229.

30 Glyn, Mills Archive, London: B/2 18, Terms with Customers. The Guinness issue consisted of £2.5m. in ordinary stock, £2.0m. in 6% preference stock, and £1.5m. in 5% debenture stock.

31 ibid.; see also Private Letter books, B.W.C. ff145, A4/8 ff113, 119.

32 ibid., A4/8 f129.

33 Vaizey, op. cit., p. 9.

34 Essex-Crosby, op. cit. p. 48.

35 Blackman and Sigsworth, op. cit., pp. 88, 94.

36 H. James, *The Red Barrel, A History of Watney, Mann*, 1963, pp. 133, 138, 144–5.

37 W. A. Thomas, *The Provincial Stock Exchanges*, 1973, p. 127.

38 J. H. Clapham, *An Economic History of Modern Britain*, III, Cambridge, 1963, p. 259.

39 Essex-Crosby, op. cit., p. 35.

40 Macrosty, op. cit., p. 181; L. F. Haber, *The Chemical Industry during the Nineteenth Century*, Oxford, 1958, p. 80.

41 A. F. Calvert, *A History of the Salt Union*, 1913, pp. v–vi.

42 ibid., pp. ix–xii.

43 See prospectus reprinted ibid., p. 25.

44 See D. R. Adler, M. E. Hidy (ed.), *British Investment in American Railways 1834–1898*, Charlottesville, Va, 1970.

45 Macrosty, op. cit., pp. 187–9; Haber, op. cit., pp. 181–4.

46 Macrosty, op. cit., p. 185; Haber, op. cit., pp. 181, 183–4.

47 *The Economist*, 3rd August 1901; quoted in Blackman and Sigsworth, op. cit., p. 93.

48 See R. J. Irving, 'British Railway Investment and Innovation, 1900–1914', *Business History*, XIII, 1971, pp. 39, 51–2.

49 Blackman and Sigsworth, op. cit., p. 94. The same pattern had occurred after the 1866 crisis. 'Thus, after the panic in 1866, events have followed their accustomed course. In 1867, frightened investors confined their operations chiefly to those stocks known or supposed to be supremely safe; and in the year 1868 they are content to place their money in securities supposed to be a degree less safe'. R. L. Nash, *Money Market Events and the Value of Securities dealt in on the Stock Exchange in the Year 1868*, 1869, pp. 12–13.

50 Harley, op. cit., p. 106.

51 S. Nishimura, *The Decline of Inland Bills of Exchange in the London Money Market, 1855–1913*, Cambridge, 1971, p. 123, table 30.

52 *The Statist*, 5th May 1894, quoted in Blackman and Sigsworth, op. cit., p. 94.

53 Blackman and Sigsworth, op. cit., pp. 94–5.

54 From table I in A. R. Hall, 'A Note on the English Capital Market as a Source of Funds for Home Investment before 1914', *Economica*, new series, XXIV, 1957, p. 61.

55 See A. E. Harrison, 'The Competitiveness of the British Cycle Industry, 1890–1914', *Economic History Review*, 2nd series, XII, 1969, pp. 287–9.

56 The above is drawn from Blackman and Sigsworth, op. cit., pp. 86–7; Essex-Crosby, op. cit., pp. 49–50; and Thomas, op. cit., pp. 129–31.

57 University of Hull Library: Mellors Basden papers, microfilm.

58 See Harrison, loc. cit., and Thomas, op. cit., p. 132.

59 Blackman and Sigsworth, op. cit., p. 87.

60 £119,000 in 1902; £404,000, 1905; £1,104,000, 1906; £772,000, 1907; £231,000, 1911; £426,000, 1912; and £1,443,000, 1913. G. L. Ayres, 'Fluctuations in New Capital Issues on the London Money Market, 1899–1913', unpublished M.Sc.(Econ.) thesis, University of London, 1934, Appendices, table 13, p. 44; Thomas, op. cit., pp. 132–3; S. B. Saul, 'The Motor Industry in Britain to 1914', *Business History*, V, 1962.

61 L. Hannah, *The Rise of the Corporate Economy*, 1976, pp. 17, 22–3; see also P. L. Payne, 'The Emergence of the Large-scale Company in Great Britain, 1870–1914', *Economic History Review*, 2nd series, XX, 1967; L. Davis, 'The Capital Markets and Industrial Concentration: the U.S. and the U.K., a Comparative Study', *Economic History Review*, 2nd series, XIX, 1966; L. Hannah, 'Mergers in British Manufacturing Industry 1880–1918', *Oxford Economic Papers*, XXVI, 1974; Utton, op. cit.; Macrosty, op. cit.

62 Thomas, op. cit., pp. 135–6; see also B. W. E. Alford, *W. D. and H. O. Wills and the Development of the United Kingdom Tobacco Industry 1786–1965*, 1973.

63 C. Wilson, *The History of Unilever*, I, 1954, pp. 45–83, 120–4; Hannah, op. cit., p. 23. See also, on piecemeal acquisition, the case of Vickers, in J. D. Scott, *Vickers*, 1962, pp. 44–5, 82–4; and below, p. 234.

64 A. G. Kenwood, 'Capital Investment in North Eastern England, 1800–1913', unpublished Ph.D. thesis, University of London, 1962, p. 248.

65 Clapham, op. cit., pp. 263–4; Essex-Crosby, op. cit., p. 98.
66 B. R. Mitchell, 'The Economic Development of the Inland Coalfields, 1870–1914', unpublished Ph.D. thesis, University of Cambridge, 1956, pp. 144, 148–9, 159–60.
67 Utton, op. cit., p. 53; Essex-Crosby, op. cit., pp. 98–9.
68 Clapham, op. cit., pp. 260–3, 269–72; S. Pollard, 'The Economic History of Shipbuilding, 1870–1914', unpublished Ph.D. thesis, University of London, 1951, pp. 449–51. With regard to Vickers, see below, pp. 233–5.
69 Ayres, op. cit., appendices, table 21, p. 53.
70 Essex-Crosby, op. cit., pp. 53–6.
71 Irving, op. cit., pp. 40–6.
72 See K. C. Smith and G. F. Horne, *An Index Number of Securities 1867–1914*, London and Cambridge Economic Bulletin, Special Memorandum no. 47, 1934.
73 See Ayres, op. cit., appendices, table 6, p. 36.
74 See F. Lavington, *The English Capital Market*, 1921, reprinted 1968, pp. 212–19; H. S. Foxwell, 'The Financing of Industry and Trade', *Economic Journal*, 1917.
75 Lavington, op. cit., p. 219.
76 J. Saville, 'Some Retarding Factors in the British Economy before 1914', *Yorkshire Bulletin of Economic and Social Research*, XIII, 1961.
77 Lavington, op. cit., p. 208.
78 Essex-Crosby, op. cit., pp. 91–2.
79 Thomas, op. cit., p. 139.
80 For a summary of the development of overseas issuing, see P. L. Cottrell, *British Overseas Investment in the Nineteenth Century*, 1975, pp. 30–5.
81 M. Edelstein, 'Rigidity and Bias in the British Capital Market, 1870–1913' in D. N. McCloskey (ed.), *Essays on a Mature Economy: Britain after 1840*, 1971, p. 86.
82 On the problems of foreign mining companies, see C. C. Spence, *British Investments and the American Mining Frontier 1860–1901*, Ithaca, N.Y., 1958.
83 M. Edelstein, 'Realized Rates of Return on U.K. Home and Overseas Portfolio Investment in the Age of High Imperialism', *Explorations in Economic History*, XIII, 1976, pp. 291, 294–5.
84 ibid., p. 314. For a criticism of Edelstein's sample see W. P. Kennedy, 'Institutional Response to Economic Growth: Capital Markets in Britain to 1914' in L. Hannah (ed.) *Management Strategy and Business Development*, 1976, pp. 174–5.
85 Thomas, op. cit., p. 139.
86 Supple, op. cit., pp. 342–8.
87 Goodhart, op. cit., pp. 134–5.
88 W. P. Kennedy, 'Foreign Investment, Trade and Growth in the United Kingdom, 1870–1913', *Explorations in Economic History*, XI, 1974, pp. 425, 434.
89 Cottrell, *Overseas Investment*, op. cit., pp. 48–9, 53.
90 The claim appears to have been made first by Essex-Crosby (op. cit., p. 47), whose statement in turn was accepted by Jeffreys, op. cit.
91 Payne, op. cit., pp. 522–3.
92 E. V. Morgan and W. A. Thomas, *The Stock Exchange: its History and Functions*, 1962, p. 138.
93 H. Osbourne O'Hagan, *Leaves from My Life*, 1929, pp. 2–29, 84–5, 149–54, 252–3.
94 Thomas, op. cit.
95 O'Hagan, op. cit., pp. 462–4.
96 Kennedy, 'Foreign Investment, Trade and Growth', op. cit., p. 433.
97 D. Burn, *The Economic History of Steelmaking 1867–1939*, Cambridge, 1940, reprinted 1961, pp. 249–56.
98 See T. H. Burnham and G. O. Hoskins, *Iron and Steel in Britain 1870–1930*, 1943; P. Temin, 'The Relative Decline of the British Steel Industry, 1880–1913' in H. Rosovsky (ed.) *Industrialisation in Two Systems*, 1966; P. L. Payne, 'Iron and Steel Manufactures' in D. H. Aldcroft (ed.) *The Development of British Industry and Foreign Competition 1875–1914*, 1968.
99 D. N. McCloskey, *Economic Maturity and Entrepreneurial Decline. British Iron and Steel 1870–1913*, Cambridge, Mass., 1973, pp. 114–27.
100 Mitchell, op. cit., p. 277; C. A. Paull, 'Mechanisation in British and American Bituminous Coal Mines, 1890–1939', unpublished M.Phil. thesis, University of London, 1968, p. 348.
101 Pollard, op. cit., pp. 70–5.

102 See D. C. Coleman, *Courtaulds, an Economic and Social History*, Oxford, 1969, pp. 10–13, 25–39, 57–60.

103 Kennedy, 'Institutional Response to Economic Growth', op. cit., pp. 168–70, drawing from Saul, op. cit., and I. C. R. Byatt, 'The British Electrical Industry, 1875–1914', unpublished D.Phil. thesis, University of Oxford, 1962.

104 For the experience of British Westinghouse, see below, pp. 232–3.

105 Edelstein, 'Rigidity and Bias in the British Capital Market', op. cit., pp. 83–4.

106 Ayres, op. cit., p. 202.

7 Banks and the finance of industry

There has been considerable controversy since the years immediately before the First World War over the extent to which commercial banks met the financial requirements of manufacturing industry. At the centre of the debate has been the provision of medium- and long-term finance, and English banks have been critized for not behaving like their continental counterparts in either sponsoring new industrial issues on the capital market or providing firms with more than working capital. These problems will be explored in this chapter by looking at the lending policies of a number of banks in industrial areas over a period from 1840 to the 1890s. However, it is important to realize that the structure of the banking system did not remain unchanged during this period. Whereas, at the outset, a manufacturer probably banked with a local concern which at the most had a handful of branches, and was generally accommodated through the discount of bills of exchange, by the beginning of the twentieth century the industrial firm, if it was still in existence, was probably a customer of a limited joint stock bank which had its head office in London, had a considerable branch network, and normally supplied its clients with the finance that they required through overdraft facilities. These structural changes had consequences for lending policies and will be considered in the first section of this chapter, while the latter part will consist of a review of empirical evidence concerning lending policies.

★

During the second half of the nineteenth century, the structure of English banking changed radically, and by the 1900s the system consisted primarily of a small number of joint stock banks which had branch networks covering every county in England and Wales. The process of concentration which had gathered pace during the 1890s accelerated during the decade and a half before the First World War to the extent that by 1917 the number of banks had fallen to about 40, of which five controlled two-thirds of the system's total resources. This development was the result of a number of interwoven strands, consisting first of the promotion of a large number of limited banks in the 1860s and 1870s, coupled with an expansion in the number of branches of both existing and new banks. This resulted in private banking, with a few major exceptions, being extinguished as a major component of the system. Bank amalgamations, a feature of the industry throughout the nineteenth century, changed in character from the 1880s. Instead of taking place between small concerns, with the one being taken over being a private institution, from the 1890s and especially after 1900, the banks involved were both large and usually limited joint stock concerns. Not only did the organizational structure of the banking system change considerably, but banks in industrial areas from the 1870s became more liquid as a result of a faster growth of deposits than of discounts, advances and other forms of accommodation. Consequently even the banks which remained unit concerns were able to hold to maturity in the 1870s a far greater proportion of the bills that they discounted, and by the 1880s no longer had to rely on rediscounting in the London money market in order to maintain adequate cash ratios. The liquid nature of the banking system in the last quarter of the nineteenth century permitted its customers to be accommodated by overdrafts rather than discounts, and together with the parallel organizational changes made for a more stable financial and monetary environment. These important structural changes in the banking system will now be considered in greater detail.

The number of joint stock banks remained more or less static at about 100 between 1840 and 1860 while at the same time the ranks of private banks were thinned considerably, mainly as a result of bankruptcy. Following the repeal of Peel's restrictive Joint Stock Bank Act and the inclusion of banks within the liberalized company law, there was a major wave of bank promotions in the 1860s and the early 1870s. Many of these fulfilled a real need, there being some consensus in the early 1860s that the 'banking of the country was...very much underdone'.[1] During the first six years of that decade 42 new domestic banks were successfully established and a further 26 were formed between 1870 and 1875.[2] Initially the joint stock banks formed before 1858 did not follow the example of their newer counterparts and take advantage of the change in the law by registering as limited concerns, since many of their directors and managers believed that unlimited liability was a necessary security for their depositors. This attitude was shattered in 1878 by the failure of the City of Glasgow Bank and consequently during the following six years 27 banks went 'limited', usually on the basis of reserved liability. By the 1890s hardly any joint stock bank was an unlimited concern.

The number of offices of banks in England and Wales almost doubled between 1858 and 1878, rising from 1,212 to 2,195. The number of both private and joint stock banks increased, but on average a joint stock concern had twice as many branches as its private counterpart. The ratio in 1861 was 3.1 offices per private bank and 6.7 per joint stock bank, and by 1881 the average number of offices per private bank had increased to 6.7 but for joint stock banks had risen to 12.9.[3] In terms of numbers of branches, private banks were only important in agricultural areas, where by the late 1870s there were 159 such concerns with 400 branches, as opposed to only 43 joint stock banks. But the latter had 380 branches. Joint stock banks, by the same criterion, had more or less a monopoly of the manufacturing districts of England and Wales by the late 1870s with 53 concerns with 460 branches compared with 37 private banks with 58 branches. The greatest growth of branches in the industrial areas occurred in the mid-1870s, following the last main wave of bank promotions. The bank-formation boom in the 1860s and the early 1870s had effects upon the metropolis, where banks began to acquire major branch networks for the first time. In this activity, the basis of future developments was laid through the emergence of five London banks with branch networks covering parts of the city and the provinces; in aggregate in 1878 these concerns had 53 branches in the capital and 394 in the rest of England and Wales.[4] However, in the late 1870s, only the National Provincial had a branch network which extended over most parts of the English economy.[5]

Balanced branch networks began to appear in the 1890s as a result of the amalgamation movement. Bank mergers had taken place throughout the first half of the nineteenth century, though such activity declined in the 1840s and 1850s. It accelerated thereafter to an average rate of four amalgamations a year between the 1860s and the late 1880s, twice the average rate of the previous two decades. The preponderant form was the absorption of private banks by joint stock concerns, caused by a number of factors including a waning of entrepreneurial drive amongst the absorbed bank's partners, financial weakness, or a simple psychological loss of faith. Both the Overend, Gurney crisis of 1866 and the City of Glasgow Bank crash of 1878 were events which appear to have crystallized the situation, with 11 private banks being absorbed in the late 1860s and 66 amalgamations taking place between private and joint stock banks during the 1880s. Similar pressures affected the smaller joint stock banks, but sometimes they were also pushed towards seeking a merger by the discovery of either a fraud or the results of mismanagement. In order to compete with their spreading and enlarging joint stock counterparts, a few private banks did band together but between 1862 and 1889 there was only one instance of a private bank taking over a joint stock concern.[6]

There was a marked increase in the number of bank amalgamations from the late 1880s. Competition through size now became of more importance, the lead being given by Lloyds, whose example was followed by the London and Midland in 1897. Previously neither of these concerns had had large branch networks; the largest banks in the early 1890s were the London and County with 174 branches and the National Provincial with 168 branches, and both these banks had had, atypically, large branch networks since the 1850s. By 1913 the Midland had 846 branches, Lloyds 673 and Barclays 599, mainly as a result of these three banks having taken over a total of 60 others at the turn of the century. Various factors were responsible for this marked increase in concentration, including the impact of the Baring crisis, Goschen's call for increases in reserve holdings, and the fall in the price of Consols after 1902, but primarily it would appear that the major form of competition within the increasingly cartel-ridden banking industry was through physical size and the amount of financial resources. Goodhart has estimated that 42% of the increase in the deposits of the large London monthly-reporting joint stock banks between 1890 and 1914 was due to the absorption of other banks. It would also appear that the London banks, which sought to maximize growth through a merger policy, had higher than average 'net' rates of growth of deposits. After allowing for the effects of amalgamations upon deposit growth, Lloyds' deposits still increased at a rate of 3.82% per annum between 1890 and 1914, and those of the Midland expanded at 4.64% per annum.[7]

Amalgamations were a way of acquiring branches and deposits. The process not only led to the almost total disappearance of private banking but eventually also reduced considerably the numbers of joint stock banks. This trend set in from the beginning of the 1880s, but initially was gradual with the number of joint stock banks falling throughout the decade from probably an all-time peak of 128 in 1880. However, by 1905 there were only 61 banks.[8] The dominant type of commercial bank in Edwardian England was a joint stock limited concern which had a branch network encompassing the metropolis and the provinces. In 1904 there were 12 such institutions with 2,721 branches between them.[9] This had some effect upon lending policies, as the higher management of these banks was based and rooted in London and controlled activity in the branches by carefully drafted regulations involving prescribed limits. Local knowledge and contacts became less important, although one of the main tasks of branch managers remained the compilation of information on credit-worthiness. The impact of the amalgamation movement upon the banks' lending policies is of considerable importance and will be examined later after considering the growth of the system's main liability: deposits.

★

While mergers between banks concentrated deposits into the hands of fewer and fewer banks, total deposits, before 1900, grew rapidly. However, owing to serious source deficiencies, it is extremely difficult to estimate with any degree of confidence the total volume of bank deposits. This is because of the banks' (especially private concerns') unwillingness before 1891 to publish informative balance sheets. Recently attempts have been made to overcome this deficiency by estimating the volume of non-reported deposits. The size of the adjustment required is open to debate but would appear to be of the order of at least 13.5 % of reported deposits held by joint stock banks in 1891. A series for total United Kingdom bank deposits has been estimated by Nishimura for the 1870s, and it shows deposits rising from £377.7m. to £491m. in 1880. The only other estimate is that of Sheppard, who aggregated reported deposits as published in *The Economist* and for the period 1881 to 1890 made a simple allowance for non-reported deposits based on the ratio of total reported bank deposits to the reported deposits held by joint stock banks in 1891. Sheppard's estimate for 1881 is £389m., some 20 % less than that of Nishimura for mid-1880, which the latter attributes both to an inadequate compensating factor for non-reported deposits held by private banks and an incomplete coverage of joint stock banks. Sheppard's post-1891 estimates are far more reliable and, although they probably are still incomplete in their coverage, this is a problem which diminishes progressively.[10]

On the basis of the best available estimates, namely those of Nishimura for the 1870s and Sheppard's post-1891 series, some impression can be derived of the growth of bank deposits. However, with the present data it is not possible to make full allowance for the impact of cyclical fluctuations on short- and medium-term growth rates. The rates of growth are shown in table 7.1. Nominal deposits show decades of alternating growth, with faster rates in the 1870s and 1890s and slower

Table 7.1   Growth of Bank Deposits 1870–1914

Nominal	% p.a.		
1870–1880	2.5		
1871–1880	1.5		
1880–1891	1.2		
1891–1901	3.1		
1901–1911	1.7		
at 1870 prices		(Rousseaux Price Index)	
1870–1880	3.4		
1880–1891	2.8	1870–1911	2.42% p.a.
1891–1901	3.1		
1901–1911	0.1		
at 1871 prices		(Board of Trade Price Index)	
1871–1880	2.1		
1880–1891	3.1	1871–1911	2.49% p.a.
1891–1901	4.2		
1901–1911	0.5		

Sources: S. Nishimura, 'The Growth of the Stock of Money in the U.K., 1870–1913', unpublished paper; D. K. Sheppard, *The Growth and Role of U.K. Financial Institutions 1880–1962*, 1971.

rates in the 1880s and the 1900s. Some of this difference may be due to the base years chosen, while the considerable variations in the price level had an effect. If the data are deflated, then the rate of increase in bank deposits appears to have accelerated until the turn of the century, but was subsequently followed by a decade of near-stagnation.

Branch expansion was one of the factors responsible for the accumulation of these deposits in the banking system. Newmarch thought that the substantial growth in bank offices in the 1860s and 1870s had led to 'banks . . . running after deposits with the offer of advancing terms on the one hand; and after active and borrowing accounts with too keen an appetite on the other'.[11] It is difficult to establish who were the main providers of bank deposits, but a breakdown of deposits held by the National Provincial in the mid-1870s revealed that sums not exceeding £100 in aggregate made up a sixth of the bank's total deposits, whereas accounts of £200 or less constituted a quarter. *The Bankers' Magazine* took great satisfaction in this distribution, pointing out that these 'small deposits', which it thought represented the floating capital of customers' savings slowly and gradually accumulating, and the small balances belonging to comparatively small tradesmen, were the most dependable type of deposits to a banker. It argued that they were less likely to be withdrawn in a panic and were less sensitive to movements in the rate of interest than larger individual sums.[12] These considerations were important because the London banks, from the 1870s, began to give up the practice of paying interest on sums held on current account. The lead was given in the late 1870s by the Union Bank and the City Bank, and their example was followed shortly by the Imperial and the Alliance.[13] By the decades before the First World War, no London joint stock bank was paying interest on current balances, although the practice continued in the provinces.[14] Increasingly, bank customers switched their credit balances from current to deposit accounts, and this movement had become well marked by the late 1880s.[15] There is little precise overall information on the division of bank deposits between current and deposit accounts, although in 1909 Charles Gow of the London Joint Stock stated that between 60% and 65% of his bank's deposits were in the form of current accounts.[16] However, data assembled by Goodhart for the decades immediately prior to 1914 indicates that information on the composition of London bank deposits is probably misleading for the country as a whole.[17]

★

The growth of bank deposits during the last quarter of the nineteenth century led to a complete reversal in the relationship between banks and their borrowing clients. This affected the whole of the English banking system including unit banks without branches in Lancashire and the West Riding of Yorkshire. Prior to the 1870s, banks in industrial areas usually had ratios of advances plus discounts to deposits in excess of 100% and had sustained this imbalance only by rediscounting bills in the London money market. After the late 1860s, as a result of either deposits increasing at a faster rate than loans and discounts, or such accommodation decreasing at a faster rate than deposits, banks in general became more liquid and ratios of advances plus discounts to deposits fell below 100%. This can be seen from table 7.2, the only exception being banks in the woollen and worsted districts which remained over-lent through the 1880s.

This change in the balance between banks' liabilities and assets had a number of consequences. First, with greater liquidity, banks in industrial areas no longer had to rely on rediscounting in order to maintain adequate reserves. Such a change can be seen clearly in the case of the Liverpool Commercial Bank, which in the mid-1860s rediscounted about a third of its bill holdings, in the boom of the early 1870s rediscounted only 15%, and thereafter, even during cyclical upswings, was able to hold bills until their maturity. This had further consequences: on the one hand, it reduced the volume of bills coming on to the London money market while on the other, it lessened provincial reliance on the metropolis and gave greater financial stability. Second, the banks' increases in liquidity were mirrored in greater holdings of cash and money at call. Last, and perhaps of the most immediate importance to industrial clients, the banks' greater liquidity led to a change in the way that they accommodated borrowing customers, discounting being replaced by overdrafts. Overdrafts allowed bank clients to take more advantage of discounts in settling their debts and led to the cheque finally replacing the bill of exchange. The volume of bills was in any case falling from the early 1870s as a result of transport improvements both nationally and internationally which collectively cut transit times drastically, reduced the need for inventories, and permitted telegraphic transfer payments. As the Bank of England found, discounting in the provinces could only be used as a way of increasing income in a very few areas by the late 1880s and the early 1890s – in some of the textile manufacturing towns and cities, and in Liverpool, Manchester and Newcastle. In Birmingham the bill had largely fallen out of use by the end of the nineteenth century.[18]

The fall in the volume of domestic bills and particularly in the amount coming on to Lombard Street was soon recognized, though initially with some surprise. *The Bankers' Magazine* in 1880 looked at the balance sheets of 20 English and Welsh banks which had aggregate resources of £95m., considered by the journal to be about a third of the system's total assets. The sampled banks' net assets amounted to £92.5m., of which 23.5% consisted of cash, 13% investments, 24.5% advances and loans, and less than 30% discounts. Discounting declined at a faster rate in the provinces than in the metropolis.[19] Dick later estimated that bills made up only 37% of provincial banks' advances in 1883 as opposed to 50% of London bank advances. These geographical differences in practice disappeared slowly, and by 1896 bills accounted for 25% of London bank advances and 21% of provincial bank advances.[20] In 1884 *The Bankers' Magazine* was remarking upon the 'constant complaint, for a long time past of the scarcity of bills in Lombard Street'.[21] At the end of the 1880s, it was apparent that money employed in the discount of bills was of diminishing importance and that bills had been scarce for the previous seven years or longer. It was seen that this shortage had pushed up their price and reduced the return on them. This situation resulted in banks employing more funds in advances and fixed investments 'for comparatively long dates', a trend which placed *The Bankers' Magazine,* for one,

Table 7.2 Banks' ratios of advances plus discounts: deposits, by region, 1865–96 (%)

	London	Cotton districts	Woollen and worsteds districts	Northumberland Durham Lancs and Yorks	Derby Notts Staffs Worcs Warwicks	Gloucs Mons and S. Wales	Rest
1865		120.9	131.5				80.0
1866		120.6					
1867	73.6	115.1	162.6				72.5
1868	74.8	96.2	168.6		109.9		67.4
1869	71.7	114.0	164.7		112.5		69.7
1870	71.2/78.6	114.8/104.6	161.2/133.7	103.5	115.3/106.6	98.3	67.8/76.6
1871	76.3	91.6	129.4	96.9	103.6	96.8	72.4
1872	76.8	91.9	122.0	96.0	98.4	91.9	75.8
1873	77.1	87.1	124.3	94.7	100.9	94.2	75.7
1874	76.5	85.0	125.4	92.5	97.3	95.3	72.7
1875	76.1	88.5	124.5	92.6	93.5	97.0	72.9
1876	74.9	87.7	125.2	86.8	94.4	96.9	75.1
1877	73.9	91.7	124.1	90.5	98.7	97.7	76.1
1878	73.0	96.4	125.2	94.2	99.8	98.4	81.9
1879	70.2	89.2	123.5	90.8	95.6	93.4	72.5
1880	65.0/70.6	85.9/90.2	112.8/124.0	96.9/88.2	90.5/92.2	94.4	68.0/71.4
1881	66.5	81.8	108.1	98.8	87.7		67.5
1882	68.9	83.8	104.2	98.0	85.9		65.5

Table 7.2   continued

	London	Cotton districts	Woollen and worsteds districts	Northumberland Durham Lancs and Yorks	Derby Notts Staffs Worcs Warwicks	Gloucs Mons and S. Wales	Rest
1883	68.9	84.5	105.0	97.1	84.0		66.8
1884	67.5	84.5	104.4	91.2	79.4		65.5
1885	66.4	78.5	99.1	87.1	76.2		62.8
1886	65.0	80.6	102.8	88.1	74.8		61.7
1887	65.6	80.2	96.0	89.7	75.2		60.9
1888	63.5	77.7	97.9	87.1	72.8		60.4
1889	62.4	82.5	103.7	76.7	72.3		60.2
1890	61.0	81.6	106.4	78.9	70.9		60.9
1891	62.3	78.7	96.7	71.2	68.7		61.1
1892	60.3	77.9	95.0	69.1	68.1		59.1
1893	60.4	78.8	99.3	77.2	68.4		59.0
1894	59.3	68.7	90.2	71.2	67.2		54.2
1895	59.0	69.6	82.1	74.4	64.9		57.7
1896	58.9	73.1	80.0	80.6	66.7		57.7

Source: S. Nishimura, The Decline of Inland Bills of Exchange in the London Money Market 1855–1913, Cambridge, 1971.

in a dilemma. While it regretted the change, as it maintained that such assets were more illiquid than bills and, with regard to advances, not homogeneous, it found such behaviour highly understandable since such assets offered a higher return than discounts. F. E. Steele remarked upon the 'notable decrease in discounts' in 1892 but pointed out that there was 'no disinclination on the part of bankers to discount; it is the supply of bills which, owing to well-known causes of a commercial nature, has fallen off'.

The comparative shortage of bills from the 1880s led to a reappraisal of their attributes as an asset, at least by some London bankers at the turn of the century. Bills discounted for customers were regarded as being synonymous with overdrafts and loans because they were just as risky, were earning assets, and involved the bank's goodwill since a refusal either to discount or to take on fresh bills when previously discounted ones matured could lead to a customer seeking accommodation elsewhere. However, bills bought in the London money market constituted an entirely different type of transaction. Generally by the 1890s the latter bills arose out of international transactions in which the bank did not have a direct stake in the form of customer relationship, and consequently they could be considered as secondary reserve assets, the amount held varying with the needs of the bank. These new attitudes in the early years of the twentieth century led to bills coming to be regarded as more liquid than bonds, particularly as foreign trade and finance bills could rightly be considered as being self-liquidating. This change in outlook was underlined by the fall in the price of Consols after 1900. The consequence in the banks' balance sheets was that their holdings of bills, as a proportion of total liabilities, fell between 1891 and 1904, while, due to the rapid growth in the number of bills arising out of international transactions, the proportion of open market bills discounted by the banks rose strongly compared with the volume of discounts for customers.[22] By the 1890s some of the emerging nationwide banks may have been pursuing a positive policy of discouraging discounts. Managers of banks absorbed by the London and Midland were requested to refrain from giving customers bill finance and instructed to provide them with advances.[23] The normal form of advance in the provinces was an overdraft, as opposed to a loan in the metropolis.[24]

By the end of the nineteenth century the London monthly-reporting banks preferred to maintain ratios of advances to deposits below 55%, and their managements became alarmed if the ratio rose and remained above 60% for any appreciable time.[25] The data that Nishimura has assembled, shown in table 7.2, indicates that the London banks in general were maintaining ratios of the desired order by the mid-1890s, whereas in the 1880s the general level had been above 60% and in the 1870s above 70%. However, the new nationwide banks in the 1890s could accommodate substantial geographical differences in the ratio of advances to deposits and give managers in new branches their head in order to obtain new accounts and customers by virtue of being 'balanced branch banks'. Through now having branches in both credit-surplus and credit-deficit areas, the new nationwide banks could offset such differences internally and maintain overall a desired margin of under-lending. The ability to make such offsetting is clearly shown in the case of the London and Midland at the end of the 1890s, for which Goodhart has been able to obtain regional ratios of advances and discounts as shown in table 7.3.[26]

Table 7.3   Ratios of advances and bills discounted to deposits for various sectors of the London and Midland Bank in the late 1890s.

	1.12.1896	5.6.1897	6.12.1897	7.6.1898	1.12.1898
London	.52	.47	.50	.60	.57
Manchester	1.12	.94	.90	.87	.83
Preston	.70	.73	.65	.66	.58
Oldham Joint Stock				.79	.66
North Western			.96	.97	.96
Huddersfield			.67	.70	.74
Midland	.57	.56	.59	.60	.55
Yorkshire	.74	.67	.60	.66	.65
Westmorland	.26	.29	.24	.26	.26
Carlisle	.91	.87	.85	.80	.68
Jersey		.54	.30	.33	.23
New branches	1.05	1.16	1.21	.99	.81

Source: C. A. E. Goodhart, *The Business of Banking, 1891–1914*, 1972, p. 159.

A fairly standardized pattern of charging had emerged amongst the London banks by the 1890s. Large advances, namely those of £40,000 or more, bore interest at Bank rate, while smaller loans and overdrafts were charged at Bank rate plus a margin of $\frac{1}{2}$% to 1%. Some banks required their customers to maintain a minimum balance which on occasion could be as large as 10% of the accommodation being provided.[27] In the provinces there was a different practice of charging a customer on the amount of turnover of his account.[28] The Barnsley Bank, a joint stock concern, appears to have charged its customers in the 1840s a commission of 5% on 'returns', with interest charged at 4% if the account was in debit but allowed at $2\frac{1}{2}$% on any credit balance. It would seem that most of its profits came from commission charges, as its directors in negotiations over accounts laid great stress on whether an account was 'active' and on its volume of turnover. This charging pattern had hidden dangers since the cost of acquiring a large account with high turnover was often bank accommodation of some form or another. It took over the account of a draper from the rival Wakefield and Barnsley Union Bank, which had an active balance of £1,500 through agreeing a temporary credit of £500. There were limits to the bank's competitive stance but they are difficult to establish. A request for an advance of £2,000 to £3,000 was considered to be too high a price for an ironwork's account which made 'returns' of upwards of £20,000 per annum. However, in 1851 the bank was prepared to give an unsecured overdraft of £1,000 to a linen manufacturing partnership with a capital of £3,000 to £4,000 in order to obtain their account, which had 'returns' of £15,000 to £20,000. Similarly in 1855 a colliery account with 'returns' of £50,000 was taken from the Wakefield and Barnsley Union through granting an advance of £9,000.[29]

Twenty years later the Swansea Bank was following a similar system of charging. It levied a half-yearly commission on the turnover of accounts. In the bank's early years the rate appears to have been set at $\frac{1}{4}$%, but during the late 1870s and in the 1880s some of its client industrial firms were able to reduce this commission to $\frac{1}{8}$% and in one case to $\frac{1}{16}$%. The much lower rates of commission were compensated to a degree by charges for discounting and other forms of accommodation. The Swansea Bank's discount rate was apparently rigid at 4%, although 5% was charged for accommodation paper. Customers tried to reduce these rates by negotiation, which led the bank to attempt to link its discount rate to Bank rate, maintaining a minimum of 4% when Bank rate was at or below 3% and thereafter a constant differential of 1%, but reduced to $\frac{1}{2}$% for first-class London bills. The bank appears simply to have charged a fixed rate of 5% on overdrafts.[30] Similarly the Cumberland Bank during the last quarter of the nineteenth century charged a commission on turnover at the rate of $\frac{1}{8}$%, and appears to have had a fairly rigid overdraft rate although it fell during the cheap money period of the 1890s from $6\frac{1}{4}$% to $4\frac{1}{2}$–5%. According to its customers, such charges were higher than those made by other local banks.[31]

The bank which combined both country and metropolitan charging practices was the London private bank of Glyn, Mills. It had a large number of provincial industrial customers and from the 1870s until the 1890s it charged them what it called 'country terms'. These would appear generally to have been a commission of 1s. 6d. (07.5p)% but with an allowance of interest credited at broker's rate on any balance kept above a specified level. Usually Glyns discounted three months bills at Bank rate, while Bank rate plus a margin of 1 %, subject to a minimum of 4 %, was charged on overdrafts. Loans were charged on similar lines. Amounts required for wage payments were charged separately and at varying rates; in one case at a commission of 2s. 6d. (12.5p) %, in another at one half of one per mille, the provision and carriage of the necessary coin being 'large and costly'.[32] The provision of cheque books was costed and charged separately; the cost for one customer being estimated at £20 a year. Inter-bank competition in the 1890s resulted in Glyns lowering its commission charges and in some cases altering the entire terms on which a customer's account was conducted. For instance, in 1899 it was agreed with one particular customer that they were no longer to be charged a commission on their general account but instead were to keep £5,000 in Glyns' hands. Glyns were prepared to pay the current broker's call rate on any balance above that level but in the case of an overdraft, or 'any deficiency below £5,000', Bank rate was to be charged.[33] Where new charging schemas were not introduced, Glyns' commission charges were reduced to either 10d. (03.5p) or 1s. (05p) %.[34] Although commission charges persisted in country banking until 1914, competition whittled them down, and the banks had to rely increasingly on interest levied on loans and discounts. Consequently, fixed interest charges disappeared and banks' charges tended to move with Bank rate, usually with a margin of 1 % or 1½ % and a floor of 4 %.

Long periods of Bank rate at panic levels of 7 % or more were an infrequent occurrence after the 1866 crisis, but the American crisis of 1907 did lead both *The Economist* and the Bank of England to investigate the effects of long periods of credit stringency upon commercial banking customers. *The Economist* solicited the views of its readers and any firms but received only 12 replies which stressed the importance of the borrowing cost effects of a higher Bank rate. Seven replies denied any deterrent to trade caused by the Bank rate being at a panic level for an appreciable period of time. Generally it would seem from the answers received that changes in the structure of domestic interest rates caused by the movement of Bank rate had by themselves little effect upon the pattern of industrial borrowing and investment. The most seriously affected groups were apparently merchants, as periods of high Bank rate usually coincided with international crises which often proved to be the upper turning point in the cyclical movement of primary product prices.[35] The Bank reached similar conclusions in the survey that it conducted through its branch agents, who appear to have gathered information from local bankers rather than their customers. The survey showed that by 1909 loan charges linked to Bank rate were common in most industrial and commercial centres, although in rural areas, especially in Yorkshire, the fixed 5% traditional charge was still in force. It was these customary charges which had attracted London banks to take over rural concerns, since they offered income with which to offset the low, almost unremunerative rates current in the metropolitan money market in the 1890s and so allowed the banks to sustain dividends of 14% to 16%. The Bank's agents discovered that most provincial banks and branches had minimum floors to interest-rate charges, which had the effect that Bank rate movements below $3\frac{1}{2}$ or 4% were of no consequence. Under such a charging system, it was only when Bank rate went above 5% that commercial banking borrowing costs on advances were affected and rose. Even so, when Bank rate had reached 7% during the American crisis, a large number of commercial banks had chosen to ignore the effect of such a rise upon their interest charges, and in many cases commercial rates had been increased to only $5\frac{1}{2}$% for 'good' customers and to $6\frac{1}{2}$% where a large risk element was involved.[36] The persistence in some areas of traditional fixed loan charges that the Bank of England survey revealed continued in some form or another into the 1920s. Lavington noted that loan rates were generally lower in the north than in the south and attributed this, possibly wrongly, to differences in the keenness of bargaining.[37] More likely it was due to the continuance in rural areas of a fixed 5% charge on accommodation.

There was little general criticism of either the availability of short-term finance from the banking system or its cost. There were complaints from provincial centres during the 1850s and 1860s about high interest rates and occasionally about the lack of credit at any price caused by an external drain of gold.[38] However, recent research has shown, for the closing decades of the nineteenth century at least, that the Bank of England attempted to shield the domestic economy to the greatest possible extent from the ebbs and flows of international financial transactions. From the late 1890s the Bank used its so-called 'gold devices' as an alternative to raising Bank rate, possibly in order not to dampen down domestic economic activity.[39] It also appears that the Bank, at least between 1890 and 1914, did not follow the 'rules of the gold standard' during a boom, to the extent that it did not attempt to contract contra-cyclically the reserve base of the commercial banks. Goodhart has found that during a boom the Bank allowed the banks to increase their balances with it, usually indirectly through discounting, in order to provide the liquidity structure with which to finance a higher level of economic activity. Such actions reduced the Bank's holdings of cash, and increased its holdings of securities, which reduced its liquidity, leading eventually to a rise in Bank rate. Accordingly Goodhart concluded that interest rates rose during a boom as a consequence of a rise, not a fall, in the reserve base of the banking system.[40] The commercial banks accommodated increases in the demand for advances by withdrawing money placed at call with the London discount market and not replacing bills in their bill cases when they matured. Such actions would eventually force the discount houses 'into the Bank'. The banks regarded domestic accommodation and bills as 'counterweights'. During a boom the banks' falling demand for bills coupled with rising interest rates had two effects. First it led to the provision of international credit being undertaken by financial centres other than London, and second it generated an inflow of short-term capital which more than compensated for the increase in the trade deficit resulting from domestic expansion.[41]

The practical reasons for the Bank of England's accommodating behaviour may lie with the Bank Act of 1892, which cut the Bank's income from the services that it rendered to the government. This fall in revenue, coupled with the low level of interest rates during the mid-1890s, curtailed severely the Bank's total earnings, reducing its dividend to a level sinificantly below that of most of the commercial banks. Consequently the Bank became more competitive in its private banking business in order to increase its total income enough to sustain a regular dividend of 9%.[42] Income from discounting at Threadneedle Street, which had been at a low level since the mid-1870s, rose steadily from 1895 until 1913. The average yearly income from discounting in London had been £35,550 between 1875 and 1895 but the average for the subsequent 20 years was £112,420. Such a change in magnitude was not simply due to variations in the price level. Similarly the Bank's income from short loans and advances rose from an average of £186,000 per annum for the period 1875–95 to an average of £354,420 per annum between 1895 and 1914.[43]

There is a very strong possibility that the Bank of England had also operated a pro-cyclical monetary policy during the 1860s and, as during the post-1890 period, that this was caused by a reduction in its income from the state. In 1861 Gladstone as Chancellor of the Exchequer cut severely the Bank's fees for managing the National Debt and, through the creation of the Post Office Savings Bank, decreased the Treasury's reliance on the Bank. Subsequently during the 1860s boom the Bank's income from discounting bills and notes reached a peak for the whole of the nineteenth century which was not surpassed until the outbreak of war in 1914.[44] This income was buoyed up by the high level of interest rates from 1864 but not to such an extent as to explain the whole rise, and it would appear that the Bank was looking for alternative sources of revenue in order to restore its income and sustain its dividend. Bill discounting by the Bank increased sharply during the second quarter of 1862, and during the next four years there were substantial periods when the volume of discounting exceeded the Bank's note reserve. As during the later decades, this activity by the Bank indirectly swelled the bankers' balances placed with it and so expanded the reserve base of the financial sector. The practical limits to the Bank's activity in the money market appear to have been reached when its holdings of bullion fell in conjunction with the note reserve declining to below the level of the bankers' balances. When this occurred the Bank curtailed its discounting after first raising the level of Bank rate. This first happened in August 1864 and the Bank was able subsequently to tackle effectively the autumn crisis of that year. The Bank's level of discounting did not begin to rise again markedly until May 1865 but was then cut in October when both the note reserve declined below the level of the bankers' balances and its bullion stock had been falling for at least a month. Subsequent peaks in the Bank's discounting before the onset of the 1866 crisis were due to the seasonal effects of the fiscal year.[45]

★

While neither contemporaries nor historians have seriously questioned the supply of short-term credit generated by the banking system, considerable criticism has been made of the commercial banks' apparent unwillingness either to provide medium- and long-term loans to industrial companies or to act as intermediaries in the capital market. Since at least the 1910s, unfavourable comparisons have been made between the services provided by English banks and those of continental, especially German, banks. Before looking at the various arguments in this particular debate, it is important to try and establish what the lending policies of English banks actually were during the nineteenth century. A substantial amount of evidence has now accumulated showing that banks during the early phases of the industrial revolution, that is up to about the 1830s, did provide long-term loans to industrial firms which often financed investment in fixed capital.[46]

Banking practice in the post-1830 period is as yet less clear. Bankers were warned of the dangers which could arise; George Rae in the guise of 'Thomas Bullion' wrote in 1850 in the following terms:

> An overdraft, if granted at all should be *temporary* only, limited in amount and duration by the occasion which it is required to meet; and there is no trade or business, however well conducted or whatever the amount of capital employed, in the course of which such

occasions may not arise. The detention of a ship, for example – the non-arrival of a letter, – the miscarriage of the mail, and other such mishaps, are clearly occasions for the interposition of the bankers with a timely advance.[47]

He was equally clear about the types of securities that a bank should take, stating: 'reject . . . everything that is not readily convertible into money. In short, turn over a new leaf, and MIND YOUR OWN BUSINESS.'[48] It is evident that many country banks did not follow this advice, though sometimes at their own peril. Black Dyke Mills was supported by a bank overdraft from the early 1830s, when it was established, until the mid-1850s.[49] Lloyds Bank in the mid-nineteenth century provided capital as well as credit to some of its customers, financing particularly building. It would appear in the case of this bank at least that such accommodation began as 'temporary' but when confidence was established in a client, then it became more long-term and in volume exceeded the requirements for solely working capital.[50] Similarly in the case of the South Wales coalfield during the 1840s and 1850s, banks were prepared to extend more than short-term credit to colliery companies, although the degree of provision varied with both the circumstances of the times and the prudence of the individual bankers. However, it has been suggested that the volume of long-term bank finance granted to this industry was of a sufficient magnitude to have limited considerably the region's dependence upon an inflow of development capital.[51]

The degree of danger incurred by banks providing long-term finance is shown clearly in the cases of two bank failures in the mid-1850s. The Derwent Iron Company, founded in 1840, which with its 18 blast furnaces was the largest iron company in England, survived only with the aid of long-term accommodation from the Northumberland and Durham District Bank. When the latter failed in 1857 it was found that the bank had advanced at least £966,381 on the security of only £250,000 promissory notes from the iron company's directors and a £100,000 mortgage on the plant. The reason for the loans would appear to have been the close personal tie between the bank and the company through J. Richardson, who was both the bank's managing director and on the board of the iron company.[52] The year before, the Royal British Bank had failed and amongst its liquidator's assets was a £100,000 advance to the Cefn Iron and Coal works, Glamorganshire, secured on the plant.[53] The iron industry also received long-term assistance during the slump of the second half of the 1870s, *The Bankers' Magazine* commenting in 1879 that 'some bankers have committed themselves heavily by advances to iron companies and when those works which they have aided in their time of distress, once more become profitable, the bankers in question may hope to realise a larger proportion of their securities with advantage'.[54] Apparently the failures of the mid-1850s had gone from memory.

The available information and evidence is patchy, and consequently it is difficult to establish in more than very general terms mid- and late-nineteenth-century banking practice.[55] One of the main reasons for this situation is the lack of the necessary source material. The archives of the Midland Bank, one of the richest in terms of overall holdings, contains material giving details of loan transactions for only a very few of its constituent banks.[56] Given this major difficulty, the records of four country joint stock banks – the Barnsley Banking Company, the Cumberland Union Banking Company, the Preston Banking Company, and the Swansea Bank – covering a period from the 1840s to the 1890s will be used to establish case studies of lending policies by fairly typical banks in industrial areas. However, records of these banks have only survived for what may be called benchmark periods and as a result it is not possible to trace over a long period quantitative or qualitative changes in lending policies of these banks. In addition there are further limitations. Although the loan books of the banks do portray the various forms of industrial finance required by their customers, any picture drawn from them will be distorted for a number of reasons. First, information is given only for the banks' customers who may be atypical and therefore unrepresentative. Second, there is seldom available parallel business-history evidence which would place the loan transactions in their proper perspective. Third, it is usually impossible to gauge the actual effect of the finance provided either upon the borrower or the lender.

The four banks to be considered had varying careers before they were absorbed into the Midland. The Barnsley and the Cumberland were amongst the earliest joint stock banks to be established but were very dissimilar in size. The Yorkshire concern was and remained a small local bank. It was founded by local businessmen in 1832 with a paid-up capital of £25,000 to replace a branch of the Huddersfield Banking Company which had closed. The Cumberland was formed in 1828 with an initial nominal capital eight times larger than the Barnsley and, unlike very many of the banks formed in the 1830s, rapidly established a branch network in the industrial region on the Cumberland coast. Both banks issued notes but the authorized circulation of the Barnsley in 1844 was only £9,563 while that of the Cumberland was £35,393. The north-western bank opened further branches in the 1860s, partly by absorbing an existing private bank, and unlike many of the established joint stock banks became a limited concern, with an issued capital of £540,000 of which £225,000 was paid up. The Preston Bank was one of the few to be formed under Peel's Joint Stock Banking Act of 1844, had initially a paid-up capital of £100,000, and in the 1850s and the first half of the 1860s opened a large number of branches in both east and west Lancashire. It survived the 1857 crisis, but the cotton famine together with the 1866 crisis caused the bank's suspension. Following an agreement with its depositors, and after raising fresh capital, the Preston Bank was reopened. The Swansea Bank was a product of the last national boom in bank formation, being established in 1872 by local merchants, many of whom were connected with the rapidly growing tinplate industry. With two branches and a capital of £90,000, its resources were soon committed, which led to a further capital issue in 1876 and an attempt by the management to reduce the volume of the bank's outstanding loans.[57] Information about loans made by the Barnsley is available for the 1840s and 1850s, by the Preston for the late 1860s, by the Swansea for the 1870s and 1880s, and by the Cumberland for the period from the late 1870s until the mid-1890s. The evidence to be considered varies considerably in source, ranging from an exact schedule of overdrafts to a manager's jotting book, but for each bank it is possible to establish some overall impression of the role that it played in the local economy.

The focus of the industrial economy of the Barnsley area changed during the first half of the nineteenth century. Until the mid-1830s, the growth of the town had been connected with the rapid development of linen weaving and finishing. Between 1770 and 1830 Barnsley's population trebled as a result of a steady influx of handloom weavers from Lancashire, Cheshire, Scotland and Ireland who were encouraged to settle by local linen bleachers. By 1836 there were 36 master manufacturers and over 4,000 handlooms in the town's linen industry. However, the industry's rate of growth started to decline during the second half of the 1820s, and from the 1830s Barnsley faced increasing competition from Scottish producers in the home market and German goods in Europe.[58] Consequently the trade was depressed and economic activity in the locality was sustained only by the beginnings of the extensive development of the South Yorkshire coalfield. The surviving loan book of the Barnsley Bank covers the period from the mid-1840s until the late 1850s when the economic base of the region was shifting from the linen trade to coalmining.

The Barnsley Bank, like many of the joint stock banks formed in the 1830s, was very much a local concern: its directors and manager knew personally most of their clients and through such knowledge determined their credit-worthiness. The nature of the relationship is illustrated by the case of a possible overdraft to a farmer: the bank's directors mentioned the transaction to the farmer's grandfather, 'who said we should be all right in letting him have it'.[59] A consequence of this mode of business was that 'outsiders' to the town and area served by the bank were generally refused accommodation. This can be seen in a number of instances. James Morton & Co., silk ribbon warehousemen of London, were refused a discount account despite their substantial business with country drapers in the locality. The bank's board took the same decision when David Duncan, a railway founder of Oakenshaw near Wakefield, wanted to open an account and obtain a credit of £500 secured on plant worth £3,000; the reason noted being that 'we think it a sufficient reason for the above coming from his own locality.' In the case of a railway contractor from Wakefield who was building a local line, the bank's directors took a year to decide to give him an advance but then gave him only a third of what he had requested. Although the bank did not deal favourably with every local request for assistance, on some occasions it went way beyond the bounds subsequently set by George Rae for an overdraft. A local surgeon with a deposit account was granted an overdraft of £300 which would enable him to lend £1,000 on mortgage. Similarly a bank shareholder obtained £100 for six months which allowed him to place his son as a partner in a newly established engineering firm without having to call in £300 which he had out at interest.

Some overall view of the bank's activities can be taken by examining the loans and credits made in two years – April 1845 to March 1846, and April 1854 to March 1855. In the former year the bank incurred a total commitment of £41,720, of which at least £29,020 (69.55 %) consisted of credits, advances, and overdrafts made to industrial enterprises. The exact type of borrowing transaction was specified in the case of £21,700, of which the majority was termed 'credits' while overdrafts totalled only £1,000. The borrowing term was given in the case of £25,750, of which all but £550 was for terms of four months or less, with the largest amount (£18,600) being for three months. However, occasionally the bank was prepared to make accommodation for periods of up to two years. In all, there were 33 transactions recorded during the year, 25 of which were for individual amounts of £500 or less, but in one case the amount involved was £18,600. The bank took a wide variety of types of security for these transactions. Personal bonds and joint promissory notes were normally associated with smaller transactions, while mortgage deeds and the bank's own shares were used generally for larger amounts, but it would seem that the bank had no hard and fast rules regarding acceptable security. In one instance an advance of £30 to a corn miller was secured on a mortgage deed, while a linen manufacturer obtained a £1,000 credit on a promissory note. Ten years later in 1854/5 the bank noted total lending of only £19,415, of which a mere £1,735 was to industrial concerns. While cyclical factors may be responsible for some of the difference in the amount of bank accommodation sought and granted, it is probable that structural change in the local economy was more important. By the mid-1850s the linen industry was declining rapidly but the coal industry, despite the coming of the railway, was as yet little developed. This transition may be responsible for both the general lack of preciseness in the bank's noted transactions and its apparent willingness to lend for longer periods. In 1854/5 the average term appears to have been four to five months, with the bank taking on more transactions involving lending over a year or a year and a half than in 1845/6. However, as in 1845/6, most loans in 1854/5, 31 out of 36, involved sums of £500 or less. Security requirements appear to have changed little though the bank in 1854/5 did allow one loan to be secured on a life policy and another on a colliery's engines and plant.

Local firms came to the bank for accommodation for a variety of reasons, and probably not all their demands for accommodation, especially if they were for discounts, reached the loans and advances book. What this source does show for the 1840s and 1850s is that the bank was prepared to grant resources for a wide range of objects, but with the local shift from linen to coal, the amounts required from the mid-1850s increased in size and were needed for a longer duration. In the mid-1840s the bank was prepared to give 'credits', each usually of £200 to £400, on a wide range of security but normally personal, to individuals either taking over existing businesses or establishing new concerns. Sons and employees were backed by their fathers and employers in requests for advances to enable them to start as drapers. Engineers, millers, coal proprietors and farmers obtained similar accommodation in proposals concerned with financing the take-over of existing concerns. Very occasionally the bank was prepared to provide capital to some of the larger textile manufacturers with, in one instance, the bank more or less converting an existing first mortgage of £5,000 provided by a private individual on premises and machinery, into a credit line.

As mining gradually became more important from the early 1850s, the bank became slowly accustomed to dealing with considerably larger loan applications which indirectly provided the borrowers with medium- to long-term finance. This change is difficult to date precisely but an application made in July 1850 on behalf of Earl Fitzwilliam for an extension of credit from £3,000 to £5,000, 'as the outlay of an ironstone works was greater and the income was less than calculated', probably marks the turning point. Extension of existing credits, followed by fresh credits, required in order to finance the sinking of colliery shafts became increasingly common from the mid-1850s. The sums involved had risen to £6,000 to

£10,000 by 1856 and 1857, and in one instance the bank was prepared to sanction a loan for £4,500 for 18 months on the security of a colliery lease. The bank gave advances to finance the construction of mineral lines to connect the new collieries with the region's growing network of railways. In addition it was prepared to give loans of between £1,000 and £9,000 to private individuals for periods up to nine months to enable them either to pay calls for capital made by colliery partnerships or to repay the capital of retiring partners in collieries. It is difficult to ascertain exactly how long the bank was prepared to allow such loans to last; in one instance it was agreed that a credit of £10,000 made to a colliery proprietor to finance the sinking of a shaft and the construction of a railway should be for five months and thereafter the balance 'was to be reduced'. Closer to 'classical' banking were advances to meet seasonal needs; in the case of the coal industry, caused by the freezing of the canal which prevented stocks from being moved before the coming of the railway. Some of the coalmasters were either local gentry or farmers, existing customers of the bank, but others were new men, often from outside the locality, and their entry into the bank's loan book appears to have been smoothed often through partnership with local men.

The decline of the linen trade by the late 1840s led to a demand for what might be termed 'disaster' banking. As the Barnsley industry lost ground to Scottish and foreign competition, the financing of yarn stocks by local firms proved difficult without bank support. This demand was then augmented by what one entrepreneur termed 'disappointing sales', but these were subsequently recast as a 'depression of trade'. The problems of the industry continued until the mid-1850s, with one manufacturer pressing each year for his line of credit to be extended. Moreover, the growth of the exploitation of the coalfield was not without its problems, even when good rail connections had been established. Shafts collapsed and sometimes new seams proved to contain substantial quantities of water, and such occurrences led to demands for financial help from the bank.

In some instances the provision of large colliery credits from the mid-1850s was balanced partially by the bank requiring minimum balances to be held. A credit of £7,000 was given to the West Silkstone and West Staveley Coal Company on the security of £3,000 promissory notes, leases, and £2,000 in cash paid into the bank. However, Smith, Carr & Smith, the owners of the Stafford collieries, failed twice to open an account in the late 1850s, despite holding out the prospect of trebling their 'returns' from £10,000 to £30,000 if a credit of £4,500 was provided for 18 months, because the only security that they could offer was a colliery lease. Therefore it would seem that there were limits to the extent to which the Barnsley Bank was prepared to lend, set by required securities, even where the prospective account offered a high commission income through a substantial turnover.

The loan data from the Preston Bank are not at all comparable with those of the Barnsley concern. Whereas the latter was a small local 'unit' bank, adapting to new demands as coalmining became more important in the area that it serviced, it is only possible to look at the activities of the Lancashire bank during an atypical period in its history, the two years after it was forced to stop payments in 1866. The Preston Bank closed its doors on 19 July 1866 after a run on its deposits during the two previous days which had caused withdrawals amounting to £40,000. The bank had been weakened by the cotton famine of the first half of the decade, during which it had tried to accommodate textile manufacturers through overdrafts and loans secured on mills. As the ripples of the Overend, Gurney failure spread out to the provinces, the bank was unable to react to the panic because it could not realize any of the advances that it had made to cotton masters during the previous four years. A preliminary balance sheet drawn up at the end of July 1866 shows that the bank's main losses arose from open accounts, which amounted to £214,000 as opposed to only £2,276 on bills held and £40,000 on bills which had been rediscounted. The bank was revived through agreements both with its depositors, who accepted repayment in instalments, and with its 113 shareholders who paid further calls on the shares that they held.[60] It began making loans again in November 1866,[61] and subsequently its directors announced that they had 'exercised great caution in avoiding any additional risk . . . while availing themselves of every opportunity of acquiring new business',[62] an understandable policy given the previous events which had necessitated the closure of two of the bank's eight branches.

The main problem that the bank's directors faced was the state of the cotton accounts and here they had to balance the feasible against the desirable. One firm obtained an agreement that its overdraft limit of £1,000, secured by a lease, would continue, providing its outstanding debt of £920 was reduced by £100 to £150 each year. Similarly another millowner was able to reach an understanding that he could have a limit of £7,000 secured on the lease of one of his mills. Such instances are not isolated cases and the bank tried generally to provide further accommodation, usually temporary, but at the same time increasing the secured portions of outstanding loans. One client, for example, managed to obtain an additional £5,000 for six months but on the condition that his outstanding balance would be reduced to £16,000, of which a further £3,000 would be secured. Some firms appear to have been in desperate straits; one owner stated in June 1867 that due to his own illness and the unfavourable state of the trade, he was unable either to bring his overdraft down to the agreed limit or to pay the half-yearly interest and commission. He hoped to meet these outstanding sums within two months but only if the bank would renew bills maturing during the next quarter. This the bank agreed to do on condition that the balance was reduced as soon as possible and a balance sheet was submitted. One further case highlights the problems which confronted the reconstituted bank. Initially it was approached for an advance of £1,000 to allow a mill to continue to run, but an investigation by one of the bank's directors revealed the overall perilous state of the applicant's affairs. Funds were required to meet raw cotton debts of £1,500 but the mill and some of its plant were pledged already to the bank and the only further security available was the remaining loose machinery. The applicant proposed to transfer his remaining free property to trustees and work under their inspection, raising capital by selling some land that he held. Other firms were working on this basis – obtaining further finance on the security of promissory notes of trustees. It is difficult to establish the precise limits to the extent to which the bank's directors were prepared to nurse cotton accounts, but they did refuse one application for an overdraft limit of £4,000 secured by a weaving shed, freehold property, and fixed machinery valued at £5,000 together with the deeds of houses and land valued at £1,500.

While the cotton famine had crippled the bank, and the ensuing depression of the second half of the 1860s had exacerbated the difficulties of cotton manufacturers who wished to borrow, some of the resulting bankruptcies created opportunities for others to enter the industry. George Brown, a wire worker and drawer, became a woollen and cotton spinner and requested an advance of £2,400 secured on deeds. Within six months he returned to the bank for a further £600 in order to lease and work a weaving shed, and the bank agreed to provide £250 to £300 without requesting further security. Some other manufacturers, with the return of American supplies, decided either to re-equip or expand and came to the bank for finance to allow them to undertake their plans. John Walker obtained £1,000 to lay down more machinery, and it would seem that the bank's favourable response to this request which extended his credit line to £5,400, was due not only to an existing guarantee provided by a Liverpool firm but also to Walker's investments in Bank stock and Consols. Another firm obtained a limit of £2,000 to finance the erection of a weaving shed and this was in addition to a previous loan of £700 which had assisted the purchase of the land and the construction of two houses. One further element, along with new entrants and extensions of existing plant, was the retirement of cotton entrepreneurs and the consequent transfer of their concerns to either their existing partners or new ones, usually their sons. The bank appears to have readily acceded to requests to maintain existing arrangements, even where they involved outstanding advances of the order of £5,000 which were being reduced only in half-yearly stages.

Such cotton business was probably exceptional – the result of the bank having to deal as sympathetically as it could with one sector of the local economy which had been badly shaken. However, it is impossible to gauge what the bank's 'normal' lending may have been, as the other local industries – coal, iron and engineering – were relatively depressed in the late 1860s as a result of the financial shock of 1866 and the collapse of the railway-building boom of the first half of the decade. The bank had the accounts of both the North of England Carriage Company and the Acadian Iron Company and was linked to the latter through John Livesey, who was a director of both the bank and the iron concern. The Carriage Company had a severe cash flow problem in the mid-1860s which the bank attempted to ease. It gave an advance of £4,000 on the security of an assignment of a debt of £6,432 owed by the Great Western Railway. However, a month later, in December 1866, the bank refused to provide a loan of £3,500 on securities of the Athens Gas and Land Company. The engineering company's difficulties grew and in January 1867 the bank agreed to advance £30,000 as a temporary loan on a variety of securities including outstanding debts, railway shares, and deeds of houses, and in the meantime provided bridging finance on wagon leases. The arrangement was finalized in the form of a fixed advance of £25,000 secured on ten guarantees of £2,000 and the wagon leases. The company obtained a further £5,000 in mid-1867 secured on a debt of £10,660 owed by the Great Western but only on the condition that it was paid off in monthly instalments of £1,500. Such accommodation in varying forms enabled the rolling stock works to ride out the aftermath of 1866. The position of the Acadian Iron Company was entirely different and Livesey's main needs consisted of 'classic' short-term self-liquidating loans to finance the import of ore. However, in two instances the bills pledged as security were renewed and the advance became effectively a medium-term loan of 12 months. In general the bank appears in the mid-1860s to have been ready at all times to make advances on metal stocks or colliery leases but not on mining shares, to which it preferred personal guarantees.

It would be highly dangerous to generalize from the activities of the Preston Bank during the three years following the 1866 crisis, its own suspension and reconstitution. Similarly objections can be raised concerning the typicality of the Swansea Bank's loan policy in the 1870s and 1880s. It was a newly created concern and probably during its early years competed agressively for business. By 1876 it was over-committed and consequently had to raise fresh capital and curtail its lending. Outside events during the following seven years probably also affected the bank's behaviour, in particular the crash of the City of Glasgow bank in 1878 and a large number of local industrial and mercantile failures in 1883 that led to the neighbouring Glamorganshire Banking company incurring losses of £168,866 which extinguished its guarantee fund.[63] The bank published a form of balance sheet from 1876, details of which are given in table 7.4. It can be seen that the bank's liquidity increased in two stages, the first in the late 1870s following the City of Glasgow failure, and the second, which is relatively a much greater shift, in the mid-1880s, and which came with local failures as well as a turn down of the business cycle. As a result of more disclosure and itemization, it is possible for 1884 and 1885 to establish the bank's advances plus discounts: deposits ratio, namely 131.2% and 120.8% respectively. This shows that the bank, despite its increased liquidity, was still 'overlent' and as such may have

Table 7.4   Swansea Bank, balance sheet (*shillings and pence omitted*)

Year ending	31.12.1876 £	31.12.1877 £	31.12.1879 £	31.12.1880 £
Capital	201,236	201,236	201,236	201,236
Reserve fund	32,623	35,000	35,000	35,000
Deposit and current account	164,502	181,425	164,722	177,702
Unclaimed divs	51	69	57	85
Rebate on bills not due	731	640	640	554
Balance on p. & l.	11,279	8,375	9,052	7,163
	410,424	426,747	410,707	421,741
Bank premises	7,018	7,039	7,214	7,165
Bills discounted etc.	370,628	386,621	363,102	376,291
Investments				
Cash in hand and at bankers	32,778	33,086	40,391	38,283
Cash: deposits	19.92%	18.23%	24.52%	21.54%
Cash: liabilities	7.98%	7.75%	9.83%	9.07%
Advances: deposits				

been atypical since the data that Nishimura has assembled, shown in table 7.2, indicates that banks in south Wales by the 1870s had generally ratios of the order of 94%. However, the relatively high mobilization of the Swansea Bank's deposits may be explained by its particular geographical location and its board's links with local industries.

The bank was established in 1873 with two branches in an area which was undergoing rapid industrialization. The original mainsprings of the growth of the local economy had been coalmining and copper smelting, and collieries, especially those raising anthracite, continued to be of growing importance, supplying both the local smelting industries and a buoyant export trade. The copper-working industry reached its apogee in the 1860s and 1870s and thereafter lead, but especially zinc, smelting became more important and some of the copper concerns were converted into smelter works. The Swansea area became also the main Welsh centre of tinplate production, using locally produced open-hearth steel.[64] The bank, through its directors, was linked intimately with these developments and can be described as an industrialists' bank. Many of its

31.12.1881 £	31.12.1882 £	31.12.1883 £	31.12.1884 £	31.12.1885 £
201,236	201,236	201,236	201,236	201,236
35,000	37,000	40,000	42,000	43,500
195,970	209,674	210,159	256,677	273,005
58	73	85	91	96
689	741	463	531	329
10,075	12,364	11,056	10,600	10,070
443,030	461,090	463,001	511,136	528,237
7,227	8,057	8,036	8,038	8,012
407,803	417,350	385,687	336,765	329,814
			67,217	100,188
27,998	35,681	69,276	99,113	90,222
14.28%	17.01%	32.96%	38.61%	33.04%
6.31%	7.73%	14.96%	19.39%	17.07%
			131.20%	120.8%

accounts, such as those of the Compagnie houillere de Graigola-Merthyr, the Cwn Bach Coal Company, the Elba Steel works, the Llandore Tin Plate Company, the Swansea Tin Plate Company, Marcus Moxham & Co., timber merchants, and the West Cwm Barrow China Clay Company, were of firms where members of the bank's board were either partners or directors. While the financial needs of such concerns may have led to the promotion of the bank, companies personally associated with the bank do not appear to have enjoyed accommodation on terms more favourable than other customers.

The evidence of the activities of the Swansea Bank comes from a general manager's jotting book,[65] which contains a wide range of miscellaneous information about the bank's client companies and the state of their banking accounts. However, it does not provide the same data as the 'loan books' of either the Barnsley Bank or the Preston Bank and therefore it is difficult to draw any direct comparisons. What can be established is the bank's charges, its security preferences with regard to loans, and its degree of tolerance with respect to outstanding debit balances.

The bank discounted bills for industrial customers and provided them with overdraft facilities. Generally it was prepared to grant overdrafts of up to £10,000 without security provided such facilities were used only occasionally, otherwise it insisted that the overdraft should be secured. It would take personal security for sums of less than £3,000, but above this level it normally took leases and occasionally mortgages, shares, or property. In one or two instances firms had overdraft limits equal to between 25% and 35% of their capital, but when their drawings rose above this level, the bank pressed immediately for a reduction of the debit balance. During the late 1870s depression the bank allowed overdrafts to run on for periods of over a year and in some cases increased customers' limits for periods up to six months, but only with the provision that the outstanding balance would then be quickly reduced. In the case of one firm only, the Swansea Tin Plate Company, in which one of the bank's directors was heavily involved, the bank provided, as a matter of course, loans for periods up to 14 months.

The bank's main industrial connections were with the rapidly developing tinplate trade, which consisted of a large number of small works involving relatively little fixed capital. Bank accommodation, such as that provided by the Swansea Bank, was generally sufficient, once available, to meet the industry's need for working capital. Its main financial problem was created by cyclical movements in both the demand for its products and the capacity of the industry. The expansion in the number of firms in the industry during the first half of the 1870s, caused by an upswing in demand and relative ease of entry, resulted in over-production during the slump of the second half of the decade. This led to widespread financial problems as profit margins were squeezed, and consequently many firms were either closed temporarily or failed. Some were assisted by their bankers. However, the Melingriffith works appears to have been totally supported by its bank, the West of England, and when that stopped in 1878, it closed.[66] During the late 1870s and the early 1880s, the Swansea Bank appears to have escaped the problems of 'depression' banking, despite its personal links with the tinplate industry. This was due to a careful monitoring of overdrawn accounts coupled with circumspect further lending in order to maintain the bank's goodwill. Only in the case of the Llandore Tin Plate Company did the bank tolerate a progressively growing overdraft which by December 1876 was fluctuating between £14,000 and £23,000.

The Cumberland Union Bank was the largest of the four banks being considered here, with deposits averaging £1.8m. during the early 1880s. The bank initially had been essentially a deposit collector but the continuing development of the West Cumberland industrial region led to a growing local demand for accommodation and by the mid-1880s it was beginning to be 'overlent', with a ratio of advances and discounts to deposits rising above 100% (see table 7.5). Its liquidity ratio in the late 1870s and early 1880s was lower than that of the Swansea Bank, and this was probably due to the bank providing substantial overdraft accommodation to local iron and steel firms during this depressed period. The Maryport Haematite Iron Company ran a continuous overdraft with the bank from at least June 1879 until December 1882, accounting for 5.7% of the bank's total advances on 31 December 1879, 3.5% on 31 December 1880, and 5.4% on 31 December 1882.[67] Similarly the four overdrawn accounts of the West Cumberland Iron and Steel Company constituted approximately 8% of the bank's advances during the early 1880s. The bank was forced to establish special directors' committees to deal with the affairs of both the Maryport and West Cumberland concerns in the 1880s and 1890s. Similarly, special committees were also formed to monitor the accounts of the Whitehaven Iron Company, the Whitehaven Harbour Trust, the Moss Bay Haematite Company and the Workington Haematite Company.[68] The loans involved were in fact highly illiquid assets and illustrate the dangers of the provision of medium- and long-term finance as they gravely weakened the bank, a situation which was only finally resolved by amalgamation.

Internal information is available of overdrafts outstanding at the bank's Carlisle branch, its head office, on 31 December 1885.[69] They amounted to £487,942, about a quarter of the bank's total advances, and the largest

Table 7.5 Cumberland Union Bank, balance sheet.

	31.12.1879 £	31.12.1880 £	31.12.1881 £	31.12.1882 £	31.12.1883 £
Capital	250,000	250,000	250,000	250,000	250,000
Reserve fund	150,000	150,000	160,000	160,000	160,000
Bank property redemption fund			2,000	4,000	6,000
Deposits & current a/cs	1,647,109	1,739,904–10– 4	1,789,453–19– 4	1,857,638–11– 7	1,852,302– 5–11
Notes	33,055	31,815	31,235	34,275	31,430
Balance of p. & l.	33,755	38,299	28,731– 4– 3	28,482– 8– 3	27,478–17– 7
	2,113,919	2,210,007– 1– 8	2,261,420– 3– 7	2,334,395–19–10	2,327,214– 3– 6
Cash	145,418	124,816– 2– 1	108,836–17– 1	174,201–16– 1	119,690– 8– 0
Cash at call & short notice	129,759	214,069– 0– 4	206,703– 4– 9	168,054– 8– 2	110,481–15– 2
Investment of reserve fund	150,000– 0– 0	150,000	160,000	160,000	160,000
Investment of bank property redemption fund					6,000– 0– 0
Bills discounted customers' balances	1,630,173– 0– 0	1,658,352–16– 4	1,715,931– 0– 6	1,758,587–10– 2	1,853,210– 9– 8
Bank property	57,522	61,903–13–11	68,916–15– 0	72,439– 4– 8	76,767–17– 4
Stamps	1,045	865–17–10	1,032– 6– 3	1,113– 0– 9	1,063–13– 4
Cash: deposits	16.7%	19.47%	17.63%	18.42%	12.42%
Cash: liabilities	13.01%	13.33%	13.95%	14.66%	9.89%
Advances: deposits	98.97%	95.31%	95.87%	94.66%	100.04%

individual category was industrial customers, who had been granted 60%
of the total. The branch's largest customer was the West Cumberland
Iron and Steel Company, whose four overdrawn accounts made up 30%
of Carlisle's outstanding overdrafts. As can be seen from table 7.6, the
other main groups of borrowers were merchants (16.5%) and farmers
(6.8%). The Carlisle branch appears to have undertaken very little
discounting by the mid-1880s: only 11 of the 659 customers who had
overdrafts also had discount accounts. They were mainly merchants and
their paper amounted to £33,025 on 31 December 1885, equivalent to
6.79% of total outstanding overdrafts.

Table 7.6 Analysis of composition of overdrafts at Carlisle branch of
the Cumberland Union Bank, 31 December 1885

To	Clients		
Unoccupied: Male			5.3%
	Female		0.4
Institutions and Public Authorities			2.2
Land			6.8
Professions			3.1
Trade and Services: Merchants			16.5
	Agents		0.7
	Retailers		1.2
	Other		0.4
Manufacturing			59.5
West Cumberland Iron & Steel Co.		30.6/	
Building			0.6
Unknown			3.2

Supporting the Carlisle schedule of overdrafts are two books recording
interviews with the manager, the first covering the early 1880s and the
second the 1890s,[70] so it is possible to piece together the bank's policy and
practice regarding lending over a fairly lengthy time-span, comparable
with the Barnsley Bank. Most of the customers who applied for overdrafts
in the early 1880s were farmers, drapers, joiners, and builders, but as has
been shown the bank's main financial commitments were to industrial
firms.

Unfortunately no record of overdraft negotiations with any of the coal,
iron and steel companies has survived for the early 1880s but several had
substantially overdrawn accounts. The security for this accommodation in
the case of the West Cumberland Iron and Steel Company consisted of a

£7,000 mortgage on its works, 500 £100 debenture bonds, and a lien on pig iron in store. The bank's other outstanding industrial overdrafts were individually much smaller than those of the Maryport and West Cumberland companies but in a number of cases relatively large compared with the fixed assets of the borrower. The bank may have been forced to grant some of these loans as a result of growing competition from the Clydesdale.[71] The Mains Manufacturing Company, for instance, a limited concern with a paid-up capital of £29,691 and fixed assets valued at £26,000, obtained an overdraft limit of £16,000, secured on the works then valued at £22,219, and the company had an outstanding balance of £9,442. Most industrial overdrafts in the early 1880s, apart from those of the iron companies, were generally for short periods but in one instance, through extensions and renewals, the bank in effect supplied long-term finance to a firm. The firm in question was Akerigg Brothers, woollen spinners of Alston, whose account the bank had obtained from the Clydesdale as a result of an introduction made by a manager of an insurance company. The firm was granted initially an overdraft limit of £3,000 secured on a second mortgage on its mills, the Kendal Building Society holding a first mortgage of £5,000 which was being repaid over seven years. The mills and their machinery were valued at that time at £13,900. In addition the woollen spinners obtained a discount account with a limit of £10,000. During the autumn of 1881 and the spring and summer of 1882 the overdraft limit was increased temporarily, but in August 1882 the bank stated that it was not prepared to extend accommodation further than the outstanding balance of £6,275. The concern was divided into two in January 1883 and an overall overdraft limit of £13,000 was agreed, secured on bills of sale on the stocks and machinery. The two separate mills were then converted into limited companies and the overall draft limit was further increased to £24,500, on the security of debentures and a bill for £2,000. By the end of 1885 the two companies' outstanding overdraft amounted to £22,152. Other local textile firms appear also to have required substantial accommodation in the mid-1880s, with J. Cowen & Sons, cotton spinners of Dalston, running an overdraft of £8,000 secured by a mortgage throughout 1885.

During the 1890s there were no approaches to the bank by textile firms and instead the overriding demand for finance came from iron and steel companies and quarrying and mining concerns. It arose from the needs of stock holding, re-equipment, and expansion. During the deep slump of the first half of the decade most of the bank's iron and steel customers were in severe difficulties and required advances even to pay the wage bill. In January 1891 the West Cumberland Iron and Steel Company required £5,000 simply to carry on from day to day, £2,700 being needed to meet the wage bill. One of its overdrafts stood at £27,640 and was secured on iron stocks with a margin of 5%. The bank agreed to provide an advance of £5,000 on debentures with a margin of 20%, provided that no more cheques were drawn by the company, that £3,620 of cheques issued were held back, and that the company sold off iron as the bank required in order to pay off its overdrafts and the fresh advance. Similarly in March 1882 the Moss Bay Iron and Steel company was running an overdraft of £31,329 and required a further £900 to meet its wages and other current bills. Its plant had been altered drastically at a cost of £33,000, of which £20,000 had been financed internally. It was hoped that this would allow the company to roll rails at 'a much greater profit'. The company's financial problems stemmed from cancelled rail orders and it was trying to reduce stocks by cutting its prices. The bank allowed its overdraft to rise by £4,000 for five months but this proved to be insufficient. In February 1893 the company obtained a further £20,000 secured on a £2 call, a charge which had been surrendered by its 'B' debenture holders in order to provide working capital. The bank had previously objected to such a security, and its change in attitude seems to have come about as a result of its confidence in the company, 'as they can now make Rails as cheap as any mill in the Kingdom'. Any competitive edge that the company may have had as a result of its recent investment was never tested in the market place, because it joined the Iron and Steel Association in January 1896, from which it received a quota of 11% of all rail orders, while Cammells and Bolckow, Vaughan each had a share of 20%.

The West Cumberland company did not survive the slump of the 1890s. It went into voluntary liquidation in 1892, and in March 1896 the options that faced the company appeared to have been either to lease the works or to sell them at the break-up value, both of which were going to result in a loss.

The local mining industry was also depressed during the first half of the 1890s, and managers and chairmen of such concerns called on the bank either to explain overdrafts or to ask for financial aid. However, in some cases the resources were required for re-equipment. A lead-mining company wanted an additional overdraft to finance the building of an electrical plant which it expected would double its output. Although its existing overdraft was utilized fully to finance stockholding, the bank appears to have agreed to supply £2,000 for a period of two years. Similarly the bank made an advance of £12,000 over three years to allow the St Helens colliery to set up a coking plant, with the provision that any profits should be applied totally to the reduction of the loan. The Southam Hematite Iron Ore company, seeking finance for the sinking of a new shaft, reconstructed its capital and obtained extended or renewed overdraft facilities.

The willingness of the Cumberland Union Bank to support local industry gradually crippled it. By 1894 it faced a loss of over £250,000 on its loans to the West Cumberland and Moss Bay companies and although it was able subsequently to reduce these 'lock-ups', it was too weak to withstand two shocks at the end of the decade. The first was the discovery of substantial frauds at its Hexham branch in 1899, followed by the second, the failure in 1900 of Dumbell's Banking company, of which the Cumberland bank was a substantial creditor. Relief came in 1901 through a merger with the York City and County Bank, a concern which had had clients in West Cumberland from at least the early 1890s.[72]

It would be extremely rash to make any general claims for the typicality of the lending policies of the four banks which have been described. However, they are pointers to the behaviour of English joint stock banks during the last 60 years of the nineteenth century. While generally they were not accustomed to lend long on a regular basis to industrial clients, they did provide overdrafts and other forms of accommodation in circumstances of which George Rae would not have approved. Their activities did make a contribution, not only to the provision of working capital but also to the finance of medium- and long-term investment projects. It would appear that they undertook such lending because their managements had a sound grasp of both the needs of their clients and their credit-worthiness. However, increasing strain was placed upon this financial system both by the growth of fixed capital, which led to individual loans becoming larger, and by cyclical forces, especially in the case of the capital goods industries. The rise of the West Cumberland iron industry led to at least one of the local banks having a grave imbalance in the structure of its loans by the early 1890s. In fact the Cumberland Union Bank's overall fortunes became tied, through substantial loans, to the prosperity of two of its customers.

The English country joint stock banks were absorbed into metropolitan concerns from the 1890s, which enlarged their capital base and may have led to a change in banking practice and attitudes in the provinces. Unfortunately little evidence is readily available concerning the lending policies of what may be termed the 'core' banks of the amalgamation movement of the quarter of a century before the First World War. The last case study to be considered is the activities of Glyn, Mills during the period 1890 to 1914, but this bank should not be regarded as typical of London banking practices. It was a private concern and even when it was turned into a joint stock company in 1885, its capital continued to be held by its 'partners'. The bank was not only uncharacteristic in terms of its organizational structure but also in the forms of banking that it undertook. On the one hand it acted as the London correspondent for a large number of country banks, holding considerable balances as a result, while on the other it behaved almost as a continental *banque d'affaires*. The bank's partners had played an important role in the railway-building boom of the 1840s which led to the bank becoming the 'railway bank', they had handled Canadian loans since the 1850s, they had assisted in the formation of a number of overseas banks in the 1860s and the 1870s, and from the 1880s undertook a number of domestic industrial issues.[73] Consequently in many varied ways, Glyn, Mills stood apart from other private and joint stock banks in the City. The uniqueness of this private bank has advantages in that its behaviour towards industrial customers may provide an indication of the 'upper limit' of metropolitan practices in the finance of manufacturing industry.

In conjunction with the transformation of the bank into a joint stock concern, it began to publish regularly balance sheets. The first revealed that the bank had total deposits of £9,459,626 of which nearly a fifth were term. Its advances plus discounts:deposit ratio was 55.2% and it had an overall cash ratio of 26.25%. Holdings of cash in the till, at call and short notice were equivalent to 30.4% of the bank's total deposits.[74] Its liquidity increased during the 1890s and 1900s with its advances plus discounts:deposits ratio falling to 47.7% by December 1895 and to 38.5% by June 1905.[75] According to its published balance sheet for 30 June 1905, Glyns had an overall cash ratio of 45.1% and a cash:deposit ratio of 50%. The changes in these ratios between the mid-1880s and the mid-1900s were the result of an increase in deposits of 46.6%, as there was only a very limited increase, 2.25%, in advances and discounts. Glyns' advances plus discounts: deposits ratio was substantially below the average of London banks during the decade after 1885.

One of the factors which may account for the increasing lack of the mobilization of the bank's deposits was the death in 1896 and 1898 of its two senior 'partners', Bertram Currie and Lord Hillingdon. They were replaced by 'very young men', some of whom had considerable preoccupations and interests outside Lombard Street, and by A. S. Harvey, the bank's secretary, who had been in the Treasury and who has been described as 'painstaking and methodical'.[76] The weakening of the bank's management occurred at the same time as other London banks grew through amalgamation. Glyns' partners did consider establishing a block of private banks as a defensive measure but the idea was rejected, one of the partners stating: 'I believe that we shall do best by preserving a characteristic which we alone of all the *large and serious* banks possess namely of having only one door.'[77] Glyns' management team was further weakened during the 1900s by Harvey's death in 1905 and the retirement due to ill-health of the second Lord Hillingdon in 1907.[78]

Glyns had a large number of industrial customers, most of them situated in the provinces, of which many like John Brown, Staveley Coal and Iron, and Vickers had been converted into public companies in the 1860s and 1870s by Chadwick. Some of Glyns' partners were major shareholders in these companies, but this relationship did not affect the terms on which they banked and received accommodation.[79]

An analysis of the loans and overdrafts that Glyns allowed its industrial customers during the period 1890–1914[80] reveals a bewildering spectrum of maturities and amounts. While a third of the transactions were for three months finance, nearly 20% were for periods of six months and 16% for periods of a year or more. About a quarter of the sums involved were £40,000 or more, while a third were £15,000 or less. The bank was prepared to consider and accept all types of security for loans and overdrafts, including Navy bills, current payments due, the proceeds of future debenture issues, calls on shares, mortgages and debentures, personal guarantees, deeds, freehold and leasehold property, War Office debts and claims, preference shares, rails and pig iron sold, underwriting letters, unissued debentures, and uncalled capital. Although Glyns went to considerable lengths to accommodate its customers, the bank's partners did have some clear idea of the types of transaction that they were and were not prepared to undertake. Charles Mills wrote to a substantial brewer in January 1898: 'I have thoroughly discussed your proposals with my partners, and we are all of the opinion that the advance suggested is quite outside our business as Bankers. We are, and always have been, most willing to assist you in the working of your business, but we think that the operation you propose is more in the nature of finance.'[81]

The question that arises is what Glyns considered to be banking as opposed to finance. This the partners never clearly spelt out in either their correspondence with clients or the internal records of loan negotiations kept by the bank's staff. However, the dividing line between the two can be established in general terms by considering the loans that the bank was prepared to make and the proposals that it turned down. The bank agreed to grant a firm of copper smelters, with which the bank was closely associated, an advance of £75,000 as and when required but 'impressed upon them that we could not go on indefinitely finding capital for them and they undertook to consider the question of the issue of capital'.[82] However, a firm of wholesale and export printers and stationers was told that the bank 'cannot make long loans',[83] which from the general evidence presented above would appear to mean longer than a year. An engineering firm had had an advance 'which has now been running so long' that the bank informed the company that, if its loans were paid off from time to time, it was prepared to allow a loan of £25,000, of which £10,000 could be uncovered, but each loan was 'to be off within six months', and six months notice was to be given by Glyns should it wish to end the arrangement.[84] Such examples would seem to indicate that the partners preferred loans to last for only six months but occasionally would favourably consider applications involving debit balances running for up to a year.

The bank did not insist that its lending should be self-liquidating, and the partners were prepared to provide accommodation for capital projects. S. Swonell & Son obtained a loan of up to £11,000 to finance the construction of a malting works over a period of a year.[85] Sums of a similar order for comparable periods were granted to other firms to allow them to absorb acquired business or to carry stocks during periods of slack trade. Not all of such transactions involved relatively small sums. One company required £30,000 to build factories and £50,000 for working capital, to which Glyns replied merely that unissued debentures were not a suitable security for such a transaction.[86] A chemical company in the north-west obtained between £100,000 and £120,000 during 1910 to enable it to build a new plant on the Manchester Ship Canal, Glyns agreeing to the loan with the provision that it was to be paid off within a year by the sale of securities which the concern held.[87] The Staveley Coal and Iron Company approached the London bank with a similar proposition involving the finance of a capital project. The company had banked with Glyns for a considerable length of time, though in December 1889 a Sheffield bank had offered to take its entire account for a fixed commission of £450 on a turnover of £1m., allowing 2% on any balance and charging 4% on overdrafts. Glyns had retained the account through a counter-offer involving a reduced commission of 10d.%, and these terms were further modified ten years later through Glyns agreeing to allow Brokers call rate on cash balances although charging Bank rate on overdrafts.[88] In 1906 the Staveley company began to build a new ironworks and sink new collieries, for which the estimated capital cost was £350,000. It received an advance of £400,000 from Glyns for eight months at Bank rate subject to a maximum of 5% and a minimum of 3%, with the loan being funded by a call on the company's shares.[89] The iron concern asked for further assistance in 1911, stating that it required advances up to £250,000, this maximum figure to be reached after two years but continuing for a further five years before being reduced by annual payments. Glyns 'explained that the period was too long for our ideas of banking [but] agreed to let them have what they want' for ten months when new arrangements would have to be made.[90]

These examples are, of course, not in any way typical of the general run of an industrial account with Glyns. The experience of British Westinghouse and Vickers will be used to illustrate the transactions of what may be called an 'average' industrial customer, although both accounts had their own unique features. Vickers had banked with Glyns since at least the early 1870s, while Glyns had been one of the underwriters to the capital issue made by the Westinghouse Electrical Supply Company to form its English subsidiary.[91]

British Westinghouse was established in July 1899 and its first approach to Glyns for accommodation appears to have been in November 1901, when it obtained between £50,000 to £100,000 for a month in the form of an overdraft. The firm's large factory at Manchester was opened in 1902, and at the end of the year its overdraft limit was raised to £150,000 with the understanding that any drawings would be repaid out of an issue of £1m. preference stock. A temporary overdraft of up to £100,000 for three months secured on Mersey Railway stock was agreed in March 1903. The interest charges were to be calculated on the amount drawn plus £5,000, in order to compensate Glyns for the absence of a credit balance in the firm's account and, as previously, it was to be funded by a fixed-charge issue. The unfavourable state of the capital market appears to have caused the postponement of the flotation, which led to the company obtaining a further advance of £200,000 in May 1903. This accommodation together with that obtained in March were to be repaid during the following 2½ months. The flotation of long-term capital was made more difficult by the firm's low profits, which led it both to pass its preference share dividend in July 1903 and to obtain a credit line of £150,000 from Glyns during the autumn of that year. Before this expired, a discussion was held by Glyns' partners with the management of British Westinghouse, who stated that they 'have undertaken more than they can manage on present capital'. The company proposed to remedy the situation by its American shareholders taking up £0.5m. preference shares and the Pittsburg company underwriting a £0.3m. debenture issue. The American parent reacted in a somewhat different way by agreeing to guarantee the issue of £0.5m. preference shares, paying 10% immediately and the balance over the next six months. This was in conjunction with an agreement with an English broker who was to advance £0.1m. against £0.4m. debenture stock which he would sell off as rapidly as possible. Glyns agreed to provide a continuing loan of £200,000 within these arrangements.[92]

By July 1904 the debentures had been issued and British Westinghouse stated that it was prepared to pay off shortly its outstanding loan. However, despite the new injection of capital into the company, it made an arrangement to have new loans, not exceeding £100,000 'from time to time', secured on £150,000 debenture stock. The first time that this facility was used was in February, when £50,000 was drawn secured against £0.5m. in payments from the Metropolitan Railway. This soon proved to be insufficient and a further £100,000 was obtained for a period of six months on £195,000 debentures issued to Glyns. The 1904 arrangement continued until the summer of 1906, when the company asked for a credit of 'up to £200,000' for six months, renewable for a further six months. This was to be repaid, as previously, from monies due from the Metropolitan Railway and was to be secured by 25,000 £10 shares of Traction and Power Securities Ltd which the American parent agreed to purchase to redeem any outstanding balance at the end of the period. Subsequently the credit was reduced to £150,000 but the length of the transaction was extended to 18 months.

Despite making an overall loss in 1907, the company was able to fund its bank advances by an issue of £0.25m. debentures in April 1908. Thereafter the company appears to have been able to meet its financial needs internally until September 1910, when it requested a temporary loan of up to £50,000. As during the winter of 1903, the demand for finance arose as a result of trying to accommodate demand, the company's directors stating 'they are rather full of work'. A similar arrangement was made in the spring of 1911, although on this occasion the request appears to have arisen out of a legal case involving a claim against the company.[93] Two main forces appear to have shaped British Westinghouse's demands for bank accommodation. One was a normal need for an occasional overdraft, but the other appears to have arisen from the company's inability to obtain long-term capital either from the market or internally, because of its low profitability between 1903 and 1912. British Westinghouse's experience was not uncommon and many of Glyn, Mill's industrial customers after 1900 obtained loans from the bank to bridge periods between debenture issues.

While British Westinghouse may stand for the so-called 'new' industries, Vickers provides an example from the staple industries. It and the Maxim, Nordenfelt company both banked with Glyns. The gun company, in which the Vickers family were substantial shareholders, had sought temporary advances during the first half of the 1890s to ease irregularities in its cash flow caused by the timing of contract payments. Glyns in 1892 placed a ceiling of £20,000 on such credits and by the autumn of that year this limit was reached. The firm got through the next four years without any difficulties, but in the summer of 1896 it asked for, and received, a loan of £37,000 at Bank rate for eight months to finance a Chinese government contract. Such arrangements with Glyns continued after the company was formally acquired by Vickers in 1897, especially loans against instalments due on foreign contracts.[94]

Vickers not only took over Maxim, Nordenfelt in 1897 but also the Naval Construction and Armaments Co. Ltd at Barrow and so became a vertically integrated munitions maker and naval shipbuilder. The acquisitions were financed by issues of debentures, ordinary shares, and preference shares and stock. At the same time the combine's overdraft limit at Glyns was increased to £100,000, at which level it remained until the spring of 1902. However, new investment which considerably enlarged the firm's capacity was financed from the late 1890s until the early 1900s by further share issues. But it would appear that by 1902 Vickers was beginning to encounter liquidity problems and in order to pay its dividend it had to borrow £250,000 from Glyns, secured by a debt due and a contract with Chile for a battleship. Similar arrangements had to be made for the final dividend payment of that year. The problem may have stemmed from Vickers' take-over of half of Beardmores' capital, which had the aim of reducing competition in the market for armour and increasing the security of debts owed by Beardmores to Vickers. Glyns did not become directly involved with Beardmores until the summer of 1904, when the firm wished to issue debentures but could not do so until it had cleared certain debts. This was managed through an issue of preference stock and a loan from Glyns to Beardmores of £250,000 to cover debts owed to Vickers, secured on Vickers shares and Beardmore preference stock. The transaction was almost a paper one because one of its provisions was that Beardmores were to open an account with Glyns, while Vickers was to place £250,000 with the London bank, with Beardmores being charged only $\frac{1}{2}\%$ interest, the normal allowance given by Glyns to Vickers on a remunerative balance.[95]

The armaments firm next came to Glyns for assistance in the summer and autumn of 1907, when it seems that it was running a number of accounts. It was agreed in July that Vickers could overdraw up to £75,000 on its Sheffield account while two months later a further overdraft facility of £200,000 was provided, to be drawn on if the firm decided not to discount Japanese government bills that it held. At this time the firm was running a major investment programme, stimulated by rising naval expenditure. In April 1908 *Vanguard*, an improved Dreadnought of the St Vincent class, was laid down at Barrow and apparently this contract, coupled with dockyard extensions, was, as in 1898, causing financial difficulties. In the summer of 1908 Vickers arranged an overdraft with Glyns to cover the payment of their dividend, which was to be extinguished by contract payments. The firm was sanguine about the future of warship-building orders after the launch of the *Vanguard* in February 1909 and made arrangements with Glyns for an overdraft of up to £0.5m. at any one time over the next three years. This was the London bank's limit and it requested Vickers to look to their other bankers should they require any further accommodation. Contract payments from the government were to be made straight to Glyns in order to reduce any outstanding balance while interest was to be charged at $\frac{1}{2}\%$ over Bank rate. This agreement was probably a special facility to be activated should the firm receive large shipbuilding orders. Actually these expectations were never fulfilled and Vickers built only two capital ships for the Admiralty before 1914 and consequently had excess capacity. Instead of using the large overdraft line, normal loans were arranged at the beginning of 1910, with a limit of £150,000 to cover an Italian contract, and even then the first drawing was used to cover the spring dividend payment.[96]

The first time that the overdraft of £0.5m. appears to have been used was August 1910, when Glyns allowed Vickers to have up to £0.4m., to be repaid by the end of the year. The facility was drawn on a second time in the summer of 1911 as a result of the tardiness of the Admiralty, possibly in connection with an expansion of submarine building by Vickers.[97]

Vickers had sought foreign orders in order to compensate for the lack of British naval contracts for battleships and cruisers. In 1910 it had begun a Canadian contract to establish a shipyard and navy for the dominion, while in 1912 a Russian order was obtained for three battleships coupled with the modernization of yards, for which Vickers was to provide the necessary expertise and supervision. It is possible that it was as a result of the Russian order that Vickers went to Glyns and asked to borrow £1m., a proposal that was met with an agreement to provide half of what was required, with the balance coming from the London, City and Midland. The main worry that Glyns had over this new facility was whether Vickers would play the two banks off against each other in order to reduce the cost of borrowing. The Midland appears to have made a fixed charge of 5% on the loan while Glyns, as previously, were going to charge Bank rate plus $\frac{1}{2}\%$. Glyns made it a condition that no repayment was to be made to the London, City and Midland while Vickers owed Glyns money. The facility was used in the summer and autumn of 1913, and by October Vickers had an outstanding overdraft of £0.5m. with Glyns. The accommodation was being used to bridge gaps in contract payments and to pay off loans from the Bank of Montreal, which had been financing the construction of the Canadian yard. It would appear that the firm had used up its credit line with the Midland by December 1913 because it asked for further provision from Glyns, who agreed reluctantly to supply £100,000 but no more.[98]

Unlike British Westinghouse, Vickers was able to raise finance in substantial amounts on the capital market. All these resources were put into expanding the firm's capacity in order to be able to cope with any Admiralty orders that it would obtain as a result of increasing naval expenditure on the fleet. These hopes were never fulfilled and the firm compensated by seeking foreign orders and diversifying into related fields such as submarines, airships and aeroplanes. It used its bankers to ease irregularities in its cash-flow position caused by 'lumpy' contract payments and the need to meet its half-yearly dividend distributions.

Glyns' behaviour with regard to industrial finance appears to have been very similar to that of the four country joint stock banks which have been considered. It went as far as it possibly could to meet the needs of its clients and did make substantial loans of a duration of a year or more, sometimes to finance capital projects. The only difference with regard to Glyns is the magnitude of its transactions, some of which were considerably larger than those undertaken by the Cumberland Union, the largest of the four country joint stock banks. Like the country banks, Glyns was closely associated with its industrial clients and in this way could accurately gauge their needs and their credit-worthiness. Its banking was not mechanical, merely matching loan against security, as often entrepreneurial judgement was called for, with one case where it was noted that 'Mr Harvey does not think well of their invention so caution had better be exercised with regard to loans in future'.[99]

★

The lack of bank support for industrial enterprise was first commented upon in forceful terms during the 1910s in a paper read by L. Joseph, perhaps significantly before the National Electric Manufacturers' Association. He critized the banks for both failing to provide industrial credit and to play a role in the establishment of industrial companies. He compared unfavourably the English situation with that in America and in Europe, especially Germany.[100] His themes were taken up by Foxwell in a lecture given six years later at the Royal Institution.[101] This latter contribution was made against a rather different background of general concern about the ability of English financial institutions to support industry in export markets against German competition when peacetime conditions returned. The provision of medium- and long-term finance and company promotion, the issues at question, are linked to a certain degree but there are advantages in considering each separately.

It has been shown in the previous section that a number of country joint stock banks and one London private bank went to considerable lengths to accommodate their industrial clients. The evidence is strong enough to refute the thesis put forward by Landes that after the 1866 crisis 'British banking eschewed speculative promotion and disguised forms of long term credit and returned to the classical tradition of short term paper and liquid assets'.[102] However, it would seem that there was a growing disquiet in Edwardian England over the role played by banks and that by the 1900s the nature of British bank lending had undergone a major change. Joseph stated that: 'True, the branch offices of the clearing banks in industrial centres grant overdrafts in some measure, but they are not of great importance; at any rate they cannot be relied upon at all times, and therefore nobody can count upon them absolutely.'[103] This suggests the possibility that the emergence of nationwide banks from the 1890s may have caused a change in banking practice.

Such a supposition is supported by a range of evidence. Lavington thought that the nature of banks' assets would change after 1914 as long loans made by absorbed banks were recovered and the resources so released were placed in 'advances both secured and more readily recoverable'. This substitution of assets was accompanied by another, namely the replacement of the 'influential and responsible local banker ... by the more mechanically trained branch manager, less well informed on local matters and closely controlled by his general manager, whose sanction must normally be obtained before the grant of an advance of any considerable size'.[104] The representatives of both the Union of London and Smith's Bank and the London Joint Stock Bank agreed in 1910 that the amalgamation movement had had the result of changing lending practice, with the result that customers were not accommodated to the same extent as previously. The control of lending had become centralized and the new nationwide banks did attempt to balance, through monitoring advances granted, accommodation given to various industries so that they were not heavily committed in any particular area. Branch managers were very restricted in the size of loan that they could grant before seeking head office approval. In the case of the London Joint Stock the ceiling was 'some few hundred pounds, according to the importance of the branch'.[105] The City Bank restricted managers initially to a maximum of £300 per customer, whether by discount or loan, and any transaction had to be reported to head office within 24 hours. These rules were revised in the mid-1890s, when the limit was raised to £1,000 in the case of nine managers and to only £500 for five managers.[106] The conservative London, County and Westminister did not raise its sanction limits for country managers until 1909, when they were doubled from £250 to £500.[107] An article on branch management in Scotland in the 1890s shows similar practices. It contained a set of rules of a bank which required managers to submit to head office applications for all loans of more than a moderate amount, together with the necessary information to determine the bank's decision. It would appear from these rules that the manager's main function was to keep an 'opinion or information book' and to 'carefully sift balance sheets and verify as far as possible the statement of assets'.[108]

The amalgamation movement led not only to more restrictive bureaucratically controlled bank lending but also to tighter security requirements for loans. It was London banking practice to make an advance only against collateral, and this spread with the emergence of national banks which had London head offices and directorates. Schuster admitted in 1910 that the new security rules were more rigid but argued that with the conversion of partnerships into companies, concerns now had in the debenture a security which a banker was entitled to require for a loan.[109] Gow, on behalf of the London Joint Stock, was more circumspect and admitted that in the case of manufacturers a bank could only lend on what collateral was available, including 'material in the process of manufacture and so on'.[110] However, there were different views regarding, particularly, the status of debentures. One commentator maintained that 'banking cover in the shape of debentures issued by public companies is, in the absence of due investigation, perhaps the most defective form of security'. He recommended that a debenture, where placed as a security, 'should be a clear document of title to sufficient assets which cannot be afterwards dealt with by the company so as to create any manner of priority over the rights of the debenture holder'. In addition, 'the company should issue a proper mortgage deed conveying such of the assets and rights as the bank may desire to trustees for the debenture holders'.[111] Similarly the Scottish correspondent of *The Bankers' Magazine* warned with regard to acceptable banking security that 'ships also share with mills, factories and stocks of goods two fatal objections, that they are not readily vendible and their value cannot always be approximately ascertained'.[112] He went on to point out that banks should make no advance without security, and stressed that overdrafts were not convertible into cash and were 'apt to drift into dead loans'. Consequently they should be exceptional, should be for limited periods, and should only be granted to either undoubted borrowers or bank shareholders, or those who deposited bills or other securities over which the bank had a lien.[113] While such admonitions were only a repetition of George Rae's warnings made fifty years earlier, by the 1890s they carried greater force because increasing numbers of managers were coming under the jurisdiction of London head offices, where directors in the wake of the Baring crisis were concerned about liquidity and the levels of reserves. If

Schuster represents the views of higher management in London, then they were entirely in accordance with George Rae's advisory letters of 1850. Schuster stated in 1910, almost repeating Rae's words, that:

> The bank ought never to supply the trader with working capital. I think it is bad for the trader. I think the banker ought to give temporary accommodation to tide the trader over the time when he is short until the time the money comes in again – for temporary purposes only. If a trader is not sufficiently provided with working capital and depends on the bank, there is sure to be trouble at some time.[114]

Although the German credit banks gave far more substantial support to domestic industry than their English counterparts, their role and function in this area was a matter of dispute in Germany, particularly after the crisis of 1901. There were six main criticisms of the performance of the German banks with regard to industrial loans, some of which were contradictory while others were very similar to those bing made of English banks. It was maintained by some that the banks had treated industrial borrowers in the same way as commercial customers by granting only short-term credit, which was held to be unsuitable and too costly for industrial needs. Close to this complaint was the charge that the banks had not catered for industrial demands, but instead had tied up their resources in speculation on the stock exchange. However, others made totally different allegations, namely that the banks had 'thrust' credit upon firms in too large a volume and at inopportune times. This argument was extended in rather different ways, with blame being placed upon the borrower rather than the lender through maintaining that industrial ventures had been taking too much long-term credit and had used it to finance improvements, extensions, or new construction, often without revealing to the bank the actual purpose of the loan.

Long-term industrial lending did lead to bank failures in Germany, especially where the institutions concerned had become heavily committed to only one particular company. The Leipziger Bank, which had a capital of 48m. marks (£2.4m.), was forced to close after lending 93m. marks (£4.65m.) to the Trebertocknungsgesellschaft, while the Dresdner Kreditanstalt für Handel und Industrie collapsed as a result of its substantial loans to the Kummergesellschaft. Such cases are parallelled in England by, at least, those of the Northumberland and Durham District Bank and the Royal British Bank in the 1850s and by the experience of the Cumberland Union Bank during the 1880s and 1890s. The difficulties that could arise were excused by one commentator as the consequences of inexperience, since generally the German banks in the 1900s were at the most only 30 years old. At the same time Riesser stressed that 'the relations of the banks to industry take the slower way of current-account credit and many forms of short term credit . . . in which the temporary demand for operating credit is satisfied. Only little by little is the long term credit developed. . . .' However, the difficulties of both German banks and industry immediately after 1901 did lead to the serious suggestion that long-term lending to manufacturers by banks should be replaced by a central institution for long-term credit, financed by the flotation of bearer debentures.[115]

It is probable that English critics of the behaviour of domestic banks had too rosy a view of the German banking system with regard to long-term lending. On the one hand they probably overestimated the amount of funds that were lent on a long-term basis to German industry, while on the other they did not take into account the dangers to financial stability caused by banks having sizeable parts of their assets in the form of illiquid industrial loans. What particularly galled Joseph was that German banks were obtaining short-term loans from English commercial banks via the London money market, with which they were sustaining long-term lending to German industry. This gave xenophobia a new twist.

German banks regarded acting as midwives to industrial security flotations as the 'natural commercial expression' of the development of a relationship with an industrial client, following on from the provision of, first, short-term and, second, medium- and long-term finance. Riesser expressed in the following way: 'the business of issuing industrial securities is the keystone of the vast structure of industrial relations between banks and industry, whose foundation is the current-account business.'[116] However, English clearing banks played a considerable role in the London capital market, and this has not previously received sufficient stress. Unlike their German counterparts, the English banks did not move into capital market operations as a consequence of current-account business but as a result of needing to obtain both short-term primary-reserve assets and higher-yielding investments than Consols.

Both London and provincial banks placed money at call and at short notice with the London discount market and the London Stock Exchange. By 1914, it is possible that half of the reported volume of money at call and at short notice consisted of loans on stock exchange security.[117] Such loans allowed speculators to carry positions in stocks and shares on from one account to another.[118] These loans were not a new feature of English banking as some country banks had been placing short-term funds with London stockbrokers since the mid-1820s.[119] The demand for this finance grew with the substantial increase in overseas lending from the mid-1850s and the consequent rise in activity on the

Stock Exchange. The further development of this business after the early 1870s gave the banks an outlet which partially compensated them for the declining volume of bills available in Lombard Street during the last quarter of the nineteenth century. This type of loan offered a considerably higher rate of return than money placed in the discount market, but the banks were extremely careful of the type of security that they would take for 14-day loans to the Stock Exchange. They were 'very chary' of new issues and generally would not lend on anything 'that is not officially quoted'. Consequently, in the 1890s, 'they would take on the rankest American rubbish simply because it happened to have got into Wetenhall's list but the best Rand shares, even Robinsons and Langlaates were tabooed'.[120]

Whereas the banks' involvement with the secondary market was of long standing, they only became important intermediaries in the new-issue market from the 1880s. Falling yields on Consols led the banks to look for other outlets for their investment funds and they began buying foreign securities, initially government and municipal bonds but after 1900 railroad bonds, too. Some of these securities were acquired through underwriting new issues, an activity which coupled with acting as dividend payment agencies led on to making flotations. The London and Westminister was a leader in this field, having issued a loan for Victoria in conjunction with Barings in 1857. During the 1880s it made issues for South Australia, Victoria and South Africa and it became almost a central bank for a number of the colonies. Parrs acted for the governments of China and Japan, while the London Joint Stock became associated with German issues. The London and Westminster, which by most criteria was highly conservative, went as far as supporting the market in the securities of some of its colonial clients and acted as a jobber of last resort for jobbers and brokers on the Stock Exchange.[121] However, the major gap in the banks' portfolios and market activities was the absence of domestic industrial securities.

The German credit banks by the 1890s were the main intermediaries in the new-issue market and, besides industrial ventures, were responsible for state, municipal and overseas issues. Here they were building upon the foundations established during the first half of the nineteenth century by private bankers, especially in financial centres such as Cologne and Frankfurt on Main. As a result of growth in both the overall volume of issues and the size of individual issues, the credit banks generally replaced the private bankers. Many of the credit banks formed in the 1850s and 1870s were specifically established to undertake industrial flotations. However, the Deutsche Bank did not become active in this section of the market until the 1890s when it founded the Deutsch-Oesterreichische

Mannesmannröhenwerke and formed a community of interests (*Interessengemeinschaft*) with the Bergisch-Markische Bank in Elberfeld and the Schlesischer Bankverein, which gave it important links with the Rhenish-Westphalian and Silesian industrial centres.[122] More typical was the Disconto-Gesellschaft, which undertook industrial promotions from its inception in the 1850s and by the 1910s had, in consequence, links with a large number of German industrial firms, including the Gelsenkirchener Bergwerks A.G., the August Thyssen group of mining and smelting companies, the Rheinische Stahlwerke, the Stumm works, A. G. Gute Hoffnungs Hütte, the Bochumer Verein für Bergbau und Gusstahlfabrikation, the Kattowitzer A. G. für Bergbau und Hüttenbetrieb, the Schmidtman potash-mining group, and various shipbuilding and engineering concerns including the Schichau shipyards and the Henschel machine works.[123]

Normally an industrial flotation took place only after mutual confidence had been established through a long period of contact between a German bank and a concern. The firm would establish its credit worthiness while the bank, as well as providing normal financial accommodation, would supervise the transformation of the client from a partnership into a private company and finally into a public company. Often one of the reasons for a public flotation was the funding of past bank accommodation to the firm. Usually the bank would take up a significant proportion of the securities that it issued on behalf of a public company, and subsequently would run a secondary market in them by trading them through its offices and branches. The significant role that the German credit banks played as promoters of industrial companies can be gauged by looking at the flotation boom of the 1890s. Between 1890 and 1900, 1,600 companies, mainly industrial concerns, were established in Germany, while during the eight years from 1895 the Dresdner Bank undertook 220 industrial security issues, the A. Schaffhausen'scher Bank Verein 187, the Deutsche 155, the Disconto-Gesellschaft 151, and the Darmstadter 151. This is, of course, not comparing like with like either in terms of timespan or type of company formation, but although the comparison is not exact, it does provide a fair pointer to the degree of the banks' involvement in the new-issue market for industrial securities.[124]

Industrial promotions, like long-term lending to manufacturing enterprise, did involve a high degree of risk, especially where banks' security portfolios were consequently rendered illiquid. For instance, the Disconto-Gesellschaft incurred losses as a result of founding the Heinrichshütte in 1857, the Dortmunder Union in 1872, and the Internationale Druckluft und Elektrizitäts Gesellschaft in 1890. The magnitude of such losses could be substantial and in the case of the

Disconto-Gesellschaft they amounted to 10m. marks (£0.5m.) between 1891 and 1894. They frequently arose when the bank made a direct participation and undertook an entrepreneurial role; Reisser commented that such 'instances . . . have for the most part not turned out to [the banks'] advantage'.[125] These experiences led to increasing use of trust and finance companies by the banks as intermediaries for industrial flotations.

It is probable that too much emphasis has been placed upon the role of the German credit banks as promoters of industrial securities, while not enough attention had been paid to their provision of what may be termed 'customer services'. Some of these activities stemmed from a firm being converted by a bank into a public company, as normally a representative of the bank went on to the company's supervisory board. The banks in this way gained links throughout substantial parts of German industry and used such connections to 'provide for the disposal of the products of client industrial companies to suitable enterprises on which the banks were able to exercise some influence'.[126] The intra-industry links of the credit banks were also used to assist the restructuring of parts of German industry, especially with regard to forward and backward vertical integration in the coal, iron, and steel industry by bringing coal and iron concerns together. The Disconto-Gesellschaft, for example, had representatives on the supervisory boards of both the Gelsenkirchener Bergwerkgesellschaft and the Schalker Graben und Hütten Verein, and consequently played an important part in the establishment of a 'community of interests' between the two firms in 1905.[127] Similarly by 1900 each of the seven major electrical combines were backed by bank groupings, of which the relationship between A. E. G. and the cluster of eight banks headed by the Berliner Handelsgesellschaft was typical.

A further aspect of customer services was the banks' attempt positively to assist German industrial exports. The lead in this area was given by the Deutsche, which established branches in both home and overseas ports and set up foreign subsidiaries, sometimes jointly with other banks. Its aim was to reduce the reliance of German exporters upon English and French banking institutions and to this end it developed a market in bills of exchange denominated in marks rather than in sterling or French francs. Initially its overseas policy was unsuccessful and it was forced to wind up some of its branches in the Far East, South America, and London, but by the mid-1880s these early reversals had been overcome and it was joined in this area of financial provision by the Disconto-Gesellschaft.[128]

The mixed banking business developed by the large German credit banks was inherently more risky than the type of transaction undertaken by most of the larger English commercial banks of the 1900s and less profitable to the banks' shareholders. German bank dividends were on average less than half those declared by English banks, because the German banks carried larger reserves and traded more on the basis of their equity capital than on their deposits. Their differing functions compared with their English counterparts were due to the differing demands placed upon them. The German banking system had developed rapidly alongside the growth of German manufacturing industry during the decades after 1840. The German industrialization was relatively faster than the English, and involved industrial sectors where from inception greater amounts of fixed capital were involved, to the extent that foreign savings had played an important role until the 1870s. The English banking system had developed over a much longer period and mainly in response to a demand for short-term credit. Unlike most other financial systems, the division of labour and specialization of function had been taken to extreme limits in the growth of English money and capital markets. In the evolution of the English financial system, at least one major developmental step had not been taken. One route whereby German banks had entered the domestic capital market had been the financing of railway construction. However, English banks had not generally been called upon to undertake such a task, which had been successfully fulfilled by private capital markets. When the English commercial banks did enter the new-issues market in a major way from the mid-1880s, it was as competitors in the flotations of foreign issues, an orientation given by the growing dominance of their London higher managements in the increasingly hierarchical systems of control that came with the amalgamation movement. While it is probable that during the 25 years before 1914 the English banking system, in peacetime at least, was more stable than the German; after the 1901 crisis the German credit banks had become aware of the dangers which arose out of a close involvement with industry and had taken out the necessary insurance. The overall balance is difficult to strike. The English banking system may have contributed just as much to economic growth through pursuing a type of banking which did not lead to financial crisis, as the German banks did by facilitating industrial capital formation and the export of manufactures.

Notes

(Place of publication is London unless otherwise stated)

1   *The Economist*, 24 September 1863, p. 1177.
2   H. A. Shannon, 'The Limited Companies of 1866–1883', *Economic History Review*, IV, 1933, table C, pp. 312–13; see also B. L. Anderson and P. L. Cottrell, 'Another Victorian Capital Market: a Study of Banking and Bank

Investors on Merseyside', *Economic History Review*, 2nd series, XXVIII, 1975.

3 S. Nishimura, *The Decline of Inland Bills of Exchange in the London Money Market 1855–1913*, Cambridge, 1971, p. 6.

4 W. Newmarch, 'The Increase in the Number of Banks and Branches ... 1858–1878', *The Bankers' Magazine*, 1879, pp. 849–61.

5 Nishimura, op. cit., p. 9.

6 J. Sykes, *The Amalgamation Movement in English Banking, 1825–1924*, 1926, pp. 30–43; see also R. S. Sayers, *Lloyds Bank in the History of English Banking*, 1957, pp. 244–56.

7 Sykes, op. cit., 48–60; C. A. E. Goodhart, *The Business of Banking, 1891–1914*, 1972, pp. 51–9; Nishimura, op. cit., p. 85.

8 Nishimura, op. cit., pp. 80–1.

9 W. F. Crick and J. E. Wadsworth, *A Hundred Years of Joint Stock Banking*, 1936, p. 37.

10 S. Nishimura, 'The Growth of the Stock of Money in the U.K., 1870–1913', unpublished paper; D. K. Sheppard, *The Growth and Role of U.K. Financial Institutions 1880–1962*, 1971, pp. 43, 116–33. See also R. P. Higonnet, 'Bank Deposits in the U.K., 1870–1914', *Quarterly Journal of Economics* LXXI, 1957, 'The Progress of Banking in Great Britain and Ireland during 1880', *The Bankers' Magazine*, XLI, 1881, and on the general problems involved, Goodhart, op. cit., pp. 25–38.

11 Newmarch, op. cit., p. 853.

12 'Banking Deposits and the Rate of Interest on Them', *The Bankers' Magazine*, 1876, pp. 712, 714.

13 'Progress of Banking in Great Britain in 1877', ibid., 1878, p. 89.

14 National Monetary Commission, *Interviews on the Banking and Currency Systems of England ...*, Washington, D.C., 1910, interview with Sir Felix Schuster, p. 44.

15 'Progress of Banking in Great Britain in 1889', *The Bankers' Magazine*, 1890, p. 529.

16 National Monetary Commission, op. cit., interview with Charles Gow, p. 64.

17 Goodhart, op. cit., p. 175.

18 R. S. Sayers, *The Bank of England 1891–1944*, 1976, I, pp. 21–2.

19 'How do our Banks employ their Money', *The Bankers' Magazine*, 1880, pp. 903–5.

20 J. Dick, 'Banking Statistics of the U.K. in 1896', *Journal of the Institute of Bankers*, XVII, 1897, p. 197.

21 'Business in the United Kingdom – Its Progress and Prospects', *The Bankers' Magazine*, 1884, p. 238.

22 Goodhart, op. cit., pp. 125, 130–3, 143–6.

23 ibid., p. 151.

24 National Monetary Commission, op. cit., interview with Charles Gow, p. 78.

25 Goodhart, op. cit., pp. 158–9.

26 ibid., p. 159.

27 ibid.

28 National Monetary Commission, op. cit., interview with Charles Gow, p. 78.

29 Midland Bank Archives, Barnsley Banking Company, A14, Loans and Credits Book.

30 ibid., Swansea Bank, V7, Manager's Notes, 1876–1892.

31 ibid., Cumberland Union Banking Company, G54, Record of Manager's Interviews, 1879–1885; G55, Record of Manager's Interviews, 1890–1898.

32 Glyn, Mills Archives, London, Private Letter Book A/4 12, f43, 29 December 1900.

33 ibid., Private Letter Book A/4 11 f68, 11 May 1899.

34 Much of the above is drawn from ibid., B/2 18, Terms with Customers, G.M.C. & Co. 1.

35 A. G. Ford, *The Gold Standard. Britain and Argentina 1880–1914*, 1962, pp. 44–6.

36 Sayers, *Bank of England*, op. cit., I, p. 44.

37 F. Lavington, *The English Capital Market*, 1921, reprinted 1968, p. 145.

38 F. W. Fetter, *The Development of British Monetary Orthodoxy, 1797–1875*, Cambridge, Mass., 1965, pp. 237–9.

39 R. S. Sayers, 'The Bank in the Gold Market, 1890–1914', in T. S. Ashton and R. S. Sayers, *Papers in English Monetary History*, Oxford, 1953, pp. 142–3.

40 Goodhart, op. cit., pp. 209–11.

41 ibid., pp. 217–19.

42 Sayers, *Bank of England*, op. cit., I, pp. 17 ff.

43 J. H. Clapham, *The Bank of England. A History*, II, *1797–1914*, Cambridge, 1944, pp. 433–4, 440–1.

44 ibid., pp. 255–6, 274.

45 *B.P.P.*, XXXIX, 1873, *Accounts and Papers, Accounts of the Bank of England . . . 1856 to the present time*, pp. 161–82. I am grateful to Professor L. S. Pressnell for bringing this data source to my attention.

46 The two major syntheses of the evidence are R. Cameron, 'England', in Cameron *et al. Banking during the Early Stages of Industrialisation*, 1967; P. Mathias, 'Capital, Credit and Enterprise in the Industrial Revolution', *Journal of European Economic History*, II, 1973.

47 Thomas Bullion [G. Rae], *The Internal Management of a Country Bank . . .*, 1850, p. 18.

48 ibid., p. 102.

49 E. Sigsworth, *Black Dyke Mills*, Liverpool, 1958.

50 Sayers, *Lloyds Bank*, op. cit., pp. 95–6.

51 J. H. Morris and L. J. Williams, *The South Wales Coal Industry 1841–1875*, Cardiff, 1958, pp. 143–8.

52 H. W. Richardson and J. M. Bass, 'Profitability of the Consett Iron Company before 1914', *Business History*, VII, 1965, p. 71.

53 *The Economist*, 6 September 1856.

54 *The Bankers' Magazine*, 1879, p. 461.

55 It was also a puzzle to contemporaries, or at least to new entrants to the industry, and the following letter is to the point: 'Your correspondent, a "Country Bank Clerk", has noticed a great and perhaps a growing want on the part of many young bank officials, viz, the difficulty of obtaining good information on practical banking; but it is easier to formulate a want than to supply the information wanted. In the first place, much of the desired advice can only be authoritatively given by those who have attained the higher positions in their respective banks, but who, having reached such positions, have no leisure nor inclination for writing on a subject of which their whole working life is full. Others think their experience should grow up with a

man's daily banking life . . .' (ibid., 1885, pp. 78–9).

56 Midland Bank Archives, London.

57 Crick and Wadsworth, op. cit., pp. 101–4, 115–34, 146–51, 215–17.

58 W. G. Rimmer, *Marshalls of Leeds. Flax Spinners 1788–1886*, Cambridge, 1960, pp. 51, 126–8, 163, 180–1, 201.

59 This section is drawn from Midland Bank Archives, Barnsley Banking Company, A14, Loans and Credits Book.

60 *The Bankers' Magazine*, 1866, pp. 926–7, 1088–9; Crick and Wadsworth, op. cit., p. 151.

61 This section is drawn from Midland Bank Archives, Preston Banking Company, AN 11–13, Directors' Considerations of Applications for Advances, 1866–7, 1867, 1867–8.

62 *The Bankers' Magazine*, 1866, p. 1017.

63 'Depression in South Wales and the Losses of the Glamorganshire Banking Company', *The Bankers' Magazine*, 1884, pp. 244–6.

64 See D. Trevor Williams, *The Economic Development of Swansea and of the Swansea District to 1921*, Cardiff, 1940; W. E. Minchinton, *The British Tinplate Industry. A History*, Oxford, 1957; H. R. Davies, 'The Industrial Revolution' in W. G. V. Balchin (ed.) *Swansea and its Region*, Swansea, 1971.

65 Midland Bank Archives, the Swansea Bank, subsequently the South Wales Union Bank, V7, Manager's Notes, 1876–1892.

66 Minchinton, op. cit., pp. 44–6, 50–2.

67 Midland Bank Archives, Cumberland Union Banking Company, G65, Pass Book of the Maryport Hematite Iron Company.

68 ibid., Acc4/2–4, Directors' Attendance Books, 11 August 1880–21 April 1897.

69 ibid., G58, Schedule of Overdrafts at Carlisle.

70 ibid., G54, Record of Manager's Interviews, 1879–1885; G55, Record of Manager's Interviews, 1890–1898.

71 M. Kita, 'The Scottish Banking Invasion of England 1874–1882, with Special Reference to the Clydesdale Banking Company's Action in Cumbria 1874–1882', *Soka Economic Studies Quarterly*, VII, 1977.

72 Crick and Wadsworth, op. cit., p. 138.

73 R. Fulford, *Glyns, 1753–1953*, 1953; P. L. Cottrell, 'Investment Banking in England, 1856–1882: Case Study of the International Financial Society', unpublished Ph.D. thesis, University of Hull, 1974, pp. 26–7, 63, 118–19, 133, 137, 181, 275–6, 391–5, 493, 551, 586, 592, 629–30, 643–6, 747–8, 824–5, 860–2. On balances held by country banks with Glyns, see Goodhart, op. cit., pp. 551–66.

74 *The Bankers' Magazine*, 1885, p. 258.

75 ibid., 1895, i, p. 451; 1905, ii, p. 248.

76 Fulford, op. cit., p. 220.

77 Quoted in Fulford, op. cit., pp. 226–7.

78 ibid., pp. 224, 228.

79 Glyn, Mills Archive, P. L. B., ff. 374, 454, 468, 469.

80 This has been drawn from a series of Advances, Engagement Books, B/3 9 1–13.

81 A/4 10 f.119.

82 B/3 10, 15 February 1900.

83 B/3 11, 14 April 1904.

84 B/3 12, 20 January 1905.

85 B/3 10, 15 February 1900.

86 ibid., 25 September 1900.

87 B/3 13, 29 November 1909.

88 A/4 11, f.20.

89 B/3 12, 13 November 1906.

90 B/3 13, 11 August 1906.

91 B/3 10, 28 April 1899.

92 B/3 12, 22 July 1904, 27 February 1905, 17 March 1905, 17 July 1906, 8 March 1907; B/3 13, 15 September 1910, 3 April 1911.

93 B/3 12, 22 July 1904, 27 February 1905, 17 March 1905, 17 July 1906, 8 March 1907; B/3 13, 15 September 1910, 3 April 1911.

94 B/3 9, 4 March 1891, 30 January 1892, 25 September 1892, 9 July 1895, 29 August 1895, 27 January 1897, 30 November 1897, 25 May 1898; see also J. D. Scott, *Vickers*, 1962, pp. 38, 39.

95 B/3 11, 12 March 1902, 8 August 1902; B/3 12, 14 July 1904; Scott, op. cit., pp. 44–9.

96 B/3 13, 20 July 1908, 14 April 1909, 30 September 1909, 8 February 1910, 23 March 1910.

97 ibid., 8 August 1910.

98 ibid., 4 October 1912, 13 August 1913, 15 December 1913.

99 B/3 10, 7 December 1897.

100 L. Joseph, *Industrial Finance. A Comparison between Home and Foreign Developments*, 1911.

101 H. S. Foxwell, 'The Financing of Industry and Trade', *Economic Journal*, 1917.

102 D. S. Landes, 'The Structure of Enterprise in the Nineteenth Century. The Cases of Britain and Germany', *XI Congrès Internationale des Sciences Historiques, Rapports*, V *Histoire contemporaine*, Uppsala, 1960, p. 113.

103 Joseph, op. cit., p. 9.

104 Lavington, op. cit.

105 National Monetary Commission, op. cit., interview with Sir Felix Schuster, p. 47; interview with Charles Gow, pp. 78, 82.

106 Midland Bank Archives, City Bank, E29, Rules for Guidance of Branch Managers.

107 Goodhart, op. cit., p. 163.

108 'Bank Branch Management', *The Bankers' Magazine*, 1891, i, pp. 640–1.

109 National Monetary Commission, op. cit., p. 43.

110 ibid., p. 75.

111 'Bankers and Public Companies', *The Bankers' Magazine*, 1899, i, p. 7.

112 'Bank Branch Management', ibid., 1891, i, p. 640.

113 ibid.

114 National Monetary Commission, op. cit., pp. 47–8.

115 J. Riesser, *The German Great Banks and Their Concentration . . .*, Washington, D.C., 1911, pp. 230–40, 366.

116 ibid., p. 364.

117 Goodhart, op. cit., pp. 120, 124.

118 On the mechanism of the transaction, see Cottrell, op. cit., pp. 749–50, 801–3.

119 Sayers, *Lloyds*, op. cit., pp. 183–5.

120 'The New Banking', *The Bankers' Magazine*, 1896, i, pp. 197–8.

121 Goodhart, op. cit., pp. 134–6.

122 Reisser, op. cit., pp. 473–4, 476.

123 ibid., pp. 118–19, 371–3.

124 ibid., pp. 118–19, 371–3.

125 ibid., p. 375.

126 ibid., p. 375.

127 C. N. Smith, 'Motivation and Ownership; History of the Ownership of the Gelsenkirchner Bergwerks-A.G.', *Business History*, XII, 1970.

128 Reisser, op. cit., pp. 421, 473–5.

8 Internal and private sources of funds

It is evident from the discussion in the preceding chapters that a considerable proportion of manufacturing concerns during the nineteenth century relied on private and internal sources of finance. Few firms took advantage of the liberalization of company law in order to raise capital externally, while banks, especially from the late 1880s, were generally very reluctant either to supply working capital on a continuous basis or more particularly to support investment in plant and machinery for any length of time. Admittedly banking practice did vary considerably but it became more uniform and more conservative as a result of the amalgamation movement in the 1890s and 1900s. Consequently, industrial firms had to look to intra-industry sources of finance or to themselves or acquaintances for accommodation. Basically this meant some form of trade credit, or the admission of a new partner, or a loan on mortgage, or profits generated by the concern. Unfortunately it is precisely for these areas of finance that little evidence is at present available and therefore the picture that can be established is partial and, with regard to profits, highly conjectural.

★

There are two basic forms of trade credit, internal and external. Internal trade credit consists of book debts of firms which if paid promptly were usually subject to a discount. Therefore the firm giving this type of financial accommodation, often called an open credit, was including an element of interest in its prices and was undertaking a quasi-banking function. In contrast, external trade credit consisted of taking a bill of exchange as payment for a debt with the seller of the goods discounting the bill with either his bank or a London discount house. Accordingly the credit need not have been created privately but could have been the product of bank accommodation extended to the seller. Often internal and external trade credit were combined with a buyer being given a period of open credit, following which payment was made in the form of a bill. Such credits could assist the provision of working capital to the buying concern and in certain situations aid the financing of fixed investment. This could arise if either the length of credit was significantly greater than the length of time taken in processing and selling the materials purchased on credit, or when a buyer received credit for a longer period than he was, in turn, granting to those who purchased his products.

The only present major study of the operation of trade credit is concerned with the West Riding wool-textile industry.[1] This found alternating phases of lengthening and shortening credit terms with credit being generally long during the first quarter of the nineteenth century, short during the next 25 years, and lengthening again after 1848. As the worsted branch of the industry was more rigidly sub-divided into specialized branches than the pure wool section, credit was more important. Until the 1860s worsted manufacturers used long-staple English wool which was more suitable for combing, and by the mid-century it was in short supply, especially for the Bradford trade. It was not until the late 1860s that greater quantities of colonial wool, suitable for machine combing, became available and that combing machines were able to process shorter-staple wool. The worsted spinner obtained his wool from a woolstapler who bought either at the colonial sales in London, where payment had to be made within seven days, or from farmers, with whom settlements were normally made in cash within 14 days. Usually staplers traded on the basis of either their own capital or bank credit but sold wool to spinners on credit. Debts between staplers and spinners for English wool were settled before 1850 by two, three or four months' bills. The length of credit given lengthened after 1848 as a result of the activities of speculators who had entered the wool trade in order to gain from the rising price of English wool used by worsted manufacturers. Longer credit was used as a competitive weapon with which to gain customers. However, it played an important part in financing the expansion of spinning in the worsted branch of the industry. This resulted from two factors: on the one hand, spinners were now receiving longer credit than previously, while on the other the mechanization of combing in the 1850s cut production time.

Speculators appear to have been able to give longer credit as a result of the accommodation that they in turn were obtaining from banks. Banks, especially new concerns in the 1860s, were anxious to obtain customers, and some of the speculative firms took up their shares in order to secure credit lines. William Cheeseborough & Son, the major speculative firm, had accounts with the Bradford Banking Company, the Halifax and Huddersfield Union Banking Company, and the Leeds branch of the Bank of England, as well as direct links with the London money market. Cheeseborough had an overdraft with the Bradford Bank and at the time of his bankruptcy owed it £44,731, of which only £2,700 was secured. The other major supplier of finance to wool speculators was the manager of the Leeds Banking Company, who without the knowledge of the bank's directors gave substantial accommodation to four or five houses.

The speculators' activities led to local financial panics in 1858 and 1864, the latter caused by the failure of the Leeds Bank. These panics resulted in agreements being made amongst woolstaplers to reduce credit terms from five to three months. They were paralleled by similar arrangements to shorten credit in the Bradford cotton warp trade and in the trade between worsted stuff manufacturers and merchants. In the former trade, credit in future was to consist of a one-week open credit, while in the latter the period was cut from eight to four months. There are indications that the post-1848 lengthening of credit terms was not limited just to worsted. Long credit was common in the Huddersfield wool trade by the 1860s, with staplers allowing terms of up to nine months to clothiers. Such credit, as in the worsted branch, may have aided the financing of mechanization because the time to process the wool and sell the cloth was normally four to six months.

Topham was able to construct two series of the average credit length actually taken by customers, mainly Scottish, of Jowitts, woolstaplers of Leeds, over the period 1848 to 1905. These show two broad movements. First, there was a cyclical fluctuation with the credit taken lengthening over the upswing of the trade cycle and contracting during the downswing. However, the pattern of the business cycle, as portrayed in the series, assumes a different form after the 1880s to that which would be expected on the basis of national indicators, with peaks in 1886, 1892, 1895 and 1900, and troughs in 1890 and 1897. Second, the series show that credit taken lengthened from the mid-1880s. Until the late 1870s, credit taken varied from about 10 weeks during the trough of the business cycle to 16 weeks at the upper turning point, but thereafter it lengthened, reaching 24.4 weeks in 1900 (peak) and 12.4 weeks in 1897 (trough).

Topham argues that long credits became common again from the 1880s in order to encourage sales, although this did lead to some unsuccessful agitation in the 1890s to curtail credit once more.[2] Generally it would appear that the power to create trade credit lay mainly in the hands of merchants rather than manufacturers, and it was based in turn on the amount of accommodation given by the financial sector.[3]

Contrary to Topham's empirical data, Lavington thought that the period of trade credit was generally contracting during the decades before 1914, which he attributed largely to improvements in transport.[4] This would suggest that he was considering primarily, not book debts but external credit involving bills of exchange. As was pointed out in the previous chapter, the volume of inland bills of exchange declined from the 1870s until the 1890s, by when their extensive use was confined to a few particular areas, of which the Yorkshire woollen district was one.[5] There is some evidence from Merseyside banks which indicates that the tenor of inland bills may have increased during the 1880s, although this may have been due to their use in financing foreign rather than domestic transactions.[6] Therefore it should not be taken as a further positive pointer to a lengthening of the maturity of domestic credit during the last two decades of the nineteenth century. In addition Lavington concluded that the main suppliers of trade credit by 1914 were merchants: 'it is a function which combines conveniently with that of holding large and varied stocks of materials required by manufacturers and retailers.'[7] Certainly in the 1900s many retailers' stocks were financed through bills which wholesalers discounted in large batches with either their own banks or a discount house.[8]

Manufacturers not only received credit from suppliers but also in turn gave it to their own customers, in varying forms, which could strain a firm's financial resources. Ironmasters from the late 1840s and particularly during depressed periods of trade were prepared to accept railway company securities as payment for rails.[9] Subsequently some locomotive builders, such as Beyer, Peacock in the 1860s, came to take stocks and shares of their clients in either full or part payment of their debts.[10] This tradition of financing the customer in the capital goods sector continued in the case of shipbuilding until 1914. Lavington stated that shipbuilders 'virtually financed shipowners' through credits ranging from one to five years. This occurred mainly in connection with domestic orders as ships exported were normally paid for in cash.[11] These long credits to domestic owners were often combined with shipbuilders taking part payment in the form of the securities of the shipowning company.[12] Close to trade credit is the leasing in various ways of plant and machinery. The earliest obvious example of the practice was the renting of 'room and power' in the cotton industry from the 1800s and in the woollen industry from the middle decades of the nineteenth century.[13] Railway wagon leasing became important from the 1860s, particularly for coal and iron companies. Typical was the North Central Wagon Company, one of a number of concerns established as joint stock companies in the early 1860s. It built and hired out wagons, usually on a purchase lease, the forerunner of hire purchase, with the annual rent ranging from £9 to £14 depending on whether the company or the hirer was responsible for repairs. The wagons were financed by short-term debentures issued by the company, with maturities which matched the terms of its wagon leases. The early principal users of the company's services were railway companies, collieries and quarries.[14] Machine hiring or purchase on credit remained common in the Lancashire cotton industry until at least 1914, and it also developed in the form of machine leasing in the Midland boot and shoe industry.[15] Such facilities could lead to manufacturers becoming tied 'hand and foot' to machinery companies.

★

Apart from trade credit, early forms of hire purchase, and leasing, one of the other main forms of external financial assistance was obtaining a new partner, either active or sleeping. This is not to suggest that all new partners recruited by firms were obtained for financial reasons; many were brought into companies in order to aid their management. It would appear from studies of firms and industries during the 'heroic' first phase of the industrial revolution that most partners were recruited either through family, religious or trade links, or from a pool of local acquaintances, some arising from no more or no less than personal friendship. This pattern probably continued throughout the nineteenth century. J. Crossfield & Sons, soap manufacturers, for instance, took in a new partner in the 1860s after it had been found that profits were insufficient to finance further investment in fixed capital.[16] However, it is probable that generally by the last quarter of the nineteenth century, if not considerably earlier with regard to specific industries such as cotton, a more formalized market in partners' capital had developed. The intermediaries in this market were usually accountants and solicitors and, as with prospectuses of limited companies, advertisements in newspapers were used. David Chadwick, as well as converting concerns into limited companies, also acted as an intermediary in the market for partnerships and mortgages. These he helped to arrange through publication of the necessary details in his *Investment Circular*.[17] Mellors & Basden, a Nottingham firm of accountants, undertook similar business in the early

1880s and published a series of handbills. One for November 1883 advertises 15 opportunities and has a footnote stating that there were others but 'some persons object to have their enquiries circulated'. Not all were requests by firms for partners; about half were on the following lines: 'a gentleman aged 25, with capital, and large experience in Practical Chemistry, desires a Partnership in a well-established Business, BLEACHING or DYEING preferred.'[18] The handbill appears to have covered mainly local ventures, although in at least two cases the requests came for companies outside of the locality, with one wanting a partner in order to consolidate a branch in a North Midlands town, while the other arose from facilitating 'paying out the Executors of a deceased partner'.

It is impossible to quantify either the size of the market in partners' capital or the flow of finance into industry in the form of mortgages, which was probably more important than the former. As with partnerships, the industrial mortgage market was institutionalized to some extent during the nineteenth century through the activities of attorneys and solicitors. They had undertaken an intermediary role in this area from at least the eighteenth century in certain parts of the country.[19] Alongside the private mortgage market was the growth of mortgage loans made by life insurance companies during the first half of the nineteenth century. By the late 1850s two-thirds of life office investments consisted of money lent to individuals and corporations secured on real property. The main avenues of this investment were loans to freehold country estates, to urban developers, especially in London, to local authorities, and to railway companies, but some industrial companies did obtain financial assistance in this way. For instance, the Royal Exchange Assurance in 1844 and 1845 lent £90,000 on the security of property mortgages and personal bonds to two colliery companies, and in 1846 and 1850 provided a brewery company with £100,000 through a mortgage of freehold estates and brewery property.[20]

★

One of the major conclusions of business histories and industrial studies is that firms have grown generally by the ploughback of their own profits into new investment. Ashton in 1948, after reviewing the experience of Wedgwood, Gott, Crawshay, and Newton, Chambers & Co., stated that 'Industrial capital has been its own chief progenitor'.[21] Subsequent work has generally confirmed this to the extent that Crouzet pointed out in 1962 that 'this fact is so obvious as to be almost a cliche and the point is not worth labouring'.[22] The practice arose out of the backgrounds of many early industrial entrepreneurs – most had common origins and were so anxious to succeed that a large minority, if not a majority, were prepared to continue the rigid personal austerity of their childhoods and early adult lives. In any case such attitudes were for many in harmony with their religious faiths; a large number were non-conformists and positively frowned upon conspicuous consumption of any kind. Thus a pattern of business behaviour was established and it continued even when the attitudes which had framed it withered away. Profits appear to have been more than sufficient to meet the financial costs of further expansion and investment. In his review of the existing literature, Crouzet found that profits were usually greater than 15% or 20% on capital employed before 1815, while he found no evidence to suggest that either gross profits or the rate of return on capital fell in the medium term after the Napoleonic wars.

Although providing much firmer and broader evidence for Ashton's earlier conclusion, Crouzet did note that the sample of firms that he had considered – those arising out of business histories written in the 1950s and 1960s – did consist principally of the 'progressive' concerns in particularly profitable industries, and he added the rider that 'no doubt many other firms had a less brilliant record'.[23] Further caution is probably necessary when considering both the industrial revolution – the period that occupied the attention of Ashton and Crouzet – and the subsequent decades of the nineteenth century. It is evident from some business histories that there could be a considerable time-lag between the foundation of a firm and the point at which profits became the main source of funds for the finance of expansion. J. Foster built his woollen mill in the mid-1830s but profits did not arise until 1842 and even then were insufficient for a further decade to provide the finance required for investment in plant and machinery. Consequently the firm was forced to rely on trade credit until the mid-1840s and continually had a bank overdraft until the early 1850s.[24] At present it is impossible to assess the typicality of Foster's experience but it is, anyway, cautionary.

There are other reasons for at least questioning the weight given to the role of profits in the growth of firms apart from their adequacy in early years. The central point at issue is again typicality. Most of the evidence regarding the relationship between profits and a firm's development has come from business histories, which are usually studies of firms which have survived, in some form at least, until the middle decades of the twentieth century. It may well be that this sample of firms is a highly misleading one as there is evidence for a few industries which points to a high rate of business mortality. Recently Chapman has assembled statistics showing a high degree of turnover amongst the concerns which made up the cotton industry during the first half of the nineteenth century.[25] Sigsworth and Blackman found a similar pattern in the woollen and worsted industries during the 40 years before the First World War. Between 1870 and 1912 the population of firms in the woollen textile industry changed drastically. Part of this was due to the final disappearance of small handicraft firms in woollen manufacturing but over the whole industry there was still a high rate of turnover, although varying between different branches. Sigsworth and Blackman did not feel confident enough, given their limited sources, to suggest reasons for this situation, but pointed out that bankruptcy certainly played a major role.[26] It would be rash to extrapolate such evidence to the whole manufacturing sector but, as with the time-lag regarding the sufficiency of profits alone to finance expansion, it is cautionary. If the two factors are combined, it does suggest that some firms, possibly a substantial number in some industries, did not survive long enough for profits to have arisen in sufficient volume to finance further growth. Lastly with regard to the role of profits, it is clear that it was the practice in some industries to distribute all profits that were generated. This was the case in Cornish non-ferrous metals mining in the eighteenth century,[27] and it also occurred amongst a considerable number of collieries throughout the nineteenth century.[28]

There is now some general agreement that the appropriate way of measuring profitability is the rate of return on capital employed and that profits should be sufficient to both cover the costs of staying in business and provide a supply of finance for innovation and expansion. Although some stress is laid upon profitability as an 'index of the net effectiveness and soundness of a business's effort', so relating it to entrepreneurship in some guise or another, the essential relationship as far as mid-twentieth-century managerial accountancy is concerned is between profits and capital.[29] Such notions were entirely foreign to most eighteenth- and early-nineteenth-century entrepreneurs, who regarded the profitability of their firms as a product of their own business ability and acumen rather than of the capital that they employed and the technology that it embodied. These two differing interpretations can be reconciled without any great difficulty. In the present world, capital is largely synonymous with plant and machinery whereas during the early stages of in-dustrialization the main constituents of industrial capital were raw materials and stocks of finished and semi-finished goods. It is difficult to measure with any precision the growth of industrial fixed capital before the 1870s but the amount of steam power employed does provide a fairly reliable guide. Such data as are at present available indicate that total industrial steam power 'can have been [no] more than 300,000 nominal h.p.' in 1850, and by 1870, including water power, had increased to

1,032,560 h.p. This power was heavily concentrated in a narrow range of industries – textiles, with cotton mills alone accounting for a third, coalmining, iron smelting, founding and forging, and engineering. Generally, power-driven machinery and with it fixed capital only became important from the 1870s with the total British industrial power rising to 9,650,000 h.p. by 1907.[30]

The very low levels of fixed capital employed in firms outside the cotton, coal and iron industries before the last quarter of the nineteenth century allowed the adoption of pre-industrial mercantile accounting practices without causing any major difficulties. Admittedly accountants did find fixed capital hard to place in the schemas to which they were accustomed, and either confused it with revenue or regarded it as an auxiliary to entrepreneurship. However, the consequent dilemmas were naturally limited to those exceptional firms and industries where fixed capital bulked large.[31] Therefore Pollard's criticisms of early industrial accounting methods, in terms of their failure to provide guidance for business decisions, is probably overdrawn since in his survey he was essentially concerned with the atypical – large firms employing relatively large amounts of fixed capital by contemporary standards.[32]

Profits were determined in most firms by comparing periodic valuations and taking any difference to be profits arising over the intervening time period.[33] Although there was no form of legal compulsion of any kind until the first decade of the twentieth century,[34] the keeping of books and accounts had become general practice in manufacturing industry by the 1820s.[35] This method of assessing profitability and the accounting practices on which it was built continued in some industries, such as the West Riding wool textiles, until 1914.[36] What was essentially being measured was the owners' stock or capital, hence Pollard's criticisms. Capital was taken to be the difference between a firm's assets and liabilities, and profits to be the increase in capital between two valuations. Usually, net profits were derived after charging interest on the partners' capital, normally at a rate of 5%. Various ways were used to calculate the partners' capital, including basing it on the original sum subscribed when the partnership had been established. The fixed 5% charge for interest, given its generality, would appear to have been derived from the legal maximum permissible under the Usury laws, but it continued unaltered even when the laws were repealed in 1854. Normally no interest was charged when a firm made a 'loss', a practice which of course minimized losses.

The ploughback of profits into the firm which gave it both the necessary liquidity to survive and the finance for expansion came about in many ways. Commonly, and particularly when a firm was small and newly established, its partners did not withdraw all the monies due to them – often not even the interest-charge element. This practice of allowing profits to remain within the firm could and did lead to problems if it continued when the firm was soundly established, because it then tended to be in receipt of an income which was much greater than its expenditure.[37] Occasionally, anticipatory drawings of profits would occur but when this took place they were normally based on previous experience and if the firm was growing caused no difficulties. Normally, and particularly before the 1850s, current and capital expenditure were confused because capital costs such as the purchase of horses, the repair or extension of buildings, the construction of machinery, or the sinking of a shaft, were charged against current revenue. This could lead to the accumulation of secret reserves since capital items dealt with in this way were written off when they were bought, with any labour involved usually being charged to the wages account.

Methods of charging depreciation had become common in some industries by at least the 1830s. A number of cotton entrepreneurs stated in 1833 that they made an annual allowance for the depreciation of capital assets.[38] Similar allowances had been made by some engineering and iron works from the 1780s.[39] Admittedly the reasoning behind the need to make allowances for depreciation was often confused and unclear – on the one hand, repair; on the other, replacement. However what does stand out is that in the industries where fixed capital had assumed some importance by the 1830s, acknowledgement was being made of the need to service it in accounting methods.[40] It is also evident that errors in accounting practice in one direction were frequently cancelled by errors in another, so that there was no overall detrimental effect upon the firm. Management may not have been positively assisted by the clerks employed in the counting house, but at the same time very few firms came to grief as a result of imperfectly conceived notions of proper accounting practice.

The ways that profits were ploughed back and the accounting conventions involved apart, the critical question, given the apparent heavy reliance on internally generated funds, is whether profits, once they arose, were sufficient to allow firms not only to survive but also to grow and adopt new technology. At present there are no general data of whatever quality on the overall course of industrial profits before the mid-1850s, let alone estimates of the industrial capital stock, which would allow a calculation of the movement of the rate of return. The general impression is that profit margins were wide, which not only compensated for inefficient costing and planning but also allowed the rapid accumulation of undivided profits and so in turn the rapid growth of firms.[41] This was the result of a number of factors. First, wage rates were relatively low for most of the first half of the nineteenth century, as a consequence of the abundant supply of labour and the low floor set to industrial wages by agricultural earnings. Thus capital accumulation through the reinvestment of profits was not checked by rising wage rates, although the abundant supply of labour may have checked the adoption of labour-saving devices.[42] Second, until the 1850s, if not the 1870s, Britain had almost a monopoly of the new industrial technology and the markets for the products which it allowed to be made so relatively cheaply. Consequently, not only did profits make up a large proportion of industrial incomes but they also contained a significant element of quasi-rents. This rent element was restricted by natural and man-created barriers to international trade and by intra-industry competition, but this latter factor was probably of some consequence only in the case of the cotton industry from 1815 and in some sections of the iron industry, such as rail-making, from the late 1840s. It is significant that it was mainly cotton masters who complained in 1833 that profits had been reduced by competition.[43]

As a result of Feinstein's major work,[44] a greater amount of evidence is available regarding the course of industrial profits and the rate of return on capital during the half century before 1914. Feinstein's estimates of the real rate of profit, by quinquennial average, for the period 1865–9 to 1905–9 are shown by table 8.1. Before either discussing these data or drawing any conclusions from them, it is important to stress that while it does portray the path of profitability in manufacturing industry, the series is based by necessity on tax data which also include profits of transport, building and distribution, and incomes from finance and professions. In the 1890s and the 1910s, these additional categories accounted for approximately two-thirds of domestic income under Schedule D gross assessments. Therefore their relative weight may have some masking effect upon variations in the profitability of the manufacturing sector. Generally, and with the exception of the railways, it is probable that they cushioned the decline in the rate of profitability portrayed for the period from the mid-1870s until 1914.

Feinstein's data show a secular fall in the real rate of return on industrial capital, a picture which is well-supported by contemporary and business history evidence. During the severe slump of the mid-1880s, the Royal Commission on the Depression of Trade and Industry collected a substantial amount of evidence for a limited range of industries which pointed to a fall in profits and profit margins from the mid-1870s to the mid-1880s. Representatives of the Oldham cotton mills spoke of depressed profits for a period of a decade after 1875, with perhaps some

Table 8.1   Real rate of profit on capital
        1865–1909

Years	%
1865–9	16.5
1870–4	18.6
1875–9	15.2
1880–4	14.7
1885–9	15.0
1890–4	15.5
1895–9	15.2
1900–4	12.7
1905–9	11.9

Source: C. Feinstein, 'Home and Foreign
Investment. Some Aspects of Capital Formation   and   Finance   in   the   U.K.
1870–1913', unpublished Ph.D. thesis,
University of Cambridge, 1960.

amelioration during 1880 and 1881. One witness claimed that spinning in
Oldham in 1885 was being undertaken only at a loss.[45] Similar comments
were made by persons appearing on behalf of the coal trade. The
representative of the South Yorkshire Coal Association claimed that a
very large number of collieries in that area had not been working at a
profit for eight to ten years.[46] A similar but rather more cautious picture
of conditions was drawn by G. B. Forster of the Northumberland Coal
Trade Association. He admitted that his body knew nothing directly
about profits but he thought that many collieries were in the red,
especially those working thinner seams.[47] Apparently, south of the Tyne
the situation was worse as the Durham representative stated that no
profits were being made.[48] A. Hewlett, talking of the position in
Lancashire, was more circumspect; he thought that very few collieries
were 'paying', while his own company, the Wigan Coal and Iron, had
earned only £6,000 on a capital of £2m.[49] These statements were
supported by evidence which the Royal Commission received from the
Inland Revenue which showed that profits of mines and ironworks had
fallen between the mid-1870s and the mid-1880s. The average assessment
in the case of mines had fallen from a peak of £4,882 in 1877 to £2,628,
while for ironworks the reduction had been from a peak of £21,804 in
1875 to a trough of £6,016 in 1880.[50] Such evidence is confirmed for
South Wales at least, by Addis's study of the fortunes of local industry.

The Dowlais company made losses on steel production in 1885, 1886, 1892 and 1894, and on coal in 1887 and 1888, with the company making an overall loss in 1887 and 1888. Similarly the Ebbw Vale concern was in the red in 1875, 1876, 1879, 1884, 1887 and 1889, while the Rymney company continually made a loss between 1875 and 1879, as did the Nantyglo and Blaina concerns from 1873 until 1879. Thereafter the Welsh companies' dividends were meagre and, with the exception of Guest, Keen and Nettlefolds which took over the Dowlais concern in 1901, only reached 10% for five years in the decade before 1914.[51]

What factors were responsible for this decline in profitability? It is evident that both cyclical and secular forces were moving in the same direction, especially between the mid-1870s and the mid-1880s, hence the contemporary outcry over the 'Great Depression'. However, even when prices began to rise from the mid-1890s, the profitability of industry in real terms began to fall again after a decade of stability. Part of the explanation of the secular fall is the removal after the early 1870s of the exceptional factors which had previously buoyed up industrial profits and consequently had assisted industrial capital formation. Profit's share of total industrial incomes started to decline from the mid-1870s, while at the same time the quasi-rents that profits had contained as a result of Britain's hegemony over industrial technology began to be reduced with the growth of other industrial economies and their appearance as competitors in international trade.

Between 1860 and 1913 money wages in the United Kingdom rose almost steadily at an annual rate of 1.03%. This gradual but almost unwavering rise in wages, especially from the mid-1880s, was coupled with a reduction in working hours which affected workers in more and more industries during the quarter of a century before 1914.[52] Consequently profit's exceptional share of industrial income during the first half of the nineteenth century was reduced to more 'normal' levels. Feinstein's data show a fall from about 46% of industrial income during the 1860s and 1870s to about 40% by the 1900s.[53] Money wages rose for a number of reasons. The cyclical shortage of labour during the early 1870s boom, combined with growing unionization, began to change the balance of power in the labour market. However, the consequence was not so much labour's ability to gain wage increases during boom periods but rather its resistance to wage reductions during the slumps of the late 1870s, the mid-1880s and the early 1890s. Although varying interpretations have been made,[54] it would appear that in terms of the experience of other industrial countries, more militant labour from the 1870s and especially by the 1890s was met with less effective opposition on the part of employers. In fact employers, who lacked in most industries effective national associations, were generally not inclined to attack organized labour but rather were prepared to work with trade unions.[55]

Britain's relative losses in international trade arising from the spread of industrialization have often been debated. The post-1870 market for Britain's manufactured exports is not at issue here but rather the consequence of foreign competition upon British profit levels and profit margins. The exact effects are difficult to unravel but, as Feinstein has shown,[56] the movement of the net barter terms of trade does provide a guide, because import prices are a proxy for raw-material costs and export prices are an indication of manufacturing prices. Both import and export prices fell from the mid-1870s until the mid-1890s but there were periods when export prices fell faster than import prices, such as the late 1870s,[57] which would suggest a general squeezing of, at least, profit margins on exports.

Technological change was a third factor affecting secularly the profitability of certain sectors of British industry. The growth of steelmaking in the 1870s and 1880s rendered puddling uneconomic. However, wrought-iron manufacture continued to expand until 1882, countering steeply falling steel prices by rationalization and reductions in wages and profits. It was precisely the development of steel rail-making with a consequent diminishing ratio of steel to wrought-iron rail prices – by 1875 steel rails were at the most 16% dearer than their iron counterparts – which led many of the Welsh ironmakers to incur losses during the second half of the 1870s on the substantial investment made in wrought-iron technology during the first years of the decade. Thereafter the wrought-iron industry contracted sharply and its output became limited to those product ranges which steel could not take over, such as anchors and anchor chains, where resistance to corrosion was important.[58] The rise of large-scale steelmaking had other, indirect effects upon the profitability of other industries, especially coalmining. Bessemer's original patent had stressed fuel economy, and such gains were even greater with the Siemen's regenerative furnace. Investment during the early 1870s had gone not only into wrought iron but also into collieries to supply ironworks with the fuel that puddling so prodigiously consumed. As a result of the switch to steel, many colliery proprietors in the late 1870s and the mid-1880s found that their industry had expanded in the medium term at a faster rate than that warranted by the growth of the main industrial users of coal. Some in the mid-1880s correctly pointed out that one of the reasons for the relatively low levels of profit current in coalmining was that the manufacture of steel had 'economised on the use of coal'.[59] Comparable to the substitution of steel for wrought iron in its effects on profitability was the replacement of the Leblanc method of producing alkalis by the Solvay process. In Britain's case, the main impact of this change was to be seen in overseas trade because except for Brunner, Mond, the domestic industry remained wedded to the increasingly uneconomic Leblanc method. Initially, as with wrought-iron production, the Leblanc trade was able to continue by more efficient production methods and some product diversification, but from the 1890s, there were no further possible avenues of retrenchment left to explore and exploit.[60]

As a result of Phelps Brown's important comparative study, it is now possible to perceive in at least general terms how British entrepreneurs reacted to the 'Great Depression'. They were confronted with contracting profit margins from the late 1870s and a falling real rate of return on capital. This they attempted to remedy by squeezing labour costs, with the result that nominal unit wage costs fell continually from the late 1870s until the late 1890s. This was in contrast to most other industrial economies, where unit costs were either static or rising. In this way, the heavy bout of investment made during the boom of the first half of the 1870s was rendered as profitable as possible, with productivity rising as a result and if anything at a faster rate from the mid-1880s. However, from about 1900 productivity growth halted, money wages continued to rise, albeit slower than elsewhere, and as a consequence unit wage costs began to rise in British industry at a faster rate than in some other industrial economies.[61] Profit margins then contracted again, after benefiting from very low raw material prices in the late 1880s and 1890s, and the real rate of return on capital, which appears to have been successfully stabilized from the mid-1880s, started to fall once more.

★

Probably the critical issue which arises in this discussion is whether a shortage of funds for industrial investment, especially of internal resources, was responsible for the post-1900 hiatus in the growth of British industrial productivity. There does seem to have been, at first glance at least, an unfavourable set of financial circumstances facing industrial manufacturers during the quarter of a century before 1914. As a result of growing competitive forces both at home and overseas in factor and product markets together with technological change, the rate of return of industrial capital declined, which reduced the amount of funds available internally to finance new investment. At the same time, banks as a consequence of the amalgamation movement were less-prepared to make available either working capital or medium-term investment finance. In addition it was difficult for small and medium-size firms to obtain long-term capital on the open market as a result of institutional difficulties, while the falling real rate of return on domestic industrial capital would not have attracted investors to hold such securities in the medium term. Such an analysis places some British manufacturers in a trap from which there was no escape. Some historians would put forward a less pessimistic interpretation. They have argued that the falling real rate of return, especially as it was masked by a recovery in gross nominal profits from the mid-1890s, was not generally sufficient either to have pushed industrialists into drastically reconsidering their position to the degree of changing either the process employed or the product produced, or to have warranted such a response.

It is held that there were only a very limited number of instances, such as the Leblanc producers and Courtaulds in the crêpe trade, where declining sales and profits made an impact. In most firms and industries it was to take the First World War, which greatly accelerated underlying trends, to change the situation dramatically and even then the new reality was masked by the false dawn of the post-war restocking boom.

In general during the period 1870 to 1914, investment in manufacturing industry was barely sufficient to maintain the amount of real capital per worker. It was just enough to keep pace with the increase in the labour force, which rose at a rate of about 14–15% per decade from the 1880s to the 1900s. The data on the employment of steam power, already considered, show that there was a qualitative change in the nature of industrial capital, but it would also appear that returns on capital were beginning to decline. The capital output ratio fell from 3.2 to 2.1 between 1880 and 1895 and, after rising sharply during the domestic boom of the second half of the 1890s, resumed its fall from the mid-1900s. The 1890s upswing in domestic investment was sufficient to put productivity back on to its trend growth of about 1% per annum but from the early 1900s there were no further productivity gains. Several commentators of what may be called the optimistic school have suggested that the post-1900 dip in productivity was due to the British economy having exhausted currently available technology. Consequently they have concluded that further capital investment would have been pointless, since it would have led to further falls in the marginal product of capital which in turn would have reduced the average.[62] In such a situation greater flows of internal or external funds to industry would have had no positive effect upon productivity. In contrast, other industrial economies continued to enjoy productivity growth but this was because of intersectoral shifts in the labour force and gains arising from the adoption of existing technology in the manufacturing sector. Industrial capital formation was proceeding more rapidly elsewhere but the effect was only to catch Britain up. Real capital per occupied person tripled in Germany between 1860 and 1913 but this resulted in the capital:labour ratio of the German economy rising from about 40% of the British level in 1860 to equality in 1913. Generally, if not at the industry level, Britain's productivity growth during the 30 years before 1900 was comparable to that of other industrial economies, most of which were in earlier phases of industrialization. Divergence only occurred from the opening years of the twentieth century.

However, doubts have been expressed and probably will continue to be aired over whether the British economy was using its productive resources to the full and exploiting all available technology. There are three general areas which prompt such questionings: one falls under the general head of 'industrial housekeeping', the second is the geographical immobility of capital and enterprise, and the third is the preference of British entrepreneurs for importing new technology in a product form rather than innovate themselves. A brief examination of at least some aspects of these topics will provide guidelines to a possible answer to the question: if entrepreneurs had been able to obtain greater quantities of finance, either internally or externally, would such funds have been utilized in a positive way?

The problem of industrial housekeeping arose essentially from the piecemeal extension of most British plant in what were increasingly congested urban areas. Consequently plant layout was seldom if ever rationalized and, instead, new capacity and new technology had to be added in a haphazard manner, which reduced its effectiveness.[63] Manufacturers seldom moved to what would now be termed 'greenfield' sites, the last main geographical shifts of technology being the erection of rail-making plants on the Cumberland coast and the building of cotton mills in the Oldham area in the 1870s. There were advantages to be gained from moving out of the established urban industrial areas, and these were not merely the advantages arising from the construction of fully integrated plants, cheap land, and closer proximity to raw materials and markets. As Hunt has shown, there were substantial regional wage variations in the British economy of the second half of the nineteenth century, which persisted until 1914 with only slight amelioration. The high-wage areas comprised London and the northern industrial counties of England joined by South Wales and Central Scotland in 1914. It was only some of the so-called 'new' industries which took advantage of the low wages current in the rural south, an area which had been almost de-industrialized during the nineteenth century. Chelmsford and Coventry provide illustrations of the process in which local economies dependent upon traditional industries, in both cases silk, declined during the nineteenth century, and only recovered from the 1890s onwards with the growth of electrical engineering, ball-bearing production, cycle manufacture, and the development of artificial fibres. As a result Coventry, through the local growth of productivity and wages, had become by 1914 almost a part of the West Midlands extension of the high-wage area of the northern counties. Similarly Chelmsford emerged as one of a number of satellite towns around London which gave the South East relative regional economic buoyancy during the inter-war years.[64]

Skill requirements in the labour force were not a barrier to capital mobility, certainly not as regards industrial growth in the rural south from the 1890s. The new techniques in manufacturing, pioneered primarily in the United States – the so-called 'American system of manufactures' – replaced skilled labour with machinery that could be operated by unskilled labour; in the American case this often consisted of immigrants, who by the 1910s were coming primarily from southern and eastern Europe. Harley has argued that there was less incentive to adopt this technology in the main industrial centres of England because 'skilled labour was relatively more abundant and consequently cheaper in Britain than in her rivals'. Accordingly, relative factor costs were such that British entrepreneurs were behaving rationally when they did not substitute capital embodying the American methods for skilled labour. However, such an explanation relies upon the hypothesis that unlike Germany and the United States, 'most of the British labour force came from urban, industrial backgrounds and had a long tradition of industrial discipline and skills'.[65] Actually it would appear that this was not the case, because part of the explanation why the main industrial areas of Britain had relatively high wages coupled with low net-migration gains was that urban workers, especially the higher-paid, were very mobile. Britain's high-wage regions experienced a steady drain of such workers to elsewhere in Britain and overseas which was offset by an inflow of labour from the rural low-wage areas and Ireland.[66] Consequently there was no steady accumulation of a pool of labour long-accustomed to industrial techniques in the main urban manufacturing areas, but instead an almost continuous training programme of labour with little knowledge of modern processes had to take place. Therefore it would seem that there was almost as much incentive arising from the availability of industrial skills to replace skilled labour with machinery in the established industrial areas as there was in 'greenfield' areas such as Coventry and Chelmsford.

Lastly, in considering whether new capital resources could have been invested effectively, one further factor has to be taken into account. The attitude of British labour to work and remuneration appears to have changed in the 1890s to the extent that Hobsbawm has seen the decade as a watershed in the development of the labour market.[67] During the closing years of the nineteenth century, workers began to question in general terms the level of wages and the division of industrial income between wages and profits. Low wages now came to be equated with low output and work effort. This change in attitude was brought about by labour being increasingly regarded by entrepreneurs as a freely marketable commodity, which led to organized labour attempting to raise wages by both restricting training in order to keep skills scarce, and enforcing rigid demarcation lines between jobs. On the one hand there was a growing number of employers who were trying to shift the determination of wage rates on to a basis of 'payment by results', a thickening of a development which had got underway in the late 1870s, while on the other hand this was countered by strikes, low output, and resistance to the introduction of new methods, especially labour-saving machinery.[68] New types of machine were not opposed directly but, rather, unions negotiated long and hard over the terms and conditions relating to their introduction. In such bargaining, employers were generally reluctant to acknowledge in wage rates the higher productivity which the new machines would bring in train.[69] This hardening of attitudes on both sides of the labour market constituted a barrier to further productivity growth flowing from new investment to the extent that some entrepreneurs may have decided not to undertake innovating capital expenditure.

★

The exact relationship between economic growth and the workings of financial markets is difficult to establish. Both theoretical and empirical studies utilizing either historical or contemporary data have as yet failed either to produce reliable methods to measure the extent and the result of the facilitating function of finance, or to determine the optimal size of the financial sector in relation to the real economy, or to distinguish effectively the contribution of different forms of financial structure to economic growth.[70] However, some theoretical guidelines have been laid down and they can be used as criteria for a general assessment of whether an economy was endowed with an efficient financial system. The provision of financial services will allow economic growth to take place when it breaks, by the creation of primary financial instruments such as bonds and shares, the direct tie between internal savings and investment for both households and economic units. However, if the introduction of primary financial securities is to accelerate economic growth, then two basic conditions have to be fulfilled. First, it is necessary that there should be an unequal distribution of entrepreneurial talent in the population. This will allow the separation of savings and investment to have a positive effect upon economic growth but only until the point is reached when the rate of net return of all investing units, whatever the quality of entrepreneurship involved, has been equalized. Second, many investments and, preferably those promising the highest returns, should be large and indivisible. This will stimulate growth because the required level of saving will then be greatly in excess of the resources of any individual unit, but only until expected returns from 'large' investments are equal to those on investments within the compass of individual economic units.[71]

Did the finance of British manufacturing industry take place in an environment where these criteria were fulfilled? Certainly at least one condition was met, namely there was an unequal distribution of entrepreneurial ability in nineteenth-century Britain. However, a large proportion of established firms apparently relied on internal savings to finance investment projects. They did not issue primary financial instruments to attract savings from surplus units and households in order to allow their concerns to grow at a rate faster than that supported by the accumulation of internal resources. Did this have a serious negative effect upon the overall rate of growth of both the manufacturing sector and the economy? Any answer to such a question is conjectural but is probably 'no' for the period before the 1860s. This is because, on the one hand, profit levels were exceptionally high owing to both a lack of competition and employers being in a strong position in the labour market, while on the other hand, most investment projects at that time were neither relatively large nor highly indivisible. Actually, for a large number of established firms the financial problem was not how to meet the needs of investment but where to place externally the flow of accumulating profits. The position changed from the 1860s, but at different times for different industries. The rate of competition increased with both the growth of industries in terms of the numbers of firms producing similar products, and the international spread of industrialization. This was coupled with the supply of labour becoming less elastic at the ruling wage, with the consequence that the position of employers weakened in the labour market. The combination of these factors led to real rates of profit declining secularly from the 1870s when an increasing number of investment projects were becoming larger and more indivisible. Responses to this new situation varied. Some investment decisions may have been shelved as a result of employers finding it difficult to negotiate what they considered to be the appropriate wage level for working new machinery. Some firms did become joint stock companies, especially from the mid-1880s, but not in order to break the tie between internal savings levels and new investment. It would appear that the predominant reason why concerns adopted the limited company form of organization was to obtain the legal privilege of limited liability so as to insure against possible future losses and ultimately bankruptcy.

So far in this discussion of the relationship between financial services and economic growth, a very simple market structure has been assumed – one without intermediation. Economic growth can be further assisted through the foundation of financial institutions. However, their creation will only accelerate development if the indirect financing of investment undertaken by them is more efficient than that arising from borrowers and savers dealing directly. Consequently, economic growth will only be positively affected if, first, the activities of financial intermediaries raise the aggregate volume of saving and investment, which will depend upon the extent to which secondary issues of securities undertaken by them are not simply substitutes for primary issues of shares and bonds. Second, it is necessary that the activities of financial institutions will increase the marginal rate of return on investment through a more efficient allocation of savings, which will depend upon their expertise and knowledge of investment outlets.[72] Theoretically the main function performed by financial intermediaries is the reduction of the cost of finance, i.e. the rate of interest, by providing through secondary financial instruments, alternative forms of debt to that arising from primary financing. This will allow savers to diversify their investment portfolios, which reduces the rate of interest since it is assumed that savers would only accept an increasing volume of primary financial instruments at a rising discount on their price. Such a description of behaviour assumes a certain level of development and the existence of perfect capital markets in order to assure responsiveness to interest rate changes.[73]

Financial intermediaries did evolve with the industrialization of the British economy. The outstanding case was the rapid development of country banking during the second half of the eighteenth century coupled with further spurts of bank formations in the 1830s, 1860s and 1870s. These institutions did issue secondary securities in the form of bank deposits and did take up the primary securities of economic units, mainly bills of exchange. However, the banking system was highly fragmented until the 1890s because most concerns had limited branch networks before the 1870s. This impeded the development of a perfect market in credit although the system was given some integration through the central role played by the institutions of the London money market from the 1830s. But it is difficult to establish whether this was sufficient to remove regional variations in the rate of interest. Data on regional borrowing costs is scanty and allowances have to be made for both the differing qualities of paper discounted and cyclical forces. Collins' work on the Liverpool money market indicates that this centre's minimum discount rate and the rate at which the local branch of the Bank of England would discount in excess of special fixed limits, remained above the average rate of the London discount market until at least the mid-1840s.[74] Although regional and local discount rates may have converged with those of the metropolis by the middle decades of the century, it is evident from the small amount of evidence presented in an earlier chapter that rates charged on overdrafts and loans varied considerably until at least the 1900s, with some variations persisting until the 1920s.[75]

Intermediation was far less developed with regard to the provision of capital and remained so until at least 1914. The lack of development and innovation in this area was primarily a reflection of the lack of demand for this type of finance, due to manufacturing industry's continuing reliance on internally generated funds. In many respects agents in the formal capital market were not called upon to provide the services of intermediation for industrial companies, which greatly retarded their development in this area. Until at least the 1880s the main forms of intermediation were the services of accountants and solicitors, who played a role in local and regional informal markets but to whom the provision of financial services was a minor function amongst the many tasks that they performed. Consequently, as 'part-timers', their expertise was limited and more often than not was placed at the disposal of the potential supplier of funds rather than the borrower, as for instance in the arrangement of a mortgage. Their knowledge of investment outlets was usually restricted to the locality of their practice. The formal capital market did develop from the mid-1880s with the growth in the number of public companies but the quality of intermediation, if anything, declined with the emergence of the so-called professional promoter.

By 1914 there was no national perfect capital for industrial needs, certainly in comparison with that provided for credit by the banking systems. Instead there was a 'Balkan-like' mosaic consisting of a number of regional bowls of savings which occasionally coalesced under special circumstances. This did occur in the 1870s to a certain extent with regard to the coal, iron and steel industries, and during the 1890s when savers' mistrust of foreign securities was so considerable that it turned their attention to domestic issues, including those issued on behalf of manufacturing concerns. However, because of the general 'thinness' of industrial securities, a secondary market for them did not become firmly established, while banks and insurance companies, as a result of liquidity requirements, did not take up industrial securities for their investment portfolios. This lack of intermediation, for whatever reason, together with its secondary consequences, did have the effect that some economic growth was forgone but the amount involved is difficult ot establish.

Historians who have discerned some degree of failure on the part of the late Victorian economy in terms of it not growing either as rapidly as other contemporary industrial economies or as quickly as allowed by internal resources, have blamed both the institutions of the financial sector and the industrial entrepreneur. In their arguments they have sometimes followed contemporary criticisms or have faulted the performance of the key decision-maker in a capitalist economy. Does the evidence support such a pessimistic view of post-1870 British economic development? It has been pointed out here that the legal environment with regard to business organization and finance before 1900 was highly permissive and gave free rein to unscrupulous company promoters to mulct both the companies that they established and the investors who placed their savings in the securities which they issued. But thereafter the grounds for what has been called damnation become less certain. Domestic industrial securities were less well-served by the institutions, especially the metropolitan instititutions, of the formal capital market. However, the lack of institutional development was largely due to the lack of a growing demand for external finance by industrial firms. This arose from most established companies continuing to rely on internally generated funds, a pattern of behaviour which had been established during, if not before, the first phase of the industrial revolution. It is surely asking too much of the financial sector to develop specialized institutions to service a demand which during the second half of the nineteenth century only reached substantial proportions during two cyclical upswings two decades apart.

After the early 1870s internal resources did not accumulate at the same rate as previously, while investment projects in manufacturing industry were becoming 'lumpier'. Entrepreneurs did become concerned about gross profitability, especially during the 1880s when falling profits were magnified by the veil of money and international competition developed for the first time in many product ranges. But prices recovered from the mid-1890s and export values not only picked up but also began to grow rapidly again. Gross industrial profits in nominal terms increased, their recovery like their previous decline being intensified by general price movements. In such a situation there was not the urgent incentive to contemplate further investment in new technology, even though it may have been warranted by unperceived falling real rates of return on capital and stagnant productivity growth.

Notes

(Place of publication is London unless otherwise stated)

1 A. J. Topham, 'The Credit Structure of the West Riding Wool-Textile Industry in the Nineteenth Century', unpublished M.A. thesis, University of Leeds, 1953.

2 The above section has been drawn from Topham, op. cit., pp. 59–69, 85–9, 91–108, 117–19, 123, 125–32, 160–1, 172, 189.

3 On the general theoretical implications, see M. S. Levitt, 'Monetary Theory and Trade Credit. An Historical Approach', *Yorkshire Bulletin of Economic and Social Research*, XVI, 1964.

4 F. Lavington, *The English Capital Market*, 1921, reprinted 1969, p. 266.

5 See above, p. 201.

6 S. Nishimura, *The Decline of Inland Bills of Exchange in the London Money Market 1855–1913*, Cambridge, 1971, pp. 40–2.

7 Lavington, op. cit., p. 267.

8 National Monetary Commission, *Interviews on the Banking and Currency Systems of England . . .*, Washington, D.C., 1910, interview with Charles Gow, General Manager of the London Joint Stock Bank, p. 77.

9 See A. Birch, *The Economic History of the British Iron and Steel Industry, 1784–1879*, 1967, pp. 220–1.

10 P. L. Cottrell, 'Investment Banking in England, 1856–1882. Case Study of the International Financial Society', unpublished Ph.D. thesis, University of Hull, 1974, pp. 341–2.

11 Lavington, op. cit., pp. 265–6.

12 S. Pollard, 'The Economic History of Shipbuilding 1870–1914', unpublished Ph.D. thesis, University of London, 1951, pp. 90–1.

13 See above, p. 21 and K. V. Pankhurst, 'Investment in the West Riding Wool Textile Industry in the Nineteenth Century', *Yorkshire Bulletin of Economic and Social Research*, VIII, 1956, p. 95.

14 *Payment Deferred 1861–1961. The Story of the North Central Wagon and Finance Company Limited*, ?Rotherham, 1961, pp. 3–5.

15 Lavington, op. cit., pp. 267–8.

16 A. E. Musson, *Enterprise in Soap and Chemicals*, Manchester, 1965, p. 64.

17 See, for example, *Chadwick's Investment Circular*, 3 September 1870, p. 8.

18 Library, University of Hull, microfilm copy of the Mellors, Basden papers.

19 B. L. Anderson, 'The Attorney and the Early Capital Market in Lancashire' in J. R. Harris (ed.), *Liverpool and Merseyside: Essays in the Economic and Social History of the Port and its Hinterland*, 1969.

20 B. Supple, *The Royal Exchange Assurance. A History of British Insurance 1720–1970*, Cambridge, 1970, pp. 317–18, 328.

21 T. S. Ashton, *The Industrial Revolution 1760–1830*, 1948, p. 97.

22 F. Crouzet, 'Capital Formation in Great Britain during the Industrial Revolution', reprinted in Crouzet (ed.), *Capital Formation in the Industrial Revolution*, 1972, p. 188.

23 ibid., p. 196.

24 E. M. Sigsworth, *Black Dyke Mills. A History*, Liverpool, 1958, pp. 174, 178, 218–27.

25 S. D. Chapman, 'Working Capital in the British Cotton Industry, 1770–1850', Ealing Business History Seminar, May 1975.

26 E. M. Sigsworth and J. Blackman, 'The Woollen and Worsted Industries' in D. H. Aldcroft (ed.), *The Development of British Industry and Foreign Competition 1875–1914*, 1968, pp. 128–32.

27 J. Rowe, *Cornwall in the Age of the Industrial Revolution*, Liverpool, 1953, pp. 22–4, 47.

28 B. R. Mitchell, 'The Economic Development of the Inland Coalfields 1870–1914', unpublished Ph.D. thesis, University of Cambridge, 1956, pp. 276–9.

29 See, for example, J. Sizer, *An Insight into Management Accounting*, Harmondsworth, 1969, pp. 78–80.

30 A. E. Musson, 'Industrial Motive Power in the United Kingdom,

1800–70', *Economic History Review*, 2nd series, XXIX, 1976, pp. 434–6.

31 S. Pollard, *The Genesis of Modern Management*, Harmondsworth, 1968, p. 271.

32 ibid., chapter 6.

33 ibid., pp. 275–6.

34 See H. C. Edey and P. Paitpakdi, 'British Company Accounting and the Law, 1844–1900' in A. C. Littleton and B. S. Yamey (eds), *Studies in the History of Accounting*, 1956.

35 Pollard, op. cit., p. 252.

36 Pankhurst, op. cit.

37 ibid., p. 102; and see Sigsworth, op. cit., p. 219.

38 *B.P.P.*, VI, 1833, *Select Committee on Commerce, Manufacturing and Shipping*, evidence of William Graham, cotton spinner and weaver, Glasgow, qq. 5548, 5550; George Smith, cotton spinner and weaver, q. 9139.

39 Pollard, op. cit., p. 284.

40 On the question of depreciation, see J. Kitchen, 'Lawrence Dicksee, Depreciation, and the Double Account System' in H. Edey and B. S. Yamey (eds), *Debits, Credits, Finance and Profits*, 1974.

41 Pollard, op. cit., pp. 285–7.

42 H. J. Habakkuk, *American and British Technology in the Nineteenth Century*, 1967, pp. 140–1.

43 *Select Committee on Manufacturing, Commerce and Shipping*, 1833; see, for example, the evidence of William Haynes, q. 5021.

44 See C. H. Feinstein, 'Home and Foreign Investment. Some Aspects of Capital Formation and Finance in the U.K. 1870–1913', unpublished Ph.D. thesis, University of Cambridge, 1960, especially pp. 23–9, 226–60.

45 *B.P.P.*, XXII, 1886, *Second Report of the Royal Commission on the Depression of Trade and Industry*, evidence of S. Andrew, Oldham Master Cotton Spinners' Association, and S. Taylor, mill owner, Oldham, qq. 4294–6, 4304; evidence of George Lord, q. 5266.

46 ibid., evidence of J. D. Ellis, qq. 3075–6.

47 *B.P.P.*, XXIII, 1886, *Third Report of the Royal Commission on the Depression of Trade and Industry*, evidence of G. B. Fowler, qq. 11,720, 11,728–30.

48 ibid., evidence of J. B. Simpson, q. 12,438.

49 ibid., evidence of A. Hewlett, q. 12,117.

50 *B.P.P.*, XXI, 1886, *First Report of the Royal Commission on the Depression of Trade and Industry*, evidence of A. West, Chairman of the Board of Inland Revenue, qq. 839–40; see also appendix 7, statement showing the gross amount of profits arising from mines, ironworks, assessed to income tax in each year ended 5 April from 1865.

51 J. P. Addis, 'The Heavy Iron and Steel Industry in South Wales 1870–1950', unpublished Ph.D. thesis, University of Wales, Aberystwyth, 1957, appendix E, pp. 22–5.

52 E. H. Phelps Brown with Margaret Browne, *A Century of Pay*, 1968, pp. 55–6, 67–82, 184.

53 Feinstein, op. cit., pp. 43, 227–31.

54 For a contrasting view, see J. Saville, 'Trade Unions and Free Labour: the Background to the Taff Vale Decision' in A. Briggs and J. Saville (eds), *Essays in Labour History*, 1960.

55 Brown with Browne, op. cit., pp. 82, 188–9.

56 Feinstein, op. cit., p. 232.

57 Between 1875 and 1880 export prices fell by 20% while import prices declined by only 7.5%: B. R. Mitchell with P. Deane, *Abstract of Historical Statistics*, Cambridge, 1971, p. 331.

58 D. S. Landes, *The Unbound Prometheus. Technological Change and Industrial Development in Western Europe from 1750 to the Present*, Cambridge, 1969, pp. 260–2.

59 *Second Report of the Royal Commission on the Depression of Trade and Industry*, 1886, evidence of J. D. Ellis, q. 3145.

60 Landes, op. cit., pp. 272–3.

61 Brown with Browne, op. cit., pp. 126–31, 180–95. See also J. Saville, 'The Development of British Industry and Foreign Competition 1875–1914', *Business History*, XII, 1970, pp. 63–5; and on the productivity issue, R. C. O. Matthews, 'Some Aspects of Post-war Growth in the British Economy in Relation to Historical Experience', reprinted in D. H. Aldcroft and P.

Fearon (eds), *Economic Growth in Twentieth-century Britain;* D. N. McCloskey, 'Did Victorian Britain Fail?', *Economic History Review,* 2nd series, XXIII, 1970.

62 Brown with Browne, op. cit., p. 183; McCloskey, op. cit.

63 Landes, op. cit., p. 336.

64 E. Hunt, *Regional Wage Variations in Britain 1850–1914,* Oxford, 1973, pp. 160–1.

65 C. K. Harley, 'Skilled Labour and the Choice of Technique in Edwardian Industry', *Explorations in Economic History,* XI, 1974.

66 Hunt, op. cit., p. 278.

67 E. J. Hobsbawn, 'Custom, Wages and Work Load in Nineteenth Century Industry', in Briggs and Saville, op. cit.

68 Brown with Browne, op. cit., pp. 185–90.

69 Habakkuk, op. cit., pp. 197–200.

70 R. W. Goldsmith, *Financial Structure and Development,* 1969, p. 401; R. Cameron and H. T. Patrick, Introduction to R. Cameron *et al. Banking in the Early Stages of Industrialisation,* 1967.

71 Goldsmith, op. cit.

72 Goldsmith, op. cit., pp. 396–400.

73 See J. G. Gurley and E. S. Shaw, 'Financial Aspects of Economic Development' *American Economic Review,* XLV, 1955; Gurley and Shaw, *Money in a Theory of Finance,* Washington, D.C., 1960. For criticisms of this view, see A. L. Marty, 'Gurley and Shaw on Money in a Theory of Finance', *Journal of Political Economy,* LXIX, 1969; B. P. Pesek and T. R. Saving, *Money, Wealth and Economic Theory,* New York, 1967; A. H. Meltzer, 'Money Intermediation and Growth', *Journal of Economic Literature,* VII, 1969.

74 M. Collins, 'The Bank of England at Liverpool, 1827–1844', *Business History,* XIV, 1972, p. 165.

75 For a contrary view, see L. Davis, 'The Capital Markets and Industrial Concentration: the U.S. and the U.K., a Comparative Study', *Economic History Review,* 2nd series, XIX, 1966.

Bibliography

Archival Sources

MIDLAND BANK, LONDON
Barnsley Banking Company, A14, Loans and Credits, 1844–1860.
City Bank, E29, Rules for the Guidance of Branch Managers.
Cumberland Union Banking Company,
G54, Record of Manager's Interviews, 1879–1885.
G55, Record of Manager's Interviews, 1890–1898.
G58, Schedule of Overdrafts at Carlisle.
G65, Pass Book of the Maryport Hematite Iron Company.
Acc 4/2–4, Directors' Attendance Books, 1880–1897.
Preston Banking Company, AN 11–13, Directors' Considerations of Applications for Advances, 1866–8.
Swansea Bank, subsequently the South Wales Union Bank, V7, Managers' Notes, 1876–1892.
NATIONAL AND COMMERCIAL BANKING GROUP, LONDON
Glyn, Mills, A/4 10–12, Private Letter Books.
B/2 18, Terms with Customers.
B/3 9, 1–13, Advances, Engagements.
PUBLIC RECORD OFFICE, LONDON
BT1 Board of Trade, Correspondence.
BT 31, Returns to the Registrar of Joint Stock Companies (for lists of company files consulted, see the appendixes to Chapters 4 and 5 above, pp. 97–101, 154–5).
UNIVERSITY OF HULL, LIBRARY
International Financial Society, Minutes of Board Meetings (I.B.) Minutes of Committee Meetings (I.C.).
Mellors, Basden papers (microfilm).

Printed Material

(*The place of publication is London unless stated otherwise*)

ANON. [?T. Joplin], *Hints by Way of Encouraging the Formation of a Joint Stock in London*, 1834.

ANON., *A History of Cooper Brothers & Co. 1854 to 1954*, ?1954.

ANON., *Payment Deferred 1861–1961. The Story of the North Central Wagon and Finance Company Limited*, ?Rotherham, 1961.

ANON., *The Story of Whitbreads*, 3rd edn, 1964.

ANON., *Trumans: the Brewers*, 1966.

J. C. A., *Limited Liability and Cotton Spinning*, ?Blackburn, 1886.

D. K. ADDIE, 'English Bank Deposits before 1844', *Economic History Review*, 2nd series, XXIII, 1970.

B. W. E. ALFORD, *W. D. & H. O. Wills and the Development of the United Kingdom Tobacco Industry 1786–1965*, 1973.

B. L. ANDERSON, 'The Attorney and the Early Capital Market in Lancashire' in J. R. Harris (ed.) *Liverpool and Merseyside: Essays in the Economic and Social History of the Port and its Hinterland*, 1969.

B. L. ANDERSON, 'Provincial Aspects of the Financial Revolution in the Eighteenth Century', *Business History*, XI, 1969.

——, 'Money and the Structure of Credit in the Eighteenth Century', *Business History*, XII, 1970.

B. L. ANDERSON and P. L. COTTRELL, 'Another Victorian Capital Market: a Study of Banking and Bank Investors on Merseyside', *Economic History Review*, 2nd series, XXVIII, 1975.

S. ANDREW, *50 Years' Cotton Trade*, Oldham, 1887.

ANGLO-AMERICAN, *American Securities*, 2nd edn, 1860.

T. S. ASHTON, *The Industrial Revolution 1760–1830*, 1948.

——, *Iron and Steel in the Industrial Revolution*, Manchester, 3rd edn, 1963.

M. BARLOW, 'The New Companies Act, 1900', *Economic Journal*, XI, 1901.

J. M. BELLAMY, 'A Hull Shipbuilding Firm. The History of C. & W. Earle and Earle's Shipbuilding and Engineering Co. Ltd', *Business History*, VI, 1963.

M. W. BERESFORD, *The Leeds Chamber of Commerce*, Leeds, 1951.

SIR H. BESSEMER, *An Autobiography*, 1905.

A. BIRCH, *Economic History of the British Iron and Steel Industry 1748–1879*, 1967.

J. BLACKMAN and E. M. SIGSWORTH, 'The Home Boom of the 1890s', *Yorkshire Bulletin of Economic and Social Research*, XVII, 1965.

M. BLAUG, 'The Productivity of Capital in the Lancashire Cotton Industry during the Nineteenth Century', *Economic History Review*, 2nd series, XIII, 1961.

S. BOULT, *Trade and Partnership*, 1855.

R. BOYSON, *The Ashworth Cotton Enterprise*, Oxford, 1970.

British Parliamentary Papers (B. P. P.), 1833, VI, *Select Committee on Commerce Manufacturing and Shipping*.

——, 1840, IV, *Select Committee on Banks of Issue*.

——, 1841, V, *Select Committee of Secrecy on Banks of Issue, second report*.

——, 1845, XLVII, *Return of all Joint Stock Companies registered as having been in Existence before the passing of 7 & 8 Vict. c. 110*.

——, 1851, VIII, *Select Committee on the Law of Partnership*.

——, 1854, LXV, *Returns of all Applications referred by Her Majesty to the Board of Trade, praying for Grants of Charters with Limited Liability under Act 1 Vict. c. 73.*

——, 1867, X, *Select Committee on Limited Liability Acts.*

——, 1877, VIII, *Select Committee on the Companies Acts, 1862 and 1867.*

——, 1878, XIX, *Royal Commission on the London Stock Exchange.* C.2157–1.

——, 1886, XXI, *First Report of the Royal Commission on the Depression of Trade and Industry.* C-4621.

——, 1886, XXII, *Second Report of the Royal Commission on the Depression of Trade and Industry.* C-4715.

——, 1886, XXIII, *Third Report of the Royal Commission on the Depression of Trade and Industry.* C-4797.

——, 1886, XXIII, *Final Report of the Royal Commission on the Depression of Trade and Industry.* C-4893.

——, 1895, LXXXVIII, *Report of the Departmental Committee appointed by the Board of Trade* (Davey Committee).

——, 1896, IX; 1897, X; 1898, IX; 1899, VIII, *Select Committee of the House of Lords on the Companies Bill.*

——, 1906, XCVIII, *Company Law Amendment Committee* (Loreburn Committee).

S. A. BROADBRIDGE, *Studies in Railway Expansion and the Capital Market in England 1825–1873,* 1970.

E. H. PHELPS BROWN with MARGARET BROWNE, *A Century of Pay,* 1968.

THOMAS BULLION [G. Rae], *The Internal Management of a Country Bank,* 1850.

D. L. BURN, *The Economic History of Steelmaking 1867–1939,* Cambridge, 1940, reprinted 1961.

T. H. BURNHAM and G. O. HOSKINS, *Iron and Steel in Britain 1870–1913,* 1943.

A. K. CAIRNCROSS, *Home and Foreign Investment 1870–1913,* 1953.

A. F. CALVERT, *A History of the Salt Union,* 1913.

R. E. CAMERON, *France and the Economic Development of Europe,* Princeton, N.J., 1961.

——, 'England, 1750–1844' in Cameron (ed.) *Banking in the Early Stages of Industrialisation,* 1967.

CHARLES CAMMELL & CO. LTD., *Cyclops Steel and Iron Works, Sheffield, England,* Sheffield, 1899.

J. D. CHAMBERS and G. E. MINGAY, *The Agricultural Revolution 1750–1870,* 1966.

S. D. CHAPMAN, *The Early Factory Masters,* Newton Abbot, 1967.

——, 'The Peels in the Early English Cotton Industry', *Business History,* XI, 1970.

——, 'Fixed Capital Formation in the British Cotton Industry 1770–1815', *Economic History Review,* 2nd series, XXIII, 1970.

——, 'Industrial Capital before the Industrial Revolution; an Analysis of the Assets of a Thousand Textile Entrepreneurs' in N. B. Harte and K. G. Ponting (eds) *Textile History and Economic History,* Manchester, 1973.

——, 'Working Capital in the British Cotton Industry, 1770–1850', mimeographed paper, Ealing Business History Seminar, May, 1975.

——, 'The International Houses: the Continental Contribution to British Commerce, 1800–1860', *Journal of European Economic History,* VI, 1977.

——, 'Financial Restraints on the Growth of Firms in the Cotton Industry', *Economic History Review,* forthcoming.

SIR J. H. CLAPHAM, *An Economic History of Modern Britain*, vols I–III, Cambridge, various editions.

——, *The Bank of England. A History*, vols I–II, Cambridge, 1944.

D. C. COLEMAN, *Courtaulds, an Economic and Social History*, vols I–II, Oxford, 1969.

M. COLLINS, 'The Bank of England at Liverpool, 1827–1844', *Business History*, XIV, 1972.

P. L. COTTRELL, 'Anglo-French Financial Co-operation 1850–1880', *Journal of European Economic History*, III, 1974.

——, 'Railway Finance and the Crisis of 1866: Contractors' Bills of Exchange and the Finance Companies', *Journal of Transport History*, new series, III, 1975.

W. F. CRICK and J. E. WADSWORTH, *A Hundred Years of Joint Stock Banking*, 3rd edn, 1958.

F. CROUZET, 'Capital Formation in Great Britain during the Industrial Revolution', reprinted in Crouzet (ed.) *Capital Formation in the Industrial Revolution*, 1972.

——, 'Editor's Introduction: an Essay in Historiography', ibid.

W. B. CRUMP, 'The Leeds Woollen Industry, 1780–1820. General Introduction' in Crump (ed.) *The Leeds Woollen Industry 1780–1820*, Thoresby Society, XXXII, Leeds, 1931.

H. R. DAVIES, 'The Industrial Revolution' in W. G. V. Balchin (ed.) *Swansea and its Region*, Swansea, 1971.

L. DAVIS, 'The Capital Markets and Industrial Concentration: the U.S. and the U.K., a Comparative Study', *Economic History Review*, 2nd series, XIX, 1966.

J. DAY, *Bristol Brass. A History of the Industry*, Newton Abbot, 1973.

P. DEANE, 'Capital Formation in Britain before the Railway Age', *Economic Development and Cultural Change*, IX, 1961.

P. G. M. DICKSON, *The Financial Revolution in England*, 1967.

D. DOUGAN, *The History of North East Shipbuilding*, 1968.

A. B. DU BOIS, *The English Business Company after the Bubble Act 1720–1800*, 1938.

M. EDELSTEIN, 'Rigidity and Bias in the British Capital Market 1870–1913' in D. N. McCloskey (ed.) *Essays on a Mature Economy. Britain after 1840*, 1971.

——, 'Realized Rates of Return on U.K. Home and Overseas Portfolio Investment in the Age of High Imperialism', *Explorations in Economic History*, XIII, 1976.

H. C. EDEY and P. PAITPAKDI, 'British Company Accounting and the Law, 1844–1900' in A. C. Littleton and B. S. Yamey (eds) *Studies in the History of Accounting*, 1956.

M. M. EDWARDS, *The Growth of the British Cotton Trade*, Manchester, 1967.

T. ELLISON, *The Cotton Trade of Great Britain*, 1886.

C. ERICKSON, *British Industrialists. Steel and Hosiery 1850–1950*, 1959.

C. H. FEINSTEIN, *National Income, Expenditure and Output of the United Kingdom 1855–1965*, Cambridge, 1972.

——, 'Capital Formation in Great Britain' in P. Mathias and M. M. Postan (eds) *Cambridge Economic History of Europe*, VII, *The Industrial Economies*, 1978.

F. W. FETTER, *Development of British Monetary Orthodoxy, 1797–1875*, Cambridge, Mass., 1965.

C. H. S. FFOOT, 'The Development of the Law of Negotiable Instruments and the Law of Trusts', *Journal of the Institute of Bankers*, LIX, 1938.

E. W. FIELD, *Observations of a Solicitor on the right of the Public to form Limited Liability Partnerships . . .*, 1854.

D. FINNIE, *Capital Underwriting*, 1934.

THOMAS FIRTH & JOHN BROWN LTD, *100 years in Steel. Firth-Brown Centenary 1837–1937*, Sheffield, 1937.

A. G. FORD, *The Gold Standard. Britain and Argentina 1880–1914*, Oxford, 1962.

H. S. FOXWELL, 'The Financing of Industry and Trade', *Economic Journal*, 1917.

C. E. FREEDMAN, 'Joint Stock Business Organisation in France, 1807–1867', *Business History Review*, XXXIX, 1960.

R. FULFORD, *Glyns, 1753–1953*, 1953.

V. A. C. GATRELL, 'Labour Power and the Size of Firms in Lancashire Cotton in the Second Quarter of the Nineteenth Century', *Economic History Review*, 2nd series, XXX, 1977.

D. GIBBONS, *Limited Liability Act, 18 & 19 Vict. c. 133*, 1855.

R. W. GOLDSMITH, *Financial Structure and Development*, 1969.

C. A. E. GOODHART, *The Business of Banking 1891–1914*, 1972.

W. R. GREY, *Investment for the Working Classes*, 1852.

A. R. GRIFFIN, *Mining in the East Midlands 1550–1947*, 1971.

H. J. HABAKKUK, *American and British Technology in the Nineteenth Century*, 1967.

L. F. HABER, *The Chemical Industry during the Nineteenth Century*, Oxford, 1958.

A. R. HALL, 'A Note on the English Capital Market as a Source of Funds for Home Investment before 1914', *Economica*, new series, XXIV, 1957.

L. HANNAH, 'Mergers in British Manufacturing Industry 1880–1918', *Oxford Economic Papers*, XXVI, 1974.

——, *The Rise of the Corporate Economy*, 1976.

C. K. HARLEY, 'Skilled Labour and the Choice of Technique in Edwardian Industry', *Explorations in Economic History*, XI, 1974.

——, 'Goschen's Conversion of the National Debt and the Yield on Consols', *Economic History Review*, 2nd series, XXIX, 1976.

A. E. HARRISON, 'The Competitiveness of the British Cycle Industry, 1890–1914', *Economic History Review*, 2nd series, XII, 1969.

J. HOOPER HARTNOLL, *A Letter to the Right Hon. E. Cardwell . . . on the Inoperative Character of the Joint Stock Companies Registration Act . . .*, 1853.

W. HAWES, *Observations on Unlimited and Limited Liability*, 1854.

G. R. HAWKE, *Railways and Economic Growth in England and Wales 1840–1870*, 1970.

H. HEATON, 'Financing the Industrial Revolution', *Bulletin of the Business Historical Society*, XI, 1937.

R. P. HIGONNET, 'Bank Deposits in the U.K., 1870–1914', *Quarterly Journal of Economics*, LXXI, 1957.

E. J. HOBSBAWM, 'Custom, Wages and Workload in Nineteenth Century Industry' in A. Briggs and J. Saville (eds) *Essays in Labour History*, 1960.

O. R. HOBSON, 'The Financial Press', *Lloyds Bank Limited Monthly Review*, January 1934.

J. MILNES HOLDEN, *The History of Negotiable Instruments in English Law*, 1955.

J. HOWELL, *Partnership Law Legislation and Limited Liability . . .*, 1869.

J. R. T. HUGHES, *Fluctuations in Trade, Industry and Finance. A Study of British Economic Development 1850–1860*, Oxford, 1960.

B. C. HUNT, *The Development of the Business Corporation in England 1800–1867*, Cambridge, Mass., 1936.

E. HUNT, *Regional Wage Variations in Britain 1850–1914*, Oxford, 1973.

A. M. IMLAH, *Economic Elements in the Pax Britannica*, New York, reprinted 1969.

R. J. IRVING, 'British Railway Investment and Innovation, 1900–1914', *Business History*, XIII, 1971.

H. JAMES, *The Red Barrel, A History of Watney, Mann*, 1963.

JAYCEE, *Public Companies from the Cradle to the Grave*, 1883.

D. T. JENKINS, 'Early Factory Development in the West Riding of Yorkshire' in N. B. Harte and K. G. Ponting (eds) *Textile History and Economic History*, Manchester, 1973.

A. H. JOHN, *The Industrial Development of South Wales 1750–1850*, Cardiff, 1949.

E. L. JONES, 'Introduction' in Jones (ed.) *Agriculture and Economic Growth in England 1650–1815*, 1967.

L. JOSEPH, *Industrial Finance. A Comparison between Home and Foreign Developments*, 1911.

W. P. KENNEDY, 'Foreign Investment, Trade and Growth in the United Kingdom, 1870–1913', *Explorations in Economic History*, XI, 1974.

——, 'Institutional Response to Economic Growth: Capital Markets in Britain to 1914' in L. Hannah (ed.) *Management Strategy and Business Development*, 1976.

J. R. KILLICK and W. A. THOMAS, 'The Provincial Stock Exchanges, 1830–1870', *Economic History Review*, 2nd series, XXIII, 1970.

W. T. C. KING, *History of the London Discount Market*, 1936.

J. KITCHEN, 'Lawrence Dicksee, Depreciation, and the Double Account System' in H. Edey and B. S. Yamey (eds) *Debits, Credits, Finance and Profits*, 1974.

J. LALOR, *Money and Morals*, 1852.

D. S. LANDES, 'The Structure of Enterprise in the Nineteenth Century. The Cases of Britain and Germany', *XIe Congrès Internationale des Sciences Historiques, Rapports*, V, *Histoire contemporaine*, Uppsala, 1960.

——, *The Unbound Prometheus. Technological Change and Industrial Development in Western Europe from 1750 to the Present*, Cambridge, 1969.

F. LAVINGTON, *The English Capital Market*, 1921, reprinted 1968.

C. H. LEE, *A Cotton Enterprise 1795–1840. A History of M'Connel & Kennedy, Fine Cotton Spinners*, Manchester, 1972.

J. A. S. L. LEIGHTON-BOYCE, *Smiths the Bankers, 1658–1958*, 1958.

L. LEVI, 'On Joint Stock Companies', *Journal of the Statistical Society*, XXXIII, 1870.

M. LEVITT, 'Monetary Theory and Trade Credit. An Historical Approach', *Yorkshire Bulletin of Economic and Social Research*, XVI, 1964.

W. S. LINDSAY and R. COBDEN, *Remarks on the Law of Partnership and Limited Liability*, 1856.

J. V. LOWE, *British Steam Locomotive Builders*, 1972.

D. N. McCLOSKEY, 'Did Victorian Britain Fail?', *Economic History Review*, 2nd series, XXIII, 1970.

——, *Economic Maturity and Entrepreneurial Decline. British Iron and Steel 1870–1913*, Cambridge, Mass., 1973.

H. W. MACROSTY, *The Trust Movement in British Industry*, 1907.

J. R. McCULLOCH, *Considerations on Partnerships with Limited Liability*, 1856.

E. C. MADDISON, *On the Stock Exchange*, 1877.

M. D. MALLESON, 'The Law of Partnership in England', *Journal of the Institute of Bankers*, V, 1884.

A MANCHESTER MAN [T. Potter], *The Law of Partnership*, 1855.

P. MATHIAS, 'Credit, Capital and Enterprise in the Industrial Revolution', *Journal of European Economic History*, II, 1973.

R. C. O. MATTHEWS, *A Study in Trade Cycle History. Economic Fluctuations in Great Britain*, Cambridge, 1954.

——, 'Some Aspects of Post-war Growth in the British Economy in Relation to Historical Experience', reprinted in D. H. Aldcroft and P. Fearon (eds) *Economic Growth in Twentieth Century Britain*, 1969.

J. MILLS, 'On the Post-panic Period, 1866–70', *Transactions of the Manchester Statistical Society*, 1870/1.

W. E. MINCHINTON, *The British Tinplate Industry. A History*, Oxford, 1957.

G. E. MINGAY, *English Landed Society in the Eighteenth Century*, 1963.

B. R. MITCHELL with P. DEANE, *Abstract of British Historical Statistics*, Cambridge, 1971.

E. V. MORGAN and W. A. THOMAS, *The Stock Exchange. Its History and Functions*, 1962.

J. H. MORRIS and L. J. WILLIAMS, *The South Wales Coal Industry 1841–1875*, Cardiff, 1958.

E. MOSS, *Remarks on the Act of Parliament 18 & 19 Vict. c. 133 for the Formation of Companies with Limited Liability*, 1856.

J. H. MURCHINSON, *British Mines considered as a Means of Investment*, 1856.

A. E. MUSSON, *Enterprise in Soap and Chemicals*, Manchester, 1965.

——, 'Industrial Motive Power in the United Kingdom, 1800–70', *Economic History Review*, 2nd series, XXIX, 1976.

T. B. NAPIER, 'The History of Joint Stock and Limited Liability Companies' in *A Century of Law Reform*, 1901.

R. L. NASH, *A Short Inquiry into the Profitable Nature of our Investments*, 1880.

NATIONAL MONETARY COMMISSION, *Interviews on the Banking and Currency Systems of England . . .*, Washington, D.C., 1910.

S. NISHIMURA, *The Decline of Inland Bills of Exchange in the London Money Market, 1855–1913*, Cambridge, 1971.

H. OSBOURNE O'HAGAN, *Leaves from my Life*, vols 1–2, 1929.

A. PACKER, *How the Public are Plundered . . .*, 1878.

K. V. PANKHURST, 'Investment in the West Riding Wool Textile Industry in the Nineteenth Century', *Yorkshire Bulletin of Economic and Social Research*, VIII, 1956.

P. L. PAYNE, 'The Emergence of the Large Scale Company in Great Britain, 1870–1913', *Economic History Review*, 2nd series, XX, 1967.

——, 'Iron and Steel Manufactures' in D. H. Aldcroft (ed.) *The Development of British Industry and Foreign Competition 1875–1914*, 1968.

——, *The Early Scottish Limited Companies 1856–1895: an Historical and Analytical Survey*, Social Science Working Paper Number 222, California Institute of Technology, Pasadena, 1977.

R. R. PENNINGTON, *Stannary Law. A History of the Mining Law of Cornwall and Devon*, Newton Abbot, 1973.

S. POLLARD, 'Fixed Capital in the Industrial Revolution in Britain', *Journal of Economic History*, XXIV, 1964.

——, 'The Growth and Distribution of Capital in Great Britain, c. 1770–1870', *Third International Conference of Economic History (Munich, 1965)*, Paris, 1968.

——, *The Genesis of Modern Management*, Harmondsworth, 1968.

F. POLLOCK, 'The Law of Partnership in England with Special Reference to Proposed Codification and Amendment', *Journal of the Institute of Bankers*, I, 1880.

M. M. POSTAN, 'Recent Trends in the Accumulation of Capital', *Economic History Review*, VI, 1935.

T. POTTER, 'On Jurisprudence in Relation to Commerce', *Transactions of the Manchester Statistical Society*, 1858/9.

L. S. PRESSNELL, *Country Banking in the Industrial Revolution*, Oxford, 1956.

——, 'The Rate of Interest in the Eighteenth Century' in Pressnell (ed.) *Studies in the Industrial Revolution*, 1960.

A. RAISTRICK, *Dynasty of Iron Founders; the Darbys and Coalbrookdale*, 1958.

A. RAISTRICK and B. JENNINGS, *A History of Lead Mining in the Pennines*, 1965.

A. REDFORD, *Manchester Merchants and Foreign Trade*, II, *1850–1939*, Manchester, 1956.

M. C. REED, *Investment in Railways in Britain 1820–1844*, 1975.

E. RICHARDS, 'The Industrial Face of a Great Estate: Trentham and Lilleshall 1780–1860', *Economic History Review*, 2nd series, XXVII, 1974.

H. W. RICHARDSON and J. M. BASS, 'Profitability of the Consett Iron Company before 1914', *Business History*, VII, 1965.

J. RIESSER, *The Great German Banks . . .*, Washington, D.C., 1911.

W. G. RIMMER, *Marshalls of Leeds, Flax Spinners, 1788–1886*, Cambridge, 1960.

R. O. ROBERTS, 'The Operations of the Brecon Old Bank of Wilkins & Co., 1778–1890', *Business History*, I, 1958.

A. J. ROBERTSON, 'The Decline of the Scottish Cotton Industry, 1860–1914', *Business History*, XII, 1970.

J. ROWE, *Cornwall in the Age of the Industrial Revolution*, Liverpool, 1953.

S. B. SAUL, 'The Motor Industry in Britain to 1914', *Business History*, V, 1962.

J. SAVILLE, 'Sleeping Partnership and Limited Liability 1850–1856', *Economic History Review*, 2nd series, VIII, 1955.

——, 'Trade Unions and Free Labour: the Background to the Taff Vale Decision' in A. Briggs and J. Saville (eds) *Essays in Labour History*, 1960.

——, 'Some Retarding Factors in the British Economy before 1914', *Yorkshire Bulletin of Economic and Social Research*, XIII, 1961.

——, 'The Development of British Industry and Foreign Competition 1875–1914', *Business History*, XII, 1970.

R. S. SAYERS, 'The Bank in the Gold Market, 1890–1914' in T. S. Ashton and R. S. Sayers, *Papers in English Monetary History*, Oxford, 1953.

——, *Lloyds in the History of English Banking*, 1957.

——, *The Bank of England 1891–1944*, vols I–III, 1976.

R. G. SCHAFFER, 'Genesis and Structure of the Foley "Ironworks in Partnership" of 1692', *Business History*, XIII, 1971.

J. D. SCOTT, *Vickers, a History*, 1962.

A. SCRATCHLEY, *Industrial Investment and Emigration*, 1851.

H. A. SHANNON, 'The First Five Thousand Limited Companies and their Duration', *Economic History*, II, 1930–3.

——, 'The Limited Companies of 1866 and 1883', *Economic History Review*, IV, 1932–3.

S. SHAPIRO, *Capital and the Cotton Industry in the Industrial Revolution*, Ithaca, N.Y., 1967.

D. K. SHEPPARD, *The Growth and Role of U.K. Financial Institutions 1880–1962*, 1971.

E. M. SIGSWORTH, *Black Dyke Mills. A History*, Liverpool, 1958.

E. M. SIGSWORTH and J. BLACKMAN, 'The Woollen and Worsted Industries' in D. H. Aldcroft (ed.) *The Development of British Industry and Foreign Competition 1875–1914*, 1968.

J. SIZER, *An Insight into Management Accounting*, Harmondsworth, 1969.

K. C. SMITH and G. F. HORNE, *An Index Number of Securities 1867–1914*, London and Cambridge Economic Bulletin, Special Memorandum no. 47, 1934.

R. SMITH, 'An Oldham Limited Liability Company, 1875–1896', *Business History*, IV, 1961.

SOCIETY FOR PROMOTING THE AMENDMENT OF THE LAW, *Report of the Committee on the Law of Partnership on the Liability of Partners*, 1849.

——, *Report of Special Committee on Partnership*, ?1857.

D. SPRING, 'The English Landed Estate in the Age of Coal and Iron 1830–50', *Journal of Economic History*, XI, 1951.

——, 'English Landowners and Nineteenth Century Industrialism' in J. T. Ward and R. G. Wilson (eds) *Land and Industry. The Landed Estate and the Industrial Revolution*, Newton Abbot, 1971.

B. SUPPLE, *The Royal Exchange. A History of British Insurance 1720–1970*, Cambridge, 1970.

J. SYKES, *The Amalgamation Movement in English Banking, 1825–1924*, 1926.

A. J. TAYLOR, 'Concentration and Specialisation in the Lancashire Cotton Industry, 1825–1850', *Economic History Review*, 2nd series, I, 1948/9.

P. TEMIN, 'The Relative Decline of the British Steel Industry, 1880–1913' in H. Rosovsky (ed.) *Industrialisation in Two Systems*, 1966.

S. E. THOMAS, *The Rise and Growth of Joint Stock Banking*, 1934.

W. A. THOMAS, *The Provincial Stock Exchanges*, 1973.

F. M. L. THOMPSON, *English Landed Society in the Nineteenth Century*, 1963.

H. THRING, *Joint Stock Companies Acts 1857*, 1858.

K. S. TOFT, 'A Mid-Nineteenth Century Attempt at Banking Control', *Revue internationale d'histoire de la banque*, III, 1970.

M. A. UTTON, 'Some Features of the Early Merger Movements in British Manufacturing Industry', *Business History*, XIV, 1972.

J. VAIZEY, *The Brewing Industry 1886–1951*, 1960.

C. WALFORD, *The Insurance Year Book*, 1870.

J. T. WARD, 'Landowners and Mining' in J. T. Ward and R. G. Wilson (eds) *Land and Industry. The Landed Estate and the Industrial Revolution*, Newton Abbot, 1971.

R. A. WARD, *A Treatise on Investment*, 2nd edn, 1852.

D. TREVOR WILLIAMS, *The Economic Development of Swansea and of the Swansea District to 1921*, Cardiff, 1940.

C. WILSON, *The History of Unilever*, vols I–II, 1954.

The Accountant
The Bankers' Magazine
Chadwick's Investment Circular
Circular to Bankers
The Economist
Hansard
Journal of the Institute of Bankers
The Statist
The Times

Theses

J. P. ADDIS, 'The Heavy Iron and Steel Industry in South Wales 1870–1950', Ph.D., University of Wales, Aberystwyth, 1957.

G. L. AYRES, 'Fluctuations in New Capital Issues on the London Money Market, 1899–1913', M.Sc. (Econ.), University of London, 1934.

J. M. BELLAMY, 'Some Aspects of the Economy of Hull in the Nineteenth Century with Special Reference to Business History', Ph.D., University of Hull, 1966.

I. C. R. BYATT, 'The British Electrical Industry, 1875–1914', D.Phil., University of Oxford, 1962.

P. L. COTTRELL, 'Investment Banking in England 1856–1882. Case Study of the International Financial Society', Ph.D., University of Hull, 1974.

A. ESSEX-CROSBY, 'Joint Stock Companies in Great Britain, 1890–1930', M.Comm., University of London, 1938.

D. B. EVANS, 'The Iron and Steel Industry of South Staffordshire from 1760 to 1950', M.A., University of Birmingham, 1951.

D. A. FARNIE, 'The English Cotton Industry, 1850–1896', Ph.D., University of Manchester, 1953.

C. H. FEINSTEIN, 'Home and Foreign Investment. Some Aspects of Capital Formation and Finance in the U.K. 1870–1913', Ph.D., University of Cambridge, 1960.

I. F. GIBSON, 'The Economic History of the Scottish Iron and Steel Industry with Particular Reference to the Period 1830 to 1880', Ph.D., University of London, 1955.

N. J. GRIESER, 'The British Investor and his Sources of Information', M.Sc. (Econ.), University of London, 1940.

R. M. HARTWELL, 'The Yorkshire Woollen and Worsted Industries, 1800–1850', D.Phil., University of Oxford, 1955.

J. B. JEFFREYS, 'Trends in Business Organisation in Great Britain since 1856 . . .', Ph.D., University of London, 1938.

D. T. JENKINS, 'The West Riding Wool Textile Industry, 1780–1835. A Study of Fixed Capital Formation', D.Phil., University of York, 1969.

A. G. KENWOOD, 'Capital Investment in North Eastern England, 1800–1913', Ph.D., University of London, 1962.

B. R. MITCHELL, 'The Economic Development of the Inland Coalfields, 1870–1914', Ph.D., University of Cambridge, 1956.

C. A. PAULL, 'Mechanisation in British and American Bituminous Coal Mines, 1890–1939', M.Phil., University of London, 1968.

s. POLLARD, 'The Economic History of Shipbuilding 1870–1914', Ph.D., University of London, 1951.

M. RIX, 'An Economic Analysis of Existing English Legislation concerning the Limited Liability Company', M.Sc. (Econ.), University of London, 1936.

R. SMITH, 'A History of the Lancashire Cotton Industry between the Years 1873 and 1896', Ph.D., University of Birmingham, 1954.

A. J. TOPHAM, 'The Credit Structure of the West Riding Wool Textile Industry in the Nineteenth Century', M.A., University of Leeds, 1953.

R. E. TYSON, 'The Sun Mill Company Ltd—A Study in Democratic Investment 1858–1959', M.A., University of Manchester, 1962.

Index to authors cited in the text

Index to banks and firms

287

Subject index